Michael Goulder is Emeritus Professor of Biblical Studies at the University of Birmingham.

JOURNAL FOR THE STUDY OF THE OLD TESTAMENT SUPPLEMENT SERIES
233

Sheffield Academic Press

The Psalms of Asaph and the Pentateuch

Studies in the Psalter, III

Michael D. Goulder

Journal for the Study of the Old Testament
Supplement Series 233

BS
1430.2
.G6850
1996

Published by Sheffield Academic Press Ltd
Mansion House
19 Kingfield Road
Sheffield S11 9AS
England

Printed on acid-free paper in Great Britain
by Bookcraft Ltd
Midsomer Norton, Bath

British Library Cataloguing in Publication Data

A catalogue record for this book is available
from the British Library

ISBN 1-85075-639-2

CONTENTS

Part I
THE PSALMS OF ASAPH

Part II
E, D, J, P

This book is the third volume of a series of *Studies in the Psalter*. The first of these, *The Psalms of the Sons of Korah*, was published in 1982, the second, *The Prayers of David (Psalms 51–72)*, in 1990.[1] The subtitle is intended to draw attention to a difference of approach from that of standard commentaries. Whereas they are preponderantly studies of the *psalms*, taken individually or viewed as members of a *Gattung*, I have taken more seriously their arrangement in the *Psalter*. Our earliest commentary on the psalms is their arrangement by anonymous Israelite tradents: in groups with differing names in the heading, *for the Sons of Korah, for David, for Asaph*, and so on; in the order in which they stand within these collections; in Books I–V; with technical notes, *Selah, for the Chief Musician*, and so on; *at the Lilies, at the Dove of the Distant Terebinths*, and so on; even the 'historical' notes, associating a psalm with an episode in David's life. Not all of these features will be guides to the original sense of the psalms, but they are the comments of people closer to the psalmists than we are, and we ignore them at our peril.

This book, then, was intended as an analysis of a third group of psalms so bound together by the tradition, *The Psalms of Asaph*. I thought of it as a third volume of the series, on a group of psalms put together (their detail suggested) in the 720s in the northern sanctuary at Bethel, and accepted (with marginal amendments) in Jerusalem thereafter. The analysis revealed a number of interesting details of Israelite life in the period, and above all it showed the profound religious tension underlying it, between faith in the God who redeemed the people in the Exodus, and the harsh reality of the armies of Tiglath-Pileser III and his successor. I also thought I could trace the outline of a pattern of festal

1. *The Psalms of the Sons of Korah* (JSOTSup, 20; Sheffield: JSOT Press, 1982); *The Prayers of David (Psalms 51–72): Studies in the Psalter, II* (JSOTSup, 102; Sheffield: JSOT Press, 1990).

worship at Bethel similar to the one I had proposed for the Korahite psalms at Dan.

However, I came to realize that if I was right in seeing the Asaph psalms as a unity, stemming from the same Bethel community in the same decade, the 720s, I had uncovered something far more significant for Old Testament studies. The Asaph psalms contain, as no other body of psalms does, the elements of a continuous outline of Israelite history, beginning from the oppression in Egypt, and going on at least as far as the Davidic–Solomonic empire. Furthermore, the detail of these historical traditions is often markedly at variance with that which we have in the Pentateuch. It seemed therefore that I had in the Asaph psalms an outline of the *earliest* form of the history of Israel, running, as we would say, from Exodus to 1 Kings; and this suggested that I should sketch an outline of how this Asaphic historical tradition developed into our Pentateuch. So the book came to be called *The Psalms of Asaph and the Pentateuch.*

The work is accordingly divided into two parts. I have put Chapter 1 in a preliminary section of its own, because the whole book depends upon the argument that the Asaph psalms are not an adventitious collection from fourth-century Jerusalem, but the composition of a community from the eighth century in Ephraim. Part I, then, is an analysis of these psalms in detail, and Part II is an attempt to set out a new and precise solution of the Pentateuchal problem. In this my basis in an eighth-century set of documents, with its name Asaph, and its inferred location Bethel, has enabled me to escape from the blur of ill-defined sigla (J, E, D, P etc.) and to attribute the different developments of the Pentateuch to three biblical families, the sons of Asaph, Korah and Merari. An analysis of the genealogies in the later Old Testament books has even enabled me to suggest the names of individuals who might be claimed as the major creative figures in the growth of the Pentateuch. I have signalled the provisionality of such proposals by entitling the last chapter, 'Concluding Unhistorical Postscript', but I think that it is worth risking the scorn of reviewers if something precise and clear is offered. Karl Popper approved the proposing of 'baroque' hypotheses: the more extravagant the detail, the more easily falsified, and the more helpful towards the final truth.

The appearance of so grandiose a scheme has presented me with problems. My major study has been the New Testament, and while I may now claim a competence in the exegesis of the psalms, the

Pentateuch is another matter. Nor is this the place in any case for a Commentary on the Pentateuch, and its enormous secondary literature, if I were able to provide one. There is therefore a difference of timbre between the two parts of the book. I have attempted in Part I a review of the Asaph psalms, and of all the significant opinions of the last century. Part II is much less heavily documented. I have presented my own scenario of the history of the Pentateuch, and have contrasted it with the theories of some eight well-known Pentateuchal scholars of the same period. I have otherwise limited the discussion to a few well-known commentaries, by Westermann, Noth, Childs, Houtman, Budd and Mayes, and to a limited number of books and articles. The important thing was to see how far my own Asaphite work corresponded with 'E', my Korahite expansion with 'J' and 'D', and my Merarite rewriting with 'P'. Thereafter the detail might vary without endangering the hypothesis.

I am grateful to friends in the Society for Old Testament Study who have helped me with questions and comments, to Ernest Nicholson for helpful discussion and kindness, and to the team at Sheffield Academic Press for their invariable support.

Michael Goulder
December, 1995

The text printed for the translation of the Psalms, and other Old Testament passages is the Revised Version margin of 1881; that is, the outvoted version proposed by the scholarly minority on the panel (hereafter RV mg; italics in the RV indicate words not in the Hebrew; their purpose throughout the book is to distinguish the biblical text that I am expounding from my own comments). Any departures from this are signalled by printing the Hebrew in parenthesis, or on occasion 'RV text'.

ABBREVIATIONS

AB	Anchor Bible
ABRL	Anchor Bible Reference Library
ATD	Das Alte Testament Deutsch
BBB	Bonner biblische Beiträge
BDB	F. Brown, S.R. Driver and C.A. Briggs, *Hebrew and English Lexicon of the Old Testament*
BETL	Bibliotheca ephemeridum theologicarum lovaniensium
BEvT	Beiträge zur evangelischen Theologie
Bib	*Biblica*
BKAT	Biblischer Kommentar: Altes Testament
BZAW	Beihefte zur *ZAW*
CBQ	*Catholic Biblical Quarterly*
ConBOT	Coniectanea biblica, Old Testament
CTA	A. Herdner, *Corpus des tablettes en cunéiformes alphabétiques*
DCH	D.J.A. Chines (ed.), *Dictionary of Classical Hebrew*
FAT	Forschungen zum Alten Testament
HAT	Handbuch zum Alten Testament
HKAT	Handkommentar zum Alten Testament
IEJ	*Israel Exploration Journal*
JBL	*Journal of Biblical Literature*
JSOT	*Journal for the Study of the Old Testament*
JSOTSup	*Journal for the Study of the Old Testament*, Supplement Series
JTS	*Journal of Theological Studies*
KB	L. Koehler and W. Baumgartner (eds.), *Lexicon in Veteris Testamenti libros*
LCL	Loeb Classical Library
NCB	New Century Bible
NTS	*New Testament Studies*
OTG	Old Testament Guides
OTL	Old Testament Library
RB	*Revue biblique*
RV mg	Revised Text (1881) margin
SBLDS	SBL Dissertation Series
SBLMS	SBL Monograph Series
SBT	Studies in Biblical Theology
SOTSMS	Society for Old Testament Study Monograph Series
VT	*Vetus Testamentum*
VTSup	*Vetus Testamentum*, Supplements
WBC	Word Biblical Commentary

WestBC	Westminster Bible Commentaries
WMANT	Wissenschaftliche Monographien zum Alten und Neuen Testament
ZAW	*Zeitschrift für die alttestamentliche Wissenschaft*
ZTK	*Zeitschrift für Theologie und Kirche*

Chapter 1

DELITZSCH'S DILEMMA

Twelve psalms in the Hebrew Psalter bear the heading note לאסף, *for/of Asaph*: 50 and 73–83. The Asaph in question is known to us principally in the traditions we find in Chronicles: the Chroniclers supposed that Asaph was David's senior musician. While it would be rash (and erroneous) to dismiss the Chroniclers' traditions about Asaph as valueless, they certainly cannot be accepted uncritically. I have attempted an analysis of all the biblical material on Asaph, but I have postponed such secondary discussion to Chapter 14. The primary evidence is in the Asaph psalms themselves.

Critics were slow to liberate themselves from the Chroniclers' tradition, but the nineteenth century saw such a movement under weigh. Franz Delitzsch, the prince of commentators from that period, still hangs on to a Davidic Asaph for some of the psalms, but his comments on the collection in itself are full of insight, and may form the basis of my own discussion. Delitzsch found himself in a dilemma (*Psalms*, II, pp. 140-43). There were a number of features which held the Asaph psalms together, and which distinguished them from the rest of the Psalter; but on the other hand the dating, as he saw it, varied from Davidic to post-exilic times. He resolved this on the basis that as 'the cymbals were inherited by [the Asaphites of Ezra's Return] from their ancestor, it is possible that a genius for poetry and a delight in it may also have been hereditary among them'.

The same dilemma has faced all commentators since, and two contrasting resolutions have been offered. The majority solution has involved minimizing Delitzsch's points in common, and attending to the variant dates and classifications; increasingly with time this has come to mean regarding the Asaph heading as insignificant. Thus Alexander Kirkpatrick (*Psalms*) still lists the features in common (II, p. 427), and groups the psalms together as all national, including 73 and 77; but they are from various periods, mostly post-exilic, and comprise the collection preserved and used by the family of Asaph, who was perhaps David's musician (I, p. xxxiii). Hermann Gunkel (*Psalmen*) credits a pre-722 northern origin to some of the collection (77; 80; 81), but they are mostly post-exilic, imitations of the prophetic style mixed with national laments, to which some personal psalms (73; 77; 78) have been added by the Asaph guild of Second Temple singers (*Einleitung*, p. 449). Sigmund Mowinckel (*Psalmenstudien, VI*, pp. 41-42; *Psalms*, II, pp. 79-82) dates 81 before 722, 74 and 79 after 587, and 50 and 73 after the exile: Asaph probably returned with Zerubbabel, and founded a guild of singers who in time were accepted as Levites. More recent, expansive, three-volume commentators, Hans-Joachim Kraus, Mitchell Dahood, Louis Jacquet, the *Word* series (Leslie Allen, Peter Craigie, Marvin Tate) dismiss the matter with a paragraph. Jacquet (I, p. 76) stresses the vigour and sublimity of the Asaph poetry; Craigie (p. 26) still thinks Asaph was David's musician.

A minority of critics has taken a different view: it could be that the whole collection was early and northern, but that when the psalms were taken south, they were adapted for use there, and references to Judah, Jerusalem and Zion were substituted for earlier northern locations. This approach was taken by J.P. Peters in 1922 (*Psalms*). Peters had an original mind, and he concluded that the Headings, *For David/Asaph/the Sons of Korah* signified the different sanctuaries, Jerusalem, Bethel, Dan, where the psalms had been used as festal liturgies. His book is brilliant but sketchy, and has been almost forgotten. He was an American, teaching in the little-known University of the South, he died before the lectures were published, and they had the misfortune to compete for attention with Mowinckel and Gunkel's battle of the giants.

A similar, but less comprehensive solution was offered by Ivan Engnell in 1963: the Asaph psalms are northern, by both content and language, but were then edited in favour of Jerusalem, especially 50 and 76: 'The image of God is very characteristic, Jahweh as God of creation and fate, but at the same time anchored firmly in the history of Israel. The tone has something of the "prophetic" view over it; it is compressed, almost passionate, and the psalms make an impression of deep personal engagement. Also the national lament predominates by type, and the "covenant" idea is to the fore. Everything speaks for our having here to do with a coherent group, and that the superscription "To Asaph" is original.'[1] Since most critics regarded the varying dates as crucial, it was an exaggeration to say that 'everything' spoke for a coherent, northern group; and Engnell did not press his case firmly enough to swing the consensus.

The idea that there was a coherence to the collection was resumed in a brief article by Martin Buss, 'The Psalms of Asaph and Korah' (1963), and was heavily criticized in a short book by a Finnish scholar, Karl-Johan Illman, *Thema und Tradition in den Asaf-Psalmen* (1976). Buss was supported by another American, Harry Nasuti, in *Tradition History and the Psalms of Asaph* (1988), but Nasuti's basic

---

1.   I owe this citation to K.-J. Illman (1976), who gives the reference as the essay 'Psaltaren' in *Svenskt Bibliskt Uppslagsverk*, II (Stockholm, 2nd edn, 1963), pp. 618-57. The English is my translation from his German translation of the Swedish.

solution remains similar to Delitzsch's—the unity lies in the 'Ephraimite' tradition. All these discussions have been useful, but Buss and Nasuti have not much affected the ruling opinion, which is substantially that of Gunkel. I take up the points of this recent debate below.

Delitzsch proposed five characteristics which held the collection together:

The Names for God

'The twelve Psalms are all Elohistic. In two of them (lxxvii, lxxxii) the Divine name יהוה does not occur at all; in the others it occurs once, or at most twice. Besides אלהים they are fond of אֲדֹנָי and אֵל; they are also specially fond of עֶלְיוֹן. Of compounded Divine names, they are the only Psalms in which אֵל אֱלֹהִים יְהֹוָה occurs (it is found also in Josh. xxii.2); and nowhere else in the Old Testament do we find אֱלֹהִים צְבָאוֹת' (*Psalms*, II, pp. 141-42).

A table may clarify the distribution of these names of God:

	אלהים	יהוה	אל	עליו	אדני	צבאות	אלוה
50	9	1	1	1			1
73	3	1	2	1	2		
74	4	1	1				
75	3	1					
76	4	1					
77	6	1(יה)	3	1	2		
78	8	2	7	4	1		
79	3	1			1		
80	5	2	1			4	
81	4	2	2				
82	4		1	1			
83	3	2	1	1			
	56	15	19	9	6	4	1

Delitzsch's case might seem rather impressive, but it has not been undisputed.

(i) As early as Kirkpatrick (*Psalms*, I, pp. lvi-lvii), it was observed that there were a number of duplications in the Psalter, with אלהים in one form and יהוה in the other; for example, Psalm 14 and part of 40, with יהוה, virtually duplicate Psalms 53 and 70, with אלהים. It seemed likely to Kirkpatrick that 'I am Yahweh, thy God' in Exod. 20.2 was an earlier form of 'I am God, thy God' in Ps. 50.8, and so arose the theory of the *Elohistic redaction*. In Book I (Pss. 1–41), יהוה outweighs אלהים by 278 uses to 15; in Books IV–V (90–150) by 339 to 9; whereas in Books II–III (42–89), if we except 84–89, the figures are reversed, 44 uses to 200. This was explained by the supposed activity of a redactor, who for some reason went through Psalms 42–83 altering יהוה to אלהים: and Gunkel, followed by Kraus and many other commentators, went through the same psalms and changed them all back.

The Elohistic redaction theory is a remarkable instance of how a speculation (for it is quite without evidence) becomes an established fact by being repeated from book to book. It does not in fact explain any-thing, for no motive is alleged: Illman (*Thema*, p. 52) concedes that it is unknown why Yahweh is so infrequent and אלהים has been substituted. There is also the unexplained mystery of how the 'redactor' managed to miss 44 instances of יהוה in the course of his activity: he must have been massively incompetent. Besides, all the evidence we have is that in later times יהוה was the preferred divine name. Gunkel hints (*Einleitung*, p. 451), that in the Chronicler's time אלהים was used in worship, but it is difficult to know what he is thinking of. In 1 Chronicles 16 the Asaphites sing a version of Psalms 105 and 96 with verses from 106, all of them יהוה psalms from Book IV, and יהוה is retained throughout; and this fea-ture predominates throughout the Chroniclers' work. Even the argu-ment from the duplicated psalms does not work. Psalm 108 virtually duplicates verses from 57 and 60, but it also has אלהים × 6 to יהוה × 1—six times out of the nine in Books IV–V! Perhaps the Elohistic redactor was trying his hand here too. Claims that 14 and 40, with יהוה, pre-date 53 and 70, with אלהים, are equally without foundation: I have discussed these in detail before (*Korah*, pp. 5-6; *Prayers*, pp. 91-92, 229-30) and will not repeat the argument here, but every difference suggests that the Elohistic forms are prior.

(ii) The occurrence figures for אדני are not remarkable, but those for אל, עליון and צבאות are surprising. The uses of אל in these twelve psalms are one third of all those in the Psalter, 19 uses as against five in the Prayers of David or six in the Korah psalms. It occurs in nine out of the twelve psalms, and is more common than יהוה. עליון similarly comes nine times out of 21 times in the Psalter (31 × in the Old Testament): the combination אל עליון occurs at 78.35, and in parallel at 73.11. With the three uses in the Korah psalms we have half the occurrences in the Psalter. צבאות is a more special case, in that it occurs in only one psalm (80), and always combined with other divine names; we find the same phenomenon in two Korah psalms, 46 (× 2) and 84 (× 3)—nine uses in all in the two series out of 15 in the Psalter. The combination 'God of Jacob' is also disproportionate in these two collections, seven uses out of 13 in the Psalter.

Illman (*Thema*, pp. 52-54) notes these figures, but discounts them. Sometimes אל is used absolutely, sometimes as a construct; sometimes with an article, sometimes without; sometimes of Yahweh, sometimes of foreign gods. עליון may be in apposition to either אל or אלהים, or in parallel, or on its own. The only legitimate conclusion is that the Asaph psalmists like to vary the divine names; though אל עליון may be an indication of use at Jerusalem.

It is difficult to see why the different ways the names are used should be thought to be relevant. The sheer figures are striking and require an explanation, and I may offer one. The Israelites did not enter the Promised Land as one people led by Joshua. Only a part of the people had become Yahweh worshippers. In time all Israelites accepted Yahweh as the national God, but the traditional names in earlier use were retained, including the Canaanite אל, the old high god spoken of as עליון at Ugarit. There was a long period of tolerance, and our psalms, as well as the Korah psalms and the others in Books II–III, belong to this time. The syncretist process became controversial with the great prophets from Elijah to Hosea, and critical in the reign of Manasseh, and from that time יהוה increasingly became normative and אלהים in retreat, as we find in Books I, IV and V. It is noticeable that in our psalms יהוה is spoken of as the *name* of יהוה: 'the enemy hath reproached Yahweh... hath blasphemed thy name' (74.18); 'I Yahweh am thy God, Which brought thee up out of the land of Egypt' (81.11); 'thou alone, whose name is Yahweh, art Most High' (83.18). I will return to עליון, with whom the issue is more complex than Illman has allowed (pp. 118, 130).

Prophetic Speeches of Divine Judgment

Delitzsch continues (*Psalms*, II, p. 142): 'As in the Prophets, God is frequently introduced in [the Asaph Psalms] speaking; we come upon elaborate prophetical pictures of the appearing of God the Judge with somewhat lengthy judicial charges (Pss. l, lxxv, lxxxii). The epithet החזֶה borne by Asaph in 2 Chron. xxix.30 fits in with this...' While there are brief oracles in the mouth of God in some 16 psalms, the Asaph psalms are distinguished by rather impressive divine speeches. God speaks three times in 50, for one (5), nine (7-15) and six verses (16-21), for probably eleven verses in 81.7-17, and for all but two verses of 82 (2-7). Most commentators also include 75, where v. 3b seems to be spoken by God, and so vv. 3-4: 'I' comes later in the psalm, but may be spoken by the king.

So much might be agreed, and again might seem to set the Asaph psalms apart: but it has proved difficult to separate the length of these divine speeches from the broader topic of their judgment theme. Mowinckel (*Psalmenstudien*, II, pp. 191-92; III, pp. 2-3, 21) saw 50, 75, 76, 81 and 82 as important elements in the autumn festival, with judgment upon Israel (50; 81), the nations (75; 76) and their gods (82); but other psalms had other themes. Buss ('Psalms') noted 'strong personal elements' (73; 78) of a 'wisdom' character, which he set alongside judgment psalms (50; 75; 76; 81) and national laments (74; 77; 79; 80; 83); so although he bracketed the whole collection (and the Korah psalms) together as Deuteronomic–Levitical, with a prophetic/homiletic common tradition, the group was far from homogeneous.

Illman (*Thema*, pp. 41-50) properly criticizes Buss's lack of definition. Only 73 can be claimed to be a 'wisdom psalm', and that in the sense of having insight. There is little didactic terminology, and the Deuteronomic expressions are not widespread outside 78: 'to walk in Yahweh's ways' (81.14); 'to walk in stubbornness of heart' (81.13); corpses as 'food for the birds of heaven' (79.2). Six of the psalms could be called didactic in the broadest sense (73; 78; with the prophetic 50; 75; 81; 82): the remainder are national laments. The judgment theme is pervasive, but in different senses: sometimes it is Israel which is judged (50; 78; 81), often Israel's enemies, once the gods (82). There is no truly common theme.

Illman's analysis is too narrowly focused. First, the 'national laments' are not about droughts, locusts and so forth, they are about acute national military peril. Psalm 74 describes the burning of the *Temple*, and of all the shrines in the land, and calls on God to plead his own cause, and remember the adversary as he did in creation. In 77 the speaker cries to God all night at the nation's trouble; but he remembers God's redeeming of his people in the Exodus, and is comforted. In 79 the Temple is defiled and the army slaughtered; God is to revenge their blood sevenfold. In 80 the vine which God planted is burned and cut down; he is prayed to turn his people again, cause his face to shine, and they will be delivered. In 83 the enemy have formed an alliance of named peoples and tribes, backed by Assyria; God is to pursue and terrify them that they may be confounded and perish.

But other psalms, even if less desperate, hint at similar peril. In 75 'the earth and all its inhabitants are dissolved'; there are arrogant and wicked men lifting up their horn, and the speaker vows to cut off all their horns; God is to give the cup of staggering to all the wicked of the earth. These are most naturally taken as the leaders of enemy armies. Psalm 76 similarly sees God as arising in judgment to cut off the spirit of princes and kings who oppress the meek of the earth; at his rebuke their chariot and horse are fallen. In these psalms God judges enemy nations; the fact that he judges Israel in 50 and 81 only thinly masks the fact of an enemy menace. Psalm 50 is a demand for national repentance, culminating in 'Now consider this, ye that forget God, *Lest I tear you in pieces and there be none to deliver*' (50.22). Psalm 81 proclaims that if Israel had hearkened to God, he *would soon subdue their enemies,* and *the haters of Yahweh would cringe to him* (81.15-16). The lengthy 78 similarly carries the double message: Israel had repeatedly forgotten God and provoked his wrath; but they should also *remember his wondrous works*, in the plagues, the Exodus, the wilderness, the Settlement and under David. It is not an accident that 78 follows 77. Behind all these psalms lurks the fear of national catastrophe. Its very impending is, to the psalmist, evidence of divine anger, and so of the people's irreligion. Repentance is the only guarantee of assuaging the divine wrath, and so of evoking the promised deliverance, as of old.

That is ten of the twelve Asaph psalms; only 82 and 73 remain. These are controverted pieces which must await a full exegesis in due course. But it may now be said that both of them are patient of interpretation against the same background of threatened national extinction. Psalm 82 prophesies judgment upon the gods; and the gods are sometimes in Scripture inferior divine powers to whom Yahweh has committed responsibility for the nations. I shall argue that here their unjust judging has consisted in loosing their peoples' armies against Israel, who are the destitute and orphaned as they were the meek of the earth in 76.10—the foundations of the earth are moved in 82.6 as its pillars were in 75.4. Psalm 73 has been widely misunderstood, largely because critics have been so quickly willing to emend it. But the text says that God is loving to *Israel*, not to the upright; that the arrogant and wicked oppress her, as they do in 75; that [their leader] will bring back his people hither and drain the waters of fullness; and the Lord will despise the image which they have set up in the city. Psalm 73 is not a wisdom psalm, still less is it about life hereafter. It is the leader's confession of trust in God's deliverance, in the face of a national military crisis.

So it is possible to see the Asaph psalms as a unity; as a sequence of calls to repentance, of laments, of prayers of confidence and appeals to the divine covenant, in face of a dire threat or series of threats. God will judge the enemy for their iniquity, and overthrow them; he will judge their gods for putting them up to it; and he will judge us if we do not obey his ordinances. The psalmist is like a weak modern prime minister: hollow threats to withdraw the whip from his dissident followers alternate with vacuous rhetoric against the opposition. Only the sons of Asaph did not fear a mere election.

I should comment on an assumption shared by Buss and Illman, and by a number of the critics I have mentioned, that the unity of a group of psalms like the Asaph or Korah psalms should consist in their being members of the same *Gattung*. This is quite unwarranted. We do not expect a book of sermons, should such be published today, to consist of homilies of the same type: perhaps the preacher will begin the Advent season with the topics of death, judgment, heaven and hell, but then turn to speak of God's grace in the Incarnation. Perhaps, similarly, an Israelite psalmist might open the festal season with a call to penitence, provide for a day's humiliation, and then turn to God's promise of blessing on the king, the army and the people. Naturally the prevailing political situation will influence his choice of theme, and a year of sharp military danger will evoke a series of laments like 74, 77, 79, 80 and 83. But the Asaph psalms are, by common assent, mostly public psalms—I should say all public psalms—and their most likely setting must be the autumn festival (cf. 81.4); and a festival must have some established liturgical form. So if, for example, the Asaph psalms were a collection for use in the festal week of Tabernacles, a variety of psalm-types is what we should expect.

History

Delitzsch goes on: 'The visionary character of the Asaphic psalms [i.e. the prophetic judgment speeches] has the historical for its reverse side; we frequently meet with descriptive retrospective glances back to facts of early times (lxxiv.13-15, lxxvii.15ff., lxxx.9-12, lxxxi.5-8, lxxxiii.10-12), and Psalm lxxviii is taken up entirely with holding up the mirror of the ancient history of the people before the present' (*Psalms*, II, p. 143).

The individuality of the Asaph psalms is even more striking than Delitzsch has indicated. Not only do half of the twelve psalms make appeal to history, on his computation 93 verses out of 262: we have also to note how rare a feature this is elsewhere in the Psalter. There are four 'historical' psalms, 105–106, 135–36, and there are 95 and 114, but beyond that it is difficult to be sure of any reference to the Exodus and wilderness themes, to Sinai or anything in Genesis. There are in fact references to the Settlement in 44, and to an apostasy in the desert in 85, and I have argued for many echoes of the David saga in 51–72. But the Exodus experience is a recurrent theme in our collection, and is constantly urged upon God as an appeal, and upon Israel as a ground for trust in 77.16-21, 78.12-14, 42–53, 80.9, 81.6-8. One might also include under this head the rather frequent references to the *covenant* (50.5, 16; 74.20; 78.10, 37), not included here by Delitzsch, which have in mind the revelation at Meribah described in 81.8-11.

A second significant feature of the Asaph historical appeals is their frequent *differences* from the classic accounts in Genesis–Samuel. The account of creation in 74.12-15 is the old Near Eastern myth, and unrelated either to the Priestly story in Genesis 1 or the Adam and Eve legend. The description of the Exodus in 77.17-20 is of God in his storm triumphing over the waters; there is no mention of the waters being divided, the Egyptian army and so forth, though these features are known in the collection and occur in 78.13, 53. Psalm 78 has a number of discrepancies with the standard history (see below). For example, the cleaving of the rock to give water (78.15-16) is not cited as a matter of Israel's tempting God; it comes before the manna and quails (78.23-29), not after as in both Exodus 16–17 and Numbers 11–20; the plagues are substantially different from the Exodus version; when the ark is lost at Shiloh, fire devours 'their young men' (78.63) in an event not mentioned in 1 Samuel 4. In 81.8-9 the covenant is given not at Sinai but at Meribah. In 83.10-11 Jabin appears to have been killed with Sisera after the Kishon battle, and their deaths took place at En-dor; neither of these details corresponds with Judges 4–5.

This accumulation, both of historical references and of discrepant details, seems to set the Asaph psalms apart. By contrast, the *Heils geschichte* as told in 105–106 begins with Abraham and is markedly nearer the Pentateuch (though still not identical), and that in 135–36 is very close. Illman correctly picks out the historical theme in our psalms, but he unwisely discounts it: only 78 is a full historical psalm—like 105–106, 135–36—and for the rest we have mere references of three or four verses in five other psalms. This is seriously to underestimate the phenomenon, by failing to set out the perspective of contrast elsewhere in the Psalter. The Asaph psalmists appealed to the Exodus, the wilderness tradition and the covenant at Meribah in a way that is unparalleled in other psalms; and it is also significant that their history begins with our Exodus 1, the oppression, and makes no open reference to our Genesis.

These features again require explaining. One line that suggests itself is a comparison with Hosea, since he cites the Exodus from Egypt (11.1; 13.4) and the covenant in the wilderness (2.14-15); and Amos, who also appeals to the Exodus and the wilderness (2.10; 5.25; 9.7). By contrast there is no reference to these themes in (first) Isaiah or Micah, their later contemporaries from Judah.[2] Also Hosea's references to Israelite history, in the case of Jacob (12.3-4), vary from the Pentateuch. We might think that the Asaph psalms come from a similar date or place to Hosea; that is, to Northern Israel in the eighth century. Perhaps the Asaph community is from the tribes which experienced the Exodus; and this would explain also their reference to Meribah, which is mentioned in the old northern Deut. 33.8, and which many scholars today think to have been the centre for the tribes which came out of Egypt (see pp. 155-56). If so, the developed version of these events which we have in the Pentateuch would not yet have been formed, and the discrepancies would be natural.

Northern Echoes

This leads on to Delitzsch's fourth point: 'If we read the twelve Asaphic psalms the one after the other, we shall also note the striking peculiarity, that more frequent mention is made of Joseph and the tribes descended from him than elsewhere (lxxvii.16, lxxviii.9,67f., lxxxi.6, lxxx.2f.).' This feature has been widely noted, and has led to the division among critics which I have outlined above. Peters and Engnell have seen it as a sign that the Asaph collection is of originally northern origin; Delitzsch, Kirkpatrick, Gunkel and most commentators have taken it to imply a core of northern psalms, later added to in Jerusalem; Illman and others have found alternative explanations for it, and sited the whole collection in the south.

The data are complex. Ps. 77.16 says, 'Thou hast with thine arm redeemed thy people, The sons of Jacob and Joseph.' The phrasing is

---

2. The references to Egypt in Isa. 10.25-26 are thought by R.E. Clements to come from a redaction in Josiah's time (*Isaiah 1–39*, pp. 116-17); only the first four chapters of Micah are commonly attributed to the prophet himself.

surprising, since in the Pentateuch *all* Israel is redeemed from Egypt, and 'the sons of Jacob' would have sufficed; the words seem to suggest that two *different* communities were in the psalmist's mind. Psalm 80 opens, 'Give ear, O Shepherd of Israel, Thou that leadest Joseph like a flock... Before Ephraim and Benjamin and Manasseh, stir up thy might, And come to save us.' It has been suggested (Kirkpatrick, Kraus, Eaton, Tate; see p. 138) that the psalmist is a Judahite in King Josiah's time, praying for the liberation of the adjacent tribes of Northern Israel; but here most critics (Delitzsch, Eissfeldt, Gunkel, Mowinckel, Weiser, Jacquet) accept the *prima facie* meaning. Ps. 80.5 prays God to cease anger with 'thy people', and this seems to be identical with 'Joseph' in 80.2, and to comprise in fact the two Joseph tribes of Ephraim and Manasseh with the related Benjamin. God 'leads' Joseph, and he is to stir up his might *before* the three tribes; that is, to go into battle at their head. Judah is not mentioned because (at the time) Judah was not part of the community. In 81.5-6 festal celebration is said to be 'a statute for Israel... He appointed it in Joseph for a testimony, When he went out over the land of Egypt.' Illman suggests that 'Joseph' was a natural name for the whole Israelite people when they were in Egypt; but again this seems a little forced. It sounds rather as if the psalmist identified Israel with Joseph, and thought of Joseph as the *only* section of the people which had been in Egypt. For a fuller discussion see p. 152.

Against these three positive passages we have two negative ones in Psalms 78: 78.9, 'The children of Ephraim, being armed and carrying bows, Turned back in the day of battle'; and 78.67, 'Moreover he refused the tent of Joseph, and chose not the tribe of Ephraim; But chose the tribe of Judah, And mount Zion which he loved.' These verses are puzzling for two reasons. First, the burden of the long psalm is that the *whole* people has continually forgotten God and been unfaithful to his covenant, not that one section of the people has failed. Secondly, the verses in question interrupt the flow of thought. Ps. 78.8 spoke of 'their fathers, A generation that prepared not their heart...', and 78.10 continues, 'They kept not the covenant of God'—'They' should be the fathers of the wilderness period, not some Ephraimites. In 78.65-66 God awakes as one out of sleep and smites his adversaries—that is, the Philistines—backward; and in 78.70-72 he chooses David to rule Israel and do the deed. Rejecting the 'tent of Joseph'—that is, the shrine at Shiloh—in favour of Jerusalem, is a distraction.

The matter is further complicated by a number of references to Jerusalem/Zion: 50.2, 'Out of Zion, the perfection of beauty, God hath shined forth'; 74.2, 'Remember...mount Zion, wherein thou hast dwelt'; 76.2, 'In Judah is God known: His name is great in Israel. In Salem also is his covert: And his lair in Zion'; 78.68-69, 'But chose the tribe of Judah, The mount Zion which he loved. And he built his sanctuary like the heights'; 79.1, 'They have laid Jerusalem in heaps.' While each of these texts will be discussed in its context, there is clearly a *prima facie* justification for Illman's conclusion that the collection belongs in Jerusalem.

We are thus faced with a dilemma. One collection of references suggests that the Asaph psalms come from Jerusalem, and another collection suggests that they come from Northern Israel. It seems a mistake to refuse either conclusion; can we not find a reconciliation? In the Psalter as a whole, it is the Joseph references which are the aberrant feature; ultimately all the psalms were used in Jerusalem, or they did not survive. We have reasons for thinking that some northern priests fled to Jerusalem after 722; and if they brought psalms with them, they would need to be adapted for use in their new home. So inevitably any references to northern sanctuaries would need to be amended to Zion/Jerusalem; and those names might well be inserted into the texts, by the northerners themselves; but we also have to reckon with some resentment by the Zadokite authorities, who would hardly relish their privileges being eroded—hence the rather jealous and petty spirit of the additions in Ps. 78.9, 67-69.

The remarkable thing is that the Jerusalem editors have left so many traces behind them of the original context of the psalms. It is a widely observed feature of redactoral overworking that editors are more careful at the beginning of their labours than at the end. It is noticeable that the Jerusalem/Zion references are limited to the first two-thirds of the collection, Psalms 50, 74, 76, 78, 79; while the Joseph references come only in its second half, Psalms 77, [78], 80, 81. Further they have left in a significant number of more subtle indications of northern provenance, such as, 'They have burned up all the places of assembly of God in the land' (74.8), or the covenant at Meribah (81.8-9).

One such significant reference is the mention of 'Salem' at 76.3. Salem was not in early times an alternative name for Jerusalem, but an independent place near Shechem, where Jacob built an altar in Gen. 33.18-20. The two sanctuaries at Salem (Shechem) and Bethel are linked in that both Abraham (Gen. 12.6-8) and Jacob (Gen. 35.1-8) journey from the first to the second, and there are reasons for thinking that the Salem priesthood moved to Bethel after the destruction of Shechem. The shrines are linked by their worship of אל, also a function of our psalms. Jacob called the altar at Salem for אל־אלהי־ישראל (Gen. 33.20), and that at Bethel for אל־בית־אל (Gen. 35.7). We have seen that אל עליון is also an Asaphic term, and Melchizedek king of Salem was the priest of אל עליון in Gen. 14.18, 22. So the *Salem* at 76.3 is part of the original northern text; it has been left in by an editor who took it, like J.M. Neale,[3] to be the same as Jerusalem, and *Zion* was introduced in parallel to confirm the fact. For a fuller discussion see below, pp. 86-88.

However, this leaves unresolved the question of why 'Joseph' should have been used for the people of God, a feature peculiar to the Asaph collection in the Psalter. Here we may think of the situation in the decade 732–722: (Northern) Israel had not included Judah since the days of Rehoboam, and in 2 Kgs 15.29 Tiglath-Pileser captured most of the cities in the north of the country, and annexed 'Gilead and Galilee, all the land of Naphtali'. What remained thereafter, until the fall of Samaria ten years later, was a rump of West Bank territory south of the plain of Esdraelon: Western Manasseh, Ephraim and Benjamin, with perhaps a part of Issachar. The greater part of the people of these territories might think of themselves as 'Joseph'.

Two features encourage us to think that this suggestion is right. One is that the people of God are also referred to as Joseph three times in the contemporary book of Amos: 'Seek the LORD, and ye shall live; lest he break out like fire in the house of Joseph' (5.6); 'it may be that the LORD, the God of hosts, will be gracious unto the remnant of Joseph' (5.15); 'they are not grieved for the affliction of Joseph' (6.5). *The remnant of Joseph* is what remains after the annexations of 732; *the affliction of Joseph* is the disastrous defeat of that year and any subsequent invasions; God was to *break out like fire in the house of Joseph* in 722. The other encouraging feature is the pervasive sense of impending catastrophe which marks these psalms, and which must have been current during this final decade of the community's history.

The only other text in the Bible in which 'Joseph' is used in this way is Obad. 18, 'The house of Jacob shall be a fire, and the house of Joseph a flame, and the house

---

3. In his hymn, 'Blessed City, Heavenly Salem'.

of Esau for stubble.' Obadiah is prophesying the recovery of the land from Edom, including the recovery of Ephraim, Samaria and Gilead (v. 19).

The assonance Asaph/Joseph (אָסָף/יוֹסֵף) has sometimes suggested a connection between the two names, and this may now seem very likely. In Gen. 30.23-24 Rachel calls her first-born son Joseph, saying, 'God hath taken away (אָסַף) my reproach.' When the collection was brought to Jerusalem, it required a label to distinguish it from the Dan psalms and the old Jerusalem psalms. It would be unacceptable to speak of them as the Bethel psalms, so 'the Joseph psalms' could be tried; but then the intention was to have them accepted as Judah psalms (76.2), Zion psalms. So perhaps they came to be spoken of as the Psalms of Asaph, for whom a high office was invented as chief musician to King David. The Dan psalms were the Psalms *of the sons of Korah*, and Korah was a real person (Goulder, *Korah*, chapter 3). Asaph was not a real person. The leading Bethel priest in charge of the psalmody was probably called Zimmah (chapter 14).

E.C.B. MacLaurin ('Joseph') suggested an Asaph-Joseph connection, but his proposal to link this with magical practices does not seem necessary.

Common Language

Delitzsch's final point is that 'the relation in which Jahve and Israel stand to one another is most generally represented under the figure of a shepherd and his flock (lxxiv.1, lxxvii.21, lxxviii.52 [cf. 70–72], lxxix.13, lxxx.2)' (*Psalms*, II, p. 143). The insistence of this image is noticeable. 'Why doth thine anger smoke against *the sheep of thy pasture*?' (74.1); 'thou *leddest* thy people like *a flock*' (77.21); 'he *led* forth his own people *like sheep*' (78.52); ['He chose David also his servant, And took him from the sheepfolds...' (78.70-72)]; 'So we thy people and *sheep of thy pasture* will give thee thanks' (79.13); 'Give ear, O *Shepherd* of Israel, Thou that *leadest* Joseph *like a flock*' (80.2). Ps. 79.13 is the last verse of 79: Ps. 80.2 is the first verse of 80. The image of Israel as the flock of the divine shepherd is limited in the Psalter to these five Asaph texts and to 95.7 and 100.3, where *the sheep of his pasture* (צֹאן מַרְעִיתוֹ) recurs, as in 74.1, 79.13. צֹאן, *a flock*, is used in all five; נהג, *lead*, comes in 78.52 and 80.2; נהה, *lead*, in 77.21; the hiph. of נסע, *remove*, is used of God's guidance out of Egypt only in 78.52 and 80.9 (also of Moses in Exod. 15.22).

The presence of a number of rare, and even unique, words and phrases in more than one of the Asaph psalms has been noted by Nasuti, and these tend to strengthen the impression that the Asaph psalms come from the same community, or even the same author. For instance, זיז שָׂדַי, usually rendered *the beasts of the field*, comes in 50.11 and 80.14, and nowhere else in the Bible; and the rare verb הופיע, *shine forth*, also occurs in 50.2 and 80.2—it comes in 94.1 in addition, in the northern Deut. 33.2 and four times in Job. But 50 is also related to 81. Ps. 50.7, 'Hear, O my people, and I will speak; O Israel, and I will testify unto thee: I am God, thy God', is nearly identical to 81.9, 11: 'Hear, O my people, and I will testify unto thee; O Israel... I am the LORD thy God.' Both psalms are prophetic challenges to obedience to the divine covenant.

Here again the *covenant*, ברית, is appealed to by name not only in 50.5, 16, but in 74.20 and 78.10, 37. Of course the term is common in post-Deuteronomic texts, but it is notoriously rare in the earlier period, where the evidence suggests our psalms arose; and further, the term is here associated with the giving of the covenant in the desert. Ps. 50.7-21 echoes our Pentateuchal covenant texts not only in the proem, 'I am God...', but in specific commandments on sacrifice, thieving, adultery and slander. Psalm 78 describes Israel's repeated rejection of the covenant in the desert. Ps. 81.8-11 mentions the site of the covenant-giving at Meribah, and the requirement of Yahweh-worship alone. Psalm 50 is also linked to 78 by the rare word מכלאות, (sheep)*folds* (50.9, 78.70; also Hab. 3.17).

Other pairs of rare expressions are more widespread. The parallel *the arrogant/the wicked* (הוללים/רשעים) comes in 73.3 and 75.5. The combination does not come elsewhere. The plural משואות, *ruins*, occurs in 73.18 and 74.3 only. God's *smoking* with anger, עשן, comes in 74.1 and 80.5 alone in the Psalter (also Deut. 29.19). The *deeds*, מעללי-, of Yah/El, are spoken of in 77.12 and 78.7 (and Mic. 2.7 only), and God *performs miracles*, עשה פלא, in 77.15 and 78.12 (also in 88.11; Exod. 15.11; Isa. 25.1). He *appoints a testimony in* his people, שים עדות ב, in 78.5 and 81.6, uniquely. He *forgives*, כפר, sins in 78.38 and 79.9, alone in the Psalter; and *drives out the nations*, גרש גוים, before his people in 78.55 and 80.9 only.

There is a marked interplay of language between the Asaph psalms and the Song of the Sea in Exodus 15, which also tends to draw the collection together:

	Exodus 15		*Psalms*
1	The horse and his rider (סוס ורכבו)	76.7	chariot and horse (ורכב וסוס)
8	The floods stood upright as an heap (נצבו כמו־נד)	78.13	He made the waters to stand as an heap (ויצב כמו־נד)...
10	The sea covered them (כִּסָּמוֹ יָם)	78.53	the sea covered their enemies (כִּסָּה הַיָּם)
11	Who is like unto thee, O LORD, among the gods? (מִי כָמֹכָה בָּאֵלִים)	77.14	Who is a great god like unto God? (מִי־אֵל גָּדוֹל כֵּאלֹהִים)
	...glorious in holiness (בקדש)	77.14	Thy way, O God, is בקדש
	...doing wonders? (עשׂה פלא)	77.15, 78.12	עשׂה פלא
13	Thou hast led thy people which thou hast redeemed (עם־זו גאלת)	77.16	Thou hast with thine arm redeemed thy people (גאלת עמך)
16	By the greatness of thine arm (זרועך)...the people which thou hast purchased (עם־זו קנית)	74.2	thy congregation which thou hast purchased of old... redeemed (קדם גאלת קנית)
17	Thou shalt bring them in and plant them in the mountain (בהר) of thine inheritance... the sanctuary (מקדש)	78.54	He brought them to the border of his sanctuary (קדשׁו) To the mountain (הר)

It is noticeable both that a considerable section of Exod. 15.1-18 is paralleled in the Asaph collection, and also that the parallels are not limited to the 'Exodus' psalms, 77 and 78, but extend to 74, 76 and 80.

The links of the Asaph collection with Exodus 15 are expounded in detail by Martin Brenner, *The Song of the Sea* (1991). Brenner concludes that Exod. 15.1-21 was written by the Asaph community about the time of Nehemiah. The strong links between the Asaph psalms and the Song are common ground to us. His reasoning for so late a date depends on (i) a late dating of these (and most other) psalms, and (ii) association of Exodus 15 with the language of other post-exilic passages. The first argument is disputed *seriatim* in Part I of this book. The second is flawed: there is much common phrasing between Ezekiel and the book of Revelation, but they do not come from the same period. While it is difficult to *prove* an early date for Exod. 15.1b-18, that is suggested by (a) 'The LORD is a man of war' (אִישׁ מִלְחָמָה, 15.3), only paralleled in Ps. 24.8, יהוה גִּבּוֹר מִלְחָמָה; (b) the archaic termination ־מוֹ after verbs, of which there are nine instances in these verses, out of 23 in the Old Testament. Brenner explains these unconvincingly as artificial. I am influenced by a third consideration. The Asaph psalmists know two versions of the Exodus story: the victory of God over the waters only (77.17-20), and the piling up of the waters to cover the Egyptians (78.13, 53). This is best explained if the former, more simple version were the community's own tradition, and if the latter has been influenced by Exodus 15.

In the nature of things, the linguistic inter-linking does not include all the Asaph psalms: there has been nothing for 82 and 83, and not much for 75 and 76. Nevertheless it may be thought that Nasuti's evidence is much more than could be explained as fortuitous, and that it reinforces the arguments above for taking the Asaph collection seriously. It increases the probability that our psalms stem from a single community in place and time.

Nasuti has attempted a more ambitious linguistic enterprise in linking the Asaph psalms' wording with 'Ephraimite' language, defined as that occurring in Hosea, E-texts, Deuteronomy and the D-history, Jeremiah, and the 'deutero-Asaphic' psalms in Book IV. While the connections he makes could be significant, they involve too much hypothesis to convince a sceptic, and I have eschewed arguments of this form, apart from an occasional link with Hosea. I think in fact that Nasuti's work is help-ful, and have argued in Chapter 15 that the Asaphites were in large measure respon-sible for the Deuteronomic revolution (the D-community were their grandchildren and later descendants). For a more ambitious but less successful attempt to isolate 'Israelian Hebrew', see G.A. Rendsburg, *Linguistic Evidence*.

The Relation to Deuteronomy

Buss spoke of the Asaph psalms as 'Deuteronomic–Levitical', and readers of them can hardly fail to be struck by the instances of Deuteronomic language. Deut. 4.45, for example, 'These are the testimonies and the statutes and the judgments (העדות והחקים והמשפטים)' is echoed in Ps. 81.5-6: 'For it is a statute (חק) for Israel, An ordinance (משפט) of the God of Jacob. He appointed it in Joseph for a testimony (עדות).' Deuteronomy 5 begins, 'Hear, O Israel...', and continues, 'I am the LORD thy God which brought thee out of the land of Egypt' (5.6). I have just cited the verses in Ps. 50.7 and 81.9, 11 which virtually dupli-cate these words. Although, as Illman says (*Thema*, p. 47), many of these expressions are not exclusively Deuteronomic, Nasuti marshals so many significant parallels that the general picture is impressive.

This is especially the case, as Illman concedes, with Psalm 78, which gives an overall view of Israelite history remarkably similar in tone to the Deuteronomistic work. Like the latter (normally), it begins with the Exodus; it presents the story as a series of divine marvels—the plagues, the Exodus, the guidance through the desert, the Settlement—punctuated by a sad sequence of rebellions, forgetting the covenant, tempting God, provoking him to jealousy and the like; this results in a series of outbursts of divine wrath, with condign punishment; and finally in a succession of acts of forgiveness, compassion and awaking as one out of sleep. In other words, Psalm 78 presents in a (large) nutshell the classic Deuteronomic *Vergeltungsdogma*: Israel's troubles are the retribution for their disobedience, and their sole hope lies in renewed obedience to the God of grace. This is expressed clearly in 81: my people did not hearken, so I let them go; if Israel walked in my ways, I should soon subdue their enemies.

The Deuteronomists have been so influential on later Israelite thinking that it has been natural for critics, Gunkel for one, to see the Asaph psalms as a post-exilic collection also testifying to their influence. But influence, of course, may run two ways. Deuteronomy did not descend from heaven in 622, and it is equally possible that the Asaph community influenced the Deuteronomists; indeed, I shall argue that they were their grandparents (Chapter 14).

Two features indicate that the Asaph group are prior. The Deuteronomic dogma has four elements: (i) divine grace (the Exodus etc.), (ii) Israel's rebellions, (iii) divine wrath, (iv) Israel's repentance and forgiveness. The D-history is written in the light of the disasters of 597 and 587, and is designed to explain point (iii). This is what the repeated homiletic matter has in mind, in Judg. 2.11-23, or in 2 Kgs 17.7-23, or in Deut. 28.15-68 above all. Israel (Judah) has suffered the ultimate punishment, but they may still turn, obey and receive God's blessing.

It is this element which is missing in the Asaph psalms. Psalm 78 alternates between calls to remember God's wondrous deeds (vv. 4-7, 'that they might set their hope in God') and warnings not to be as their forefathers (vv. 8, 10-11). The story starts with the miracles in Egypt (v. 12), and it ends with the Lord awaking out of sleep and smiting the Philistines backward through his chosen David (vv. 65-72). Things are bad as the psalmist writes, and he naturally attributes this to God's wrath, and so to national disobedience. But his message is one of hope. There has been no loss of the people's independence. They are to remember God's wondrous deeds of old, and expect him to repeat them, as he did in the Exodus period, and with David. It is noticeable that even the present, glossed form of the text does not know of the fall of Jerusalem: God 'forsook the tabernacle at Shiloh, The tent which he placed among men' (78.60), and 'built his sanctuary [in Zion] like the heights, Like the earth which he hath established for ever' (78.69).

It is the same throughout the collection. The speaker of Psalm 77 is perplexed, and passes the night in prayer, but he resolves his doubts by reflecting that the right hand of the Most High does not change—what he did in the Exodus, he will do again. In Psalm 75 the speaker vows to cut off the horns of the wicked, and in Psalm 76 God is terrible to the kings of the earth, and stuns their chariots and horses. In Psalm 80 God's hand is to be on the man of his right hand; he is to quicken us, to turn us again and we shall be saved. In Psalm 81 if Israel would hearken, their enemies would soon be subdued. Psalm 83 can envisage victories over the surrounding invaders such as were won over Sisera and the Midianite princes. Even Psalms 74 and 79 can look for revenge on the spoilers of their sanctuaries, which are still under Israelite control, and the site of national prayer. There is no psalm in the collection whose text implies the loss of national sovereignty: the references to Jerusalem in Psalms 74 and 79 are problematic, as will be seen.

A second important feature of the Deuteronomic charge is that Israel has been idolatrous. Their principal sin has been that they 'feared other gods' and burned incense 'upon every high hill, and under every green tree' (2 Kgs 17.7-12); in other words, that they worshipped at local shrines away from Jerusalem, and this involved other gods than Yahweh. Now local worship was undoubtedly a feature of pre-Deuteronomic Israel, and the worship of the host of heaven, with hideous rites, is attributed to Manasseh (2 Kgs 21.1-18); but neither of these matters seems to be felt as a major cause of guilt by the Asaph psalmists.

So far as the local shrines are concerned, Ps. 74.8 says, 'They have burned up all the meeting places of God in the land.' The מועדי־אל are nothing else than local shrines (see pp. 66-67); and so far from being seen as sinful, they are *God*'s meeting places, and their destruction is appealed to as a gross insult to his dignity, which he is expected to avenge. Nor is idolatry apparently a current problem, Ps. 78.58 says, 'they provoked him to anger with their high places, And moved him to jealousy with their graven images', and this refers to lapses into iconic worship during the Settlement period, now past. Ps. 81.10 refers to the interdict on alien worship at Meribah, 'There shall no strange god be in thee...', and the verses following show that this was not observed: 'But my people hearkened not to my voice...'—probably with special reference to the apostasy now associated with the Golden Calf. But Psalm 50 gives us a better idea of the current situation. It delivers a series of clear charges against 'my people', and idolatry is no part of them. What is said is that sacrificial worship has been superficial and without true thanksgiving; that there has been collusion with theft and adultery, and slandering within the family. This is similar in tone to the nearly contemporary Korahite Psalm 44: 'If we have forgotten the name of our God, Or spread forth our hands to a strange god, Shall not God search this out?' (44.21-22).

So despite the general similarity of Psalms 78 and 81 to the D-history, there are marked differences. The Asaph psalmists, unlike the Deuteronomists, do not regard the loss of national sovereignty as the ultimate punishment for its apostasy, expressed in the worship of other gods in local shrines. They have not experienced the loss of national sovereignty (even if they are looking it in the eye); they were not conscious of worshipping other gods; and they regarded local shrines as God's meeting places, whose destruction he should avenge. It is the Asaph psalmists who have influenced the Deuteronomists, not *vice versa*.

Conclusion

Delitzsch's five points seem, on examination, to bind the Asaph collection *together* even more firmly than he had thought. The dominant use of אלהים and the comparative rarity of יהוה set the group apart from Books I, IV and V. It belongs with the Korah psalms and the Prayers of David (51–72) in Books II–III, which have roughly the same proportionate uses of these two names, but its uses of אל and עליון are notably more frequent than in the rest of Books II–III, or of any other group of psalms, and suggest that the Asaph group have some inner cohesion. The political situation presupposed by the texts is also strikingly univocal. Sometimes (74; 79; 82) disaster has struck, but the end is not yet. More often it threatens, but there is hope (77; 80; 81, 83—and, I shall argue, 73). Sometimes it calls forth the prophetic challenge to return to the covenant, and the enemy will be defeated (50; 78; 81). Sometimes the psalmist meets it with bluster (75; 76). But the pervasive theme of judgment, whether on Israel or their foes, bespeaks the same Damoclean sword suspended above their head.

There are numerous other features which bind the collection together. The appeal to history (74; 77; 78; 80; 81; 83) is far more widespread and detailed than is to be found in any other collection, if we exclude the two pairs of historical psalms, 105–106 and 135–36. There is no mention of the Exodus elsewhere in Books I–III, but it is the basis of 77, 78, 80 and 81. It is striking besides that the Exodus is associated in 77, 80 and 81 with Joseph as the people of God, specified in 80 as Ephraim, Benjamin and Manasseh; and the same use comes, in a perverse sense, in 78, but nowhere else in the Psalter. There are also considerable linguistic links between the Asaph psalms and the Song of the Sea in Exodus 15, and a number of rare and unique expressions, like זי שׁדי, occur more than once in these psalms alone.

Many of these features not only bind the Asaph group together, but suggest a time and place for them in *Northern Israel* in the decade 732–722. It was in this period that Israel was reduced to a core, comprising the tribes of Ephraim, Benjamin and Manasseh, with perhaps Southern Issachar, the Assyrians having annexed the northern and East Bank territories. The country is three times referred to as Joseph by Amos in this decade. It was in this period that Israel suffered a fatal defeat at the hands of the Assyrian army, which marched at will through Palestine creating havoc. So we have a ready-made explanation for the burning of the national shrine, the slaughter of the army, and the ever-present fear of the unthinkable. The Assyrians are specifically mentioned in 83, along with numerous jackal allies; we hear of their setting up their 'images' or 'signs' (73; 74) in their victory inscriptions; and their burning of 'all the meeting places of God in the land' (74) belongs most easily in the pre-Deuteronomic north.

Other features seem to confirm this picture. The preference for אלהים over יהוה is best explained as coming from an early period, before the prophets had forced the issue on syncretistic worship. The frequency of אל and עליון, with their Canaanite overtones, invites an early date, as does the link with Salem; and the polytheistic picture in 82, and the primitive creation myth in 74, are alike signs of antiquity—the former being the clearest piece of non-orthodoxy to survive in the Bible. The historical traditions, too, are frequently not quite the ones we find in our Pentateuch: there is an Exodus tradition in which God acts in nothing more than a thunderstorm (77), the plagues are different (78), the water from the rock is a gift, not a temptation (78), the covenant is given at Meribah, not Sinai (81), the details of the Settlement battles differ from Judges (83). This is most easily explained if they are drawn from an early tradition outside Jerusalem. The theology of the collection, similarly, seems to be pre-Deuteronomic: it has much in common with the

D-tradition, both in language and in thought, but it is missing the important elements of the abomination of local worship and idolatry, and the
nation's sovereignty is still intact.

These considerations form a powerful cumulative case for siting the
whole Asaph collection in a northern shrine, most probably Bethel, in
the 720s. The counter-arguments which weighed so heavily with
Kirkpatrick, Gunkel and Mowinckel seem to stem from a failure of
imagination. It is naive to assume that a psalm which refers to the
defilement of the Jerusalem Temple must have been *composed* for that
event. Psalm 74 uses early names for God, and the old Near Eastern
creation myth, and it deplores the burning of all the meeting places of
God in the land. This should surely suggest to us that it was composed
as a lament for some earlier, northern disaster, and then applied to the
situation of 586 in Jerusalem by the addition of a few words. References
to Babylon in Isaiah 40–55 (and before) do not prove that the entire
book of Isaiah stems from the Babylonian period. Any ancient northern
psalms had to be *edited* to make them usable in Jerusalem after 722; and
the solution proposed by Peters and Engnell deserved a proper
consideration.

A general overview of the evidence, such as I have offered in this
chapter, can never suffice to close the case. What I hope to have done
here is to propose a plausible working hypothesis: the Psalms of Asaph
were composed in Northern Israel in the 720s in response to the
Assyrian threat, and were then taken and re-used in a (slightly) edited
form in Jerusalem. The only way in which such a hypothesis can be
made convincing is by a detailed exegesis, such as Peters, Engnell and
Nasuti did not provide; and that will occupy the rest of Part I. Perhaps
my wary readers suspect that hard work lies ahead for small reward.
They have not hitherto much regarded the sons of Asaph. Let them not
fear. Three great prizes lie ahead. First, we are able to descry numerous
details of Israelite life in the 720s, and to see into the hearts of a deeply
religious people on the verge of catastrophe. Secondly, the psalms reveal
the outline of worship at the autumn festival of the period. Thirdly, they
provide the key to a long quest: the riddle of the history of the
Pentateuch.

Part I

THE PSALMS OF ASAPH

Chapter 2

BEFORE THE FESTIVAL

Psalm 50

50.1   A Psalm of Asaph
      God (אל), *even* God (אלהים), *the* LORD, hath spoken,
      And called the earth from the rising of the sun unto the going
         down thereof.

2   [Out of Zion] From the fullness of splendour (מכלל־יפי) God
      hath shined forth.

3   Our God cometh, and shall not keep silence:
      A fire devoureth before him,
      And it is very tempestuous round about him.

4   He calleth to the heavens above,
      And to the earth, that he may judge his people:

5   Gather my saints together unto me;
      Those that make covenant (כֹרתי) with me by sacrifice.

6   And the heavens declare his righteousness:
      For God is judge himself.   (Selah

50.1. The psalmist begins with a revealing complex divine name. God is known first by the old name, אל, by which the Joseph/Benjamin tribes first knew him (p. 157); and it was at Salem by Shechem that Jacob set up his altar to אל־אלהי־ישראל (Gen. 33.20). These tribes have with time adapted to the worship of Yahweh established by their predecessors, and his name has now been glossed in to form the impressive triple אל אלהים יהוה. We find the same combination in only one other context, Josh. 22.22, where the Transjordanian tribes defend their having built an altar beyond Jordan for אל אלהים יהוה. It was from this area that the Joseph tribes immigrated into West Bank Israel, and Joshua 22 comes shortly before the Shechem covenant of Joshua 24.

God calls the whole world, not just Israel, to his judgment. This again is traditional. Powerful kings in the ancient Near East presided over national festivals at which their clients were expected to attend and present their annual tribute. In the tenth century the Israelite poet could say, 'Because of thy temple at Jerusalem Kings shall bring presents unto thee... Princes shall come out of Egypt, Ethiopia shall haste to stretch out her hands to God' (Ps. 68.29-31; cf. Goulder, *Prayers*, pp. 191-216); and in the high days of the Omrids the psalmist can write, 'O clap your hands, *all ye peoples*... He shall subdue the peoples under us' (Ps. 47.1-3). They are to clap their hands and rejoice that they have become subject to Israel; and he can even say, 'The princes of the peoples are gathered together *To be* the people of the God of Abraham'—they are being assimilated into the Israelite empire (Goulder, *Korah*, pp. 153-59). Such ideas are nothing but nostalgia now. It soon becomes evident that 50 is addressed to Israel alone. There are no client princes when one's back is to the wall.

50.2. A further traditional theme has been carried over in the storm theophany. Just as Baal-Hadad made his voice heard in the thunder, and came in storm from Mt Zaphon, so does God *call* the world. The end of the long Levantine summer drought is marked by the first thunder of autumn, and that is the sign for the Israelite king to summon the people for the festival (חג יהוה, 1 Kgs 8.2; Lev. 23.39; Hos. 9.5; Judg. 21.19). The slightly elastic Israelite year, with twelve moons totalling 354 days, could be amplified with an additional leap-moon every three years or so, and the seasonal thunder was among the signs which told him that the festal month of Bul (harvest) was due. Baal-Hadad came from Zaphon, and in later times the Judahite tradition was to bring God from Sinai in the south; but the Joseph tribes had been settled at Kadesh in the Edomite hills, and it is for that reason that the older, northern traditions ascribe him a home there. 'The LORD came from Sinai [so the later Judahite glossator], And rose from *Seir* unto them; He shined forth (הופיע) from mount *Paran*, And he came from the ten thousands of holiness (קדש, LXX καδες): At his right hand was a fiery law unto them' (Deut. 33.2); 'LORD, when thou wentest forth out of *Seir*, When thou marchedst out of the *field of Edom*, The earth trembled, the heavens also dropped, Yea, the clouds dropped water' (Judg. 5.4). This has been also carried over in, 'God cometh from Teman, And the Holy One from mount *Paran*' (Hab. 3.3).

Our text reads, 'From Zion, from the perfection of splendour God hath shined forth.' Gunkel notes the inappositeness of this: God *is coming*, not *from* Zion but *to* Zion (where the psalm was later to be at

home)—he is coming with thunder and lightning from his mountain
home in the south. Furthermore, the psalm is regular in its metre: 3.3 for
most of it, but there are five stresses in v. 2. Gunkel and Kraus delete
אלהים to give a balanced 4.4 with v. 3a, but it would be preferable to see
מציון as a later Jerusalem gloss, introduced to domesticate the psalm. We
would then have a reason for the second 'from' (מכלל־יפי), and God
would be 'shining forth' (הופיע) from *heaven*, as he does in Deut. 33.2;
that is, in the lightning. This is a more plausible notion of a theophany
(cf. Kraus) than the claims of a pietistic, visionary 'theophany' in the
Temple, and Ps. 80.2, 94.1 should be taken in the same way. יפי should
be rendered 'splendour' rather than 'beauty'. In Ps. 48.3 the divine
mountain is said to be יפה נוף, *splendid* rather than beautiful in height,
and the word is used of Pharaoh's cows in Gen. 41.2 and the great
cedar in Ezek. 31.3—Delitzsch gives the root meaning of יפה as *tower
forth, be high* (*Psalms, ad* 48.2). So God shines forth from the fullness
of splendour in heaven. The lightning we see is but a ray from the fullness of his sun-like glory. The glossing of 'From Zion' was done in the
seventh century when the Asaph psalms were adapted for Jerusalem
use: by the sixth century we read, 'Is this [Jerusalem] the city that men
called The perfection of beauty?' (Lam. 2.15).

50.3-6. It was traditional not only to see the autumn thunderstorms as
the sign of God's coming to judge the world, but also of the universe as
his court of law. Micah's prophecy begins, 'Hear, ye peoples, all of you:
hearken, O earth, and the fulness thereof: and let the Lord GOD be witness against you, the Lord from his holy temple. For, behold, the LORD
cometh forth out of his place, and will come down...' (1.2-3); but he
later continues, 'Hear ye now what the LORD saith: Arise, contend thou
before the mountains, and let the hills hear thy voice. Hear, O ye mountains, the LORD's controversy, and ye enduring foundations of the earth:
for the LORD hath a controversy with his people' (6.1-2). Isaiah opens
similarly, 'Hear, O heavens, and give ear, O earth, for the LORD hath
spoken...' (1.2). So now the psalmist has God call to the heavens and
the earth, the *enduring foundations* of the world which were there long
before humanity. They are to be witnesses of God's judgment of Israel,
and the heavens will testify to the *righteousness* of God's case—for God
is judge himself, *qui nec falli nec fallere potest.*

The heavens and the earth are not just witnesses in the great Assize,
they are also ushers, bidden to *Gather my saints together unto me.* Israel

gathered each year for the festival when summoned by the autumn thunder in heaven and the completion of the harvest on earth. Three times in the year was all Israel to appear before God, or to see his face; and the great, autumnal festival, the festival *par excellence*, was the turn of the year when God was seen as settling accounts and renewing his people's life. Those who are gathered are חסידי, the people of God's covenanted love. They are 'those who cut my covenant upon sacrifice'. They are 'all Israel' who are pledged to be loyal to God, and he to them, who come to the national sanctuary and participate in the national sacrificial rites by which that covenant is renewed.

Selah. The surprising feature of Psalm 50 is the division which now appears between the apparently righteous of vv. 7-15, who maintain the sacrificial tradition, and the 'wicked' of vv. 16-21, whose immoral living shows their religion to be a hypocrisy. Duhm and Gunkel will not accept such a division, and relegate v. 16a, 'But unto the wicked God saith', to a later gloss. But we have the evidence of just such a division in the ritual described in Deuteronomy 27. There Moses ordains that after crossing Jordan Israel is to set up plastered stones on Mt Ebal, on which the 'words of this law' have been inscribed. They are to build there an altar of unhewn stones, and offer burnt offerings and peace-offerings. The Levitical priests are to divide the people in two, half to stand on Mt Gerizim 'to bless the people', and half on Mt Ebal 'for the curse'. They are then to answer and say to all the men of Israel with a loud voice the twelve commandments, each of which opens with the formula, 'Cursed be he that...' The commandments cover idolatry (v. 15), dishonesty (vv. 17, 19), sexual sins (vv. 20-23) and other matters.

No doubt the present form of the account is late, being full of D/Dtr expressions, and various tensions (Mayes, *Deuteronomy*, pp. 353-55), but the acute contradiction between the worship on mounts 'Gerizim' and 'Ebal' ordained here and in Deut. 11.29-30, and the worship at Jerusalem alone specified in 2 Kings 22–23, shows that the tradition behind the passage is ancient. As it stands, the division between the two mountains is on a fixed tribal basis: Simeon, Levi, Judah, Issachar, Joseph and Benjamin on Gerizim; Reuben, Gad, Asher, Zebulun, Dan and Naphtali on Ebal. This corresponds with the situation in the decade 732–722. Assyria had occupied 'Gilead and Galilee, all the land of Naphtali' (2 Kgs 15.29), so Reuben and Gad on the East Bank (Gilead), and Asher, Dan, Naphtali and Zebulun, the northern tribes (Galilee), had been lost. The still independent tribes are put in the traditional order of Genesis 49: Simeon, Levi, Judah first, although Simeon had long since disappeared; Issachar, Joseph and Benjamin, the rump of Israel south of Galilee under King Hoshea.

The ritual of Deuteronomy 27 corresponds with Psalm 50 in a number of respects: (i) the whole people is assembled for it (Deut. 27.1; Ps. 50.5, 'Gather my saints unto me'); (ii) sacrifice is to be offered in ratification of the divine covenant (Deut. 27.6-7; Ps. 50.5, 'those that make a covenant with me by sacrifice'); (iii) a form of the Law is to be recited (Deut. 27.14; Ps. 50.17-20, 'What hast thou to do to recite [ספר] my statutes?'); (iv) the people are divided into two parts, one apparently good, the other bad; (v) the Asaph psalms and Deuteronomy 27 both presuppose worship at a northern shrine, Salem for the former, Shechem for the latter; this can be more closely defined (see below, pp. 46-49).

Now in *The Psalms of the Sons of Korah* and in *The Prayers of David* I argued consistently that the occurrence of *Selah* in the text was a sign that the psalm should be broken off (διάψαλμα) for the cantillation (סֶלָּה) of a relevant text. When 44.1-8 has spoken of 'what our fathers have told us', for example, the Selah after v. 8 provides for the chanting of a text like Joshua 24, a number of whose phrases occur in the psalm; or when 87.2 reads, 'Glorious things are spoken of thee, O city of God', the Selah following permits the recital of the city's (Dan's) foundation legend. So now we have a Selah after v. 6, and this will have given opportunity for the recitation of the Commandments, in whatever form. There is only one Selah in the psalm, and the recital of commandments is specifically mentioned in v. 16 (ספר), so we have the possibility of something like a (duo-)decalogue being recited at this point.

The connection of early decalogues with Deuteronomy 27, and so with festal worship at Shechem/Salem, was made by Albrecht Alt in 1934. Alt conjectured a seven-yearly festival (Deut. 31.10) with apodeictic laws which disappeared early from regular use. Gerhard von Rad accepted this (1938), and saw the setting as an annual festival of covenant-renewal, but he saw the Sinai tradition as lying behind the implied Commandments of the covenant. Kraus, and almost all modern commentators, see some similar liturgical setting for the psalm: the presence of 'From Zion' sites it in Jerusalem, and some (e.g. Eaton) posit an earlier use in Shechem.

Mowinckel (*Psalmenstudien*, III, pp. 41-45), Johnson (*Cultic Prophet*, pp. 22-30) and Craigie take the theophany as mediated by the rising sun (הופיע). Craigie takes 'from the rising of the sun unto the going down thereof' (1b) in a temporal sense. But הופיע is used of Yahweh's coming in the storm in Deut. 33.2, and the festival for renewing the covenant lasted not a day but a week. It is also good to avoid pietist, visionary concepts of theophanies in the temple. Thunderstorms are more impressive, and one is implied in v. 3.

Despite Gunkel's reservations on the unsuitability of Zion as the source of the theophany, it is almost universally accepted (cf. Jacquet, *Psaumes*, II, p. 132: 'une note de grâce et de sérénité'). But the 5-stress colon suggests a gloss, and even more the parallel in Hab. 3.3, 'God cometh from Teman, And the Holy One from mount Paran. His glory covereth the heavens... And his brightness is as the light.' That is where the perfection of glory is.

50.7	Hear, O my people, and I will speak;
	O Israel, and I will testify against thee:
	I am God, *even* thy God.
8	I will not reprove thee for thy sacrifices;
	Nor for thy burnt offerings, which are continually before me.
9	I will take no bullock out of thine house,
	Nor he-goats out of thy folds.
10	For every beast of the forest is mine,
	And the cattle upon mountains where thousands are.
11	I know all the fowls of the mountains:
	And the wild beasts of the field are in my mind.
12	If I were hungry, I would not tell thee:
	For the world is mine, and the fulness thereof.
13	Will I eat the flesh of bulls,
	Or drink the blood of goats?
14	Offer unto God the sacrifice of thanksgiving;
	And pay thy vows unto the Most High:
15	And call upon me in the day of trouble:
	I will deliver thee, and thou shalt glorify me.

The divine complaint is not the *absence* of sacrifices; indeed they *are continually before me*, and God's saints *make covenant with me by sacrifice*. It is rather that the spirit is wrong: Israel is supposedly worshipping on an *ex opere operato* theory—they have performed the ceremonial, and that should be enough. What is missing is the *thanksgiving of the heart*: *offer* (זבח) *unto God* תודה, which means 'immolate' it, and hence not songs of *thanksgiving*, but the *sacrifices of thanksgiving*. The same thing is required in v. 23. Their worship is superficial and unacceptable: they are supposed to think (i) that God is in need of offerings, and (ii) that he is hungry and drinks the blood of goats.

It is not really to be supposed that Israel had become a nation of hypocrites, or that the primitive view of a hungry God lapping up the sacrificial blood was still rampant. God seems captious and grumpy in these verses, despite their noble eloquence; and the reason for this comes out in v. 15. Israel is face to face with *the day of trouble* (יום צרה) when the Assyrian armies will destroy Samaria and deport all of the aristocracy; Israel is in dire need of God's *deliverance*. The view into the abyss is uninviting, and the psalmist turns away. It surely cannot be that God has brought us so close to disaster for no reason. Something is amiss with our worship, and that will be its genuineness. Such a conclusion may be felt to be widely satisfying. All Israelites knew that catastrophe was at the door, and that they must do what they could to stop it: no one could know whether the national spirit was sufficiently thankful, and everyone could suppose that the fault lay with a neighbour.

The same structure of thinking underlies Isaiah 1. The Assyrian army which had overwhelmed Israel in 732–722 has now wrought havoc in Judah: 'Your country is desolate; your cities are burned with fire; your land, strangers devour it in your presence...' (1.7-8). We know this, the pious Judahite might answer, yet we have been faithful in offering Yahweh's sacrifices. To which the prophet much in wrath replies, 'To what purpose is the multitude of your sacrifices unto me? saith the LORD: I am full of the burnt offerings of rams, and the fat of fed beasts...' (1.11-15). Lacking a traditional liturgy in which those on one mountain are blessed and those on the other cursed, Isaiah generalizes the moral onslaught. The whole people is involved: 'your hands are full of blood...seek judgment, set right the oppressed, judge the fatherless, plead for the widow' (1.15, 17). Where the northern psalmist saw a half of the nation as ethically righteous, but their worship vitiated nevertheless by a lack of true thankfulness, the Jerusalem prophet takes moral iniquity to be universal, and the subverter of festivals and offerings. There is a not dissimilar attack in the first chapter of Micah, where the worship of both Samaria and Jerusalem is said to be marred by their graven images and idols, and divine retribution is promised (Mic. 1.5-7). For all three military defeat is the incontrovertible evidence of spiritual inadequacy.

50.7. The passage is one of the speeches of God favoured by the Asaph psalmist: 50.5, 7-15, 16b-23, 81.8-17, 82.2-7. The opening line, שמעה עמי ואדברה ישראל ואעידה בך, is closely similar to 81.9, שמע עמי ואעידה בך and its conclusion, אלהים אלהיך אנכי to 81.11, אנכי יהוה אלהיך. God 'witnessed against' Israel (העדתה בנו) in Exod. 19.23 that it was not holy enough to ascend Sinai to his presence; and this was immediately before he delivered the Ten Commandments, starting אנכי יהוה אלהיך (Exod. 20.2). Since this text continues 'who brought thee out of the land of

Egypt', its associations are with the Joseph tribes (cf. 81.6-7), and since the sins reproved in vv. 16-21 bear a general similarity to the later commandments in the Exodus 20 table, we should probably think of this passage as being the first part of the proclamation signified by the Selah after v. 6. The Deuteronomy 27 text provides a series of imprecations beginning, 'Cursed be he that...', and ending with the people's Amen; and we may think of these as spoken to those who 'stand upon mount Ebal for the curse'. The more positive form of the Commandments has already been given in a recitation of Exod. 20.2-17, and this will represent the liturgy as spoken to those who stand upon Mount Gerizim, to bless them. (We may except the Third and Fourth Commandments, on which see pp. 294-96.)

50.8-15. God's reproof (אוכיחך) again recalls Isa. 1.18, 2.4. The sacrifices in question are זבחיך and עולתיך, the latter being 'burnt-offerings'. In Deut. 27.6 the offering of עולת is commanded, and in the following verse it is said 'זבחת שלמים and thou shalt eat there; and thou shalt rejoice before the LORD thy God'. Lev. 7.11 suggests that the peace-offerings (שלמים) were the same as the thank-offerings (תודה), so we may think that Psalm 50 and Deuteronomy 27 are referring to the same actions. Naturally Psalm 50 concentrates on God's part in the sacrifices, but it is not to be thought that the people did not have their share besides. The verses express with sublimity God's transcendence over all his creation. Gunkel writes with characteristic feeling of the wild and the birds as especially the divine realm, beyond the reach of petty human control. The meaning of the Hebrew is a little uncertain in vv. 10-11. Kraus renders הררי־אלף 'the cattle-mountains', and Kirkpatrick thinks זיז שדי means 'the creeping things of the country'; but the latter phrase recurs in the Asaph psalm, 80.14 (alone), where they ravage the vine of Israel—like the little foxes of Cant. 2.15.

Earlier critics, including Delitzsch and Gunkel, took the psalm to be an attack on the sacrificial system as such, and this continues with Weiser ('not ritualism borrowed from the Canaanite environment, but humble testimony in praise of God', *Psalms*, p. 393). This is now generally abandoned (Eaton, Dahood, Anderson, Jacquet). The participle in v. 5b naturally means 'those who *make my covenant* upon sacrifice', and זבה in v. 14a is a root implying the slaughter of an animal. Kraus is typical in seeing in the verses a prophetic critique of sacrifice as buying off Yahweh's anger. But this line leads easily into contextless sermonizing—'The true worship of Yahweh is ethical sacrifice... a prophetic declaration of law and judgment.' It is easy to miss the latent menace of the coming 'day of trouble' which is the dynamic of the 'prophetic critique', and to suppose that the prophets whose writings we have are the force behind the reform of popular priest-led religion. Kraus dates the psalm in Josiah's reign, Gunkel and Mowinckel (*Psalmenstudien*, III, p. 42) after the exile. Mowinckel saw the psalm as the protest of the Temple singers with their *song of praise* (תודה) against the priests with their sacrifices.

Eaton sees the psalm itself as the work of an outstanding prophet, speaking at the renewal of the covenant (*Vision*, pp. 6, 43-45), and he also saw the renewal ceremony as 'the setting where the tradition of the great prophetic admonitions took its origin' (*Psalms*, p. 137). These seem to me to be crucial insights. Every commentator notes the parallels with Isaiah 1 and Micah 1 and 6, but Eaton locates these prophetic rebukes in a plausible cultic context, and he reverses the simplistic view that the writing prophets were the inspired innovators of the moral critique of sacrifice. Commentators also note the echoes of Exodus 20/Deuteronomy 5–6, and sometimes draw the conclusion that the psalmist is familiar with the Sinai tradition. This goes beyond the evidence. The Asaph psalms do indeed have a desert tradition in which God delivers the covenant, but that tradition is located in 81.8 at Meribah, not at Sinai; and even the Deuteronomic tradition does not mention Sinai but Horeb as the mountain of the covenant. We should think of the Asaph covenant as rooted in some primal experience at Meribah, and that these traditions were later assimilated to the Jerusalem orthodoxy that the place of revelation was Mt Sinai.

50.16	But unto the wicked God saith,
	What hast thou to do to recite (לְסַפֵּר) my statutes,
	And that thou takest my covenant in thy mouth?
17	Seeing thou hatest correction,
	And castest my words behind thee?
18	When thou sawedst a thief thou consentedst with him,
	And thy portion was with adulterers.
19	Thou givest thy mouth to evil,
	And thy tongue frameth deceit.
20	Thou sittest and speakest against thy brother;
	Thou givest a thrust against thine own mother's son.
21	These things hast thou done, and I kept silence;
	Thou thoughtest that I was altogether such an one as thyself:
	But I will reprove thee, and set *them* in order before thine eyes.
22	Now consider this, ye that forget God,
	Lest I tear you in pieces, and there be none to deliver:
23	Whoso offereth the sacrifice of thanksgiving glorifieth me;
	And prepareth a way that I may shew him the salvation of God.

The psalmist turns to those 'standing upon mount Ebal for the curse', referred to here as 'the wicked'. Perhaps in happier times Israel had stood on the mount of blessing (Deut. 27.12, 'upon mount Gerizim to bless *the people*'), and curses had been heaped on 'the nations' for their wicked ways (e.g. Amos 1.2–2.3), symbolized by the dark, more northerly mountain. But now the crisis has come, and the prophetic movement, voiced by cultic prophets (Johnson, *Cultic Prophet*), has seen its advent as Yahweh's wrath with Israel for its moral disobedience no less than its superficial worship. The wicked on 'mount Ebal' are Israelites no less than those in v. 7 addressed as 'my people...Israel'; they too *recite my statutes* and *have taken my covenant in thy mouth*. It is easy to see behind these words some such liturgy as in Deuteronomy 27, with the people separated into halves, and all replying 'Amen' to the recited catalogue of statutes.

Deuteronomy 27 specifies worship on Mounts Ebal and Gerizim; but both the D-history (1 Kgs 12.25-33; 13) and the contemporary prophets, Hosea and Amos, make clear that the national sanctuary of the 720s was not Shechem but Bethel. How then is this to be reconciled? Shechem was the most powerful fortress in central Palestine, and as such both a claimant to national hegemony and a target for its rivals. G.E. Wright ('Shechem', pp. 1092-93) lists five violent destructions of the city between Abimelech (Judg. 9) and 722. In addition to these we may note that 'Jeroboam [re]built Shechem' in 1 Kgs 12.25, so the place was apparently in ruins then. Also Ps. 60.7, 'I will divide Shechem, and mete out the valley of Succoth' implies that Shechem is an enemy in a civil war, and I have argued that the Shechemite priesthood took sides against David in Absalom's rebellion, and suffered for it afterwards (*Prayers*, pp. 141-51).

In these circumstances it would clearly be impracticable for Shechem to have retained its position as Israel's national shrine, and Jeroboam's choice of Dan, and later Bethel, for the honour proves that it did not. The people had reconvened there in 1 Kings 12, for tradition's sake, but that was all. Later indications give the impression that the Shechem priesthood has removed semi-permanently to Bethel. In Gen. 12.6 Abram passes through the land 'unto the place of Shechem, unto the terebinth of Moreh', and in 12.8 he 'removed from thence unto the mountain on the east side of Bethel', building an altar between Bethel and Ai. In Gen. 35.1-8 Jacob follows the same itinerary, burying his 'strange gods' under the terebinth at Shechem, and building an altar at Bethel to El-beth-el. Shechem, it seems, is being left behind as a place where Israel worshipped Canaanite idols. The permanent altar to the Israelite God was at Bethel.

This impression is strengthened by the three Deuteronomic passages which prescribe worship at Ebal and Gerizim. At Deut. 11.29-30 Moses says, 'thou shalt set the blessing upon mount Gerizim and the curse upon mount Ebal. Are they not beyond the Jordan, behind the way of the going down of the sun, in the land of the Canaanites which dwell in the Arabah, over against Gilgal, beside the terebinths of Moreh?' We are immediately surprised to be given such elaborate directions. We are never told how to find Mt Zion. But then, although Gerizim and Ebal are indeed beyond the Jordan, the other details do not suggest Shechem at all. 'The way of the going down of the sun' means *the road west*, which runs from Gilgal-Jericho up the valley to *Bethel*. It is *Bethel* which is 'over against Gilgal', not Shechem, which is thirty kilometres further north. Nor is Shechem close to the Arabah, as Bethel is, and Shechem was famous for its single 'terebinth of Moreh'—this site appears to have a copse of such terebinths.

We find similar hesitations with Deuteronomy 27. Moses says, 'It shall be on the day when ye shall pass over the Jordan...that ye shall set ye up great stones...and thou shalt write upon them all the words of this law...ye shall set up these stones in mount Ebal' (27.2-4). It is thirty kilometres to Bethel, and it would be conceivable that such instructions be obeyed *on the day when ye shall pass over the Jordan*. Sixty kilometres in a day passes the bounds of credulity.

The instructions are in fact obeyed, after a more considerable lapse of time, in a puzzling passage in Josh. 8.30-35. In the earlier part of the chapter Joshua has defeated the king of Ai, setting an ambush between Bethel and Ai (8.9, 12). No sooner has he captured Ai (8.28-29) than we read, 'Then Joshua built an altar unto the LORD, the God of Israel, in mount Ebal, as Moses commanded' (8.30), with the altar of unhewn stones, the sacrifices, the writing of the law on the stones, the dividing of the people for blessing and curse and so forth, as provided in Deuteronomy 27. The only thing that is missing is any account of the march to Shechem and the capture of that city. We have the strong impression that Mounts Ebal and Gerizim have been mysteriously removed to between Bethel and Ai.

That, we seem forced to conclude, is what has happened. When a religious community is forced to move, it may commonly transfer the name of its old home with it, as in Mount Zion Temple, Chicago, or Christchurch, New Zealand, or Ripon College, Cuddesdon. When the Shechemite priests were driven out, they settled at Bethel, at the head of the valley leading down to Jericho. Bethel was on the main spinal road north, and unlike Shechem did not lie between two mountains. But two kilometres down the road, 'between Bethel and Ai', as we so often hear, the valley descends steeply, with the Judaean hills on the south and Baal-hazor rising darkly to a thousand metres on the north. Here was a site that was like Shechem, with terebinths, and an ancient altar, and they named the mountains Ebal and Gerizim after the hills at home. It was *behind, north of, the road west, in the Arabah over against Gilgal, beside the terebinths of Moreh,* the Levite priest in whom was vested the תורה (Deut. 33.10), and there the tribes could be marshalled on the hillside of *Ebal and Gerizim* and hear the proclamation of curse and blessing.

The three Deuteronomic texts are a source of mystification. E. Nielsen (*Shechem*, pp. 42-43) omits 'over against Gilgal' from Deut. 11.30, but Mayes (*Deuteronomy*, pp. 218-19) sees that this still leaves other problems. He amends *terebinths* to a singular, to bring it into line with Gen. 12.6, and follows L'Hour ('Législation') in assimilating the site to Gilgal. But where, then, are the mountains? Gilgal is in the Jordan valley. John Gray (*Joshua, Judges and Ruth*) thinks that Josh. 8.30-35 is 'quite out of context'. Magnus Ottosson (*Josuaboken*, pp. 76-80) draws an ingenious parallel between Exodus 12–17 and Joshua 3–8, in which the victories at Rephidim and Ai, and the subsequent altar-building are set alongside each other, but this does not seem to resolve the problem. A. Alt, in a famous article, 'Die Wallfahrt von Sichem nach Bethel', explained the Genesis 12 and 35 texts as echoes of a pilgrimage between the two sanctuaries, but they are better explained as echoes of the transfer of national worship from the one shrine to the other.

50.17. The motivation for this second rebuke at once becomes clear: those addressed *hate correction* (מוסר). Correction, in ancient Israel and until quite modern times, was normally administered corporally (Prov. 13.24; 15.5; 22.15; 23.13), and God's correction takes the form of personal or national disasters (Prov. 3.11; Job 5.17; Isa. 26.16; 53.5; Jer. 2.30; 5.3; 7.28; 30.14; Hos. 5.2). The defeat of 732 and the massive loss of territory are probably in mind, or perhaps Shalmaneser's ravaging invasion of 725. These should have led to penitence and virtue, but in fact the divine chastisement has been *hated,* and *his words cast behind* them. However, God is not mocked: *I will reprove thee and set them in order before thine eyes* (v. 21). The unrepented sins will come home to roost in further and yet more dire catastrophes, when God will, like a lioness, *tear you in pieces, and there* will *be none to deliver* (v. 22). How justly has the psalmist been called a prophet! He could read the writing of 722 on the wall.

The Psalms of Asaph and the Pentateuch

50.18-20. The sins with which the people are charged are so mild that they ought to be taken more seriously than with a casual reference to the Ten Commandments. They consist of consenting to theft, going along with adultery, and speaking evil against one's family. There is no reproof for the theft and adultery implied, let alone the more grievous sins which are the prophets' staple. We may contrast the contemporary Hos. 4.2: 'There is nought but swearing and breaking faith, and killing, and stealing, and committing adultery; they break out, and blood toucheth blood.' The psalmist is not exaggerating, and we should take his comments as in earnest.

It looks as if there has been a moral breakdown of an extraordinary kind, which has alarmed both Hosea and our psalmist, and we may see a parallel, and an explanation for this, in events of our own day in Bosnia. The annexation of Gilead and Galilee in 732 is likely to have resulted in expropriations, deportations and, in consequence, a flood of refugees to the rump West Bank lands. Hence there has come a sharp pressure on resources. Order has been hard to maintain, and there has been violence and the forcible taking of property, perhaps in desperation. Further, as has been so evident in Sarajevo, the breakdown of society and the imminent threat of death leads to a relaxation of sexual inhibitions. If we may die tomorrow, we will gather what roses we may today. Nor can domestic peace be expected to survive the sudden billeting of large numbers of penniless relations *sine die*. Such a situation would account for both Hos. 4.2 and our text. The prophet is scandalized by the individual acts of violence, murder and sexual laxity. The psalmist is concerned that such things have become socially accepted. Property is filched, or commandeered with a high hand, as may have been widespread in the desperate 720s, and no one has raised an objection. With the break-up of so many families, the men killed in battle or enslaved, women have been driven to loose relationships, and the bulwarks of social disapproval have given way. And there is nothing like a permanent incursion of starving relatives into his home for bringing a man to *give* his *mouth to evil*, or *giving a thrust* (דפי) *to thine own mother's son.*

We may suspect that the same situation underlies the mysterious twelve-curse liturgy of Deuteronomy 27. Here again there is no general curse on the murderer, the thief or the adulterer. The offences reprobated are: idolatry, setting light by parents, removing landmarks, misdirecting the blind, wresting judgment, sleeping with one's stepmother, sister or mother-in-law, bestiality, secret and hired killing; and general disobedience to 'the words of this law'. The opening verses of the chapter have required the inscribing of 'all the words of this law' on plastered stones, in which case the curse-liturgy may be a special amplification.

The twelve curses will be appropriate for the twelve tribes marshalled in 27.11-13. Idolatry is a constant threat, and comes first, in line with other tables of Commandments (Exod. 34.17; Deut. 5.8), and something similar is true of honouring one's parents (Exod. 21.17; Deut. 5.17). There are three indications of injustice over property: the removing of a neighbour's landmark, the deprivation of widow, orphan and גר in lawsuits, and 'making the blind to wander out of the way'. The last can hardly be malicious jesting. It is more likely that the blind man is directed away from property to which he has a just claim. There are four sexual interdictions, which have given rise to some surprise (it is not often that a man must be forbidden from sleeping with his mother-in-law). But these may again be a reflection of the breakdown of a society in crisis. In face of extinction inhibitions fade. Not only rose-buds are gathered, but even rather overblown roses. There are two kinds of murderer cursed, 'he that smiteth his neighbour in secret', and 'he that taketh reward to slay an innocent person'. We are no longer concerned with murder generally, but with particular kinds of covert killing, which may again be signs of social disintegration (we may compare Ishmael the son of Nethaniah in Jer. 41).

50.22-23. Such troubles do indeed cause people to *forget God*, for the need to survive is rather pressing. But he will have the last word. Hosea knew it too: 'I will be unto Ephraim as a lion... I, even I, will tear and carry away, and there shall be none to deliver' (5.14). The image of Assyria as a ruthless, powerful wild animal was no exaggeration, and his red teeth and claws are the teeth and claws of God. The only hope lies in a genuine worship, *sacrificing thank-offering*, which means the offering of animals with integrity. In this way one *prepares a way* (שׂם דרך) *that I may shew him the salvation of God*. Those who live in obedience to the divine statutes will find deliverance from the most formidable of enemies; this is the *way* they must *set* if they are to see God save them from massacre, rape and enslavement.

The Hebrew is difficult in vv. 21, 23. הַיוֹת, which RV takes as an abs. inf. ('altogether'), is pointed הַיוֹת by Dahood (cf. הַוּוֹת, Gunkel), 'destructions' (cf. versions); but the sense is not so easy. Kirkpatrick suggests a play on Exod. 3.14, where אהיה is the name of God. Gunkel puts תם for שׂם, 'pure of way', but the unamended text gives sense, as in RV.

The mildness of the faults reproved in vv. 18-20 is generally not noted. The peculiarities of the Deuteronomy 27 Dodecalogue are a mystery (cf. Mayes, *Deuteronomy*, pp. 353-55). A number of the forbidden deeds are secret, but this is not mentioned for most of them, and does not apply to making light of one's parents, or leading the blind to wander out of the way.

Dating has been varied. Delitzsch still favoured the tenth century, taking Asaph to be David's musical director. The later Mowinckel, von Rad, Weiser and Anderson ascribed Psalm 50 to the eighth century, often influenced by parallels in Hosea. Kraus and Jacquet thought a seventh-century date more likely, under Josiah, when prophetic/Deuteronomic influences were strong. Gunkel thought that the gathering of v. 5 was addressed to the Diaspora, and the prophetic style was a post-exilic imitation. We may accept the arguments of Weiser and others for the eighth century (and the eighth decade thereof) for the psalm as a whole, and Kraus's view for its acceptance, with the gloss מציון, in Jerusalem.

Psalm 73

73.1   A Psalm of Asaph.
        Surely God is good to Israel,
        Even to such as are pure in heart.

2   But as for me, my feet were almost gone,
        My steps had well nigh slipped.

3   For I was resentful (קנאתי) at the arrogant (הוללים),
        When I saw the success (שלום) of the wicked.

4   For there are no torments (חרצבת) in their death:
        And their belly is fat (ובריא אולם).

5   They are not in the trouble of men;
        Neither are they plagued like *other* men.

6   Therefore pride is as a chain about their neck;
        Violence covereth them as a garment.

7   Their eyes stand out from the fat (מחלב):
        The imaginations of their heart overflow.

8   They scoff, and in wickedness utter oppression:
        They speak from on high.

9   They have set their mouth in the heavens (בשמים),
        And their tongue walketh through the earth.

10   Therefore he brings back (ישיב) his people hither:
        And waters of a full *cup* are drained by them.

11   And they say, How doth God know?
        And is there knowledge in the Most High?

For most critics 73 has been a wisdom psalm. It has been bracketed with Psalms 49 and 37, and has been compared with the book of Job. The speaker has been the much spoken of 'poor', oppressed Israelite, puzzled and fretted by the arrogance of the wealthy oppressor, so colourfully pictured in the verses above. His faith was trembling in the balance, but it was restored by a visit to the Temple, where he received a revelation (sometimes in a theophany). There he realized two things. One was that the success of the wicked was a temporary thing; in the end God

would see them off. But the other, and spiritually profound, insight was
that he had the sole thing that mattered, fellowship with God. The
'wisdom' interpreters divide at this point. A majority of them glory in
the depth of such a spirituality, which is content to press on in unre-
lieved earthly misery, in the confidence that God is with the sufferer. A
minority see the divine consolations as continuing after life here, whether
on the model of Enoch who was 'taken' by God, or in some form of
post-mortal existence.

The mainline wisdom interpretation is taken by Kirkpatrick, Gunkel, Mowinckel,
Jacquet and Tate. Delitzsch, Kraus and Dahood thought in terms of God taking the
speaker as he 'took' Enoch. Weiser, Rogerson and McKay, and Anderson keep open
a variety of possible forms of the hereafter. Because Psalms commentators have so
often been good men with high spiritual aspirations, 73 has drawn a marked enthusiasm: Gunkel speaks of the glorious sentences ('herrliche Sätze') in vv. 25-26 which
reach the height of the New Testament, and Jacquet says, 'cette Foi atteint à un haut
degré de ferveur religieuse'. It has not been obvious how to envisage a setting for the
psalm, which Gunkel calls a didactic poem and Kraus an account of a spiritual experience. Sometimes it is seen as an individual lament (Gunkel), and sometimes as
more an individual thanksgiving (Mowinckel, *Psalms*, II, pp. 35-39). Weiser calls it
a confession and says, 'It may be assumed that the psalm was recited before the congregation in the sanctuary where the worshipper was granted the insight that released
him from his doubts' (*Psalms*, p. 507).

The wisdom interpretation has not been universal, and it is studded
with problems. First, an alarming amount of the text does not fit it, and
has to be emended. Gunkel has 27 emendations, some of whole phrases,
with two verses misplaced in addition, and three or four probable
glosses. It has proved extremely difficult to find any sense in particular
for vv. 10 and 20, the draining of the waters of fullness and the despis-
ing of the image in the city. Second, the psalm seems not to be concerned with a *division within* Israel, between the poor oppressed and the
wealthy oppressors, but with Israel as a whole—'Surely God is good to
Israel' (emended by some to *the upright*, אֵל יָשָׁר לְ for לְיִשְׂרָאֵל). The
speaker seems not to be a poor individual, but to have a responsibility
for the nation. His near lapse of faith would have been treachery to 'the
generation of thy children'. He has access to 'the sanctuary of God'.
God holds his right hand, guides him, and afterwards 'takes' him glori-
ously. It is not easy to see this language as suitable for any pious Israelite. It fits more naturally in the mouth of a national leader. We should
also do well to be suspicious both of private revelations, theophanies and

testimonies, so beloved of Protestant commentators, and of the fashionable God-is-on-the-side-of-the-poor theology, which has so easy an appeal to the preacher.

There are two further difficulties, one of which concerns the presumed setting. Weiser has offered (above) a conceivable scenario, but is it at all a plausible one? Could anyone go into the sanctuary and give a testimony or confession of his experience? If so, was it normally 20 to 30 verses of balanced poetry? Did sympathetic priests stand by and ask to retain a copy for the Temple files? Did such confessions form part of a liturgy, and if so what liturgy? Or were there continually groups of 'poor' pious Israelites standing round in the hope either of a personal revelation, or at least of hearing some new thing? Many critics have thrown stones, some of them well-aimed stones, at the lack of direct Old Testament evidence for the New Year Festival hypothesis, but it would become them to remember that they live in temples made almost wholly of glass.

The final problem concerns the content of the experience. Critics are divided over this because both options seem so unlikely. It is true that God's 'taking' the psalmist in glory carries an echo of Enoch and Elijah, but can Delitzsch, Kraus and others really be right in thinking that an ordinary Israelite had such an expectation? If so, would he not express so bold an idea rather more clearly? Or if, as Duhm, Weiser and others suppose, we have here a more vague hope of post-mortal life, how is that different from the standard expectation of life in Sheol? It is hard to think on so thin a base that Daniel-style resurrection is in view; and I have argued strongly that such an interpretation is impossible for Psalm 49 (*Korah*, pp. 181-95).

But is the 'spiritual' alternative any more likely? The speaker receives two insights in the Temple, and one of them is the standard, self-comforting delusion that the wicked always come to a bad end: Job has seen through that, and places its glib shallowness on the lips of his friends. The other is that a life of persevering misery is no harm if one has fellowship with God. Such a conclusion would be unique in the Old Testament, and I simply do not believe that any Israelite could think like this. Israelites felt that the Lord of hosts was with them when they beheld what desolations he wrought to enemy bows and chariots; when they saw their children like olive plants round about their table, they experienced the Lord as building their house. It is a mistake for Gunkel and Kirkpatrick to cite Rom. 8.18 as a parallel: Paul had seen the risen

Lord, and could look forward with confidence to a glory which would be revealed.

A more straightforward exegesis takes the Hebrew as it stands. In 732 Tiglath-Pileser's armies defeated the Syrian–Israelite allies, captured Ijon, Abel-beth-maacah, Janoah, Kedesh and Hazor, and imposed humiliating terms. Half the national territory was annexed to Assyria—Gilead and Galilee, all the land of Naphtali. Pekah, the king of Israel, was deposed and killed, and replaced, according to Assyrian sources, by Hoshea as an Assyrian nominee. An enormous annual tribute was required. Tiglath-Pileser, or his Rabshakeh, is not likely to have bargained with the Israel-ites; they will have treated them as Hitler treated the French in 1940. Nor was this the end. Tiglath-Pileser meant to conquer Egypt, and marched across Israelite territory to Gath. His records are fragmentary and may have included accounts of further incursions. His successor Shalmaneser V invaded Israel again in 725. There was no rest for the godly.

A minority of critics have maintained that the speaker is the king and the situation the liturgy, normally at the autumn festival. These include Birkeland (*Feinde*), E. Würthwein, H. Ringgren, and (most fully and convincingly) Eaton (*Kingship*, pp. 75-78).

73.1. Against such a context our psalm gives a clear sense. *Surely*, despite all (אך), *God is good to Israel*, and will preserve his people in their hour of peril. This applies especially when they have gathered for the festival and have consecrated themselves to be *pure in heart*. In v. 14 the leader—we may suppose the king—says that he has *washed his hands* for the occasion; and this recalls the specification of those who may process through the Temple gates in Psalm 24, 'He that hath *clean hands and a pure heart*' (נקי כפים ובר־לבב, 24.4); or the speaker of 26.6, 'I will wash *mine hands in innocency*; so will I compass thine altar, O LORD'. Of course a silent pretension to purity of heart would not suffice: the worshippers would no doubt have to pledge their loyalty to the divine commands in word as well as in ritual; and we may think of some such ceremony as I have suggested to be implied in Psalm 50/ Deuteronomy 27.

There is no support in any Hebrew MS or version for emending ישראל; the 'correction' is made simply in favour of the Wisdom interpretation.

73.2-3. Surely God's promise is dependable; but military realities are impressive too, and it is the duty of kings to give heed to them also.

Hence the speaker's closeness to a failure of faith; his *steps had well nigh slipped* when he considered in sober rationality the odds he was up against. The prospect was in fact formidable. The unbroken sequence of Assyrian victories when Tiglath-Pileser ruled, had Hoshea known the full history, might have driven him to a wiser despair. As it is he is filled with resentment (rather than envy, קִנֵּאתִי, cf. 1 Kgs 14.22; Anderson, *Psalms*) as he *sees the peace of the wicked*. Their unvarying success (שָׁלוֹם) is a challenge to God's covenant to protect his people; and they are suitably spoken of as *wicked* (cf. Isa. 14.5), in view of their cruelty and unprovoked destructiveness, and *arrogant*. We find the same pair of adjectives used in parallel in 75.5, where the context is plainly of the Israelite king facing down *wicked* and *arrogant* foreign enemies. The behaviour of the Rabshakeh in Isaiah 36–37 is certainly הוֹלֵל.

We probably do best to retain the more difficult K נָטוּי, שָׁפְכָה, cf. v. 7 עֵינֵמוֹ; in each case the dual is accompanied by an irregular form. Dahood explains the latter as an archaic 3f. dual, and we may have here indications of a deviant Northern Hebrew.

73.4-5. The Assyrians were terrible enemies: they held the elders of any town responsible for failure to surrender, and when the siege was completed would torture to death the surviving leaders *pour encourager les autres*. The pitiful tale of such cruelties, inflicted on his own faithful lieutenants, comes first to the king's mind: *there are no* חַרְצֻבּוֹת, *torments*, to the Assyrians' *death*. The contrast with *their fat bellies* is forcible and disgusting. How pathetic to think of so many fine Israelites, men and women, driven from their homes, reduced to grinding poverty and slavery (Ps. 44.11-13), while these swaggering oafs *have no part in human trouble*, or *the plagues of mankind*.

לְמוֹתָם, *to their death*, is surprising but not impossible Hebrew: לְמוֹת לָמוֹ would have been more comfortable. But there is no justification for emending to לָמוֹ תָם, *they have no pangs; perfect and healthy is their body*. It is quixotic to begin one's complaint against a wealthy and oppressive landowner that he is bursting with health! The MT gives forceful sense in view of the well-known horrors of Assyrian cruelty; and the final phrase means naturally *and their front (belly) is fat*.

73.6-9. We may picture the Assyrian officers as war-films present the caricature Nazi generals—hardfaced nightmares of uniformed arrogance. The Tartan, Rabsaris and Rabshakeh of 2 Kings 18 do not have jackboots and iron crosses, but they will have worn the contemporary equivalents. *Haughtiness goes round their neck: Violence covers them as a garment* (Delitzsch): we may think of the necklaces of precious metal with which ancient warriors consecrated themselves for battle, the crescents and the pendants and the purple raiment that was upon the kings of Midian in Judg. 8.26. Nor is it only their *belly* which is so disgustingly gross. *Their eyes go forth from fat* (*ex adipe*, Delitzsch): their double chins and rolls of surplus flesh contrast with the emaciated Israelites, starved by siege and the ravaging of their crops.

The Rabshakeh's speech to the defenders of Jerusalem puts the following lines into *oratio recta. The imaginations of their hearts overflow; they scoff, and in wickedness utter oppression; they speak from on high.* Let not Hezekiah deceive you saying, The LORD will surely deliver us. Thus says the king of Assyria. Make your peace with me until I come and take you away to a land of corn and wine...that you may live and not die. *They have set their mouth in the heavens, and their tongue walketh through the earth.* Hath any of the gods of the nations ever delivered his land out of the hand of the king of Assyria? Where are the gods of Hamath and of Arpad? Will they deliver Samaria out of my hand? Are not my princes all of them kings?

We should resist the temptation to revocalize the surprising תָּמֹקוּ; such traditional pointings may be precious indications of old Northern Hebrew.

73.10. The presence of a 'difficult' verse is often a sign that the accepted interpretation of the psalm is in error. We cannot escape the presence of a singular, עמו, *his* people, for which there is no referent, and will do better to stick to the predominant ישוב which requires the same, and not emend anything. Behind the הוללים, the dictating generals, stands the terrifying figure of the great king himself. *His imaginations overflow, his tongue walks through the earth,* he boasts of his conquests and is set on more. *Therefore he brings his army back here—* עם, his people = his army as in Ps. 3.7 and often—*and the waters of fullness are drained by them*—they take everything we have. Water in arid Palestine was the symbol of life. When God's anger was turned away Isaiah could say, 'Therefore with joy shall ye draw water from the wells of salvation' (Isa. 12.3). We should probably be content with a symbolic understanding: all the resources of our land, *the waters of fullness,* they drink up and exhaust. A more literal interpretation would be in line with the rumours preceding Xerxes' invasion of Greece in 480: so large a host was drinking the rivers dry.

73.11. The psalmist returns to the deputation he knows with, *And they say*... They deride the God of Israel as if he were the gods of Sepharvaim; but *there is knowledge* indeed with אל עליון. God Most High, and he knows *their latter end*.

73.12	Behold, these are the wicked;
	And, being always successful (שלוי), they increase in
	strength (חיל).
13	Surely in vain have I cleansed my heart,
	And washed my hands in innocency;
14	For all the day long have I been plagued,
	And my chastisement was every morning.
15	If I had said, I will speak thus;
	Behold, I had dealt treacherously with the generation of
	thy children.
16	When I thought how I might know this,
	It was labour in mine eyes,
17	Until I went into the sanctuary of God,
	And considered their latter end.
18	Surely thou settest them in slippery places:
	Thou castest them down to ruins.
19	How are they become a desolation in a moment!
	They are utterly consumed with terrors.
20	As a dream when one awaketh, O Lord,
	Thou shalt despise their image in the city.

73.12-14. *These men*, the arrogant Assyrians, win every battle; they are for ever successful (שלוי, adj. from שלום), and with every victory they increase their strength (חיל), capturing our supplies of food and armaments and gaining slave-labour. *Surely*, says the speaker, despite my years of trust in him, God has let me down; I have made my ritual vows of faithfulness, and I have kept them, and it has been for nothing. *And all the day long have I been plagued*...: it is like Ps. 44.15, 'All the day long is my dishonour before me.' One tale of disaster has followed another, morning after morning has come news of more towns taken, more defences overwhelmed, harsher and harsher demands from the victors.

73.15-16. As in modern times the British Parliament is opened by the Queen's speech, in which the government's policies for the coming year are set out, so must it have been in ancient Israel. The people assemble for the feast, and the king must declare whether they are to go up to

Ramoth-Gilead or no. No doubt the king took counsel beforehand, with
or without the aid of Zedekiah the son of Chenaanah; and many years
his responsibilities must have weighed heavily upon him. What should he
do: accept the bitter Assyrian terms or defy them? More often he may
have chosen to put off the evil day. But still he must address the
assembly, the מוֹעֵד. Should he say in effect, They are too strong for us?
Our talk of God's protection has been a delusion; we must face reality,
lest worse befall us? He nearly did say this, but if he had done so, he
would have betrayed (בָגַדְתִּי) the generation of God's children, the
people of his time whom God had entrusted to his rule. He wrestled
with this appalling dilemma, *and it was labour in his eyes*.

73.17-19. Enlightenment came, however, at last. He came to preside
over the festival, and then, as he *went into the sanctuary of God*,
מִקְדְּשֵׁי־אֵל, the complex of the sacred site, it became clear. The Temple
was a charred ruin (74.3-10); all that remained was God's holy ground.
As he looked out on the desecrated ruins, the conviction came to him
overwhelmingly. The enemy had gone too far: they had blasphemed the
name of Yahweh; they had hacked down and burned his shrine; and
God would avenge his honour (74.18-23). Ancient armies, and especially
siege-armies, were liable to typhoid and cholera, to the pestilence that
walketh in darkness and the destruction that wasteth in the noonday.
What came to King Hoshea in his hour of crisis was the *fata morgana* of
light-headed hope, the doomed consumptive's mirage of health; the
daydream of Israelites in other sieges. Perhaps the Lord would make the
Assyrians hear the sound of chariots and the sound of horses and they
would flee, leaving the spoil of their tents to the lepers; or perhaps the
angel of the Lord would smite a hundred fourscore and five thousand of
them in the night, and in the morning, behold, they would be all dead
corpses. So would be אַחֲרִיתָם, *the latter end* of the enemy. The חֲלָקוֹת,
the *slippery places*, would be such trials leading to their *ruin*. They
would sink to *desolation in a moment*, as they were *utterly consumed
with* panic, בַּלָּהוֹת.

73.20. The solution to this long puzzling verse is suggested by Tiglath-
Pileser's account of his capture of Gath: 'As to Hanno of Gaza, who
fled before my army and ran away to Egypt, [I conquered] the town of
Gaza...[and I placed] (the images of) my [gods] and my royal image in
his own palace...and declared them to be (thenceforward) the gods of
their country' (*ANET*, p. 283). He set up the images, no doubt in fact in

the *temple* at Gath, to affront the defeated Philistines, and to assert his supremacy. Such symbols would be a scandal to the defeated: they were an insult to their god, and yet to touch them would bring certain and hideous vengeance on the leadership. They would be bitterly resented. If such a gesture pleased the Great King in Gath, perhaps it did in Bethel too; and the Israelite might comfort himself that his God would not have to suffer such an indignity for long. *As a dream when one awaketh, O Lord, so shalt thou despise their image in the city.* The Hebrew בעיר means *in the city*; the proposed equivalence בחעיר, *when one awakes*, is a speculation. We meet the Assyrian images again in 74.4.

It is a great advantage to dispense with *subjective theophanies*. Many commentators suppose a purely private experience: Weiser (*Psalms*, p. 511) at least speaks of 'an experience in the Temple, an encounter with his God that was brought about by the theophany, assumed to have taken place in the cult of the Covenant Festival'. But Weiser's psalmist is but a private worshipper: the king, who must guide 'the generation of thy children' in the face of a victorious and arrogant enemy, is a more plausible candidate for a change of heart at the festal worship. 74 shows there was no Temple building, which suggests a more plausible scenario.

73.21	For my heart was in a ferment,
	And I was pricked in my reins:
22	So brutish am I, and ignorant;
	I was *as* a beast with thee.
23	Nevertheless I am continually with thee;
	Thou hast holden my right hand.
24	Thou shalt guide me with thy counsel,
	And afterward receive me with glory.
25	Whom have I in heaven *but thee*?
	And there is none upon earth that I desire with thee.
26	My flesh and my heart faileth:
	But God is the rock of my heart and my portion for ever.
27	For, lo, they that are far from thee shall perish:
	Thou hast destroyed all them that go a whoring from thee.
28	But it is good for me to draw near unto God:
	I have made the Lord GOD my refuge.
	That I may tell of all thy works.

73.21-24. The king's heart was indeed *in a ferment* (יתחמץ), and properly so: the fate of his people was in his hands, and he was about to take a disastrous decision. He was *pricked in* his *reins*; he knew the sinking feeling so familiar to everyone who must put his fate to the touch, to win or lose it all. He castigates himself unfairly for his faithlessness, as *brutish* and *a beast with* God. He bethinks himself of his royal position

and divine grace: *But I, I am continually with thee*—as king, he has
continual access to God's presence in the shrine. It was the kings' prerogative that God should hold (אחז) their hand, and they often took
names with this root, Ahaz, Ahaziah, Jehoahaz (Eaton, *Kingship*, p. 77).
God would *guide him with his counsel* in the diplomatic and perhaps
military decisions that lay ahead; counsel was especially associated with
kings (Prov. 8.14; Isa. 9.5; 11.2). Then, when the crisis was over, when
the enemy had withdrawn or been defeated, God would *receive him
with glory*. אחר refers to the same future event as אחריתם in v. 17, the
coming *bouleversement*: there would be a victory march as in Psalm 68,
with the king in the centre of the procession going up in triumph (כבוד)
to God's temple. So did General Rommel dream of the La Scala company singing *Aida* for him in Cairo, before the Battle of Alamein.

73.25-28. The king thinks of the heavenly court as in Psalm 82, a cabinet of self-willed rebel gods, one of whom has let the Assyrian plague
loose upon him. *Whom* has he *in heaven*? El alone. But with him as
guide and mentor *on earth*, he is like a Homeric hero who *desires no*
other. Weak as his own knees feel, God is his *rock*, and his *portion for
ever*. This was the divine covenant, and the enemy are *far from* God,
and *go a whoring* from him after their own gods. It is these whose presence in the Bethel shrine is an unforgivable affront, and those responsible can expect only to *perish* and *be destroyed*. *It is good* for the king to
draw near to God, whom he has made his *refuge*; he will be able in due
course to testify to the people of *all* God's works in resolving the crisis.
He goes forth to war like a Homeric hero; like Hector to fight Achilles
in the twenty-second book of the *Iliad*, encouraged by Athena in the
form of his brother Deiphobus, and deceived to his death.

Psalm 74

74.1   Maschil of Asaph.
    O God, why hast thou cast us off for ever?
    Why doth thine anger smoke against the sheep of thy pasture?
2   Remember thy congregation which thou hast purchased of old,
    Which thou hast redeemed to be the tribe of thine inheritance.
    [*And* mount Zion, wherein thou hast dwelt.]
3   Lift up thy feet unto the perpetual ruins;
    The enemy hath wrought all evil in the sanctuary.
4   Thine adversaries have roared in the midst of thine assembly;
    They have set up their ensigns for signs.

74.5   He made himself known (יִוָּדַע) as one that lifted up
        Axes upon a thicket of trees.
   6   And now all the carved work thereof together
        They break down with hatchet and hammers.
   7   They have set thy sanctuary on fire;
        They have profaned the dwelling-place of thy name even to
            the ground.
   8   They said in their heart, Let us make havoc of them
            altogether:
        They have burned up all the places of assembly in the land.
   9   We see not our signs;
        There is no more any prophet,
        Neither is there among us any that knoweth how long.
  10   How long, O God, shall the adversary reproach?
        Shall the enemy blaspheme thy name for ever?
  11   Why drawest thou back thy hand, even thy right hand?
        Pluck it out of thy bosom and consume *them*.

Like 73, Psalm 74 evokes a limited unanimity. It is a national lament,
and it was composed for the burning of the Jerusalem Temple, to be
used on a day of public fasting. Which burning of the Temple is, however, less clear, Gunkel points out the problems. It can hardly be the
Babylonian capture of the city in 586. The disaster here described is
apparently limited to the Temple; there is no reference either to the
large-scale loss of life or the deportations following, as there is, for
example, in Psalm 44. It would be peculiar to complain of the absence of
prophets when so celebrated a prophet as Jeremiah was around. We
may add that since Josiah had destroyed all the meeting places of God in
the land only a few years before, it is surprising that any survived to be
burned up by the enemy. The absence of prophets is not a problem if
the disaster described was the work of Antiochus IV in 167, since this is
commented on in 1 Maccabees (4.46; 9.27; 14.41). But then Antiochus
set up an altar to Zeus, and forbade circumcision and other Jewish religious practices, and there is no reference to anything of this kind. The
'places of assembly' are not likely to be synagogues (RV text), because
the LXX does not translate מוֹעֲדֵי־אֵל by συναγωγάς but by ἑορτάς;
also we have no evidence of synagogues in Palestine so early. In any
case Maccabaean datings for psalms have fallen under a cloud since the
days of Duhm, as both the LXX and the Qumran psalms are uncomfortably close in date. Gunkel escapes the difficulty by supposing a rather
hypothetical third destruction of the Temple in the fourth century.

Kraus avoids the problem over the absence of prophets by postulating a date around 520; or a slightly earlier setting is suggested by W.A. Young (*Psalm 74*, p. 227). This would be in line with the time gap suggested by v. 3 *perpetual ruins*, v. 9 the absence of *signs* of divine intervention, and so forth, and would agree with Lam. 2.9, 'her prophets find no vision from the LORD'. But the impression given by the psalm is of a comparatively *recent* outrage: will the enemy's roaring in the sanctuary be the first remembered sixty years after the event, and will Babylonian ensigns still be in position a decade after the Persian victory? There *are* prophets about, too, in Lam. 2.14. Another remote possibility, favoured by Dahood, is a supposed sack of the Temple in the 480s.

A different possibility is suggested by v. 2. The metre of the psalm is fairly regular, seventeen verses being 4.4, and apart from v. 2 there are two cola in each verse. In v. 2 there is a third colon: הר־ציון זה שכנת בו. The syntax with v. 2ab is clumsy. God is asked to remember his *congregation* which he has redeemed to be the *tribe of his inheritance; Mount Zion*. But a congregation or tribe is not a mountain. Furthermore the loose זה appears elsewhere in what look like adaptations of northern psalms to Jerusalem use: 68.9 זה סיני, and in Judg. 5.5 the same. Gunkel proposes the omission of a whole colon before our v. 2c, and many other scholars suggest other emendations. But the simplest solution would be to see v. 2c as an expansion to adapt the psalm to Jerusalem use, like 50.2 מציון, or others still to be considered. The psalm would then have been originally composed for use in a northern shrine, Bethel in fact, which was pillaged and burned in the invasions of 732–722. It will be seen that the detail supplied in the psalm fits well with such a supposed context.

74.1-2. The psalm is full of echoes of the laments which opened the two Korah series. *Why hast thou cast off for ever?* (זנחת לנצח): cf. Ps. 43.2, 'Why hast thou cast me off (זנח)?'; 44.9, 'But now thou hast cast us off'; esp. 44.24, 'Arise, cast not off for ever' (אל־תזנח לנצח, no object); 85.6, 'Wilt thou be angry with us for ever?' The same catastrophe which overwhelmed the priesthood at Dan has afflicted their colleagues at Bethel, and meets with the same response. The language is also echoed in other psalms in the Asaph series: 'Why doth thine anger smoke (עשן) *against the sheep of thy pasture?*—cf. Ps. 80.5, 'How long wilt thou be angry (עשן)...'; 79.13, 'we thy people and sheep of thy pasture'. *Which thou hast purchased* (קנית) *of old, which thou hast redeemed* (גאלת): cf. Ps. 77.16, 'Thou hast with thine arm redeemed (גאלת) thy people'; 78.35, 'the Most High God their redeemer (גאלם)'; also Exod. 15.13, 16,

'the people which thou hast redeemed (נאלת)...which thou hast purchased (קנית).'

In all these parallels God's *purchase* and *redemption* of his people
refers to the Exodus, and that is in mind here also with *of old* (קדם). The
term *congregation* (עדה) is widely used of the people in the desert
(especially in P material). Although Israel is once described in Jeremiah
as *the tribe of thine inheritance* (10.16; cf. 51.19; Isa. 63.17, *tribes*), in
77.16 *thy people* is identified as 'the sons of Jacob and Joseph'; and it is
likely that, in line with Pss. 80.2-3 and 81.6, *the tribe of thine inheritance* is here intended to be Joseph. It was Joseph (and perhaps
Benjamin) who was *purchased* and *redeemed* from Egypt to become the
tribe of God's inheritance: Jacob was the earlier group of immigrants.
By Jeremiah's time the Exodus legend has been appropriated by the
whole people, Israel.

The dignified public lament which opens with this moving appeal
poses a problem in itself: what situation does it presuppose? We might
naturally think of a national gathering, *thy congregation*, come together
to plead with their God. The lament is apparently spoken by a national
leader (*my King*, v. 12), and the place seems to be the national Temple
complex. Ancient temples were small, and even in good times the people
did not enter them at festivals: they gathered in massed tribal formations
(Ps. 68.27; Deut. 27) and saw and heard what they could, and joined in
the procession. Here we seem to understand that the traditional national
symbols have been displaced from their familiar positions (*we see not
our signs*), and the hated enemy symbols have been substituted for them
(*They have set up their ensigns for signs*). These must surely be in the
Israelite national centre. The lament is then the more pointed in that the
burned out shell of the temple buildings is before the people's eyes, and
God's, and can be appealed to as a monstrous insult to his *Name*.

Mowinckel and others appeal to the Israelite custom of holding occasional national fasts in times of military defeat, and so forth, citing Joel
2.15-16 as a likely background to psalms like 74. But this seems unlikely
after 587, which Mowinckel assigns as the most probable setting for
Psalm 74, when the country was in chaos. Eighty men, who had shaved
and slashed themselves and rent their clothes, tried to bring offerings to
the Jerusalem Temple, and were massacred by Ishmael ben Nethaniah
(Jer. 41.5-7). The governor, Gedaliah, was murdered; and even the reluctant Jeremiah took refuge in Egypt. The pitiable picture of the lawlessness and misery of the next generation is painted with remorseless

vigour in Deuteronomy 28. In time a regular calendar of liturgical fasts
came to be held in memory of the siege and fall of the city (Zech. 7.1-7;
8.18-23); but Psalm 74 seems to belong to a recent catastrophe, and yet
to presuppose an ordered liturgical occasion. It would be more at home
in Bethel in the 720s when the shrine had been ravaged and desecrated,
but the king and government were still in place, and the national festivals, including a preliminary fast, could be celebrated with dignity.

74.3-4. The divine abode is probably Mt Paran (Deut. 33.2; cf. Ps. 50.3),
whence God is urged to *lift up his feet* upon the high places of the earth
(Mic. 1.3) to his ruined shrine, The *ruins* (מַשֻּׁאוֹת, as in 73.18 with plene
וֹ) are *perpetual* because the Assyrians burned the shrine in 732, and the
glory is departed from Israel. *The enemy* totally wrecked *the sanctuary*.
They came in *roaring* like lions (Lam. 2.7), shouting and blaspheming in
the assembly place (מוֹעֲדֶךָ) where there should be the praise of God, or
else a respectful silence (Hab. 2.20). As at Gath, *they have set up their
ensigns for signs*, for symbols of their mastery (see on 73.20). Tiglath-
Pileser set up his own statue and that of his god at Gath, and these will
be the אוֹתֹת referred to here, the צֶלֶם of 73.20: אוֹת is used of a religious
symbol at Deut. 6.8, Ezek. 4.3. They are intended as manifest signs of
Israel's humiliation, and are felt to be so with all the resentment of the
powerless.

74.5-7. The Assyrians will have behaved as Nebuchadnezzar did following the siege of Jerusalem in 597. He deposed King Jehoiachin and
replaced him with Zedekiah, as they deposed Pekah and replaced him
with Hoshea. He 'carried out all the treasures of the house of the
LORD...and cut in pieces all the vessels of gold which Solomon king of
Israel had made for the temple of the LORD' (2 Kgs 24.13), as they
broke down all the carved work here *with hatchet and hammers*. No
doubt they carried away any gilding or ivory from the פִּתּוּחֶיהָ as spoil
for their own temples. As in Ps. 73.10, the psalmist moves from plural to
the nameless and abominated singular leader, the Rabshakeh. He had
seemed a proud and dignified man; but *he made himself known* as no
better than a coarse peasant, *lifting up axes on high in a thicket*. Finally
they put God's holy place to the torch, and desecrated it to the ground.
The same ambiguity applied at Bethel as at Jerusalem. Bethel was the
house of God, his abode in happy times, where he was enthroned upon
the cherubim (Ps. 80.2), even as Yahweh of Hosts sat on his throne on

Zion in Isaiah 6. But when disaster befell and the temples were
destroyed, it was better to think of him as away on Mount Paran or
Mount Sinai. The heaven and the heaven of heavens could not contain
him—how much less a house that humans have built. God has merely
caused his name to dwell in Zion (1 Kgs 8), made Bethel *the dwelling
place of thy name*. Like the covenant theology, the name theology was
not invented by the Jerusalem Deuteronomists: it was carried there by
their fathers, the Elohist priests from Ephraim.

74.8-9. As at Ps. 83.5, the psalmist imagines the wicked in their plotting,
and in both cases it is the extirpation of Israel that is in their minds. They
have already set their plans into action by attacking Israelite religion:
they have burned up all the meeting places of God in the land, and so
attempted to cut the lifeline between the people and God. Amos and
Hosea show that there were many מוֹעֲדֵי־אֵל in the land in the 730s—
Dan, Shechem, Tabor, Mizpah, Gilgal, beside Bethel—and their destruction is the first sign of the coming assimilation into the Assyrian empire.
The familiar symbols of the worship of Yahweh are no more to be seen.
These will have included the bull-cherub figures which sustained the
divine throne in the Bethel shrine, and which Hosea derided ('Men kiss
calves!'); the famous silver ephod with the teraphim which had been at
Dan and Nob; the steles and altars of sacrifice; and no doubt many other
precious cultic foci.

There is no more a prophet either. Amos had prophesied back in the
days of Jeroboam II in the 750s, and Hosea is supposed to have been
active from as early (Hos. 1.1); the latter's writing reflects the situation
after 732, but 1.1 suggests that he soon removed to Jerusalem. We hear
of no successors to these two formidable figures; and for all their tones
of menace, they were felt to mediate the will of God—while they were
around, there was someone *among us that knoweth how long*. Hosea
did say that the children of Israel should abide many days without
sacrifice and without pillar, and without ephod and teraphim, but after-
ward should return and seek Yahweh their God, and David their king
(3.4-5).

We should have expected נִיְנֶם (from ינה, to oppress) for MT נִיְנָם; and should probably
suspect old northern Hebrew: Delitzsch compares נֶרַם in Num. 21.30, an ancient
fragment. כל־מוֹעֲדֵי־אֵל בָּאָרֶץ should mean *all the meeting places of El in the land*.
מוֹעֵד meant this in v. 4, and El is a frequent name for the God of Israel in the Asaph
psalms. Gunkel and Kraus take בָאָרֶץ as 'in the world'; but Israelites did not think

that the temples in Nineveh and Babylon were meeting places of El, and would not have been greatly disturbed if they had all been burned up. Anthony Gelston ('Psalm 74.8') discusses four possible solutions to the problem—Gunkel's foreign temples, local Israelite shrines, the Temple complex of buildings, and non-sacrificial places of prayer. He inclines to the last, and is followed by Tate; but the only evidence offered is 1 Macc. 3.46, which is unconvincingly late. Kirkpatrick denied that אות could mean a religious symbol, and took it to mean an *ensign*, as in Num. 2.2; but the term is used for a religious arm-band in Deut. 6.8, and Tiglath-Pileser's inscription about Gath strongly suggests that it would be in order for a more public religious 'sign'. Kraus understands the word to mean signs of Yahweh's intervention in the holy war; but *our signs* could hardly bear this meaning.

73.10-11. The theme of the adversaries' reproach (יחרף) and the *enemy's blasphemy* (ינאץ) once more echoes Psalm 44: the middle section of that psalm is given to the topic, especially 44.17, 'From the voice of him that reproacheth (מחרף) and blasphemeth (מגדף); By reason of the enemy and the avenger.' The question 'How long?' had not yet arisen in 42–44: the Korah psalms come from Dan, and the disastrous defeat of 732 has only just happened. Psalm 74 stems from Bethel four or five years later, and the ruin, and the disgrace of Israel's God, appear to be permanent (לנצח). God's *hand* and his *right hand* were also appealed to in 44.3-4, and the pressing requirement of divine action in 44.24. There the urgency has taken a toll in reverence, 'Awake, why sleepest thou, O Lord?'; here it has made short work of the syntax, 'Why do you withdraw your hand? And your right hand— from within your bosom, destroy!'

RV mg follows the Q 'your bosom' against the meaningless K חוקך, 'your ordinance'. Young, followed by Tate, sees an extensive Canaanite background to the first half of the psalm: the attack of the Babylonians on Yahweh's Temple is understood to be set against the Ugaritic myth of the gods' attack on the palace of El. This seems far-fetched, even given the connection of Leviathan with Ugarit; and we might have expected some reference to such a palace in vv. 12-17.

74.12   Yet God is my King of old,
        Working salvation in the midst of the earth.
  13   Thou didst break up the sea by thy strength:
        Thou brakest the heads of the sea-monsters in the waters.
  14   Thou brakest the heads of Leviathan in pieces,
        Thou gavest him to be meat to a people, to beasts (לציים).
  15   Thou didst cleave fountain and torrent (נחל):
        Thou driedst up ever-flowing rivers.

74.16   The day is thine, the night also is thine:
             Thou hast prepared the luminary and the sun.
   17   Thou hast set all the borders of the earth:
             Thou hast made summer and winter.

74.12. As Psalm 44 began with an appeal to God's 'salvations' (ישועות),
and to God as 'my King' (44.5) in the days of old (קדם, 44.2), in the
Settlement, so does our psalmist turn now to God as *my King of old*
(קדם), and the *salvations* (ישועות) which he wrought at Creation. This
was done *in the midst of the earth*: somewhere in the East, in Eden, as
the Israelites were later to express it (Gen. 2.8).

God's *victories* in creation are not introduced by accident. Psalm 74,
like Psalm 44, is headed 'Maschil', a clever psalm (שכל). Commenting
on 44, I noted that the ישע root was used four times in the opening lines
of the psalm, and suggested that the repetition was due to the accession
of a new king whose name, Hoshea, meant *Saviour* (*Korah*, pp. 88-91).
Similarly, the root כון, *establish*, is found four times also in the Maschil
Psalm 89, which can be dated to the period just before the fall of
Jerusalem, when the (true) king was called Jehoiachin, Yahweh will
establish (Goulder, *Korah*, pp. 218-19). There are a number of Maschil
psalms in the Prayers of David (51–71), and I was able to make suggestions of similar plays on the name of some central character implied in
the situation (*Prayers, passim*). So here, when the king is again Hoshea,
we find God spoken of as *my King of old working salvations*. Like
Jehoshaphat and Uzziah, Nabal and Solomon, his name is looked upon
as an omen of what is to come.

74.13-14. The recall of the battle with Leviathan is not an accident
either, and will necessitate a short excursus. Leviathan is the name of a
river monster, here equated with the Euphrates, and her shattering of
old is intended to suggest the coming shattering of the latter-day
Euphrates power, Assyria.

EXCURSUS: LEVIATHAN

Leviathan is an extremely ancient mythical water-monster, which occurs in the
Ugaritic Baal texts. Mot says to Baal: 'Because you smote Leviathan (*ltn*) the twisting serpent (*btn. brh*), (and) made an end of the crooked serpent (*btn. 'qltn*), the
tyrant with seven heads, the skies will become hot (and) will shine' (*CTA* 5.I.1-3).
Similar language is used by Anat in *CTA* 3.IIID.34–IV.47: 'What foe has risen up

against Baal, (What) enemy has arisen against the Rider of the clouds? Surely I smote Yam, beloved of El, surely I made an end of River, the mighty god. Surely I lifted up the dragon (*tnn*), I... (and) smote the crooked serpent (*btn. 'qltn*), the tyrant with seven heads. I smote Ar[s] beloved of El, I put an end to El's calf Atik...' (translation by John Day, *Conflict*, pp. 13-14).

The situation appears to be clear:

(i) 5.I.1 begins abruptly, and there is a lacuna at 3.IIID.37; so it is likely that parallel descriptions were in the original. Baal (in 5.I) and Anat (in 3.IIID) both defeated *ltn* 'the twisting serpent/crooked serpent, the tyrant with seven heads'. Since Baal also defeated Yam and Nahar in a contest described at length (IIIAB), it is probable that this was referred to in the missing matter before 5.I, as it is by Anat in 3.IIID.

(ii) Yam and Nahar are the primary enemies of Baal and Anat. Litan (as J.A. Emerton argues the name should be vocalized, 'Leviathan') is the first of a series of subsidiary opponents (Ars, Atik, etc.). Litan is never paralleled with Yam, and is not another name for the Sea; the name occurs only once in the surviving text, and is implied once more (in 3.IIID).

(iii) The various monsters correspond with major features of life at Ugarit. Just as Mt Zaphon 'is' Mt Casius, so is Yam the Mediterranean Sea and Nahar the Nahr el-Aksy, the Orontes, the great river of Syria whose estuary lies north of Mt Casius, not far from Ugarit.

(iv) Litan, Ars and Atik are likely then to be subsidiary river-powers. This is implied by several features of the description. Litan is twice spoken of as a serpent; and rivers look like snakes when seen from a hill. They twist and bend as Litan is said to be twisting and crooked (for the translation of *'qltn* see Day, *Conflict*, p. 142). The similarity to a snake is widely obvious: in the Hereford *Mappa Mundi* the rivers are all portrayed as snakes with heads and eyes. It was after Baal smote Litan that the skies became hot: that is after the river-waters begin to subside in May, the high summer begins. It may be that further enemies smitten in the list in 3.IIID, Ishat and Dhabib, are river-powers too, rather than fire-powers (Caquot *et al.*, *Textes*, p. 168).

(v) This suggests that Litan is the name of a secondary river in Syria. After the Orontes the biggest river in Syria–Lebanon is the Litani, which follows a tortuous course southwards between the Libanus and Antilibanus ranges before taking a sharp turn west to flow into the Mediterranean north of Tyre. It has numerous tributaries, which may suggest the seven heads. So Litan is the eponymous name of the twisting, bending, many-tributaried river-serpent, the Litani. In an ephemeral world it is a comfort that some things approach permanence, and that the river of the Beqaa valley has been known by the same name for four millennia.

The modern Litani is spelt with a ט, whereas Leviathan has a ן, transliterated Λευιάθαν by Aquila and Symmachus. ט and ן are rarely confused in Hebrew texts, though there are instances, for example, Ps. 60.6, where קשֹׁט, *truth*, should be קשֶׁת, *bow*. But spelling changes in names are widespread with shifting populations over millennia.

(vi) A remarkable survival of Ugaritic phrasing into Israelite texts a thousand years on is often noted at Isa. 27.1: 'In that day the LORD with his sore and great and strong sword shall punish leviathan the twisting (ברח) serpent and leviathan the crooked (עקלתון) serpent; and he shall slay the dragon (תנין) that is in the sea.' The coincidence of four terms (including לויתן) in so similar a context is very striking. The insertion of the ו into ליתן is usually attributed to a connection with the Hebrew verb לוה, to twist (BDB, KB).

Isaiah 27 is an obscure chapter, but the concluding verses offer an interpretation: 'And it shall come to pass in that day, that the LORD shall beat out *his corn* from the flood of the River unto the brook of Egypt, and ye shall be gleaned one to another, O ye children of Israel. And it shall come to pass in that day, that a great trumpet shall be blown, and they shall come which were lost in the land of Assyria, and they that were outcasts in the land of Egypt; and they shall worship the LORD in the holy mountain at Jerusalem' (27.12-13). In this view, God means to gather his scattered people for festal worship at Jerusalem, those exiled in Assyria and those who have fled to Egypt; and to ensure this he will punish (visit upon) the twisting Leviathan and the crooked Leviathan, the two rivers standing for the two great empires on the Nile and the Euphrates. This would then parallel the adaptation of the sea-monster Rahab killed at creation (Ps. 89.10-15; Job 26.12-13; 9.13; Isa. 51.9) into Rahab the symbol of Egypt (Ps. 87.4; Isa. 30.7; 51.9-10); and Rahab is also a 'twisting serpent' (נחש בריח) at Job 26.13, so the Nile is the link here too.

Opinion on Isa. 27.1 has been very various. Mediaeval Jewish commentators, Kimhi and Rashi, saw the two leviathans as Assyria and Egypt, and took the תנין to symbolize Tyre, as the contemporary sea-power, and I should be content to go along with this. Day (*Conflict*, p. 142) says, 'The Ugaritic texts cited above make it clear that Isa. 27.1 is describing one monster, not three'; he insists, properly, that some political power is meant, and he follows H. Wildberger (*Jesaia*, II, p. 1004) in identifying this as Egypt. They offer good reasons for dating the chapter soon after the exile. However, the Ugaritic texts themselves certainly do not settle the matter for 'one monster', since there Yam stands for the Mediterranean Sea and Litan for the Litani River; and although in Ps. 104.26 Leviathan has become a (domesticated) sea-monster, and a fire-breathing water-monster in Job 41, Isaiah 27 seems to differentiate *two* Leviathans, 'leviathan the twisting serpent and leviathan the crooked serpent'. Also, for reasons set out above, a serpent is a natural symbol for a river, not for the sea; so the two leviathans do sound like the two great rivers, as is indicated by Isa. 27.12-13. We should take the twisting river as the Nile, as in Job 26.12-13, since the lower Nile, more familiar to Israelites, is extremely sinuous; and the bending river as the Euphrates, as the upper Euphrates, more familiar to Israelites, takes a sharp bend to the east. There were Judaean exiles on both Euphrates and Nile after the exile; and Tyre was a sea-power then too (Ezek. 26–28), but without known exiles. Hence only Assyria and Egypt are mentioned in 27.12-13.

(vii) We may trace a history then of these symbolic monsters. In Ugaritic times Litan was the river-serpent shattered by Baal and Anat in the creation myth, and a river-serpent it remains in eighth-century Psalm 74 and fifth-century Isaiah 27. The sea-monster was called Yam (Sea) at Ugarit, and sometimes the Dragon (*tnn*), and this name also continues in Israelite texts including Isaiah 27. An alternative, non-Ugaritic name for the sea-monster was Rahab, which is found in this sense from the ninth-century Psalm 89a (Goulder, *Korah*, pp. 211-28) to Job. With time the Canaanite creation myth was amended, and eventually forgotten. Litan has ceased to be the local Litani by Psalm 74, and has become the more fearsome Euphrates. With Isaiah 27 there are two Leviathans, the Nile and the Euphrates. But it has also been equated with the sea-monster. By the seventh century it is a large fish taking its pastime among the ships in the sea (Ps. 104.26) as a part of Yahweh's creation. In Job 41 it is Yahweh's creation too, but not so tame; it is fearfully and wonderfully made. In Job 3.8 it seems to be a symbol of darkness (Day, *Conflict*, pp. 44-48). So here is the end of Yam and Rahab and Leviathan, humbly demythologized.

This excursus enables us to gain a firmer grasp of the force of 74.12-17. God's victories of old were when he *broke up the sea by* his *strength*; when he *brake the heads of the* תנינים *in the waters*. We are still in the world of the Canaanite myth, but the Ugaritic monster *tnn* has been debased into a school of sea-dragons. Where Baal shattered the head of Yam/Nahar with his magic clubs, God breaks the heads of the *tanninim*. Perhaps we should think of God's *strength* (עזך) as in line with Baal's club Yagrush. All this happened somewhere in the East. The major river-monster was Leviathan. God *brake* his multiple *heads* also, like the seven heads of Litan. The savages (ציים) of the vast desert which then stretched across North Arabia and into Iran, the ancestors of the modern Assyrians, were *given* his corpse *to be* their *meat*. God is my King of old: he can work salvations for us against the same wretched enemy now.

To an earlier commentator as acute as Kirkpatrick the passage referred to Israel's passing of the Red Sea 'of course'; but Gunkel saw that it was the *Chaoskampf* even before the discovery of the Ras Shamra texts (*Schöpfung*, pp. 44-45). Kraus thought both traditions were in mind, and Ps. 77.15-21 may be cited in support (see below); but the Exodus is not clearly referred to at any point, even v. 15. The suggestion that the 'people inhabiting the wilderness' (עם לציים) might be an animal 'people' is improbable. The ants and the rabbits are spoken of somewhat playfully as peoples in Prov. 30.25-26, and the locusts less playfully in Joel 2.2, because they are seen as working together for the common good and living in community. At 72.9 the ציים are, as here, humans, and, as here, live between the River and the Sea. The normal meaning of the word elsewhere (Isa. 13.21; 23.13; 34.14) is wild beasts of the desert. The English word *beasts* comprises both wild men and wild animals, and there can be little doubt that the term which covers both is intended pejoratively. There is no need of an emendation to yield *sharks*. The feared Assyrian enemy is being belittled as mere *beasts of the steppe*, whom God provided for with the disgusting sustenance of the flesh of Leviathan: they were like a pack of hyenas.

74.15. God imposed order on 'the mighty world of waters dark and deep', as in Psalm 104 or Job 38.8-11. He clove (בקעת) the spring-holes and the torrent-beds to enable the waters to run away. The latter are a familiar sight in Israel today: a dry wadi may fill to flooding in a matter of hours, and even minutes, carrying away the melting snow on the hills. So, in the psalmist's imagination, did God at creation *dry up the ever-flowing rivers*. The water from the rock story has nothing to do with it (Emerton, 'Spring').

74.16-17. The story of creation continues to what Genesis 1 will make the fourth day: the forming of moon and sun to govern night and day, summer and winter. Perhaps the account is without prejudice: this was how God completed his handiwork. But perhaps we should not suppress our strategy of suspicion. It may be that the psalmist wishes to stress that God *set all the borders* (גבולות, as in Deut. 32.8) *of the earth*, and intended the Assyrians to keep to Assyria; and that the *moon and the sun*, which are worshipped by such heathens, are in fact only God's creations. The moon (the luminary, מאור) comes before the sun, perhaps a reflection of Mesopotamian moon-worship.

74.18	Remember this, that the enemy hath reproached the LORD,
	And that a foolish people hath blasphemed thy name.
19	O deliver not the soul of thy turtledove unto the wild beast
	(RV text):
	Forget not the life (RV text) of thy poor for ever.
20	Have respect unto the covenant:
	For the dark places of the land are full of the habitations
	of violence.
21	O let not the oppressed return ashamed:
	Let the poor and needy praise thy name.
22	Arise, O God, plead thine own cause:
	Remember how the foolish man reproacheth thee all the day.
23	Forget not the voice of thine adversaries:
	The tumult of those that arise up against thee which
	ascendeth continually.

The echoes of Psalm 44 are insistent. Ps. 44.16-25, '*All the day long* is my dishonour before me...For the *voice* of him that *reproacheth* and blasphemeth; by reason of the *enemy* and the avenger... Neither have we turned back from thy *covenant*... Awake, why sleepest thou, O Lord, Arise... Wherefore *forgettest thou* our *affliction* and our oppression?' The general tone and the specific language are very close over the final verses of the two laments.

74.18-19. The standard appeal to God's injured honour is repeated throughout these verses. The *foolish people*, the wilfully ignorant Assyrians, *has reproached Yahweh*: the name of God is used, in parallel with *thy name*, because the blasphemous invaders have shouted (v. 4; *the voice of thine adversaries, the tumult of those that rise up against thee*, v. 23) his name derisively as they hacked down his shrine. The image of Assyria as *beasts* (v. 14) *roaring* (v. 4) is now developed. Israel is God's precious *turtle-dove*, as in Ps. 68.14 (cf. Goulder, *Prayers*, p. 198), and the enemy is a *wild beast* (חית), perhaps an eagle, which almost has her life (נפש, חית by a word-play) in its claws. Assyria is a wild animal again in 80.14, a boar. God's people have become 'the wretched ones' (עניּיך), and in v. 21 *the oppressed* (דך), the wretched and impoverished (עני ואביון), a defeated, harried, desperate community, with an unpayable indemnity round its neck.

74.20. Appeal is made to the covenant, as was done in Ps. 44.18, a recurrent theme of the Asaph psalms (pp. 23, 31). The breakdown of law and order, discussed above on 50.18-20, is hinted at again here. *The dark places of the land* are remote corners as Laish once was, quiet and secure till the Danites came and slaughtered the inhabitants (Judg. 18.7-28). Now the authority of the central government has collapsed, and every man does what is right in his own eyes. Such places are *full of the habitations of violence*. Refugees from the East Bank and from Galilee are an intolerable incubus on their relatives, and resentment leads to quarrels, force and sometimes death.

Anderson takes v. 20b to refer to the murder of refugees in hiding, a similar and possible view; the violence could stem from marauding Assyrian bands. Dahood notes the pun on חית in v. 19ab (meaning first *wild beast* and then *life*): the first will be an old absolute form, another instance of old northern Hebrew. There is a second pun in vv. 13, תנינים, *dragons*, and 14 תתננו, *thou gavest him*; and perhaps a third between חרף, *reproach*, and חֹרֶף, *winter* (v. 17). Such word-plays are recurrent in the Asaph psalms.

A Liturgical Hypothesis

The Asaph collection begins with three psalms, 50, 73 and 74, which give the impression of the opening of a liturgical sequence. All three are public psalms. The first [50] suggests its setting as the beginning of a festival, because it includes the command, 'Gather my devoted ones together unto me, Those that make my covenant with sacrifice.' It also proclaims God's coming in judgment, which was a central theme of the autumn festival. So although Psalm 50 has become separated in the Psalter from the rest of the Asaph psalms, there can be little doubt that it originally stood first in some sequence: God's חסידים must be *gathered together* to renew *his covenant with sacrifice* at the beginning of some occasion. The most likely occasion for such a renewal of the covenant would be *the* feast, the autumn festival, Tabernacles.

We have two other psalms in the Psalter which must similarly have been introductions to festivals, Psalms 42 and 84. Both of these are pilgrimage psalms. In 42 the speaker 'goes mourning' to the shrine; his 'soul thirsteth for the living God' like the hinds he can see panting after the water-brooks; he is 'coming to see the face of God'. The shrine where he is to 'remember thee' is in 'the land of Jordan' under 'the Hermons', on 'the little hill'; that is, at the national sanctuary at Dan, where the main source of the Jordan rises, and 'deep calls to deep at the sound of thy waterfalls', almost the only waterfalls in Israel. His mourning is 'because of the oppression of the enemy', who have 'a sword in my bones', and 'continually say, Where is thy God?' Psalm 42 is the opening psalm of the main collection of the Psalms of the Sons of Korah, 42–49. It would find a natural context at the time of the Assyrian invasion about 732 (Goulder, *Korah*, pp. 23-33).

Psalm 84 is also spoken by a national leader, perhaps a priest, whose soul similarly 'longeth, yea, even fainteth for the courts of the LORD', crying out also to 'the living God'. He is accompanying a group of men 'in whose heart are highways', and who 'pass through the Valley of Baca' to 'see the face of God', as in Psalm 42. He prays God to 'behold our shield, And look upon the face of thine anointed'. There is no mourning, and no suggestion of any threat from enemies. The present text applies the psalm to Zion (v. 8), but the similarities of phrasing to Psalm 42, and the geographical details, both suggest an earlier use in Dan (Goulder, *Korah*, pp. 37-50). If so, the confident background would suggest happier times than 42, perhaps in the ninth century. Psalm 84 is the first psalm in the second collection of the Sons of Korah, 84–85, 87–88.

A likely setting for the three psalms, then, 50, 42, and 84, would be the opening of the autumn festival, held in the harvest month of Bul (October–November) in Northern Israel. The actual festival began with the full moon, on 15th Bul, so the royal party, and the people generally, must have arrived a little before. The trumpet announcing the feast was probably sounded at New Moon in Bul, and it might take a week or ten days to travel to Dan, or to Bethel. When he arrived, the Israelite needed to cut some branches, find a site and build his tabernacle, his home for the week. We cannot give a precise day to the pre-festival psalms; but we may note that in later time the 10th of the festal month (Tishri in Jerusalem) came to be used as the day of the fast before the feast, the Yom Kippur.

Psalm 42 is closely linked to Psalm 43, where the speaker still 'goes mourning', and uses the same refrain (42.6, 12; 43.5); but now he is to be brought to 'thy holy hill', and will 'go unto the altar of God' with music and sacrifice. This is succeeded by Psalm 44, a noble national lament. But Psalm 85, the psalm after the pilgrimage psalm 84, is also a national lament. In the past God forgave the iniquities of Jacob: he is prayed now to cause his indignation against his people to cease—'Wilt thou be angry with us for ever? Wilt thou draw out thine anger to all generations?' It is his mercy and salvation which are asked for. But, as with Psalm 84, there is no suggestion of invasions or defeats. Salvation means that 'Truth springeth out of the earth: And righteousness hath looked down from heaven'. We are again back in happy times when the worst enemies were General Drought and General Locust.

But then the Asaph collection also opens with an initiating psalm, 50, and (as I have been arguing) two national laments, 73 and 74. This suggests that we ought to consider the same liturgical possibility for which I set out evidence in *The Psalms of the Sons of Korah* and in *The Prayers of David*. It could be that the Asaph collection was not merely a *significant* collection, coming from the same shrine and the same historical context (as I urged in Chapter 1), but also an *ordered* collection: not like an anthology of modern prayers, from which the minister may select as he or she pleases; more like the Book of Common Prayer, where the Collects are set to be read in a given order round the year.

A liturgical hypothesis of this kind is at first sight difficult to establish: for we have no direct evidence of the pattern of Israelite festal worship even at Jerusalem, let alone Dan and Bethel. However, what we do have is a cumulative argument. It may perhaps be an accident that both Korah series begin with (i) a pilgrimage psalm (42–43, 84), followed by (ii) a national lament (44, 85). On the other hand it is rather plausible that the festival at Dan should have been preceded by a pilgrimage and a day of humiliation; and when we find that the Asaph collection also begins with an initiatory psalm ('Gather my devoted ones...', 50), and

two national laments (73, 74), a hunch becomes a speculation. For it to
be more than a speculation, we should need to find the sequence to
continue. If Psalm 45 corresponded with Psalm 75 we should have a
hypothesis, and if Psalm 46 corresponded with Psalm 76 we should have
a theory. But in such matters there is always an element of judgment.
Psalm 85 is like Psalm 44 in pleading to God to cease from his anger,
but unlike 44 in that there is no military defeat to bewail. 'Correspondence' is always going to be a relative matter: but I shall hope to
offer reasons for the differences as well as the similarities.

For the moment we may be content to note how close Psalms 44 and
74 are. Both are in three sections: the people's plight after defeat (74.1-
11; 44.10-17); a recall of God's earlier 'salvations' (in creation, 74.12-17;
at the Settlement, 44.2-9); an appeal for God to arise and act (74.18-23;
44.18-27). The recall of a particular, relevant, earlier divine incursion is
a rare element in public laments (contrast Psalms 79, 90, 120 for
example). The language is often close:

74.1	why hast thou cast off for ever (זנחת לנצח)?
44.24	cast not off for ever (אל־תזנח לנצח); also v. 10.
74.2	thy congregation which thou hast purchased of old (קדם)
44.2	what work thou didst in their days, in the days of old (קדם)
74.3	the enemy hath wrought all evil (הרע)
44.3	Thou didst wreak evil on the peoples (תרע)
74.10	How long, O God, shall the adversary reproach (יחרף)?
	Shall the enemy (אויב) blaspheme thy name for ever?;
	(also vv. 18, 22)
44.17	For the voice of him that reproacheth (מחרף) and blasphemeth;
	By reason of the enemy (אויב) and the avenger.
74.11	Why withdrawest thou thy hand, even thy right hand
	(ידך וימינך)?
44.3-4	the nations with thy hand (ידך)... thy right hand (ימינך)
74.12	God is my King (מלכי) of old, Working salvation (ישועות)
44.5	Thou art my King (מלכי), O God, Command salvation (ישועות)
74.22	Arise (קומה), O God
44.27	Arise (קומה) for our help.

Both psalms appeal to the *covenant* (44.18) and God's *name* (44.20).

These features are sufficiently strong to make it not absurd to think
that the same psalmist has composed both pieces; though such a conclusion is not obvious. What is clear is that they stem from the same

tradition, and reflect very similar national situations. In Psalm 44 Israel has suffered a severe military defeat; the army has been slaughtered; the people carried off in slavery; the towns are covered with the shadow of death. But in the face of this there is a spirit of robust religious self-confidence: we have not been unfaithful to the covenant, it is because of thee that we suffer all the day long; awake, why sleepest thou, O God? Such was the independent mood still in the 730s. Psalm 74 represents the more chastened tone of seven or eight years later. The Assyrians have now repeatedly established their hegemony: they have annexed half the country, they have desecrated the national sanctuary at Bethel and every other shrine in the land, their blasphemous images are every-where. There is still place for hope and prayer, but the chutzpah is gone; we are on the road to Psalm 90, 'Thou hast set our secret sins in the light of thy countenance.' 'The jading and jar of the cart / Time's task-ing, it is fathers the asking for ease / Of the sodden–with–its–sorrowing heart.'

So we have the suggestion of three parallel liturgical sequences, one at Dan in the palmy days of the ninth century, or of Jeroboam II's time, in the Korah appendix, Psalms 84–85, 87–88 (89A); one at Dan after the disaster of 732, in the main Korah series, Psalms 42–49; and one at Bethel in the Asaph collection, Psalms 50, 73–83:

	Dan, 9th c.	*Dan, 730*	*Bethel, 725*
?13th Bul	84	42/43	50
14th Bul	85	44	73, 74

The 14th Bul was a long day. When times were bad, there was leisure for *two* national laments.

Note on Lamentations 2

Commentators, Kraus for example, often note parallels between Psalm 74 and Lamentations 2:

Lam. 2.2   He hath brought down, to the ground hath he profaned
            (לארץ חלל) the kingdom and the princes thereof.
Ps. 74.7   To the ground have they profaned (לארץ חללו) the dwelling
            place of thy name.
Lam. 2.3   He hath cut off in fierce anger (אף) every horn...
            He hath drawn back his right hand (השיב אחור ימינו)...
Ps. 74.1   Why doth thine anger (אפך) smoke...?
Ps. 74.11   Why drawest thou back thy hand, even thy right hand
            (ידך וימינך תשיב)?

Ps. 75.11   the horns of the righteous shall be exalted.

Lam. 2.6   He hath destroyed his place of assembly (מועדו).

Lam. 2.7   They have made a noise in the house of the LORD, as in the
            day of solemn assembly (מועד).

Ps. 74.4   Thine adversaries have roared in the midst of thine assembly
            (מועדך).

Lam. 2.9   ... among the nations where the law is not (אין תורה);
            Yea, her prophets (נביאיה) find no vision from the LORD.

Ps. 74.9   There is no more any prophet (אין־עוד נביא).

Lam. 2.15   Is this the city that men called the perfection of beauty
            (כלילת יפי)?

Ps. 50.2   Out of Zion, the perfection of beauty (מכלל־יפי)...

The echoes are insistent, but the relationship is different from that with
Psalm 44. Psalm 74 is a lament composed in the anguish of recent
bereavement and in the fear of worse: Lamentations 2 is an artificial
composition, an alphabetic lament written in the leisure of prolonged
desolation. The editor of Psalm 50 called Zion the perfection of beauty;
in Lamentations 2 men used to call her that, in improved Hebrew. In
Psalm 74 the shrine at Bethel was really profaned to the ground; in
Lamentations 2 Israel's kingdom and princes are metaphorically profaned to the ground. In Psalm 74 God turned his right hand; in
Lamentations 2, more clearly, he turned it back. In Psalm 74 the enemy
roared like lions in God's place of assembly; in Lamentations 2 they
more decorously made a noise, and the מועד is no longer natural for a
place of assembly, and is soon glossed as a time of assembly. In the days
of Psalm 74 there was no longer a prophet—Amos and Hosea were
gone; in Lamentations there was no law where the exiles had gone,
there were prophets, but they saw no visions.

Lamentations does not at all reflect the same situation as Psalm 74,
nor are its phrases independent parallels to the usages of Psalm 74. The
author is used to Psalm 74 (and 50) in the liturgy, and he reproduces
and glosses its language in imitation.

Chapter 3

THE OPENING OF THE FESTIVAL

Psalm 75

Before the festival began it might be suitable to go humbly with one's God, to fast and to have one's soul cleave to the dust (Psalms 42–44, 84–85, 73–74); but when the 15th arrived, the order of the day was rejoicing and praise, never mind how black the clouds on the horizon. Psalm 75 is a psalm of praise, shot through with apprehension.

75.1   For the Chief Musician. Do not destroy (אל־תשחת).
        A Psalm of Asaph. A Song.

2   We give thanks unto thee, O God;
    We give thanks, for thy name is near (RV text):
    They recite (ספרו) thy wondrous works.

3   When I take the appointed time,
    I will judge uprightly.

4   The earth and all the inhabitants thereof are dissolved:
    I have set up the pillars of it (RV text)   (Selah

5   I said unto the arrogant (RV text), Deal not arrogantly:
    And to the wicked, Lift not up the horn:

6   Lift not up your horn on high;
    Speak not insolently with haughty neck.

7   For neither from the east, nor from the west,
    Nor from the wilderness *cometh* lifting up (RV text).

8   But God is the judge:
    He putteth down one, and lifteth up another.

9   For in the hand of the LORD there is a cup, and the wine foameth
        (RV text);
    It is full of mixture, and he poureth out of the same:
    Surely the dregs thereof, all the wicked of the earth shall drain them
        and drink them.

10   But I will declare for ever,
    I will sing praises to the God of Jacob.

11   All the horns of the wicked also will I cut off;
    But the horns of the righteous one (צדיק) shall be lifted up.

Once more general agreement is limited. It is common ground that Psalm 75 is a public psalm, and has its place in a national liturgy. It opens as a hymn in the first person plural (*We give thanks unto thee...*), and closes similarly on a note of praise, now in the first person singular (*I will declare...I will sing praises...*). But problems arise partly from vv. 3-4, which are commonly taken to be spoken by God through a prophet (Gunkel, Mowinckel), or perhaps a priest (Kraus): only God, presumably, can set in order the pillars of the world when there is an earthquake. As Kraus comments, this makes a curious hymn, with the unheralded delivery of an oracle; the more so, as this is followed by five verses of warning to the arrogant/wicked. But there is something similar in Ps. 46.11 ('Let be, and know that I am God...'); Gunkel calls it a prophetic liturgy, and sees it as a prophecy of God's final (eschatological) judgment on the nations.

Mowinckel takes the psalm in the same general sense as Gunkel, but he disputes the eschatological sense, and proposes a more plausible setting in the autumn festival (*Psalmenstudien*, III, pp. 47-49). Israel was constantly at war, and God's ordered world, as it was seen, was for ever under threat from the invasions of the nations; and this paralleled the threat of chaos which he quelled in creation. So the festival each autumn marked the ascent of Yahweh to his throne to bring judgment on the world: the tale of his wonders in creation was recited, and hymns like Psalms 75 and 76, 46 and 48, were sung, reassuring the worshippers that all was well; and prophets might suitably deliver oracles in the same sense.

The difficulty for such approaches is in v. 11, *All the horns of the wicked also will I cut off*: surely this was not a part of the prophet's responsibility? Gunkel feels the uncomfortableness, and sees the speaker as in a moment of elation: 'Yes, he himself in his inspiration feels strong enough...to break off their horns.' So does Kraus, but he has a quicker solution: after v. 8 (*God is the judge*) the text (*I will cut off*) is impossible, and one must read יגדע, He *will cut off*. But we do better to be faithful to the text we have, and not to write our own psalm; and the obvious answer is that the main speaker is the king. Gunkel concedes that such language was 'originally' proper to kings, and Eaton (*Kingship*, pp. 55-56) cites Ps. 101.8 as an apt parallel, where the king vows, 'Morning by morning will I destroy all the wicked of the land.'

Eaton thus has a royal psalm, in which the king begins as spokesman for the people (*We give thanks...*), and goes on to threaten the wicked,

and to promise his personal testimony and praise; but the psalm is a dialogue between him and the prophet, who delivers the oracle in vv. 3-4.
While such an arrangement is conceivable when the psalm was first
spoken, it requires a clumsy and artificial stage-managing if (as Eaton
supposes) the psalm was in regular liturgical use; and he himself considers the possibility that the king spoke the whole text (though he prefers
the dialogue theory). I will suggest reasons for thinking that the whole
psalm was spoken by the king, including vv. 3-4.

75.1-2. The tension under which the psalm is composed is evident from
the beginning. It is a שׁיר, a *song*; with Psalms 76 and 83, the only songs
in the whole Asaph series. Psalms 45 and 46 were songs, and it was
traditional to open the festival with such a note of joy: Isaiah, foretelling
the defeat of Assyria, says, 'Ye shall have a song as in the night when a
feast is hallowed; and gladness of heart, as when one goeth with a pipe
to come unto the mountain of the LORD' (Isa. 30.29). The opening
words are of gratitude, the repeated *We give thanks*; and the reason
offered for this (it is just ו, *and*, in the Hebrew) is that God's *name is
near*, that is, his protective presence. The same passage in Isaiah begins,
'Behold, the *name* of the LORD cometh from far, burning with his
anger...' (Isa. 30.27).

It is a good thing that God's name is arriving at last, for it has not
been much in evidence recently (Pss. 73, 74), and the present text soon
reveals that *the arrogant* have been *dealing arrogantly*, and *lifting up
their horn on high*. Things have in fact come to such a pass that the
heading provides for a ceremony known as אל־תשׁחת, *Destroy not*. The
same provision is noted in the headings of Psalms 57, 58 and 59, which
marked the nadir of David's fortunes (Goulder, *Prayers*, pp. 116-39);
and its significance comes out in Deut. 9.11-29. There Israel has provoked Yahweh's wrath with the Golden Calf, and he threatens to
destroy them; but Moses fasts and intercedes for them—'So I fell down
before the LORD the forty days and forty nights that I fell down;
because the LORD had said he would destroy you. And I prayed unto
the LORD, and said, O Lord GOD, destroy not (אל־תשׁחת) thy people'
(Deut. 9.26-27). For all its thanksgiving and praise for God's imminent
presence, Psalm 75 is preceded by fasting and a rite of prostration such
as is ascribed to Moses: national annihilation has become a daunting
possibility.

For the significance of *the Chief Musician* see below on vv. 3-4. Weiser translates the verbs of v. 2 as perfects, and infers a preceding cultic liturgy with hymns and recitals; but it seems easier to understand these features as current with the psalm (see below). The LXX has καὶ ἐπικαλεσόμεθα τὸ ὄνομά σου, from which it is conjectured that the original Hebrew was וְקֹרְאֵי בִשְׁמֶךָ, *they that call on thy name*, for וְקָרוֹב שְׁמֶךָ. But the correspondence is not exact, and the Greek looks like an attempt to make sense of a lost idiom.

75.3-4. Many commentators speak of a sudden, unheralded oracle (Jacquet, '*ex abrupto*') in vv. 3-4, or even 3-6, but there is in fact a plain heralding at the end of v. 2, *they recite thy wondrous works*. The psalm provides an interval for such a recital in the Selah, marked after v. 4. So now the *wondrous works* of God are to be recited, in fact the wondrous works of creation which have already been hinted at in the Leviathan passage in Ps. 74.12-17. But before the king gives place to the מנצח who will chant the recital, he quotes the essential message himself. *When I shall take the set time, I will judge uprightly*: God has had enough of the misrule of the sons of El, the gods whom he has left in charge of the nations (Ps. 82). The time is at hand when he will judge himself (Ps. 50.6), and justice will be done, and his people vindicated. *The earth and all the inhabitants thereof are dissolved* (or perhaps, *sway*): the world is lapsing into chaos as the borders which God set (Ps. 74.17) are overrun, and evil and blasphemous Assyrians openly defy Yahweh and defile his sanctuary. *I have proportioned its pillars*: God set the universe in order, measuring it out in the hollow of his hand, and establishing it on pillars in the subterranean floods (Ps. 24.1-2; Job 9.6). The Chief Musician may now take over, and chant the traditional creation story in detail. We have an outline of his recital in Job 38.

The linking of the מנצח with the Selah is speculative, but is the best, indeed the only, suggestion on offer. Elements in the headings, and Selahs, were not understood in later tradition, and tended to drop out, as 'For David' is usually thought to have dropped out from the headings of Psalms [1], 2, 10 and 33: so we cannot reasonably expect complete correspondence of fact with theory. Nevertheless the correspondence of *For the Chief Musician* in the heading with *Selah* in the body of the Asaph psalms is high enough to be impressive, both in presence and in absence:

	50	73	74	75	76	77	78	79	80	81	82	83
למנצח	–	–	–	1	1	1	–	–	1	1	–	–
סלה	1	–	–	1	2	3	–	–	–	1	–	1

Thus the hypothesis is that the Chief Musician was required to chant the recital marked Selah, and his presence was noted in the heading. The theory corresponds with the text on nine occasions out of twelve, which is enough to make it plausible. We should have to suppose that a Selah has dropped out of Psalm 80 (where there is an open reference to the Settlement, and Davidic–Solomonic empire), and a למנצח from the headings of Psalms 50 and 83.

For all the unanimity of modern commentators, Coverdale's translation of vv. 3-4 still deserves consideration: *When I receive the congregation, I shall judge according unto right. The earth is weak, and all the inhabiters thereof: I bear up the pillars of it.* (1) מועד is used in Ps. 74.4, 8 as the place rather than the time of assembly of the people, and could suitably bear the related meaning, *assembly*, here. (2) לקח, *take*, is a little strained in the RV mg translation, *When I take the appointed time* (BDB gives no justification for this: KB gives 'wählen'); but it means receive at Ps. 73.24. (3) The speaker will then be the king, as in the rest of the psalm, speaking for himself, and following on with *I said*...in v. 5, naturally. (4) The king's vow to judge *according unto right* (מישרים) is part of his divine vocation, stressed a number of times in royal psalms (Pss. 45.7-8; 72.1-2, 12-14; 101.2-7). Such judgments would be especially in need when the people came to the festival and could see the king (Ps. 122.4-5). (5) The dissolution (מוג) of the mountains/earth is symbolic, as in Ps. 46.3-4, of the raging of the nations, as in Ps. 46.7, where מוג is also used: the real trouble, in both psalms, is the human enemy. (6) The עמודים, *pillars*, of the earth, could be metaphorical; as God says to Jeremiah, 'Behold, I have made thee this day...a pillar (עמוד) of iron.' In New Testament times Peter and the other Jerusalem leaders were known as pillars (Gal. 2.9, στῦλοι); and kings were sometimes spoken of in a similar metaphor as 'the shields of the earth' (Pss. 47.10; 89.18). The strongest point in favour of such an interpretation is (3), which enables the whole psalm to proceed without artificiality. Its weakness is תכנתי, *I measured, proportioned*; which has to be strained to mean, *I organized them into an alliance.* The 'oracle' interpretation is much eased by the realization that *they recite thy wondrous works* refers to the coming Selah recital.

75.5-7. The text says, *I said unto the arrogant, Deal not so arrogantly*; but fortunately the king had done nothing of the kind, or he might have been flayed alive. The רשעים/הוללים are the same *arrogant/wicked* who were described in Ps. 73.3 and the verses following: they are the ever-victorious Assyrians, and once more they are likened to wild beasts. In Ps. 74.5 they *roared* like lions, in 74.20 they were a *wild beast* after *the soul of thy turtledove*, in Psalm 80 they are *a boar out of the wood*; here they are like the wild ox, the master of a harem of cows, who *lifts up his horn on high* and defies all comers to take his females from him. But such *lifting up* (הרים) is vain. Self-exaltation will achieve nothing.

Exaltation does not come *from the east*, from Assyria, *nor from the west, nor from the desert*. We have a list of the Assyrians' client-allies in Ps. 83.7-9: 'The tents of Edom and the Ishmaelites; Moabites and the Hagarenes; Gebal and Ammon and Amalek; Philistia, with the inhabitants of Tyre; Assyria also is joined with them: They have been an arm to the children of Lot.' Old scores are being settled, and peoples whom the Israelites had dominated in the palmy days of Jeroboam are getting their own back. Some of them live to Israel's *east*, the *children of Lot* for whom Assyria *has been an arm*; some on Israel's *west* coast, *Philistia with the inhabitants of Tyre*; while others are the implacable *desert* tribes, Edomites, Ishmaelites, Hagarenes, Amalekites. But it is God who does the lifting up in this world: he *is the judge, he puts down one and sets up another*.

BHS takes הרים as the hiph. inf. constr. of רום: Delitzsch cites Rashi and Kimhi as saying that this is the only place in Scripture where the word does not mean *mountains*, and their view gives the best sense. Many MSS give מִדְבָּר rather than the construct מִדְבַּר, *the wilderness of mountains*. Contrast Dahood ('Cardinal Points'), who maintains that here and at Joel 2.20 the four points of the compass are indicated. MT בְּצַוָּאר, *with [haughty] neck*, is to be preferred to LXX κατὰ τοῦ θεοῦ = בְּצוּר, *against the Rock*; cf. Ps. 73.6.

75.9. The image of the *cup* of divine wrath *in the hand of Yahweh* is widespread in the prophets. It is not a cup of poison, as is sometimes said, but 'the bowl of the cup of staggering' (Isa. 51.17), which Israel has now drained, and is to be passed into the hand of Babylon (Isa. 51.22-23). Israelites were impressed with the power of alcohol, which did so much to make glad the heart of man, but might also degrade him (Isa. 5.22; 28.1-13; Amos 6.6). Here the *cup* is made extra-alcoholic; it is *foaming*, and *full of mixture*, with herbs and spirits added. The image may be drawn from the custom of forcing a defeated king to drink such a draught to the *dregs*, and watching him reel and stagger in impotence to the amusement of the victors. Such a fate has Yahweh now in store for *all the wicked of the earth*, the Assyrians and their cruel and blasphemous allies.

J.P. Brown ('Vocabulary') writes interestingly about Mediterranean drinking, drawing on Greek and Ugaritic sources as well as Hebrew (pp. 153ff). He stresses the peril of מָסַךְ, *mixing* one's drinks (Prov. 23.30-31; Isa. 5.22; 65.11), which he takes to be adding weak wine to strong wine. But human ingenuity might do worse than that. R. Tournay ('Notes') thinks they mixed wine with water.

75.10-11. The king *will declare for ever* the marvellous turn of fortune which God will now bring about. His vocation was in part to be a witness of the divine blessings on Israel (Eaton, *Kingship*, pp. 182-95), and we often hear him undertake this task: for example 'O God, thou hast taught me from my youth; And hitherto have I declared thy wondrous works... My lips shall greatly rejoice when I sing praises unto thee... My tongue also shall talk of thy righteousness all the day long' (Ps. 71.16, 23-24). Here also there is both spoken *declaring* and sung *praises*, and the context again shows that the *wondrous works* have nothing to do with creation or the Exodus, but are the miracles of deliverance now so earnestly prayed for. The king gave a kind of state-of-the-Union address each year, mentioning (at considerable length) the earlier blessings of his reign, and leading the Hallelujahs.

The royal vow closes with the promise to *cut off all the horns of the wicked* (pl.) Assyrians; but *the horns of the righteous* (s.) *shall be lifted up.* The Israelite king is devoted to God's law, and he is *righteous* (Eaton, *Kingship*, p. 151). So speaks the voice of faith; but alas, God was on the side of the big battalions.

אַגִּיד, *I will declare*, is sometimes read as *I will rejoice*, אָגִיל = LXX ἀγαλλιάσομαι, an easier reading, as the translator was not familiar with the tradition of the king's spoken witness. The emendation to *He will cut off* goes back to Duhm, and is supported by Kraus, Weiser and Jacquet, but is without justification. Tate tries to save the text by reintroducing God as speaker of v. 11, but this is artificial.

Earlier critics, including Gunkel, associated the psalm with the Assyrian attack on Jerusalem in 701; they were not in fact far wrong, though the link with Isaiah 30, strongly put by Kirkpatrick, is if anything a sign of dependence on the psalm. LXX introduced the psalm πρὸς τὸν 'Ασσύριον (Theodoret), and Vulgate *Ad Assyrios*. Jacquet favours the sixth century on the frail basis of parallels in Isaiah 2 and Jeremiah. Mowinckel, Anderson and others are content to take the psalm as a regular piece of cultic liturgy without a precise historical origin, much as F. Willesen ('Cultic Situation') did with Psalm 74; but the tone and the detail fit well with the rest of the Asaph group, in the 720s.

Psalm 76

76.1   For the Chief Musician; on stringed instruments. A Psalm of Asaph, a
        Song.
2   In [Judah] {*Joseph*} God makes himself known (נוֹדָע):
        His name is great in Israel.
3   In Salem also was (וַיְחִי) his covert,
        And his lair in [Zion] {*Gerizim*}.

76.4   There brake he the lightning shafts (רִשְׁפֵי) of the bow;
              The shield, the sword and the battle-weapons (מִלְחָמָה).   (Selah

Psalm 76 is widely seen as a companion to Psalm 75. God's name is near in Ps. 75.2; it is great in Ps. 76.2. He is the judge in 75.8; he arises to judgment in 76.10. The horns of the wicked were to be cut off in 75.11, their armouries are destroyed in 76.4, 6-7. The earth swayed but its pillars were confirmed in 75.4; it fears and is still in 76.9. The wicked of the earth are to drink the cup of wrath in 75.9; God saves the meek of the earth in 76.10, but is terrible to the kings of the earth in 76.13.

Psalm 76 is in fact a hymn of praise for victory in war, and celebrates the divine deliverance of Israel in a battle at Salem near Shechem. As the existence of this place in the eighth century is disputed, we shall need a short excursus.

EXCURSUS: SALEM

Salem, שָׁלֵם, which is mentioned here in Ps. 76.3, is not, for any information we have, an early alternative name for Jerusalem. That city is referred to in the Amarna letters as Urushalim, and is never called Shalem in any text in the prophets or in the D-history, but always Jerusalem. (The name is spelt *Shalem* in Hebrew, but Σαλήμ, Σαλείμ in Greek; hence the variant English.) There is a quite different place today, Salim, five kilometres east-south-east of Shechem. This place is referred to in *Jub.* 30.1 as Salem, a town in the proximity of Shechem, interpreting Gen. 33.18; and that verse is understood in the same way by LXX, Vulgate and Syriac. Jud. 4.4 mentions 'the valley of Salem' in a context implying that it is not Jerusalem, and Jn 3.23 speaks of John baptizing 'at Aenon near to Salim', apparently near Samaria. It seems clear that there was a Salem near Shechem in the late BCE period. It is possible but not certain that this should be identified with *sh–r–m* mentioned in an Egyptian text of the thirteenth century, which would be a form of the Semitic שׁלם (Emerton, 'Salem', p. 49). Apart from the present text, the name occurs in Gen. 14.18, and probably in Gen. 33.18.

Gen. 33.18 opens, וַיָּבֹא יַעֲקֹב שָׁלֵם עִיר שְׁכֶם, translated by RV mg, 'And Jacob came to Salem, a city of Shechem', but by RV text, 'And Jacob came in peace to the city of Shechem'. שָׁלֵם is an adjective, normally meaning *complete*, but it means *peaceable* in Gen. 34.21. It is not likely to mean *peaceably, in peace*, at 33.18 (cf. Westermann, *Genesis*, II, p. 528), for the author never considers the possibility of any patriarch coming other than peaceably (unless strongly provoked, as in Gen. 14). It could more plausibly mean *in safety*, since Jacob made a vow in Bethel if God should bring him home in safety, בְשָׁלוֹם (Gen. 28.21), and with 33.18 he has made peace with Esau, and reached the West Bank. However, of the many towns (עִיר) visited by the patriarchs in Genesis, none is ever spoken of as 'the town of X'; they are all merely 'X', and the same is true throughout the Bible. We do hear of עיר as a subsidiary town: 'Heshbon and all her towns' (Josh. 13.17), 'this town and all her towns' (Jer. 19.15), עריה in both texts. We also hear of עיר מבצר־צר, *the fortress of Tyre*, but that is a special case. Thus the natural translation of Gen. 33.18 is '...to Salem, a [subsidiary] town of Shechem'. Shechem was the most important and most heavily fortified town in central Palestine in the late second millennium (G.E. Wright, 'Shechem'), and controlled a considerable surrounding area of smaller towns.

Gen. 33.18-20 describes Jacob as buying a plot of land at Salem, and erecting an altar there to אל אלהי ישראל, El the God of Israel. In the course of time the Israelites made Shechem itself the centre of their confederacy (Josh. 24), and there was there a great stone under the terebinth in Yahweh's sanctuary (Josh. 24.26; Gen. 12.6, 'the terebinth of the giver of *torah*' in the מקום at Shechem; Gen. 35.4). Judges 9 gives a picture of Israelite and Canaanite living in uneasy cohabitation in Shechem, and there can be little doubt that Shechem was an important centre for Israelite adoption of Canaanite religious traditions (Kraus, *Worship in Israel*, pp. 134-46). The Shechemite God was known as אל־ברית, *God of the Covenant* (Judg. 9.46), and this is a link with the Asaphite preference for אל, and its repeated references to *the covenant*. The Asaph psalms also favour עליון, and combine אל עליון (p. 19).

The development of the Pentateuch was at first in the hands of northern tradents, as the Exodus was their community's history (see Part II); and in consequence there was no reference to Jerusalem. But the development of Genesis took place in Jerusalem, mainly under Josiah, and the Zadokite priesthood did not take kindly to having their religious capital ignored. The move was accordingly made to interpret the Shechemite Salem as being a shortened form of Jeru-salem. Abram is returning from Dan to Hebron in Gen. 14.17 via 'the King's Vale', and there was such a valley near Jerusalem (2 Sam. 18.18); so the Jerusalem editor inserts a little scene in his own interest. Melchisedek king of Salem (i.e. Jerusalem) kindly brought out supplies of bread and wine for Abram's tired forces; he was the priest of אל עליון, and Abram accepted his blessing, and gave him a tenth of his spoil. The name Melchisedek has been manufactured on the lines of Adonisedek king of Jerusalem (Josh. 10.3), and the occasion is dignified by making him priest and king at the same time. Salem was the name of a seldom mentioned northern sanctuary where El was worshipped as the supreme God (עליון) and creator of the world; and these details will go very well for ancient Jeru-salem. The priest's blessing and Abram's vow alike testify to the ultimate authority of the Zadokite priesthood over Abraham's descendants; we are reminded of the success of the second-century Roman church in electing St Peter as its posthumous first bishop.

The insertion of the Gen. 14.18-22 paragraph is probably from the exilic period, being an embroidery on Abram's battle with the Mesopotamian kings, itself a late addition to Genesis 12–25. It will thus be considerably later than the acceptance and adaptation of the Asaph psalms in Judah: for the armies which overwhelmed Samaria were soon at the gates of Jerusalem. Words which must have touched the heart of God in the 720s might move him in 702; and if Israel had been victorious at Salem then, perhaps the same might happen at Jeru-salem now. So any original obviously northern names like Joseph, Shechem or Gerizim could come out and be replaced by Judah and Zion; but Salem was retained, a sign that it was accepted as a form of Jerusalem. In this way the ground was prepared for Melchisedek king of Salem in times ahead.

Psalm 110 is in Book V, virtually all of whose psalms come from after the exile. The person addressed is not (despite earlier assertions) a king, but a priest: 'Thou art a *priest* for ever After the manner of Melchisedek' (110.4). He is a warlike priest, and spoken of as 'my lord'; we may think of Jeshua ben Jehozadak, for whom Zechariah made a crown, and of whom he spoke as the Branch (Zech. 6.9-13). He is thought of as no mere priest, but one who will be king also, as Melchisedek had been in the legend in Genesis 14; as a martial figure he will, under divine guidance, make his enemies his footstool and re-establish Jewish independence.

The question of Salem has been widely discussed, and recently it has had an authoritative overview by J.A. Emerton ('Salem'). Emerton gives, helpfully, an exhaustive list of ancient references to Salem, and he outlines and refutes the many poor arguments adduced by a number of modern critics between 1938 and 1977, supporting the site near Shechem or an identification with Shechem. He himself defends identification with Jerusalem.

The main weaknesses of Emerton's position are: (i) his uncritical acceptance of Ps. 76.3 as the original form of the text ('where the parallel Zion shows that Salem must be Jerusalem', p. 45); (ii) his assumption that Psalm 110 provides an early link betweent Melchisedek and Jerusalem (p. 70); (iii) failure to note the absence of the form, עיר + X, meaning *the town of X*, in Genesis and elsewhere; (iv) denial of the form, עיר + X, meaning *a subsidiary town of X* (pp. 65-66).

The psalm is a *Song*, a triumphal psalm: only the opening two psalms of the festival, Psalms 75 and 76, are Songs, and Psalm 83, which closes the sequence on the final day. It is chanted *to stringed instruments*, which give a joyful accompaniment; it is the only psalm in the Asaph collection to have this privilege, and indeed is the only truly festal piece in the series. Psalms 54, 55, 61 and 67 are similarly accompanied on stringed instruments (in 61 on a single string), in an atmosphere of rising confidence (Goulder, *Prayers*, pp. 93, 152, 187). The *Chief Musician* is at hand to recite the two Selahs.

76.2-3. The form of the psalm which we have is naturally the version used in Jerusalem worship, and *Judah* and *Zion* have been introduced to replace unacceptable northern locations: that this is so is evident from the retention of *Salem*, which was not in early times another name for Jerusalem. This is the only reference to Judah in the Asaph collection, and Judah is paralleled with Israel elsewhere in the Psalter only in Ps. 114.2, a text in Book V. However, Ps. 81.5-6 reads, 'it is a statute for *Israel*... He appointed it in *Joseph* for a testimony', and Psalm 80 opens, 'Give ear, O Shepherd of *Israel*, Thou that leadest *Joseph* like a flock'; and this suggests an original opening here, 'In Joseph God makes himself known: His name is great in Israel.' Such a beginning would call naturally for amendment in favour of Judah; the problem is really why Ps. 80.2 was allowed to stand, especially the reference to 'Ephraim, Benjamin and Manasseh'. But the form *Yehoseph* (יהוסף) at Ps. 81.6 is probably a witness to an attempt to substitute יהודה there also; and fatigue is a regular phenomenon with those amending extended texts.

A similar problem awaited the Jerusalem editor with v. 3, but this was solved by assimilating *Salem* to Jerusalem. *Zion* will be his replacement for some northern holy place, *Bethel* perhaps, or *Gerizim*, the mountain of blessing.

God is not so much *known* (RV) as *makes himself known* (נוֹדָע) in his people: that is, he shows his providential hand in awarding them deliverance, a thing unknown among other nations. *His name is great* among them too: as in Ps. 75.2 God's name is his protecting presence, *near* and powerful in time of emergency. He is thought of as a lion, with his *lair* (מעונה) in the *covert* (סֹךְ). The area round Shechem was thickly wooded (Judg. 9.48-49), and was known as the Forest of Ephraim (2 Sam. 18.6; Goulder, *Prayers*, pp. 201-202); it was full of wild animals, which, according to the Succession Narrative, devoured more of Absalom's troops than Joab's army did (2 Sam. 18.8). סֹךְ is normally used for a covert (Ps. 10.9) and מעונה for a lair (Ps. 104.22; Amos 3.4; Job 37.8). The imagery arises from Israel's experience of being the *prey* (v. 5) of the invaders, and is repeated in Jer. 25.30-38.

Mowinckel (*Psalmenstudien*, II, pp. 58-59), Eaton and others, see God as *making himself known* in the liturgy of the festival: while this is psychologically possible, it is unnecessary here since God's action is plainly presupposed in the divine victory described in vv. 4-10.

76.3. It was at Salem, or at the mountains close by, that the decisive victory was won. Israelite history was of semi-continuous war, so we are not in a position to identify or date the battle. It may have taken place in an earlier generation, and the psalm celebrating it have become an established part of the Shechem, and so later the Bethel liturgy; or it may be a recent dramatic event. Assyrian records make it plain that there was much military activity in Israel between 733 and 721, and the Israelites will not have lost every engagement. That Salem was God's *lair* in his *covert* does not require that it was the *national* shrine at the time: Hosea makes it plain that there were many *lairs* of Yahweh in the

land then, including Shechem (Hos. 6.9). The psalm will have much
more force if the victory is recent. The description is not specific. God
brake the lightnings of the bow (רִשְׁפֵי־קָשֶׁת), probably the swift-flying
arrows rather than burning shafts; *the shield, the sword and the battle*
(מִלְחָמָה), no doubt the weapons of battle. In Hos. 2.20 God vows similarly to 'break the bow and the sword and the battle out of the land'.
With this the מַצֻּנָה takes the floor for the Selah; no doubt the story has
taken on a miraculous tone, as befits a divine victory, perhaps something
on the lines of 2 Kings 7, or 19.35-37.

To Delitzsch, Kirkpatrick and Jacquet, Psalm 76 was a clear echo of the events of
701, and the LXX heading πρὸς τὸν 'Ασσύριον seemed a confirmation of this.
Hardly anyone but Peters has suspected an earlier, northern setting for the original
psalm; and the LXX tradition will be simply an inference, like Delitzsch's, on the
assumption that Salem = Jerusalem. Twentieth-century commentators have been less
willing to commit themselves to a particular battle. Gunkel (with considerable emendation) thought the battle was eschatological. In *Psalmenstudien*, II (pp. 58-59),
Mowinckel took it to be a real battle, for which thanks was regularly given at the
feast, to celebrate Yahweh's coming to judgment; but in *Psalms* (I, pp. 149-51) the
experience is entirely of the myth in the liturgy, and in this he is followed by Tate.
Kraus sought to have the best of all three worlds, but taking the historical base to be
David's victory in 2 Samuel 5; Eissfeldt ('Lied Moses') included 2 Samuel 8, where
David defeated Hamath (see below); Dahood similarly combines the historical and the
eschatological.
    In v. 3 וַיְהִי should be allowed its normal past sense: God's covert *was* in Salem,
and it was there that he *made himself known* in Israel's victory; the present of many
translations comes from the assumption that God's name is *eternally* great in Zion. In
v. 4 Tate prefers *fiery arrows*, on the analogy of Ps. 7.14.

76.5   Glorious art thou *and* excellent,
        More than the mountains of prey.
   6   The stouthearted are spoiled, they have slept their sleep:
        And none of the men of might have found their hands.
   7   At thy rebuke, O God of Jacob,
        Both chariot and horse are cast into a dead sleep.
   8   Thou, even thou, art to be feared:
        And who may stand in thy sight when once thou art angry?
   9   Thou didst cause sentence to be heard from heaven;
        The earth feared, and was still,
  10   When God arose to judgment,
        To save all the meek of the earth.   (Selah
  11   For (כִּי) the wrath of Edom (אֱדֹם for אָדָם) shall praise thee:
        The residue of Hamath (חֲמָה for חֵמֹת) shall celebrate to thee
             (ἑορτάσει σοι).

76.12 Vow, and pay unto the LORD your God:
Let all that be round about him bring presents unto him that ought to be feared.

13 He shall cut off the spirit of princes:
He is terrible to the kings of the earth.

For the most part the psalm is straightforward, and closely parallel to Psalm 46. The difficult verse, and the one which provides the key to the closer context, is v. 11. The RV text translates, 'Surely the wrath of man shall praise thee: The residue of wrath shalt thou gird upon thee' (RV mg: restrain): but despite heroic attempts by earlier commentators this must be resigned as yielding nonsense. In 1934 Hans Schmidt proposed an ingenious revocalization: as at Amos 9.12 LXX and elsewhere the name *Edom*, אֱדֹם, could have been misread as אָדָם, *man*; and the presence of חֵמָה, *wrath*, in v. 11a could have led to the false reading חֲמֹת, *wraths*, in v. 11b, in place of a second name, חֲמָת, *Hamath*. With an unvocalized text, and the passing of an ephemeral event into oblivion, such a process would be plausible, and it is accepted by Kraus, Jacquet, NEB, REB, and viewed sympathetically by Eaton, Anderson and others. At the same time it is difficult to see how God could *gird himself* with the *residue* of either Hamath or *wraths*, and the LXX here reads ἑορτάσει σοι, rendering תֶּחְגָּך, *will celebrate to thee*, in place of תַּחְגֹּר, *will gird himself*. Delitzsch cites Isa. 51.9, 59.17 of Yahweh girding himself; but it is with righteousness, strength, and so forth, not the residue of v. 11. It seems suitable therefore to think with Kraus that the MT has fallen into disarray, and that we do best to follow LXX for once, and to accept Schmidt's two changes to the vowels. Kraus notes that *all that be round about him* in the following verse seems to confirm the suggestion that some neighbouring peoples were referred to in v. 11.

J.A. Emerton ('Problem') commends an earlier proposal to resolve the difficulty. He translates, 'Surely thou dost crush the wrath of man: Thou dost restrain the remnant of wrath', reading תָּדוֹך or תָּדוּך, *thou shalt crush*, for תּוֹדֶךָ (the roots דכך and דוך mean *crush*). This would fit well with v. 13, and the image of the terror of God more generally in the psalm; but questions remain about the translation *restrain* and *the residue of wraths*. Emerton is followed by J. Day.

Schmidt and Kraus understood Hamath and Edom to be symbols for the north and the south; but this proposal seems weak for other suggested texts, such as Pss. 75.7 (p. 84), 89.13 (Goulder, *Korah*, pp. 213-14); cf. on Ps. 80.3 below. We should rather understand the names literally, as one would expect. The picture that we have of the 720s is coloured by retrospective accounts. It was Assyria which deported the nobility of Israel, and made the land of Omri an Assyrian province; and it was Assyria which attacked Judah twenty years later. But to Israelites at the time, the enemy was a local confederation with Assyria backing it: Edom, first, and the Ishmaelites, Gebal nearby, and Ammon and Amalek (83.6-9). We have to think of them as of the Russians in 1941, attacked by Hungarians, Finns and Rumanians as well as Germans, and later by Lithuanians and Cossacks—all those who had earlier been savaged by Stalin. So now the people of Hamath remembered that Jeroboam II had 'recovered' Hamath (2 Kgs 14.28), and 'restored the border of Israel from the entering in of Hamath unto the sea of the Arabah' (14.25). 'The entering in of Hamath' was our Beqaa Valley, which had never belonged to Israel except for a few years under David; and 'the sea of the Arabah' was our Dead Sea, and the land of Edom. While Israel was strong, down to the middle of the eighth century, their vine took root: the mountains were covered with the shadow of them, including the Libanus and Antilibanus ranges; they sent out their shoots to the River, the Euphrates. But now it is not just the boar out of the forest, Assyria, which ravages them; but all they which pass by the way pluck them, and break down their fences, like hyenas on a wounded zebra. Settlers from Hamath were among those who were awarded Israelite land by the conquering Assyrians after 721 (2 Kgs 17.24, 30); and Edom was an implacable enemy of Israel as well as Judah in the days of Amos—'his anger did tear perpetually, and he kept his wrath for ever' (Amos 1.11-12).

76.5-7. This gives a better meaning to v. 5. God's little 3,000 ft *covert*, the wooded slopes of Gerizim, did not look much beside the great 10,000 ft peaks of Lebanon; we have the same thought at Ps. 68.16-17, where the 'mountain of peaks, the mountain of Bashan', Mt Hermon in the Libanus range, is urged not to be jealous of Mt Zion which 'God hath desired for his abode' (Goulder, *Prayers*, pp. 202-204). But God's dramatic victory (v. 4) has been a demonstration of his glory (נֵאוֹר like נוֹדָע in v. 2, *Thou hast shown thyself glorious*); *majestic beyond the mountains of prey*. The higher levels of the Lebanon mountains were notorious for their wild life. The king can say playfully to his bride in Cant. 4.8, as he moves from her breasts to consummate their marriage, 'Come with me from Lebanon, *my* bride... From the lions' dens, From the mountains of the leopards.' So now Hamath is seen as *the mountains of prey.* The jackals of the north came into Israelite territory in search of what prey they could get, and they met with a divine lion.

The MT טֶרֶף *prey*, thus gives good sense, and should be preferred to LXX, Syriac עַד, *eternity*, which is supported by Gunkel, Kraus and others: a relatively common phrase, *the eternal mountains*, has been substituted for the obscure original. For the Assyrians as wild animals rending their prey, cf. Nah. 2.11, 3.1. In the next verse, however, we have to take אֶשְׁתּוֹלְלוּ as a scribal error (Tate) for הִשְׁתּוֹלְלוּ.

The stouthearted, the formidable warriors of the enemy, *are spoiled*; they came for *prey* and they have become prey themselves—the gold and finery in which ancient fighters consecrated themselves for battle made valuable *spoil* (Judg. 8.24-27; Ps. 68.13-14). Now, says the psalmist ironically, *they have slept their sleep*; the big sleep of death; as in Nahum again, 'Thy shepherds *sleep* (נָמוּ), O king of Assyria, thy worthies (אַדִּירֶיךָ) are at rest' (Nah. 3.18). They *did not find their hands* for the battle; we may compare Josh. 8.20, where the men of Ai had no *hands* to flee, or 2 Sam. 7.27, where David *found* his heart to pray. *At thy rebuke*, at God's (probably fictional) thundering, *both chariot and horse are cast into a dead sleep*. Would that battles were won so easily! The phrasing recalls Exod. 15.1 where 'The horse and his rider hath he thrown into the sea', by stretching out his right hand, sending out his wrath, and so forth. Kraus plausibly translates רֶכֶב as *rider*, as at Ezek. 39.20; Exod. 15.1 has סוּס וְרֹכְבוֹ.

76.8-10. The victory is ascribed to God alone. He is *to be feared*, insupportable *from the time of his wrath* (מֵאָז אַפֶּךָ). *From heaven* he *made sentence heard*, no doubt again in an imaginary thunderclap; and *the earth* is pictured as *afraid and falling silent*. Here is the awesome spectacle of the omnipotent *God rising for judgment*; and that means he is to *save all the oppressed* (עֲנוֵי) *of the earth*, that is, his people Israel who have humbly (עָנוּ) kept his covenant and suffered for it. We may notice the difference of mood from Psalm 50. Then, when the thought was the imminence of catastrophe, and the need was for national penitence, God called to heaven and earth that he might *judge his people*: now that the thought is of a blessed victory, and hope has grown, God has *arisen to save* his people, and their enemies *cannot stand when once he is angry* (מֵאָז, *since*, as at Ruth 2.7; cf. *DCH*, *ad loc.*).

The psalm has a second Selah after v. 10, and it is natural to think that with two enemies mentioned in v. 11, Edom and Hamath, there is a

recital for each of two battles. They come from opposite points of the
compass, and are unlikely to have been able to combine. Rather the one
may have taken advantage of the distraction caused by the other, as
Grant did of Lee when Sherman marched through Georgia; but Israel's
Appomatox was not yet. The first Selah will have covered the invasion
by Hamath, being followed by the reference to the *mountains of prey*;
the second celebrated the Edomite battle, with Edom mentioned in the
next line, probably at a different site.

76.11-13. The *wrath of Edom* was proverbially implacable (Amos 1.11),
but with their recent disastrous defeat they will find themselves sending
a royal delegation to take part in the Israelite festival at Bethel, *praising*
and *thanking* (תודך) Yahweh. So will the people of *Hamath*, what
remains of them, their *residue*; only as Hamath is on the Orontes, about
250 miles from Bethel, it will be quite a long pilgrimage for them—they
will go on pilgrimage for thee (reading תְחָגֶּךְ with LXX ἑορτάσει σοι,
as above) to join in Israel's celebration. We may compare the paradox of
Psalm 47, 'O clap your hands, all ye peoples; Sing unto God with the
voice of triumph... He subdueth the peoples under us, And the nations
under our feet.'

Praise and thanksgiving will be quite acceptable; but it would show
sincerity if the vanquished peoples put their hands in their pockets as
well. They should *vow and pay unto Yahweh, and bring tribute* (שי)
unto the terror (למורא); and the same goes for *all that be round about
him*, the Tyrians, Ammonites and the rest whose loyalty is so dubious
(Ps. 83). In the hour of disaster the defeated will naturally *vow* large
tribute (cf. Judg. 11.39; 2 Sam. 15.7-8); the important thing is that they
should *pay*, 'cringing with their pieces of silver' (Ps. 68.31).

76.13 opens with a surprising expression, *He will cut off* (יבצר) *the
spirit of princes*. בצר is used of *cutting off* grape clusters; or more
commonly of *cutting off* a town by making it inaccessible: it is an
unusual word here. We may think that once again the psalmist is making
a play on words. Just as the attack by *Hamath* (חמת) suggested to him
the *wrath* (חמה) *of Edom*, and just as there was a series of plays on
words in Psalm 74, so now we may suppose that the Edomite invasion
has brought to mind its principal city Bozrah (בצרה), the *cut off* town.
We may compare Obadiah's oracle against Edom: 'If thieves came to
thee...would they not steal till they had enough? If grape-gatherers

(בצרים) came to thee, would they not leave some gleanings of grapes?' (Obad. 5). Call your capital Bozrah and you are asking to be *cut off*. The *spirit* of the Edomite *princes* has been *cut off* in death on the battlefield, and the *kings* of Edom and Hamath alike have been terrified before Yahweh.

The Liturgical Hypothesis

Virtually every commentator notes the similarities between Psalms 76 and 46 (and often 48 also). In Ps. 46.5 an assault has been made on the tabernacles of the Most High: here the battle has been at Salem, God's lair in his covert. The nations rage and the kingdoms are moved to attack Israel in 46.7; the God of Jacob utters his voice and the earth melts. So here the stouthearted descend on Israel from the mountains of prey; but at the rebuke of the God of Jacob both chariot and horse lie stunned, the earth fears and is still. In 46.10 God broke the bow and snapped the spear in sunder and burned the waggons in the fire; here he breaks the arrows of the bow, the shield, the sword and the weapons of battle. In 46.11 the enemy is bidden to be still, for God will be exalted among the nations; here all the peoples round about are called to bring tribute to him. The parallel with Psalm 46 is closer than with Psalm 48, where there is a procession round the city, whose walls and towers are to last for ever, a feature missing from Psalm 76. On the other hand Ps. 46.10 appears to imply a victory bonfire of the captured weapons, as in Isa. 9.5 (Goulder, *Korah*, pp. 144-49), and the same may be true of the broken weapons here also.

I have cited above the points made by Delitzsch and others linking Psalms 75 and 76; but no critic aligns 75 with 45. Nonetheless these two psalms share an important theme, the responsibility of the king for leading his army to victory. The king has no special position in Psalms 46 and 76, which are spoken in the name of the people: the LORD of hosts is with *us*. Psalms 45 and 75 are royal psalms, addressed *to* the king in 45, spoken *by* the king in 75. Psalm 45 describes a triple ritual. First the king girds his sword on his thigh, his glory and majesty, that is his breastplate and helmet; he rides out in procession for truth, meekness and righteousness; his right hand will teach him terrible things, as the peoples fall under him, his sharp arrows in their heart. Second comes his (re-)enthronement, anointing, and entrustment with the sceptre of equity. Finally comes his marriage to a new wife, a Tyrian princess.

Psalm 45 comes from the high days of Israelite power: I have argued that the king is Ahab and his wife Queen Jezebel (*Korah*, pp. 121-37). Psalm 75 comes from more than a century later, and the times have changed. The liturgical hypothesis does not claim that the Asaph and Korah psalms furnish parallel sequences of exact counterparts; only that the same central themes can be discerned in them, *mutatis mutandis*. With the writing on the wall, Hoshea was not going on a bombastic war parade; and the days when Israelite monarchs had kings' daughters among their jewels, and a new wife each year (Goulder, *Korah*, pp. 125, 132-35), were long past. What was central to the first day of the festival proper was the reconsecration of the king as the nation's leader; and in the 720s, as at all times, this meant especially in war. In Psalm 45 the peoples are to fall under him with his sharp arrows in their heart; in Psalm 75 he is seen as rebuking enemy arrogance and cutting off the horns of the wicked.

So the argument accumulates for the liturgical hypothesis:

	Dan, 9th c.	*Dan, 730*	*Bethel, 725*
?13th Bul, Pilgrimage	84	42/43	50
14th, Pre-festal Lament	85	44	73, 74
15th, King Consecrated	45	45	75
16th, Victory Hymn	46	46	76

Psalm 76 thus emerges as partially justifying both Delitzsch and Mowinckel. It celebrates a real victory, as Delitzsch said, with real horses and chariots and arrows; and although the actual occasion of its composition was probably at Bethel in the 720s, the Asaph psalms were transferred to Jerusalem, and in its present, revised form it was a hymn for the deliverance of Zion in 701. But it was also a key-unit in the liturgy of the autumn festival, as Mowinckel saw. It was used not once, but year after year, both at Bethel and later at Jerusalem: the horses and the kings have become mythical figures, symbols of the never-ending threat of the hostile nations to oppressed Israel; and the God who arises to judge them is the God who never fails the faithful—not in 722, nor in 587, nor in all the pogroms, nor in the Holocaust.

Chapter 4

THE VIGIL

Psalm 77

With Psalm 77 we return to the depressed mode of Psalm 74. Ps. 74.1, 'O God, why hast *thou cast off for ever?* Why doth thine *anger* smoke...?'; Ps. 77.8, 10, 'Will the Lord *cast off for ever?* And will he be favourable no more?... Hath God *forgotten* to be gracious? Hath he in *anger* shut up his tender mercies?' Ps. 74.23, '*Forget* not the voice of thine adversaries...' The pathetic pleas in fact dominate both psalms (74.1, 10-11, 21-23; 77.1-10); and both resolve the dilemma by remembering the *strength* of God (74.13; 77.15) in his salvations/wonders *of old*, 74.12-17 in creation, 77.17-21 in the deliverance from Egypt.

The most striking difference between the two psalms is the repeated reference in Psalm 77 to the night-time: 'My hand was poured out in the night... Thou hast held mine eyes watching... I call to remembrance my song in the night.' The fact that the speaker has a song of his own (*my song*, v. 7), and that this song is concerned with the national deliverance (*thy people, The sons of Jacob and Joseph*), suggests that once more he is a national figure, in fact the king; and this is confirmed by the presence of no less than three Selahs in the course of the psalm. He is not a private pious man, unable to sleep because of personal trouble: he is the same leader as in Psalm 74, observing a vigil because his nation is in crisis, like King George VI leading a National Day of Prayer before Dunkirk.

Such a conclusion is controversial. Earlier critics, including Gunkel, and more recent commentators too like Weiser and Kraus, think in terms of an individual religious man. Kraus, like Kirkpatrick, sites the psalm during the Exile; the latter suggests the theme, 'As from Egypt, so from Babylon.' Gunkel, noting the mention of Joseph, places the psalm more sagely in Northern Israel before 722. But the form-critical riddle is difficult for these views: Psalm 77 opens for them with an individual lament which then turns for some reason from v. 14 to a hymn; and Weiser and

Kraus stress the liturgical setting of the latter. Verses 17-20 are of a triple-three rhythm, against a dominant double-three elsewhere, and may stem from an independent hymnic origin; but the psalm leads up to these verses, as Kraus saw. Mowinckel (*Psalms*, I, p. 227; II, p. 139) and Eaton (*Kingship*, p. 79) argue convincingly for a public liturgical setting throughout, with the king as speaker; Eaton concedes that the speaker shows no special royal traits, unless (optimistically) *Thou leddest thy people like a flock by the hand of Moses* suggests a more modern leadership. Mowinckel (*Psalms*, II, p. 152) like Gunkel, opts for a northern setting; but most commentators prefer the Exile.

77.1   For the Chief Musician; at Jedithun (עַל־יְדִיתוּן); a Psalm of Asaph.
   2   I will cry unto God with my voice;
          Even unto God with my voice, and he will give ear unto me.
   3   In the day of my trouble I sought the Lord:
          My hand was poured out (נִגְּרָה) in the night, and slacked not;
          My soul refused to be comforted.
   4   I will remember God (אֶזְכְּרָה), and be disquieted (וְאֶהֱמָיָה);
          I will complain (אָשִׂיחָה), and my spirit fainteth.   (Selah

Again the *Chief Musician* is at hand, this time to cantillate *three* Selahs; and the minstrels strum an accompaniment (מִזְמוֹר) on their zithers. The psalm is referred to as נְגִינָתִי in v. 7, a song accompanied on strings, and all the Asaph psalms have some accompaniment, each being spoken of as a מִזְמוֹר (even the most depressed ones), a מַשְׂכִּיל or a שִׁיר.

The more puzzling element in the heading is עַל־יְדִיתוּן, as it is spelt in the Kethib and LXX, against יְדוּתוּן in the Qere' and Targums. As the וֹ-form is common elsewhere (Ps. 62.1; and as the name of a minstrel, Jeduthun, 1 Chron. 16.42; 25.1; cf. some MSS of 62.1 לִידוּתוּן), we should suspect assimilation of the unfamiliar to the familiar. There are similar notes in the headings of two other psalms, 39 and 62 (also with spelling differences in the MSS and versions), and it is noticeable that these three psalms share certain features. Psalm 39 opens with a period of *silence*: 'I will keep a bridle (or muzzle) for my mouth. I was dumb with silence, I held my peace, and had no comfort... I was dumb and opened not my mouth; Because thou didst it.' *Had no comfort*, Heb. 'away from good', probably implies fasting. This boils over into a *plea for God to cease his anger*: 'While I was musing the fire kindled: *Then* spake I with my tongue... Remove thy stroke away from me... Hear my prayer, O LORD, and give ear unto my cry.'

Psalm 62 similarly opens with the *silence* theme: 'My soul is silent unto God... My soul, be thou silent unto God' (vv. 2, 6): there is no mention of divine anger, but again the hope is in God alone—'From

him *cometh* my salvation. He only is my rock and my salvation...'
(vv. 2-3, 6-7).

It is therefore striking to find the same *silence* in Psalm 77: 'I am
troubled and do not speak... I will remember my song in the night with
my own heart'; and also the suggestion of fasting, 'My soul refused to
be comforted.' The climax of the psalm is dependence on the God who
has brought salvation before, in the days of the Exodus. We may think
therefore that under circumstances of crisis a national leader spent a
period in silence before God, before presenting his plea; and that Psalms
39, 62 and 77 are such pleas, being linked by the silence theme and the
עַל־יְדִיתוּן heading note. As I have suggested numerous explanations in
Psalms of the Sons of Korah and *Prayers of David* for other עַל־ heading notes as locations (e.g. Ps. 45 'At the Lilies', the courtyard at Dan
ringed with lily-engraved portico lintels; Ps. 56 'At the dove of the far
terebinths', the hill-top camp by Bahurim where there was a copse of
terebinths visible from Jerusalem), we should probably render 'At
Jedithun'. The noun could be derived from יָדָה, 'to confess', and would
then mean 'At the confessional', a location in the Temple complex
where the king held his silent vigil. The psalm will then probably be
spoken at dawn; cf. Ps. 88.14.

A derivation from יָדָה is urged by Mowinckel and Eaton (*Kingship*, p. 59): in 1 Kgs
8.33-36 Solomon twice refers to national disasters, defeat and drought, which Israel
may survive by turning and *confessing* (הוֹדוּ) Yahweh's name.

77.2-4. The opening verse of the psalm also recalls Ps. 39.13, 'Hear my
prayer, O LORD, and *give ear unto* my cry'; and we have similar
phrasing at Ps. 102.2, 'Hear my prayer, O LORD, and let my cry come
unto thee. Hide not thy face from me *in the day of my trouble*'—Psalm
102 is also 'A Prayer of the afflicted', and there are references to
'watching' (v. 8), and 'eating ashes like bread' (v. 10). A parallel psalm
in the Korah collection is Psalm 88, 'O LORD, the God of my salvation,
I have cried day and night before thee. Let my prayer enter into thy
presence; Incline *thine ear* unto my cry'. Here again the speaker is on
his own and through the night; he is not silent, but he expects his prayer
to come before God in the morning (v. 14).

In Psalm 77 the king's *hand is poured out in the night, and slacks
not*: the verb is surprising, and should be understood as of repeated
movement in a downward direction, pleading for *mercies. My soul
refused to be comforted*: there was no respite, perhaps no break for

food. *I mean to remember God and to moan* (cohortatives): the continuous groaning and crying which is to move the all-powerful national protector has still a long way to go. He *will complain, and* his *spirit faints* at his community's predicament. I comment on the Selah below, on v. 16.

Kirkpatrick and Kraus say the tenses are difficult and (with RV mg) translate as presents; but the cohortatives should be allowed their proper force, with Delitzsch. They are themselves an indication of a national *ritual* leader performing his liturgical duty, rather than the supposed private speaker in distress—even suffering from insomnia (Jacquet). The surprising 'My hand is *poured out*' should not be emended; the Targums' 'My *eye*...' is intended to avoid the difficulty, and Lam. 2.18, where לא־תפוג recurs, and is used of tears, comes from a chapter which I have already argued to be a gloss on the Asaph psalms (esp. Ps. 74, pp. 77-78). Eaton (*Kingship*, p. 49) suggests that water may have been poured out at public confessions of sin, as at 1 Sam. 7.6; such a ritual may have influenced the wording. Delitzsch derives תתעטף from עטף II, *to veil* 'like a widow', rather than עטף III, *to faint*.

77.5	Thou hast held (אחזת) mine eyes watching:
	I am troubled and I do not speak (ולא אדבר).
6	I have considered the days of old,
	The years of ancient time.
7	I will call to remembrance (אזכרה) my song in the night with
	my own heart:
	I will complain (אשׂיחה), and my spirit shall make diligent
	search (וַיְחַפֵּשׂ).
8	Will the Lord cast off for ever?
	And will he be favourable no more?
9	Is his mercy clean gone for ever?
	Doth his promise fail for evermore?
10	Hath God forgotten to be gracious?
	Hath he in anger shut up his tender mercies? (Selah

77.4-7. Thou hast held the lids of my eyes: God has set him aside for the night's vigil. The Hebrew says, *I am distressed and I do not speak*, not '*so*...that I *cannot* speak' (RV). Gunkel is mistaken in suggesting that silence has nothing to do with distress, and that the speaker soon finds tongue in vv. 8-10: he has spent a protracted period in silent vigil, and the psalm, with its series of anxiety-laden rhetorical questions, marks his verbal expression of the hours of meditation and moaning (שׂיח). He has, in the silence, *considered* (perfect, חשׁבתי) *the days of old*; the centuries-old experience of the Joseph-tribes' escape from Egypt in *the years of long ago*. He means now to *call to remembrance* (cohortative,

אזכרה) *his song in the night by himself.* The Hebrew tradition divides
the line here, after עם־לבבי, and this gives a satisfying contrast. Psalm 77
is a vigil-psalm, a *song in the night*, now *remembered with his own
heart* and chanted at dawn with a small company of minstrels (נגינתי, a
string-accompanied psalm); the public psalm, addressed to *my people*, on
the same theme, will follow in Psalm 78. In the meantime he will continue to moan (אשׂיחה), and his *spirit will make diligent search* for an
answer in history for the riddle of present disaster. Psalm 78 shows that
his diligence was amply rewarded.

77.8-10. The questions which the king asks show that his mind is on the
covenant which God made with his people during the Exodus journey.
It is his *mercy* (חסדו), and in parallel his *promise* (אמֶר), on which all hope
depends. If he has *forgotten to be gracious* (חנות), they are finished; if he
has *shut up his tender mercies* (רחמיו), covenanted in the desert, where
will they go? It is to this story of *the years of long ago* that his meditation has been tending: it is recited in the Selahs, adumbrated in vv. 17-20
(see below on v. 16), and expounded in the following psalm.

The singular form in which the Exodus story appears in vv. 17-20 (with the waters,
not the Egyptians, as the enemy) has led many commentators to see *the days of old*
as the creation, as in Ps. 74.12 where קדם is also used (so Gunkel). There is similar
phrasing ('as in the *days of old*, the generations *of long ago*') in Isa. 51.9, where the
prophet first speaks of Yahweh cutting up Rahab and piercing the dragon, and then
of drying up the sea as a way for the redeemed to pass over (v. 10). The two stories
have been coalesced into a single myth.
עם־לבבי is used in Deut. 8.5, Eccl. 1.16, of private meditation; v. 7a is overlong,
but the traditional division makes good sense, and each colon can then begin with a
cohortative verb in the 1st p.s. These cohortatives can then be given their natural
force (against RV presents), and form a transition from the perfects of vv. 5-6, covering the preceding silent vigil, to the intention to voice the searching questions of
vv. 8-10.

77.11   And I said, This is my infirmity,
         That the right hand of the Most High doth change.
   12   I will make mention of the deeds of Jah (יה);
         For I will remember thy wonders of old.
   13   I will meditate also upon all thy work,
         And muse on thy doings.
   14   Thy way, O God, is in holiness:
         Who is a great god like unto God?
   15   Thou art the God that doest wonders:
         Thou hast made known thy strength among the peoples.

77.16   Thou hast with thine arm redeemed thy people,
             The sons of Jacob and Joseph.   (Selah

77.11. The translation is notoriously difficult; I have followed RV mg hesitantly, taking חַלּוֹתִי as piel inf. of חלה I, *to be sick, weak*, with termination, and שְׁנוֹת as qal inf. cstr. of שנה I, *to change*. This yields good sense, in that the speaker has been questioning the faithfulness of God—*Hath he in anger shut up his tender mercies?*—and now turns to rely on his immutability: the idea of *the changing of God's right hand* was his own *weakness*. Furthermore it has a marked parallel in Psalm 73, where the king also began to wonder if there was *knowledge in the Most High*, but realized that such talk was his own *foolish ignorance*, and would have *dealt treacherously with* his people; so there too he turned to faith once more.

There is support for *my affliction...have changed* in the Targums and Versions, but the piel of חלה normally means to *make sick*; a change of vowels to חֲלוֹתִי, qal inf. would make things easier, and would have the support of Aquila, ἀρρωστία μου. Eaton interestingly suggests a derivation from חלה II, to *seek the favour of, entreat*, and takes שנות as from שנה III, to *repeat, recite*: the prayer of propitiation will then be the recital of the mighty deeds of the Most High. But שנה means *repeat* only in late texts (Job 29.22; Prov. 17.9; Ecclus. 42.1), and is normally followed by ב; *to repeat the right hand of the Most High* is strained. Emerton ('Psalm lxxvii') suggests a double emendation to תֹחַלְתִּי *my hope*; but 'This is my hope, The years of the right hand of the Most High' seems forced. Delitzsch too, and others, prefer to take שנות as *years*, as in v. 6; but this involves inserting 'I will remember'. The Asaph psalms are full of plays on words (cf. p. 73), and the dual meaning of שנות may well have appealed to the author—cf. also יֹסִיף v. 8, יוֹסֵף v. 16.

    Note *Hath* אל *forgotten to be gracious?...that the right hand of* עליון *doth change*: we had אל עליון in parallel in 73.11 also, and he comes in a single phrase in Ps. 78.35. With *the right hand of the Most High* compare v. 16, *Thou hast with thine arm redeemed thy people*, and Isa. 51.9, 'Awake, awake, put on strength, O arm of the Lord...' God is thought of as classically hurling his *arrows* (v. 18), his *lightnings* (v. 19), with his *right hand*; and the right hand of the Most High does not change.

77.12-15. The king will *make mention of*, even *proclaim the deeds of Jah*, first briefly in vv. 17-21; *for* he *will remember* them, call them to mind in the present crisis. In fact he *will meditate on all* God's *work*, and this more extended reflection will occupy seventy verses of Psalm 78, for there is more to be learned than just God's changeless power. His *way is in holiness*, and what he has bound himself to he will perform (though he will insist on obedience from his people too); *Who is a great god like* אלהים? We have the same picture as in Psalm 82, where אלהים, that is Yahweh, takes his stand in the council of the lesser gods, and declares their judgment. It is he, not they, *that doest wonders*; he has *made known his strength among the peoples*, in particular the Egyptians.

The Kethib אֶזְכִּיר is to be preferred to Q אַזְכִּיר in v. 12a, avoiding the empty repetition of *I will remember* in v. 12b: Weiser is right to insist on the liturgical context, even if his own individual interpretation is open to objection. פְלָאֶךָ in v. 12b is a collective (Tate), as in v. 15.

77.16. The sons of Jacob and Joseph come as a surprise, for we are familiar with Joseph as a son of Jacob, and he seems unnecessary. But a parallel in Obadiah should warn us: 'And the house of Jacob shall be a fire, and the house of Joseph a flame, and the house of Esau for stubble...' (Obad. 18). Joseph was not always a sub-group of Jacob, his (favourite) son. They were an independent wave of Israelite immigrants, who settled latest of all in Palestine: they came from Egypt via Moab, and occupied the rich lands in the centre of the country. By contrast the previous immigrants had come from Midian and from areas of the Negev, and had settled under the name of Jacob: the Korah psalms, which were composed at Dan, never use the name *Israel* for the people of God, but always *Jacob*. So there were two major settlements, by *the sons of Jacob* and *the sons of Joseph*; and it took the trials of the Philistine wars and other troubles to weld them into a united people, Israel. For further discussion see below, Chapters 9 and 11.

Many commentators have noticed a relationship between Psalm 77 and the Song of the Sea in Exodus 15; and this is already indicated by the use of the rare יָהּ in v. 12. It may be convenient to set out the details here:

Ps. 77.12   I will make mention of the deeds of *Jah*
Exod. 15.2   *Jah* is my strength and song
Ps. 77.14-15 Thy way, O God is *in holiness*: *Who is a* great *god like unto* God?
              Thou art the God that *doest wonders*
Exod. 15.11   *Who is like unto* thee, O LORD, among the *gods*? Who is like
              thee, glorious *in holiness*, Fearful in praises *doing wonders*?

Ps. 77.15   Thou hast with thine arm *redeemed* thy *people*
Ps. 77.21   Thou *leddest* thy *people* like sheep
Exod. 15.13 Thou *in thy mercy hast led the people* which *thou hast redeemed*
Ps. 77.16   *The depths* also trembled
Exod. 15.5   *The depths* cover them.

The relationship is sufficiently close, especially with Ps. 77.11-15, that we may think that the third Selah, following these verses, in fact consisted of Exod. 15.1b-18, the Song of the Sea. This passage is a *proclaiming* of *Jah's wonders of old,* and *meditates upon* God's *making his strength known among the peoples*, first the Egyptians, and then the Edomites, Moabites, Canaanites and Philistines. It continues the story beyond the Reed Sea to the *leading* through the wilderness to the mountain of God's sanctuary, unnamed; just as Psalm 78 pursues the story to his holy mountain-land, and the defeat of the Philistines.

What then are we to think of the previous two Selahs? The first comes after v. 4, when the speaker has *cried unto God with his voice in the day of his trouble*; the second after v. 10, when he has *considered the days of old, the years of ancient times, and meditated* on God's *mercy* and *promise*. We know that these themes were familiar to the Asaph psalmist as in connection with Egypt from Ps. 81.7-8, 'I removed his shoulder from the burden: His hands were freed from the basket. Thou calledst *in trouble*, and I delivered thee'; and we might suitably think that the first two Selahs were the community's accounts of the Egyptian oppression and God's promise of deliverance. We have an elaborated version of the first in Exodus 1–2: 'the children of Israel sighed by reason of their bondage, and *they cried,* and their *cry* came up *unto God* by reason of the bondage' (2.23).

It is the *language* of Psalm 77 which alone can be our guide, and for the second Selah we require something that will answer to the word אָמֶר, God's *promise* or *utterance* in v. 9, which leads up to it. The psalmist asks: 'Is *his lovingkindness* (חֶסֶד) clean gone for ever? Doth his promise fail for evermore? Hath *God* (אֵל) forgotten to be *gracious* (חַנּוֹת)? Hath he in *anger* (אַף) shut up his *tender mercies* (רַחֲמָיו)? (Selah'. It is difficult not to think of Yahweh's famous declaration to Moses in Exod. 34.6: 'The LORD, the LORD, *a God* (אֵל) *merciful* (רַחוּם) and *gracious* (חַנּוּן), slow to *anger* (אַפַּיִם) and plenteous in *lovingkindness* (חֶסֶד) and truth'. The terms are common, but it would not be easy to find them so concentrated in a single significant *utterance*.

The three Selahs will then follow the mood of the psalm rather convincingly: the king's present *crying unto God* (vv. 2-4) finds an echo in
the crying of Israel in oppression (cf. Exod. 1–2); his *remembering* of
God's *promise in the days of old* (vv. 5-10) recalls the great words of
the divine promise which we have in Exodus 34; while the *musing on
God's wonders* in vv. 11-16 corresponds closely to the wording of our
Exodus 15, the 'Song of the Sea'.

I owe the suggestion of Exod. 34.6 to an interesting article by Kselman ('Psalm 77');
I had thought of the less impressive parallel in Exod. 6. Kselman was not thinking
about the Selah, but saw the strong verbal connection.

77.17	The waters saw thee, O God;
	The waters saw thee, they were in pain:
	The depths also trembled.
18	The clouds poured out water;
	The skies sent out a sound:
	Thine arrows also went abroad.
19	The voice of thy thunder was heard in the whirlwind;
	The lightnings lightened the world:
	The earth trembled and shook.
20	Thy way was in the sea,
	And thy paths in the great waters,
	And thy footsteps were not known.
21	Thou leddest thy people like a flock,
	By the hand of Moses and Aaron.

77.17-20. These four verses desert the hitherto rather regular 3:3
bicolon rhythm for a sequence of tricola 3:3:3. They are distinctive in
other ways. They purport to describe the *redeeming of* God's *people*, as
he *made known his strength among the peoples,* in *leading* them
through the Reed Sea; but there is no reference in them to the
Egyptians. In many ways they echo the primal battle of creation in
which God's enemies are the waters. With his thunder and lightning
God terrifies and overwhelms them in ways which recall Baal's victory
over Yam/Nahar in the Ugaritic myth; the waters see, writhe and
tremble just as the Canaanite divine powers are stricken with trembling,
panic and micturition. It seems likely that we have here therefore an
older piece of mythical poetry which has long been part of the festal
liturgy, and which has been applied to the Joseph-tribes' Exodus experience. No doubt the pursuing Egyptians are a later legendary accretion,
already present in Exodus 15, and included in the account in Psalm 78.

The community's memory of the Exodus event is of an escape through the shallows of the Reed Sea in a thunderstorm, thus bypassing the frontier defences. The events of the historical exodus were in time mythicized in line with creation, as was the deliverance of David in 2 Sam. 22.8-16/Ps. 18.8-16.

Jefferson ('Psalm LXXVII') points to the large coincidence of vocabulary with the Ugaritic texts. There are some unique Hebrew elements too: זֹרְמוּ poel, the reduplicated חֲצָצִים, the mysterious גַּלְגַּל, which could mean a *whirlwind*, but Gunkel took to be the wheels of Yahweh's war-chariot. The former sense recurs at Ps. 83.14; Aben-Ezra thought it meant a peal of thunder. See further Day (*Conflict*, pp. 96-101), G. von Rad (*Theology*, I, pp. 137-38).

77.21. With the final verse we return to the 3:3 rhythm which dominated the psalm until v. 16; and also to the earthly plane, with Moses, Aaron and their human flock. The latter image is congenial to the Asaph psalmist (cf. pp. 28-29). It is often said that the psalm closes somewhat abruptly; but this is because there is to be a rich deployment of the wilderness tradition later in the day, with Psalm 78.

What is more singular, and revealing, is the mention of Moses and Aaron as the two leaders. It is noticeable that although there are extensive traditions about the desert period in the Asaph psalms, especially in Psalms 78 and 81, these names do not occur elsewhere in the collection; whereas the name of David does occur at Ps. 78.70. But Moses is associated with the shrine at Dan: the founding priest there was Jonathan son of Gershom son of Moses (Judg. 18.30). In *Psalms of the Sons of Korah* (pp. 51-84), I argued that the Danite Levites drew their legitimacy from an incident at 'the waters of Massah' where under Moses' leadership they had slaughtered the non-Yahwist members of the clan (Deut. 33.8-9; Exod. 32.26-29). Aaron, however, is associated with a different rebellion at 'the waters of Meribah' near Kadesh on the route from Egypt, as well as with the Egyptian plagues; and it is likely that he was the leader of the Joseph Exodus. In time the two traditions have been assimilated to one another, the waters of Massah to the waters of Meribah, for example. The exodus of Joseph (Ps. 81.6-8) has become the redemption of *the sons of Jacob and Joseph* (Ps. 77.16); and the Jacobite leader, Moses, and the Josephite leader, Aaron, have become the shepherds of a combined flock. See further below in Part II.

Psalm 78

78.1   Maschil of Asaph
Give ear, O my people, to my teaching:
Incline your ears to the words of my mouth.

2   I will open my mouth in a parable;
I will utter dark sayings of old:

3   That which (אשר) we have heard and known,
And our fathers have told us,

4   We will not hide from their children,
Telling the generation to come the praises of the LORD,
And his strength, and his wondrous works that he hath done.

5   For he established a testimony in Jacob,
And appointed a law in Israel,
Which he commanded our fathers,
That they should make them known to their children:

6   That the generation to come might know *them*, even the children
which should be born;
Who should arise and tell *them* to their children:

7   That they might set their hope in God,
And not forget the works of God,
But keep his commandments:

8   And might not be as their fathers,
A stubborn and rebellious generation;
A generation that did not make firm (הכין) their heart.
And whose spirit was not stedfast with God.

9   [The children of Ephraim, being armed and carrying bows,
Turned back in the day of battle].

10   They kept not the covenant of God,
And refused to walk in his law;

11   And they forgat his doings,
And his wondrous works that he had shewed them.

Psalm 78 makes a smooth transition from Psalm 77. Both psalms are about *the deeds of Yahweh, thy wonders of old* (77.12; 78.7, 4), God's *doing wonders* and *making known his strength* (77.15; 78.11, 4); that is, his *redeeming his people* from Egypt in the Exodus (77.17-20; 78.12-13, 42-53), and *leading* them through the desert *like a flock* (77.21; 78.52-53). But there are marked differences between the two psalms. In Psalm 77 the king searches his heart for a solution to his nation's crisis, and finds encouragement in God's mighty deeds of old. In Psalm 78 he takes a more ponderous and didactic tone, as befits a king addressing *my people*; he has a double message to reveal to them—God steadily

delivered Israel in the days of old, but an equally regular feature of those
times was Israel's rebellions. It is just such rebellions of which the people
must repent now (cf. Ps. 81) if God is to show his strength once more.
In Psalm 77 the problem was private and insistent, *Will the Lord cast
off for ever?*; and the answer was, *that the right hand of the Most High
should change* was his own *infirmity*. Now he has his *people* to carry
with him, and they need seventy verses of measured exhortation.

The difficulty of isolating the *Gattung* of Psalm 78 is a reflection on the helpfulness
of form criticism. Gunkel says properly that it is a historical psalm, like Psalm 105 or
the sermons in the D-history; but it is also in part a hymn praising God's wonders in
history, it opens like a wisdom poem, and it exalts the Temple and the house of
David. Kraus aligns it more closely with the Levitical sermons in Chronicles; it will
have a liturgical setting at one of the festivals, and the wisdom type opening also
suggests a late date. But the closest parallel, noted by Kirkpatrick and many, is
Deuteronomy 32, which is early. Wisdom preachers rarely take Israel's history as
their theme; and they never presume to address *my people*. Nor do the prophets, for
that matter, or the priests invoked by Kraus and Weiser. It is God who normally says
my people (Ps. 50.7; Hos. 1–2, etc.); and the king is his closest surrogate (1 Sam.
15.30; 2 Sam. 22.44; 1 Kgs 22.4; 2 Kgs 3.7; 1 Chron. 28.2; 29.14; 2 Chron. 18.3;
Gen. 41.40; Exod. 12.31; the only prophetic uses are Isa. 16.20 and Jer. 51.45).

78.1-2. The king was responsible for administering God's תורה (vv. 5,
10; Ps. 45.7), and תורתי, *my guidance*, was his application of it. What he
is intending is to draw on the traditions מני־קדם, from history *of old*; and
to apply them by means of a parallel, משל, to the present situation.
Notoriously משל has many equivalents in English, but the basic meaning
is the setting of one matter alongside another (Gk. παραβολή). Kings
used such devices in Israel for centuries before Sages took them over:
Solomon was famous for his three thousand משל (1 Kgs 5.12, EV 4.32),
and our Proverbs are said to be משלי שלמה (Prov. 1.1); we may think
also of Jotham (Judg. 9.7-20), Jehoash (2 Kgs 14.9-10), and Lemuel
(Prov. 31). King Hoshea means to set God's miraculous deliverances of
old alongside his present expected actions; while at the same time pointing to Israel's faithlessness in the desert as a warning of what lies behind
his present inaction. But the lessons of history are not obvious: they are
חידות, *dark sayings*, obscure matters which have been revealed to him
only after deep ponderings through the night (Ps. 77.2-10). He will now
utter them, more graphically *belch them out*; they have been forming in
the depths of his being, and they are now to be revealed.

78.3-4. The history of the community has been made familiar by being *heard and known*, being *told* by *our fathers*, the nation's elders, at the annual festivals. These recitals (ספרו), marked in the psalms by the direction Selah, have been the means of forging a united nation. We have a close parallel in Ps. 44.2, 'We have *heard* with our ears, O God, *our fathers have told us*: What work thou didst in their days, in the days *of old*'; Ps. 44.3-9 describe the Settlement in words strongly recalling Joshua 24, which is likely to have constituted the Selah at the end of v. 9 (Goulder, *Korah*, pp. 92-94). Such a power of nation-building is recognized by the king in Psalm 78: one generation passes the national myth on to the next, so that there is faith in *the Lord* as a source of supernatural *strength* and a *doer of wondrous works*.

Maschil. Psalm 78 is a Maschil, and Psalm 74 seemed to be a 'clever' psalm (שׂכל) by virtue of a play on the name of the king, הושע, in the opening verse of the hymnal section, 'Yet God is my King of old, Working salvation (ישׁועות)' (cf. pp. 67-68 for other references to such plays in the Korah and David psalms). Psalm 78 is substantially a psalm celebrating the Exodus and the journey through the wilderness, and Ps. 77.21 tells us that by the time of our psalms these events were thought of as under two national leaders, *Moses and Aaron*. However, as I hinted above, and argued in *Psalms of the Sons of Korah*, Moses was in fact the leader of an earlier 'Jacob' invasion; his grandson was the founder-priest at Dan, and the Levitical priesthood there drew its legitimacy from having massacred their heathen relatives, at Moses' behest, at the waters of Massah (Deut. 33.8-9; Exod. 32.26-29). The suggestion is therefore that the leader of the Exodus of the Joseph-tribes from Egypt was in fact Aaron, who takes an important share in the story in Exodus–Numbers, but who has later been overshadowed by Moses; and if we are looking for a name in Psalm 78 on which the heading *Maschil* promises a play, then we should expect to find it on the name Aaron. Aaron, אַהֲרוֹן, is in fact a name without obvious derivation; but the sound is close to אַחֲרוֹן, *later*, and we find this word twice in the opening verses of Psalms 78:

Telling the generation to come (דור אחרון) the praises (v. 4)
That the generation to come (דור אחרון) might know (v. 6).

Hebrew tolerated the difference between sounds as close as ה and ח: in *b. Šab.* 105a a Tanna composes an acrostic (Notariqon) on the phrase

אב המון, and for the ה uses חביב, *loved one*—as Freedman, the Soncino translator, notes (p. 505), 'ה and ח interchange'. (Cf. also the play אהב/אחאב in the Maschil Psalm 45 [Goulder, *Korah*, pp. 131-32].).

78.5-11. The means by which the tradition was to be handed down was the divine *law, establishing a testimony in Jacob.* This עדות consisted of the national festival when *our fathers* were *commanded* to *make his wondrous works known to their children* in recitals; in time this would develop into a full-blown rehearsal of the entire תורה tradition every seventh year (Deut. 31.9). There is a similar use of עדות at Ps. 81.6, referring to the blowing of the trumpet and other elements of autumn festal worship.

The purpose of this institution is set out here with a ponderous emphasis which owes everything to the Assyrian crisis. God intended that the chain of tradition should go on from generation to generation, to *the children which should be born, Who should arise and tell their children.* But in the present national predicament realists were facing the fact that the enemy seemed to be invincible; like the Turks before 1565, they never lost a battle. So indeed the people need to *give ear to* Hoshea's *guidance.* First there must be an end to alarm and despondency: they must *set their hope in God,* they must expect *wondrous works,* miracles, for that is what Yahweh showed he could do throughout the classic Exodus–wilderness period, and that needs reciting. But second, things have come to their present pass because of repeated national apostasy: so a second insistent theme is that the people *might not be as their fathers, A stubborn and rebellious generation.* The warning continues from vv. 7-8 into vv. 10-11: *A generation that did not make firm their heart, And whose spirit was not stedfast with God* (v. 8cd)... *They kept not the covenant of God, And refused to walk in his law* (v. 10). *That they might not forget the works of God* (v. 7b)... *And they forgat his doings, And his wondrous works that he had shewed them* (v. 11). It continues unremittingly to the end of the psalm.

78.9 is 'inconvenient and enigmatical' (Delitzsch). The psalm is about *Jacob/Israel,* about the whole people, not about a single tribe, *the children of Ephraim;* it is about a religious failure to trust God, not about cowardice in battle—contrast the Philistine section in vv. 59-64, where defeat is imputed to God's anger, not to martial failure. The verse is an insertion into a consistent statement of theme in vv. 5-8, 10-11; and it is easy to understand why it has been introduced. Psalm 78, like the rest of the Asaph psalms, was of northern origin, and was taken over into Jerusalem use: we have already noted at Pss. 50.2, 74.2c, 76.2-3 the need felt by the Jerusalem authorities to adapt the psalmody for use in *Zion, Judah*, and so forth. So here they are glad to rehearse the *wondrous works* of God; but they are very conscious that it was not Judahites who were involved in the sins of the wilderness. There is a familiar human desire to have things both ways. The Exodus–wilderness story is being accepted as *our* story, God's act of redemption for *us*, his people; but the sins committed on the way were not committed by us, but by *the children of Ephraim*, that is, the Joseph–Benjamin tribes, who were in fact the group of the Exodus, and no doubt did actually *turn back in* some *day of battle* in the 720s. So v. 9 is not so very inconvenient or enigmatical; it is just one more instance of the wish to have one's cake and eat it.

The Jerusalem editors experience the same feelings when they reach the Philistine tale in vv. 59-66, 70-72, to which I return below.

These verses pose a problem for every commentator, and a variety of solutions are offered. (i) Cohen cites mediaeval Jewish sages who taught that the Ephraimites broke away from the main Exodus, and were defeated at Gath. (ii) A.F. Campbell ('Psalm 78') takes the loss of the ark in vv. 59-64 to be recent history; or Weiser and Eaton suggest that *Ephraim* stands for Saul, and the *turning back in battle* was at Mt Gilboa: for either view this then leads on to *God's choice of David and Mt Zion* in vv. 68-70. (iii) Duhm and Anderson (hesitantly) see the references to Ephraim as a polemic against the Samaritans and their rebuilding of the Mt Gerizim temple in the late fourth century. (iv) Gunkel and Jacquet saw a corruption of the text, which they rewrote. (v) Kraus, correctly, saw a gloss, though he gave no explanation for it; and there are similar suggestions of an earlier text being revised after 722 by R. Carroll ('Psalm LXXVIII') and Tate. Junker ('Entstehungszeit') sees v. 9 properly as a general reflection on the catastrophe of 722, but misses the fact that the main body of the psalm is about the whole people, not one tribe. D. Mathias (*Geschichtstheologie*, pp. 48-57) argues on dubious criteria for vv. 5, 7c and 10-11, as well as 9, as later glosses.

The problem of vv. 9, 67-69, broadens out into the bigger problem of the psalm's relation to the Deuteronomic writings, and so to its date. Psalm 78 is clearly related in many ways to the D-corpus. Its references to *giving ear* and *not forgetting*, to the *testimony, law, commandments* and *covenant*, and its interest in carrying the tradition from *fathers to children*, have already been evident in these opening verses, and such ideas pervade the D-writings, especially in the opening, homiletic chapters of Deuteronomy, notably Deuteronomy 6. The impression is confirmed by the long historical survey, with its insistence on Israel's disobedience to God as a constant spur to divine anger, which, however, is later followed by instances of God's grace. The story begins with God's bringing his people out of Egypt, and ends with his bringing them in to possess the land. Here is the central theme of the whole D-history, and we have it set out *in nuce* in many of the sermonic passages, like 2 Kgs 17.7-23, which press the *Vergeltungsdogma* on the hearer.

The response of Gunkel, Kraus and others has been to conclude without discussion that Psalm 78 has been influenced by Deuteronomy: the 'wisdom poem' opening has often seemed to be an indication of a late date, and so the same direction of influence. But such an inference is hasty. There is a marked difference between Psalm 78 and the D-sermons. They—and indeed the whole D-history—stress the prosperity–sin–divine anger–defeat syndrome because they are attempting a theodicy after 586: there is no description of the Exodus, or the plagues of Egypt, and the story ends in disaster. Psalm 78 offers a double emphasis, both the retribution syndrome and the celebration of God's deliverances, and it is the latter which complete the recital; for the psalmist the last act has still to crown the play. Weiser, Anderson and others note that there is no reference to the destruction of the Temple, which would have been almost inevitable given the retribution theme, had the date been after 586. An influence from the Asaph community on the Deuteronomic school seems equally possible therefore: the Exodus community were the Joseph (/Benjamin) tribes, and the Exodus–wilderness saga is their saga; this was accepted in Jerusalem in Hezekiah's time, but with vv. 9, 67-69 as protest glosses, and in time found expression in the D-theodicy. As we shall see, the details and order of the Exodus and wilderness events differ sharply from that given either in D or in Exodus–Numbers, a feature noted by Rogerson and McKay, and by Campbell.

The dating of Psalm 78 varies enormously, and is often dependent on the view taken of vv. 9, 67-69. Eissfeldt ('Lied Moses'), Campbell, Dahood and Jacquet go for a tenth-century date, soon after the secession of 'Ephraim' by Jeroboam I. Kirkpatrick, Weiser, Carroll and Tate give a post-722 date; Junker ('Enstehungszeit') and Anderson connect it with the Deuteronomic movement in Josiah's time. Gunkel sets the psalm after the Exile and Kraus with the Chronicler, both on grounds of Deuteronomic influence.

78.12	Marvellous things did he in the sight of their fathers,
	In the land of Egypt, in the field of Zoan.
13	He clave the sea, and caused them to pass through;
	And he made the waters to stand as an heap.
14	In the day-time also he led them with a cloud,
	And all the night with a light of fire.
15	He clave the rocks in the wilderness,
	And gave them drink abundantly as out of the depths.
16	He brought streams also out of the rock,
	And caused waters also to run down like rivers.
17	Yet they went on still to sin against him,
	To rebel against the Most High in a dry land.
18	And they tempted God in their heart
	By asking meat for their lust.
19	Yea, they spake against God;
	They said, Can God prepare a table in the wilderness?
20	Behold, he smote the rock, that water gushed out,
	And streams overflowed;
	Can he give bread also?
	Will he provide flesh for his people?

Gunkel thought that Psalm 78 drew on our Pentateuch, and had no independent tradition. Differences of order arose because the psalmist had no interest in order; differences of substance, as in v. 19, were free inventions. I do not think this can be supported. The only clear aberration of order is the placing of the plagues in vv. 42-53 as a flashback, and the reason for that is not far to seek. The exordium, vv. 1-11, has introduced the twin themes of God's miraculous power (vv. 3-7) and Israel's repeated disobedience (vv. 8, 10-11). Verses 12-16 give examples of the former, and vv. 17-20 bring us to the latter: had the psalmist stuck to chronology, he would have begun with ten verses of plagues (vv. 42-51) and five verses of desert wonders (vv. 12-16), and the disobedience theme would have been swamped. As it is, he has balanced the two themes skilfully. Where we can be confident of the order of events, Psalm 78 has them in sequence: the plagues (vv. 42-51), the Exodus (vv. 52-53), the Settlement (vv. 54-58), the loss of the ark, and of Shiloh (vv. 59-64), the defeat of the Philistines (vv. 65-66) and the reign of David (vv. 70-72). Such a sequence does not occur with writers not concerned with chronology.

The accounts of Israelite history given in the Asaph psalms, and in particular by Psalm 78, diverge in many small matters from the Pentateuchal and Former Prophets versions; and encourage us to explore the possibility that they are in fact earlier. From our present section we may note:

1. The sojourn in Egypt is said to have been *in the field* (district) *of Zoan.* צֹעַן, LXX, is a city on the eastern branch of the Nile delta, and is not mentioned in the Pentateuch. Zoan occurs in the eighth-century text Isa. 30.4 and later.

2. The account of the Exodus itself, v. 13, is, like that in Psalm 77 (cf. pp. 103-105), closely related to the hymn in Exodus 15: *he made the waters stand as an heap* (13b), cf. '...*the waters*: The floods *stood as an heap*' (Exod. 15.8). The people's faithlessness, Moses and his rod, angelic manoeuvres with the cloud and fire, and so forth, are all later developments in Exodus 14.

3. Then come the *cloud and fire* (v. 14), by which God *leads* the Israelites on their way (right from the start in v. 52). Ps. 105.39 has developed this: 'He spread a cloud for a covering; And fire to give light in the night'—the cloud was to *hide them from the Egyptians*, the fire to give them *illumination.* In Exod. 13.21-22 the feature seems more developed still: 'And the LORD went before them by day in a pillar of cloud, to lead them the way; and by night in a pillar of fire, to give them light.' The amorphous, natural, cloud and fire of Psalm 78 have been tidied into defined *pillars*; the point of the fire is as in Ps. 105.39b.

4. To anyone even thinking of desert travel the first concern is water; and in vv. 15-16 God provides *drink in abundance as out of the depths.* There is no question of any sin here, any tempting of God or contention: the *water* is provided by God's bounty, and is accepted as such. By contrast the water from the rock in Exodus 17, and again in Numbers 20, is the occasion of sin. The people murmured against Moses, and tempted Yahweh in Exod. 17.1-7; they assembled themselves together against Moses and against Aaron at the waters of Meribah in Num. 20.2-13. This water trouble does not come at the beginning of the journey, but after some time (Exod. 17)/an enormous time (Num. 20), since Meribah was near Kadesh by the Negeb. There is an incident in which God provides sweet water after the passing of the sea, in Exod. 15.22-26, the waters of Marah; and there are the springs of Elim at Exod. 15.27: but in neither case does God provide water out of the rock.

In v. 15 God *clave the rocks* (צֻרִים): Gunkel infers that the plural is a later inference from the presence of *two* cleavings of rock in the Pentateuch, צוּר in Exodus 17 and סֶלַע in Numbers 20. More likely Psalm 78 saw the divine action as bringing the water bursting *between the rocks* (cf. בקע, *divide* in v. 13), and the Pentateuchal authors have increased the miracle.

5. The *tempting of God* then follows in vv. 17-20, as a consequence of the gift of water. *Yet went they still on* (ויוסיפו) *to sin*: the *stubborn and rebellious generation* had been like that from the beginning (v. 8). Their sin takes the form of a challenge to God: *Behold, he smote the rock... Can he give bread also? Will he provide flesh for his people?* The sequence of events is quite different in both Exodus and Numbers. In Exodus the quails-and-manna temptation comes in Exodus 16, immediately *before* the water-from-the-rock incident in Exodus 17 (though after the Marah/Elim water provision in Exod. 15). In Numbers the manna-and-quails story is told in ch. 11, long before the Meribah contention in Numbers 20. In neither case is the food temptation directly correlated to the water temptation, or vice versa.

There is a fuller account of the development of these traditions in Part II below. It may well be that the plural צרים, and *they went on still to sin*, have been interpreted to yield the twin accounts in Exodus 17 and Numbers 20.

78.21   Therefore the LORD heard, and was wroth:
        And a fire was kindled against Jacob,
        And anger also went up against Israel;
22   Because they believed not in God,
        And trusted not in his salvation.
23   And (ו) he commanded the skies above,
        And opened the doors of heaven;
24   And he rained down manna upon them to eat,
        And gave them of the corn of heaven.
25   Man (איש) did eat the bread of the mighty:
        He sent them meat to the full.
26   He led forth the east wind to blow in the heaven:
        And by his power he guided the south wind.
27   He rained flesh also upon them as the dust,
        And winged fowl as the sand of the seas:
28   And he let it fall in the midst of their camp,
        Round about their habitations.
29   So they did eat, and were well filled;
        And he gave them that they lusted after.
30   They were not estranged from their lust,
        Their meat was yet in their mouths,

78.31   When the anger of God went up against them,
             And slew all the fattest of them,
             And smote down the young men of Israel.

The sequence of events is quite different from Exodus 16, where the quails come first and then the manna, and there is no divine anger except for sabbath-breakers; but it is strikingly close to Numbers 11–12, with some interesting differences.

1. The challenge of Ps. 78.18-20 is met with Yahweh's wrath, *fire and anger* (vv. 21-22). Nothing is made of the fire, which stands in parallel to the anger, and the latter expresses itself in the disaster of v. 31. It seems therefore that the fire is not literal, but a symbol of the divine wrath, as in v. 63 (so *DCH*, p. 400; cf. Deut. 32.22; Isa. 30.27; 65.5, etc.). By contrast there is real fire in Num. 11.1-3, which 'devoured in the uttermost part of the camp'; it is evoked by some unspecified 'murmuring'; and it takes place at a place called Taberah (= Burning). It looks as if the author in Numbers has interpreted the Psalm 78 tradition: he has supplied a bit of stock murmuring, he has understood the fire as burning people, and he has made this an aetiology for the place Taberah.

2. In Ps. 78.20 the people challenged God to provide both *bread* and *flesh*; and he does provide both these things, but he does so to their destruction. (Heb. ו is not adversative here [RV 'Yet']: the rain of manna and birds is the medium of his wrath.) He pours down on them *manna, the corn of heaven, the bread of the mighty* (i.e. the gods of Ps. 82); he raises the *east* and *south winds*, and *rains upon them winged fowl as the sand of the seas*. So they *did eat* to the full; and as *their meat was yet in their mouths, the anger of God went up against them.* Man eats divine food at his peril (אִישׁ at the end of the clause is contrasted with the divine אַבִּירִים at the beginning), and meat which he has gained by faithlessness. So God's anger brings about the death of the *stoutest* of the people, and the flower of *Israel's youth*.

Again Numbers 11 seems to be an interpretation of this. We have had a murmuring at 11.1, but that has been punished by the fire, so there is a second, rather clumsy murmuring at 11.4-6, debited to 'the mixed multitude'. As they have been going a good time through the desert, and must have been eating something, the manna is assumed, and is made the basis of the complaint—they are sick of manna, and want flesh. Moses (it is Moses now) takes the complaint to God, who sends out a wind and brings quails from the sea in fabulous quantity—a day's journey on either side of the camp, and two cubits deep. While the flesh was between their teeth, the anger of the LORD was kindled against the people, and the plague kills them, at Kibrot-hattaavah, the Graves of Lusting. So the Numbers author seems to have adjusted and elaborated the Psalm 78 story. The manna has had to become the basis of complaining instead of a medium of punishment; the wind, the birds, the meat in the people's mouths as the occasion of their smiting—all this is the same; the fanciful multiplication of the divine provision, and its specification as quails, are the author's imagination; the place name is once more an aetiology.

With אַבִּרִים, *mighty ones*, cf. Yahweh's titles אֲבִיר יַעֲקֹב, Ps. 132.2, 5; אֲבִיר יִשְׂרָאֵל, Isa. 1.24; 49.26; 60.16; see *DCH*; Johnson, *Cultic Prophet*, p. 52 n.1.

78.32	For all this they sinned still,
	And believed not in his wondrous works.
33	Therefore their days did he consume in vanity,
	And their years in terror.
34	When he consumed them, then they inquired after him:
	And they returned and sought God earnestly.
35	And they remembered that God was their rock,
	And the Most High God their redeemer.
36	But they flattered him with their mouth,
	And lied unto him with their tongue.
37	For their heart was not stedfast with him,
	Neither were they faithful in his covenant.
38	But he, being full of compassion, forgave *their* iniquity,
	and destroyed *them* not:
	Yea, many a time turned he his anger away,
	And did not stir up all his wrath.
39	And he remembered that they were but flesh;
	A wind that passeth away, and cometh not again.
40	How oft did they rebel against him in the wilderness,
	And grieved him in the desert!
41	And they turned again and tempted God,
	And limited the Holy One of Israel.

Although the language is allusive, we may distinguish three elements in these verses: (1) In vv. 32-33 the people do not *believe in* God's *wondrous works*, and are punished by having *their days consumed in vanity* and *terror*. We are reminded of Numbers 14. Joshua and Caleb have pioneered an expedition into Palestine, and brought back an encouraging, though realistic report. The people refuse to accept this, and the LORD says, 'How long will this people despise me? and how long will they *not believe in me*, for all the *signs which I have wrought* among them?' (Num. 14.11). God's sentence is on the whole generation, from twenty years old and upward: '*in the wilderness* they shall be *consumed*, and there shall they die' (Num. 11.35; cf. 29). It is to be forty wasted years.

Again, Numbers seems to offer a developed account of the Psalm 78 tradition. No doubt historically the Israelites tried to force their way into Palestine from the south by the direct route, and only the Calebites succeeded in gaining a foothold; the Joseph/Benjamin clans remained as nomads for a further generation, and eventually came in from the east, via Moab. The echo of this failure has survived into Psalm 78, with a theological explanation, and in time this has been elaborated as Numbers 13–14. There were two faithful spies, Joshua (who ultimately led the Benjaminites into their tribal inheritance) and Caleb, eponym of the Calebites: they were excepted from the otherwise general condemnation.

(2) In vv. 34-38 the people are driven to a shallow repentance: they *inquire after God and seek him earnestly, remembering that* אל עליון *was their rock, their redeemer* (from Egypt). However, this did not last long: *they were not faithful in his covenant,* but failed to keep their promise (*flattered, lied, not stedfast*). This time God *did not destroy them* for some reason, but *being full of compassion, forgave their iniquity.*

It is difficult not to associate these verses with Psalm 81, where God 'proved thee at the waters of Meribah... I am the LORD thy God which brought thee up out of the land of Egypt. But my people hearkened not to my voice' (81.8, 11-12). In the Asaph tradition the covenant was made at *Meribah*, not at *Sinai*. It was there that there was *contention*, because some of the clans accepted that עליון אל was the God who had brought them out of Egypt, and others not. Psalm 78 has no mention of Sinai because Sinai was the divine locus in the Judah tradition only. There has been no reference to *the covenant* hitherto because the Joseph-tribes, who worshipped עליון at Bethel, placed the covenant rather late in the desert sequence, at Meribah near Kadesh. It is also noticeable that in Psalm 78 (as opposed to Ps. 81), the name for God is insistently (עליון) אל, rather than Yahweh.

Once again we are able to see the hand of the Exodus–Numbers author revising the Asaph tradition. Israel reaches Meribah only at Numbers 20, as is required by geography; and Aaron dies soon afterwards (grossly unfairly). But the real significance of the place is wished away: 'the waters of Meribah' are assimilated to 'the waters of Massah' in a repetition of the tale of Moses striking the rock (Num. 20.1-13). The actual *contention* has been fused into the Golden Calf story, as part of the covenant at Sinai in Exodus 32. Moses (inevitably Moses) intercedes for the people, and God announces himself 'Yahweh, Yahweh, an אל *full of compassion* and gracious, slow to *anger*, and plenteous in mercy and truth; keeping mercy for thousands, *forgiving iniquity* and transgression and sin' (Exod. 34.6-7). It is the same covenant pronouncement which we saw echoed in the language of Ps. 77.8-10, and proclaimed in the Selah there. Of course Yahweh in his justice punished the first three generations for the fathers' sins, much as he does in Numbers 14; but he generously forgives their great- grandchildren, who will inherit the land.

(3) In vv. 40-41, anticipated by v. 38b, there are general statements of rebellions: *Yea, many a time, How oft...* It is difficult to have any confidence what traditions, if any, were in the psalmist's mind here. We might think that the title *the Holy One* (קְדוֹשׁ) *of Israel* is a name associated with the place Kadesh (קָדֵשׁ), which is where the waters of Meribah were (Num. 20.1); God reproves Moses and Aaron there, 'ye believed not in me *to make me holy* (לְהַקְדִּישֵׁנִי) in the eyes of the children of Israel', and 'he *shewed himself holy* (וַיִּקָּדֵשׁ) among them' (20.12-13). Holiness implies the demand for unreserved loyalty, and the verbs הִתְווּ, יְנַסּוּ probably indicate the worship of other gods. This was the point of 'stubbornness' known to the Asaphite tradition in Psalm 81: God said, 'There shall no strange god be in thee', but 'my people hearkened not' (81.10, 12). Once more we may suspect the interpreting hand of the Numbers author. In the tradition known to the psalmist, Israel (led perhaps by Aaron) failed to worship the Holy God of Kadesh alone, and that is why Aaron was condemned to death in the desert (Num. 20.12), and died soon afterwards (20.24-29). The Pentateuchal author has had to place the covenant-giving at Sinai, and so much earlier in the story; and Aaron's faithlessness, and the worship of other gods, are described in Exodus 32. So he is left with a problem when he comes to Meribah, and the need to have Aaron die. Ps. 78.41, *they turned again and tempted God*, suggests a second version of the waters of temptation (Exod. 17 being the first); and Aaron is implicated in a manner reminiscent of Soviet justice, with God behaving like Stalin.

The result of this examination of the wilderness story is striking. At every point Ps. 78.13-41 seems to represent the primary tradition; which indeed is not surprising, since it is the product of the Joseph community which had actually experienced the Exodus and wanderings, and it belongs in the eighth century. For the greater part the closest Pentateuchal parallel to this tradition is not in Exodus but in Numbers; and it represents a consistent development of the Asaphic story—'improving' the order, tidying (the pillars of cloud and fire), (mis)interpreting (the burning, the temptation), adding colourful legend (Joshua and Caleb) and aetiologies (Taberah, Kibrot-hattaavah), adapting to the Sinai tradition (the Meribah covenant, Aaron's death). The Numbers narrative follows the same order as Psalm 78: God's anger/fire (11.1-3), the quails (11.4-34), the consuming of years in vanity (13–14), the disobedience at Meribah/Kadesh (20.1-13). I shall return to this in Part II.

Most commentators align vv. 32-33 with Numbers 14, and Kirkpatrick notes the parallel of v. 38 with Exod. 32.10, 12; 34.6-7, and of v. 41 with Num. 20.12-13; but the connection with an independent tradition of the covenant at Meribah-Kadesh is absent. התוו in v. 41 is hiph. of תוה, *repent*; most commentators prefer RV text translation, *provoke*.

78.42   They remembered not his hand,
         Nor the day when he redeemed them from the adversary.
43   How he set his signs in Egypt,
         And his wonders in the field of Zoan;
44   And turned their rivers into blood,
         And their streams, that they could not drink.
45   He sent among them swarms of flies, which devoured them;
         And frogs, which destroyed them.
46   He gave also their increase unto the caterpiller,
         And their labour unto the locust.
47   He killed their vines with hail,
         And their sycomore trees with great hailstones.
48   He gave over also their cattle to the hail,
         And their flocks to hot thunderbolts.
49   He cast upon them the fierceness of his anger,
         Wrath and indignation and trouble,
         A sending of angels of evil.
50   He levelled a path for his anger;
         He spared not their soul from death,
         But gave their life over to the pestilence (RV text);
51   And smote all the firstborn in Egypt,
         The beginning of their strength in the land of Ham:
52   But he led forth his own people like sheep,
         And guided them in the wilderness like a flock.
53   And he led them safely, so that they feared not:
         But the sea overwhelmed their enemies.

78.54   And he brought them to his holy border,
         To the mountain-land which (הר־זה) his right hand had purchased.
55   He drove out the nations also before them,
         And allotted them for an inheritance by line,
         And made the tribes of Israel dwell in their tents.

Attempts to reconcile this account of the Egyptian plagues with those in
Psalm 105 and Exodus are vain. The plagues here are not counted; they
are described poetically, and if we insist on counting, we should probably reckon with five—the Nile into blood; people attacked by flies and
frogs; vegetation destroyed by insects; hailstorms (perhaps subdivided,
with frost for the trees and thunderbolts for the cattle); and pestilence.
The picture is simple and graphic, and the other accounts are later
elaborations:

78.43-44. The Nile branches and canals (יאריהם) are turned to blood, so
that there is no water to drink. In Ps. 105.29 a secondary inference has
been drawn: 'And slew their fish'. Exod. 7.14-25 has expanded this into
a fairy-tale: Moses and Aaron meeting Pharaoh by the river-brink,
Aaron's rod, the fish dying and the river stinking, the pools and ponds
included, the magicians, the need to dig for water... The gloating has got
under weigh.

There is a significant point at Ps. 105.27. Ps. 78.43 reads *How he*
[God] *set his signs in Egypt, and his wonders in the field of Zoan*;
Psalm 105 has introduced Moses and Aaron in v. 26, and writes 'They
set among them the words of *his signs, And wonders in the* land of
Ham'. The parallel structure, the use of שם, and the presence of *in the
tents of Ham* at Ps. 78.51, all suggest a direct relationship; and the plural,
the insertion of דברי, and the artificiality of 'They set the words of his
signs', indicate the use of 78 by 105.

78.45. The Egyptians are eaten (ויאכלם) by a vast swarm of flies (ערב)
and destroyed (ותשחיתם) by frogs. Of course frogs do not destroy
people, and when we say we are being eaten by midges we are speaking
hyperbolically; this is a divine plague, and the flies and frogs are excep-
tionally potent, but the destruction is still intended to fall short of death.
Egypt is a lower-lying country than Israel, with more waterways, and
travellers might well be impressed with its unpleasant flies and numerous frogs. Ps. 105.30-31 has reversed the order. The frogs come first
because they have been driven out of the blood-waters, the first step

towards the rationalist exegesis of the nineteenth century; they no longer, unrealistically, eat people, but merely cause gross embarrassment by penetrating even to 'their kings' chambers'. The flies have a verse of their own (105.31), and are paralleled with 'lice' (more probably *gnats*, כנים), intended as a specification. Exod. 7.26–8.11 (EVV 8.1-15) accepts the Psalm 105 order: the frogs are the second plague, and there are again suitable elaborations—the frogs cover the land, die, are gathered in heaps, the land stinks, and so forth. This is then followed by a third plague of lice/gnats (כנים) on man and beast, made out of the dust at Aaron's blow. In 8.16-28 (EVV 20-32) the flies make a distinct fourth plague. At each step the Hebrew poetic parallelism is being interpreted as a pair of distinct elements. The two plagues of Psalm 78 have become the four of Exodus 7–8.

78.46-48. These preliminary plagues are now succeeded by the loss of crops. ארבה in v. 46b is the normal word for locust; חסיל in v. 46a, the 'consumer' is probably a variety of locust rather than RV's *caterpiller*. First then it is the greenery; then the trees. The *vines* have been stripped, but now they are *killed* (יהרג) *with hail*, and the *sycomores with* חנמל, variously rendered *great hail-stones* (RV mg), *frost* (LXX, Tate), *torrents of rain* (NEB, REB), *sleet* (NIV). The first is the most plausible: it takes a lot to kill a sycamore, and the *hail* (ברד) continues into v. 48, where it destroys the cattle, and the sheep with thunderbolts (רשפים).

Two MSS, and Symmachus, read דבר, *pestilence*, for ברד, *hail*, and this is commended by Tate, since רשף may also mean the divine lightning of sickness (cf. the arrows of Artemis in *Iliad* 1); but the *varia lectio* is better explained as a more usual affliction of cattle. The דבר actually arrives in v. 50.

Ps. 105.32-35 reverses the order of the hailstorms and locusts. Storms may damage but they do not normally kill trees, and the locusts are a more formidable enemy, as every Israelite farmer knew. So God first 'gave them hail for rain, flaming fire in their land', which 'smote their vines and their fig-trees, And broke (sc. the branches of) the trees of their borders'. Fig-trees, the Israelite's pair to his vines, are now included, and the *sycomores* have become *trees* more generally. The cattle have been forgotten. Psalm 105 is counting seven wonders: waters to blood, frogs, flies, hail, locusts, first-born, the Exodus. By taking the hail before the locusts/'cankerworm' (ילק, another species of locust), it has bypassed the animals.

All this has been re-thought by the Exodus authors. They have preferred the (more recent) Psalm 105 order, with hail/fire as the seventh and locusts as the eighth plague; they have interpreted Psalm 105's darkness as the ninth plague, and thus obtained a climax of horror, leading up to the death of the first-born. With their earlier expansions this already makes eight plagues, and they have rounded the total up to ten with murrain on the cattle and boils on man and beast. The reader may work out the detail of the embroidering interpretations for her or himself: the 'very grievous' unparalleled fire, for instance, in the seventh plague, the exclusion of Goshen, the mighty thunders, the limit of damage to the flax and barley, so as to reserve the wheat and spelt for the locusts, Pharaoh's equivocation. I have added some more general comments in Chapter 11.

78.49-51. The final blow, as God really gives his anger free rein, is a *pestilence*, delivered by a *sortie of angels of bain*, which *spares not from death the soul of all the firstborn in Egypt*. We have a similar (? derived) picture of the sword-bearing angel presiding over the pestilence in David's time in 1 Chronicles 21. The blow is delivered in almost the same words in Ps. 105.36, '*He smote* also *the firstborn in* their land, *the firstfruits of* all *their potency*'. This later psalmist thus knows Psalm 78. He has cut out 78.49-50 on God's anger so as to leave space for the spoiling of the Egyptians, the universal health of the Israelites, and the fear of the former for the latter—all gloating expansions. The extended expansions of Exodus 12 are familiar. It should be noticed that Ps. 78.51, *He smote all the firstborn in Egypt*, has become 'the LORD *smote all the firstborn in* the land of *Egypt*, from *the firstborn* of Pharaoh...unto *the firstborn* of the captive that was in the dungeon; and *all the firstborn* of cattle' (Exod. 12.29).

RV mg translates v. 50c 'gave their beasts to the murrain': at Exod. 9.3 the cattle are smitten with 'a very grievous murrain (דבר)'. This is unlikely to be right, since the rest of vv. 49-50 reads like the approach to the climax of v. 51, and RV text's 'gave their life to the pestilence' forms a smooth part to this climax. On the other hand such an interpretation was possible, and it is this which has inspired the fifth plague, the murrain of Exodus 9. RV mg has fallen into the standard error of interpreting Psalm 78 in the light of Exodus, and not vice versa.

78.52-53. God *led his own people* (ויסע) as in v. 14, there with the cloud and light of fire, and the same is understood here. The leading followed the sea at v. 13, but it precedes it here, and no doubt this is intended in both passages. The *sheep/flock* image is a favourite with the Asaph psalmist: cf. vv. 70-71; 79.13; 80.2. The passing of the Sea is again related to Exodus 15: with *the sea overwhelmed* (כסה) *their enemies*; cf. Exod. 15.10, 'the sea overwhelmed them (כסמו)'.

78.54-55. God brought the people to the גבול קדשו; RV mg's *his holy border* would be better as *his holy territory* (RSV: 2 Sam. 21.5; 1 Kgs 1.3, etc.). Similarly הר is the *mountainous land* of Israel: we can refer once more to the Asaphites' familiar Exodus 15, 'Thou shalt bring them in and plant them in the הר of thine inheritance' (15.17); cf. Isa. 11.9; 57.13 (Delitzsch). Delitzsch also renders זה as *which*, following Prov. 23.22. The references are not to Zion or Gerizim but to the whole land, as may be seen from v. 55, where *the nations are driven out* to give *Israel an inheritance*. Psalm 78 is assimilating the Joseph experience to the whole of *the tribes of Israel*, all of whom had taken part in the Settlement.

78.56	Yet they tempted and rebelled against the Most High God,
	And kept not his testimonies;
57	But turned back, and dealt treacherously like their fathers;
	They were turned aside like a deceitful bow.
58	For they provoked him to anger with their high places,
	And moved him to jealousy with their graven images.
59	When God heard this, he was wroth,
	And greatly abhorred Israel:
60	So that he forsook the tabernacle of Shiloh,
	The tent which he placed among men;
61	And delivered his strength into captivity,
	And his glory into the adversary's hand.
62	He gave his people over also unto the sword;
	And was wroth with his inheritance.
63	Fire devoured their young men;
	And their maidens had no marriage-song.
64	Their priests fell by the sword;
	And their widows made no lamentation.
65	Then the Lord awaked as one out of sleep,
	Like a mighty man that shouteth by reason of wine.
66	And he smote his adversaries backward:
	He put them to a perpetual reproach.
67	[Moreover he refused the tent of Joseph,
	And chose not the tribe of Ephraim;

78.68 But chose the tribe of Judah,
The mount Zion which he loved.

69 He built his sanctuary like the heights,
Like the earth which he hath established for ever.]

70 He chose David also his servant,
And took him from the sheepfolds;

71 From following the ewes that give suck he brought him,
To feed Jacob his people, and Israel his inheritance.

72 So he fed them according to the integrity of his heart;
And guided them by the skilfulness of his hands.

78.56-58. The normal explanation for the reverses experienced in occupying the land was the rebellion–divine anger–mercy–victory syndrome, which we have here, and which dominates in the D-work; see especially Deuteronomy 32. *They provoked him to anger with their high places, And moved him to jealousy with their graven images* is close to Deut. 32.21, '*They have moved me to jealousy with* that which is not God; *They have provoked me to anger with* their vanities.' What folly to *provoke the Most High God* (אלהים עליון), who can both deliver and punish to the uttermost! Verse 57 takes up v. 8 with *rebelling like their fathers*; the *deceitful bow* is one that is twisted or slack, and causes the arrow to fly off at an angle, or short.

78.59-64. God abhors *Israel*, the whole people, not the Northern Kingdom; and Shiloh was the sanctuary of the whole people, and the repository of the ark. Shiloh was not a *tent* but a temple (1 Sam. 3; Jer. 7.12), but it has been demoted into being a temporary affair, a tent, not by the author of the psalm but by its Jerusalem editor, who has used the similar phrase, *the tent of Joseph*, in v. 67 (see below). God's *strength* and *glory* (תפארתו) was the ark, which was *delivered into the adversary's*, that is the Philistines', *hand*; we may compare the name given to Phinehas's postumous son, Ichabod, No-glory. The Israelite army was butchered by *the sword* at the battle of Ebenezer; as at v. 21h *fire* is a symbol for God's *wrath*—the Israelites were slaughtered, not burnt alive. In consequence *their maidens were not praised* with their husbands' customary marriage song: we have an example of such a *praising* in Cant. 4.1-7, 'Behold, thou art fair, my love...', which follows the princess's marriage procession (Cant. 3.6-11), and precedes the marital union (Cant. 4.8–5.1; Goulder, *Song*, pp. 32-34). *Their priests*, Hophni and Phinehas for example, *fell by the sword*; but 1 Samuel 4

gives no suggestion that in the panic evacuation *their widows* had no
time to *make lamentation*. Once more Psalm 78 is nearer reality than
the D-history, which has suppressed the loss of Shiloh (Jer. 7.12).

78.65-66. The crude images betray the early date of the writing: God is
first like *one asleep*, and then like *a mighty man shouting* (hithpoel of
רנן, *shouting vigorously) from wine*, that is, a drunken bully. The contemporary Ps. 44.24 can ask, 'Awake, why sleepest thou, O Lord?', but
by the time of the D-history it is a joke that Baal may be asleep (1 Kgs
18.27), and the God of Israel neither slumbers nor sleeps. In the text
the Lord *smote his enemies backward* (אחור), that is he defeated them at
the hand of David (vv. 70-72). But the Hebrew permits the possibility of
his *smiting them in the hinder parts*; and mediaeval Jewish commentators took this to refer to the 'emerods' inflicted on the Philistines
in 1 Samuel 5. (Gunkel and Tate take this interpretation seriously.) Once
more we seem to have an instance of the historian *interpreting the
tradition of the psalm*: Psalm 78 meant that the Philistines were forced
by David to retreat, but the Deuteronomist has combined אחור with
perpetual reproach, and seen the implication of a widespread attack of
piles.

78.67-69. These three verses are the gloss of the ill-natured Jerusalem
community, just like v. 9. (i) They break the general sense of the psalm,
which is a reflection on the history of Israel as a whole, not of Joseph
contrasted with Judah. (ii) They interrupt the immediate context, which
is concerned with God's defeat of the Philistines (v. 66) and his election
of David for the purpose (vv. 70-72), not with alternative centres of
worship. (iii) Ephraim is rejected, as in v. 9, in opposition to Ps. 80.3,
where God is to stir up his might before Ephraim, and Joseph is the
people of God (cf. Pss. 77.16; 81.6). (iv) There was a temple at Shiloh,
not a *tent* (see on v. 60): the word is used pejoratively, to contrast its
ephemeral use with the permanence of the *sanctuary* on *Zion*.
 The wording of the gloss is suggested by the context. 'And he chose
(ויבחר) David' (v. 70, the next verse after 66) suggested *And he
refused...and chose* (בחר) *not the tribe of Ephraim, But chose* (ויבחר)
the tribe of Judah. Verse 54, *he brought them to the border of his
sanctuary* (RV text, גבול קדשו), *To the mountain* (RV text, הר) *which his
right hand had purchased*, suggested *the mount* (הר) *Zion which he
loved, And he built his sanctuary* (מקדשו). Ps. 87.3 also has the gloss,

'The LORD loveth the gates of Zion.' Zion is glorified as being as permanent as *the heights*, that is, heaven, *Like the earth which he established for ever,* in contrast with *the tent of Joseph.*

78.70-72. The defeat of the Philistines was accomplished through God's choice of *David*, whom *he took from the sheepfolds* to *feed* and *guide his people. He pastored them* (וירעם) *according to the integrity of his heart, And led them* (ינחם) *by the skilfulness of his hands.* The psalmist sees David as both a religious (תם) and an understanding (תבונה) king, who in the strength of these virtues drove the Philistines back. He had risen from humble but symbolic beginnings, as a shepherd. The D-historian has developed and idealized the psalm picture into the legend of 1 Samuel 16. The seven older sons of Jesse pass before Samuel, but God says of the first, 'I have *refused him* (מאסתיחו)', and the prophet pronounces 'Neither hath the LORD *chosen* (בהר) this'; the son to be anointed is David the youngest, of whom it is said, 'Behold, *he keepeth the sheep*' (בצאן רעה, 1 Sam. 16.11). So the adult shepherd of Psalm 78 becomes the favoured youngest son of folklore, ruddy and withal of a fair countenance.

It is sometimes thought that the mention of David implies a southern provenance, but this is not so. The D-historians portray David as a Judahite, born in Bethlehem, against whose grandson the northern tribes rebelled, and seceded; rather as the western Catholic Church made Peter its first bishop, and saw the eastern churches as schismatic and excommunicate. But David's family came in fact not from Bethlehem, but from Ephratha (1 Sam. 17.12); and Ephratha (despite Judahite attempts to identify it with Bethlehem as a village with two names, Gen. 35.19, Mic. 5.2) was the place where Rachel died bearing Benjamin (Gen. 35.16-20), and her grave was in the territory of Benjamin at Zelzah (1 Sam. 10.2). David was a Benjaminite; the 68th psalmist says of him in the victory procession after Absalom's rebellion, 'There is little Benjamin their ruler' (68.28, Goulder, *Prayers*, pp. 191-216, esp. 208-211). So Israel, the Northern Kingdom as we call it, knew David as their king; and Hosea, the northern prophet, can speak of the children of Israel returning to 'David their king' (3.4).

Psalm 78 is widely misunderstood. First, as not even Kraus concluded, vv. 67-69 are as flat against the general tenor as v. 9, and they show various signs of being Jerusalem glosses on a northern original; all attempts, such as Duhm's or Weiser's, to interpret it in the light of these verses are unconvincing. Second, the psalm is not, as Gunkel thought, a later reflection of our Pentateuchal and D-history narratives. At point after point we have seen signs that hints in its text have been interpreted, and often misinterpreted, both in the later Psalm 105 and in our Exodus–Numbers–1 Samuel; and this fact is crucial for establishing a sound foundation for an account of Pentateuchal development, as will appear in Part II.

A third error has been to see the psalm as a reflection of the Deuteronomistic writings, with which its language and theology have so much in common (Gunkel, Kraus, Mathias, *Psalmen*, pp. 61-66). Here the crucial feature is not the lack of any mention of the disaster of 586, but the high note on which the psalm ends. The speaker is drawing two lessons from history, two *riddles from of old* (v. 2). The first of these is Yahweh's *strength and his wondrous works that he hath done* (vv. 3-7), and the second that *stubbornness and rebellion* call down God's *wrath* (vv. 8, 10-11). But it is the first of these which dominates the end of the psalm. Its message is: Do not forget God's covenant and rebel, or he will vent his anger on us; God did miracles delivering Israel in the past, finally through David, and he can do the same for us with the Assyrians now. He will come round, like a boxer dozing off his beer, bawl them out and thump them.

The Liturgical Hypothesis

With Psalms 50, 73–76 I have tried to show substantial thematic agree-ments with the Korah psalms 42–46, 84–85, and in the same order. Psalm 50 was a call to *Gather my people unto me*, as Psalms 42–43 (and 84) were pilgrimage psalms, sung as the national gathering made its way to the shrine at Dan. Psalms 73 and 74 were pre-festal laments, with much to bewail, and had both theme and language in common with 44. Psalm 75 was the king's vow to *cut off the horns of the wicked*, to defeat the enemy, in the same way that 45 was a psalm for the king to see his *sharp arrows in the heart of his enemies*. Psalm 76 saw God *breaking the arrows of the bow, the shield, and the sword and the battle*, much as in 46 he *breaketh the bow, and cutteth the spear in sunder, and burneth the chariots in the fire*.

We have the same thematic correspondence between Psalms 77–78 and 47, but it is not so striking because the political/military situation is so different. Psalm 47 was composed in the high days of the Omrids

(Goulder, *Korah*, pp. 151-59), when all the peoples could be urged to clap their hands and triumph in God, as their princes gathered to be assimilated to the people of the God of Abraham. Such times were a distant memory, more than a century since, when Shalmaneser's armies roamed at will devastating the land. So perhaps it was not so suitable to chant 'He subdueth the peoples under us, And the nations under our feet' (Ps. 47.4), or 'God has taken up his reign over the nations' (Ps. 47.9).

Nonetheless the basic theme of the three psalms is the same. Psalm 47 sings praises to יהוה עליון, the LORD Most High, who subdues the nations under Israel; who chooses their inheritance for them, the pride of Jacob which he loves. Yahweh is the supreme God who has given Israel the land to inherit and defeated the peoples who had occupied it, or tried to take it from them. It is this thought which comforts the heart of the distraught Hoshea in Psalm 77, and which he teaches his dispirited people in Psalm 78. God is repeatedly said to be the Most High (Pss. 77.11; 78.17, 35, 56), אלהים עליון, אל עליון, עליון. What is dwelt upon is his wonders of old, which are the centre of both psalms—the Exodus (Pss. 77.15-21; 78.13, 53), the plagues in Egypt, the deliverances in the desert, in the Settlement, from the Philistines: 'He drove out *the nations* also before them, And allotted them for *an inheritance* by line' (Ps. 78.55). The land is God's holy territory (v. 54), and the Jerusalem glossator adds 'the mount Zion *which he loved*' (v. 68). Psalm 78 is fundamentally, as Gunkel saw, a hymn to the supreme God. The rebellion–punishment–grace syndrome has been imported on a large scale because it is necessary to provide a theodicy, an explanation for God's failure to live up to his covenanted expectations. When Ahab was exacting the wool of a hundred thousand lambs from Mesha king of Moab, such excuses were not required.

The Korah series also has a night-psalm, 88, in which the national representative, a priest perhaps, spends the night in an underground chamber of horrors, among the ghosts, crying pitiably to God, but confident that 'In the morning shall my prayer come before thee' (88.14; Goulder, *Korah*, pp. 195-210). In Bethel in the 720s the king takes this duty on himself, for the national situation is critical; but, as befits a monarch, the personal ascesis is more relaxed. There is no 'affliction', 'terrors', or 'shutting up'; it is a plain, night-long vigil in the Temple 'confessional', without the comfort of food or rest. But I have argued above that the speaker is the king in both Psalms 77 and 78; who first seeks to reconcile the national crisis with God's covenant in Psalm 77, and finds the answer in his wonders in Egypt; and then continues in Psalm 78 to give his teaching to *my people*, expanding the same theme at leisure.

So the serial pattern seems to be maintained:

		Dan, 9th c.	*Dan, 732*	*Bethel, 725*
13th Bul	Pilgrimage	84	42, 43	50
14th	Pre-festal Lament	85	44	73, 74
15th	King consecrated	45	45	75
16th	God victorious	46	46	76
17th	God's wonders	47	47	77, 78

Chapter 5

THE DAYS OF PETITION

Psalm 79

79.1   A Psalm of Asaph.
    O God, the nations are come into thine inheritance;
    Thy holy temple have they defiled;
    [They have laid Jerusalem on heaps.]

2   The dead bodies of thy servants have they given to be meat unto the
        fowls of the heaven;
    The flesh of thy saints unto the beasts of the earth.

3   Their blood have they shed like water; [round about Jerusalem]
    And there was none to bury them.

4   We are become a reproach to our neighbours,
    A scorn and derision to them that are round about us.

5   How long, O LORD, wilt thou be angry for ever?
    Shall thy jealousy burn like fire?

6   Pour out thy wrath upon the heathen that know thee not,
    And upon the kingdoms that call not upon thy name.

7   For he has devoured (אכל) Jacob,
    And they have laid waste his pasture.

8   Remember not against us the iniquities of our forefathers:
    Let thy tender mercies speedily prevent us:
    For we are brought very low.

9   Help us, O God of our salvation, for the glory of thy name:
    And deliver us, and purge away our sins, for thy name's sake.

10   Wherefore should the heathen say, Where is their God?
    Let the revenging of the blood of thy servants which is shed
    Be known among the heathen in our sight.

11   Let the sighing of the prisoner come before thee;
    According to the greatness of thine arm preserve thou the children
        of death;

12   And render unto our neighbours sevenfold into their bosom
    Their reproach wherewith they have reproached thee, O Lord.

13   So we thy people and sheep of thy pasture
    Will give thee thanks for ever:
    We will shew forth thy praise to all generations.

The similarity of Psalm 79 to Psalm 74 is obvious. Both psalms lament the recent desecration of God's sanctuary, and they are the only psalms in the Psalter to do this: Psalm 137 remembers 'the day of Jerusalem' from the rivers of Babylon. *How long, O LORD, wilt thou be angry for ever?* (79.5) recalls Ps. 74.1, 'O God, why hast thou cast off *for ever*?' and 74.10, '*How long, O* God, shall the adversary reproach...*for ever?*'. *We are become a reproach to our neighbours* (79.4), and *render unto our neighbours sevenfold... Their reproach wherewith they have reproached thee, O Lord* (79.12) repeat the theme of 74.10, 'How long, O God, shall the adversary *reproach?*' and 74.18 'Remember this, that the enemy *hath reproached the LORD*'. The honour of God's name is at stake: *Help us...for the glory of thy name...for thy name's sake* (79.9); 'Shall the enemy blaspheme *thy name* for ever?' (74.10), 'a foolish people have blasphemed *thy name*' (74.18). In 74.21 'Let the poor and needy *praise thy name*' parallels 79.13, *We will shew forth thy praise*. Both psalms favour the same animal imagery. *So we thy people and sheep of thy pasture* (79.13), *the flesh of thy saints to the beasts of the earth* (79.2), echo 74.1 'Why doth thine anger smoke against *the sheep of thy pasture?*' and 74.19, 'O deliver not the soul of thy turtledove unto *the wild beast*'. The uncommon יִוָּדַע, *make himself known*, occurs in 79.10 and 74.5.

It seems very likely that the two psalms, both Asaph psalms, refer to the same occasion, and are composed by the same author. Psalm 79 gives more emphasis to the slaughter the Israelite army has suffered (vv. 2-3, 10b), and to the existence of prisoners awaiting sentence of death (v. 11). Psalm 74 describes the desecration of the sanctuary in detail—the setting up of alien religious symbols, the breaking up of carved wood and ivory work, the burning of the shrine. But Psalm 79 has as its principal focus the defilement of the *holy temple*, and there can be little doubt that such an event will have been preceded by a disastrous defeat, even if Psalm 74 does not mention this.

The principal discussion of Psalm 79 has concerned which desecration. Although Duhm and other earlier commentators argued for Antiochus's defilement of 167, most scholars—Delitzsch, Kirkpatrick, Mowinckel (*Psalms*, II, p. 95), Jacquet, Anderson, Tate—have preferred 587. Gunkel objected to this: there was no mention of war, of siege, of king, of the burning of the Temple, of deportations. But the combining of 79 with 74 yields a single picture which does include the firing of the Temple, and we cannot expect every detail of a historical description, such as we have in 2 Kings 25, to recur in a contemporary lament. There can be little doubt that the psalm as we have it is a lament following the fall of Jerusalem in 587.

Kraus notes the dramatic irregularity of the metre, so great that it is difficult to trace any distinctive pattern of rhythm, and suggests that the text has experienced repeated adaptations in the decades after 587; he and Tate give a final date closer to the rebuilding of the Temple. However, there is an element of immediacy in most of the psalm. It is plainly a recent enormity that the heathen should have defiled the sanctuary, and that the dead are lying unburied; and there are prisoners expecting the death sentence. It is difficult to see how a national lament of this kind could have been publicly chanted, with its imprecations upon the invaders, in the situation following the disaster of 587. Nebuzaradan was governing the city, despoiling and burning the Temple, and sending the senior priests to execution at Riblah; some tens of thousands of the educated classes were being marched off to the Euphrates. It is difficult to imagine a scenario for the public recital of Psalm 79 in such an atmosphere. It is better to follow Kraus's suggestion back rather than forward from 587. In the 720s Shalmaneser's armies, and those of their local allies, roamed (Northern) Israel at will. At some critical point they took Bethel, slaughtering the defenders and executing the leading prisoners (probably with torture). But they did not capture Samaria till 722, and having taken what they could from other places they would move on. So the surviving priests would be in a position to give voice to a lament like Psalm 79 in their wake, and to include it in the liturgy of the succeeding autumn festival. Sadly there were to be many subsequent parallel disasters, culminating in Jerusalem in 587, when adaptations could be made, and the text reach its present, apparently contradictory form.

79.1-4. Thine inheritance is probably the land of Israel (Kirkpatrick) rather than the Temple itself: first God's holy land has been invaded, then his *holy Temple* defiled. The third colon mars the climax: *They have laid Jerusalem on heaps* expresses the desolation facing the survivors of 587, but its devastation was a lesser outrage to God than what happened in the היכל קדשך. The third line has been glossed in from the wording of Mic. 3.12, 'Jerusalem shall become heaps (עיין)'. Similarly in v. 3 the RV translation would give a 5:2 rhythm, and *BHS* divides 3:4, against the sense. It is better to think that the original was 3:2 , with סביבות ירושלם glossed in on the basis of לסביבותינו in v. 4.

The situation is grim. Israelites faithful to the covenant (*thy servants, thy devoted ones*—חסידיך) have been slaughtered and left unburied, a prey for vultures and jackals. It is unclear whether the glossed 'round about Jerusalem' was understood of those killed in battle or those executed afterwards (Gunkel). 2 Kings 25 says that Zedekiah's army was defeated near Jericho, and the executions took place at Riblah; the impression given is that the city was undefended, and surrendered from famine, as against the carnage outside the walls here. So the indication is that the original context of Psalm 79 was not 587.

What hurts most, and can be most pressingly urged on Yahweh as a matter for his honour, is the glee of the surrounding peoples, *our neighbours*. No doubt Jeroboam II's successes in the early part of the century had brought loss and humiliation to those *round about*—to Edom and the Ishmaelites, Moab and the Hagarenes, Gebal and Ammon and Amalek, Philistia and Tyre (Ps. 83.7-8). No doubt they had prayed to their gods to *render unto* Israel *sevenfold into their bosom*; and it is hardly surprising that when their hour came they rejoiced, and praised their gods of wood and stone. But to the defeated revenge is bitter.

The power of these verses made them familiar to later generations. Deut. 28.26, 'And thy *dead body* shall be *meat unto* all *fowls of the heaven and unto the* animals *of the earth, and there* shall be *none to* fray them away'. The singular נבלתך is a collective like נבלת in Ps. 79.2; the more normal בהמת replaces the old northern חיתו־ארץ, also found at Ps. 50.10 (Tate). The LXX version of Ps. 79.2-3 is cited at 1 Macc. 7.17 and alluded to in 1 Macc. 1.37. Lam. 1.10 echoes Ps. 79.1, 'For she hath seen that *the heathen are come into* thy *holy* place.'

79.5-9. The description of national humiliation and disgrace now leads on to a plea for divine vindication. The saints' cry, *How long?*, came in Ps. 74.10 and will recur in Ps. 80.4 and later in Ps. 89.47. Yahweh is called upon to direct his *jealous anger* and *wrath* where it belongs, on *the heathen that know* him *not*; his name is used, in place of Asaph's usual *God*/אל, because they are *the kingdoms that call not upon thy name*. The reason is then suitably supplied. *He has devoured Jacob*: the singular אכל is the harder reading, and corresponds with the similar singular reference to the anonymous enemy general in Ps. 73.10. *They have laid waste his pasture* (נוהו) corresponds to the national devastation of Ps. 74.8, and the *pasture* image to *the sheep of thy pasture* (מרעיתך) of Ps. 79.13 (cf. Ps. 80.2).

The importance of this exposition of Ps. 79.6-7 as a clear sequence of thoughts, natural to its context, is that the verses have a close parallel at

Jer. 10.25, '*Pour out thy wrath* upon *the heathen that know thee not, and upon* the families *that call not upon thy name; for* they *have devoured Jacob,* yea, they have devoured him and consumed him, *and have laid waste his pasture*'. Jeremiah is secondary. (1) The context is loose: the verse follows a prophecy of coming desolation (10.22) and prayer for the prophet's personal correction to be 'not in thine anger' (10.23-24). (2) Ps. 79.6a's preposition אל, *to*, is improved with על, as in 79.6b. (3) Psalm 79's ממלכות, *kingdoms,* is replaced by משפחות, *clans,* as used also in Jer. 1.15. (4) The singular אכל is improved to the more natural plural. (5) The singular *he has devoured* is expanded with *yea, they have devoured him and consumed him.* We should conclude that Psalm 79 was in liturgical use in Jeremiah's time/that of his D-redactor, and that is why its wording was so influential, not only on him, but on Lamentations 1 and Deuteronomy 28.

The psalmist falls back on the standard explanation of disaster, God's punishment of sins. In v. 9 Yahweh is prayed to *purge away our sins.* In v. 8 they are the עונת ראשנים, taken by RV, Delitzsch, Gunkel, Kraus and others to be *the iniquities of our forefathers*, and by Eaton, Tate and others to be *our former iniquities.* The RV rendering is more likely in view of the stress on the disobedience of the forefathers in the desert in Psalm 78, and the same theme recurs in Ps. 81.12, 'But my people hearkened not to my voice [at Meribah]'. The sense of corporate guilt over generations will come to frequent expression as the *Vergeltungs-dogma* of the D-corpus; but there is an important difference. In the D-history Israel's sin is the worship of alien gods, on high places, and so forth. There is no clear sign of such a charge in the Asaph psalms, and it is markedly absent from the reproaches of Psalm 50; indeed in the virtually contemporary Korah psalms it is said, 'If we have forgotten the name of our God, And held up our hands to any strange god, Shall not God search this out?' (Ps. 44.21-22). The charge of alien worship is a development of the seventh century, associated especially with Manasseh; it was not relevant in eighth-century Israel, and the Asaphic form of the *Vergeltungsdogma* precedes and lacks this element. In the same way the Asaph psalms appeal to Yahweh's *name* (79.6, 9); but the Deuteronomists have still to develop a Name theology, whereby Yahweh's Name is a virtually independent hypostasis, dwelling in the Temple while he is in heaven.

79.10-13. In Psalm 44 'the enemy and avenger'/'the adversary and they which hate us'—that is, the Assyrians—are distinguished from 'our neighbours/them that are round about us'—that is, Edom, etc.—for whom Israel has become a reproach, scorn, byword and shaking of the head. No such distinction between lioness and jackals is to be perceived in Psalm 79. The invading גוים of v. 1 can hardly be different from the reproachful, scornful neighbours of v. 4, for the גוים of v. 10 ask the scornful question, *Where is their God?*; the divine revenge for the massacre is to be *made known among the* גוים in v. 10bc, and *our neighbours* are to have *their reproach rendered sevenfold into their bosom* in v. 12. The insistence with which the poet returns to this theme is itself evidence of the military involvement of the local states. There are Assyrian armies in the country, as Shalmaneser's inscriptions show. But the Israelites' experience is as in Psalm 83. Moabites and Ammonites remembered when Israel had made them lie down on the ground in defeat, and inflicted hideous penalties; now they had come to get their own back, and Asshur was an arm to the children of Lot.

The recent date of the disaster is again shown by v. 11. *The prisoner*, usually understood as a collective, אסיר, is *sighing* in his manacles; he is taken to be the same as *the children of death* in the parallel colon. In Psalm 68 David held a victory parade after the battle of Zalmon in the forest of Ephraim; he led his captives in triumph, before smiting through their hairy scalps, and dipping his foot in their blood (68.19-24), but he spared Amasa, their general (2 Sam. 19.13). Psalm 49, a Korah psalm from a closer date (Goulder, *Korah*, pp. 181-95), warns the invader, 'None can by any means redeem his brother, Nor give to God a ransom for him' (49.8): prisoners of war might hope to be ransomed from their captors, but ruthless bloodlust was the victor's prerogative, and the psalmist's preference. In 587 Nebuchadnezzar put the leading priests and the princes to death, but spared Zedekiah, merely blinding him (2 Kgs 25.6-7, 18-21); so it could be that here too the *prisoner* is distinguished from *the children of death*.

The psalm closes with a vow. God is to see the prisoners released (v. 11), the Israelite army victorious (v. 9), the invaders given their own back sevenfold (v. 12) in the sight of his people (v. 10), his honour vindicated after the enemies' blasphemies (v. 12b), and he will have performed his side of the covenant. There will be peace in perpetuity; and his festivals will resound with our *thanks* and *his praise* in public recitation and psalm (נספר), in place of lament and reproach. The petition is

moving to human ears; but the heavens were as brass, and there was
neither voice nor answer.

Psalm 80

80.1   For the Chief Musician; at (אל) the Lilies, a testimony. A Psalm of
        Asaph.

2   Give ear, O Shepherd of Israel,
        Thou that leadest Joseph like a flock;
        Thou that sittest upon (RV text) the cherubim, shine forth.

3   Before Ephraim, and Benjamin, and Manasseh, stir up thy might,
        And come to save us.

4   Restore us, O God;
        And cause thy face to shine, and we shall be saved.

Psalm 80 is a natural successor to Psalm 79: 'So we thy people and
sheep of thy pasture Will give thee thanks for ever' (79.13); *Give ear, O
Shepherd of Israel* (80.1). It is a national lament like Psalms 74 and 79.
With v. 5, *How long wilt thou blaze* (עשנת)?, compare Ps. 79.5, 'How
long, O LORD, wilt thou be angry for ever?'; 74.1,'Why doth thine
anger blaze (יעשן) against the sheep of thy pasture?'; 74.10, 'How long,
O God?' With 80.7, *our neighbours...our enemies laugh among themselves*, compare Ps. 79.4, 12. With 80.19, *we will call upon thy name*,
compare the vow in Ps. 79.13 'we will give thee thanks for ever', in
contrast with the heathen in 79.6 'that do not call upon thy name'.
There are links too with other Asaph psalms: God's *shining forth* (הופיע)
comes also in Ps. 50.2; the phrase זיז שדי of 80.14 recurs only at 50.11;
and the leading of the people like a flock was found at 78.52.

     The historical situation presupposed by Psalm 80 is also that of the
720s which we have found to be the probable background of the other
Asaph psalms. The people of God is *Joseph*, as in Ps. 81.6, 'the sons of
Jacob and Joseph' of Ps. 77.16; but now they are specified. God is
prayed to *stir up his might before Ephraim and Benjamin and
Manasseh* (v. 3): that is, he is to be their leader (נהג, v. 2), going into
battle at their head (לפני), and *thy people* (v. 5) consists of these three
tribes. This implies the situation between 732 and 722: Gilead (that is,
Reuben, Gad and E. Manasseh), and Galilee (that is, Dan, Naphtali,
Zebulon, Asher and Issachar) have been annexed by Tiglath-Pileser to
be an Assyrian province, and Judah does not belong. There is no suggestion of exile. The land has been *ravaged* and despoiled (v. 14), *burnt
with fire* (v. 17, as in Ps. 74.7), its people *perish* (v. 17, as in Ps. 79.2-3);

but there is still hope of *victory* (ישׁעות, v. 3), and the repeated prayer is that God will *restore us...and we shall be saved.* For what it is worth, the LXX has a Heading note ὑπὲρ τοῦ 'Ασσυρίου.

Such a historical setting seems clear, and it was clear to Delitzsch, Eissfeldt ('Psalm 80'), Mowinckel (*Psalms*, II, p. 153), Weiser, Jacquet and—at least for a pre-722 northern setting—Gunkel. There has, however, been a natural reluctance to exclude Judah from a psalm which must have been used in Jerusalem; and the third person in v. 6, *Thou hast fed them with the bread of tears*, has seemed a hint that Judah is praying for her northern brothers. So Kirkpatrick aligns Psalm 80 with the prayers of Jeremiah and Ezekiel for a reunited Israel, and dates the psalm c. 570, during the Exile; Kraus thinks of the reign of Josiah, when there were thoughts of expanding north, and Bethel was part of Judah, and there are similar suggestions by Eaton and Tate. Beyerlin ('Schichten') has a complex hypothesis with layers going back into the second millennium.

But although Psalm 80 fits so comfortably in this way into the Asaph sequence, it is also strikingly different from Psalms 74 and 79. It has a complex heading which they lack. It has a marked refrain in vv. 4, 8, 20, for which they have no comparable feature. There is a detailed reference to God's throne in v. 2, and a fourfold use of the ancient name צבאות. These features combine to give a note of urgency, even of desperation, more acute than that of the earlier Asaph psalms.

Lilies, a testimony is not the name of an old Israelite melody (Kirkpatrick), like *Cwm Rhondda*, nor a lost musical instrument (Anderson), nor an indication of taking omens from flowers (Mowinckel, *Psalmenstudien*, IV, pp. 29-33; *Psalms*, II, pp. 214). Lilies were a royal symbol in Israel as in France, and they were engraved on capitals over the portico surrounding the royal court. Thirty-four such capitals have been discovered, all from royal centres in ninth-/eighth-century Israel; the design is originally Egyptian, and is developed into the Proto-Aeolic (and later the Ionic) capital in Greek architecture. We have such masonry referred to in the description of Solomon's great pillars outside the Temple: 'And the chapiters that were upon the top of the pillars in the porch were of lily work, four cubits' (שׁושׁן מעשׂה, 1 Kgs 7.19, cf. 22). So, אל־שׁושׁנים means *At Lilies* (אל being the equivalent of the normal Hebrew על, as at Ps. 79.6 אל־הגוים, where the parallel in Jer. 10.25 has על־). *Lilies* was the name for the courtyard of the royal shrine at Bethel; as Amaziah its priest said to Amos, 'prophesy not again any more at Beth-el: for it is the king's sanctuary and the temple for the kingdom' (ובית ממלכה, Amos 7.13).

The remaining psalms of the series have no indication of a particular location, and will have been chanted in the great natural theatre between the slopes of 'Ebal' and 'Gerizim' (Deut. 27.11-14, cf. above pp. 47-49). Psalm 80 is different: it is chanted *at Lilies*, the Temple courtyard being named after its principal architectural feature, like the Unter den Linden in Berlin or the Arc de Triomphe in Paris. Psalm 45 was similarly sung על־שושנים at Dan, with the king taking his 'eternal' throne, and the hand of his less permanent new wife, to the strains of stringed instruments from his ivory-decked palace; only in this case Biran has excavated the site and uncovered the throne-base, and three of its four carved pillar-holders (Goulder, *Korah*, pp. 123-24). For the same heading to Psalms 60, 69, see Goulder (*Prayers*, pp. 142, 218).

There is a photograph of a proto-Aeolic capital from Hazor in Yadin ('Excavations', pl. 9B, reproduced opposite p. 147 in my *Korah*); Yadin dates the capital to the reign of Ahab (p. 79). Other examples survive from Samaria, Megiddo and Ramath Rahel. W.B. Dinsmoor traces the Greek capital back to Egyptian fleur-de-lys patterns, and associates Solomon's 'lily-work' with it (*Architecture*, pp. 59-61). The identification of the motif as a lily is not universal: see Y. Shiloh, who takes the design to represent a palm-tree (*Proto-Aeolic Capital*, pp. 26-28).

Psalm 80 is headed also עדות, normally rendered *A testimony*. We have already met the term in Ps. 78.5, 'For he established *a testimony* in Jacob, And appointed a law in Israel', that there should be a recital of his wondrous works from generation to generation: thus a testimony in the sense of a permanent witness to the divine providence. It recurs in Ps. 81.6, 'He appointed it in Joseph for *a testimony*', where the matter referred to is the blowing of the *shofar* in the festal month. Here the witness is given not by a verbal recital, but by a ritual act: the sounding of the *shofar* is an acted witness to the presence of the God of insistent demand and ultimate succour at his feast. This gives a clear meaning to the present heading also. Psalm 80 is a *ritual* psalm, celebrated in the Temple courtyard, whose action is *a testimony* to the presence and action of God.

The ritual element accompanying the psalm is suggested by the repeated reference to the cultic symbol within the Bethel shrine. God is *enthroned upon the cherubim* (ישׁב הכרובים): there is inside the בית (or was before the Assyrians burnt and defiled it), a throne such as we have portrayed in ivories from the Euphrates, with sphinx-like figures to left and right supporting the central seat. Such were the six-winged seraphim in the Jerusalem Temple as seen by the prophetic eye of Isaiah;

and their features are alluded to in the great vision of the throne in Ezekiel 1, as of lion, bull, man and eagle. We may think of such a throne of the invisible God as the cultic focus at Bethel also. Perhaps the bull symbol was more greatly emphasized than the lion and the man; for the libellous D-historian can defame Jeroboam as making 'two calves of gold', and representing them as idols, one in Bethel and the other in Dan (1 Kgs 12.25-33; cf. Goulder, *Korah*, pp. 60-65).

The nature of the divine throne, and the use of the name יהוה אלהים צבאות in its variant forms, have been extensively studied by T.D.N. Mettinger (*Dethronement*; 'YHWH Sabaoth'; *In Search of God*. The 1982 article is particularly relevant).

Bulls were dangerous symbols in view of their history in Canaanite religion, and others before the D-historian saw idolatry lurking in them. Hosea can say, 'And now they sin more and more, and have made themselves molten images of their silver, idols according to their own understanding, all of them the work of the craftsmen: they say of them, Let the sacrificers of men kiss the calves' (Hos. 13.2-3). The 80th psalmist is worshipping God enthroned upon the cherubim; but the prophet senses that to many the bull-figures are themselves of divine power, and are nothing but silver idols. Perhaps the Israelite's prostration and kissing of the base of the divine throne was as innocent as the pious Catholic kissing the bronze toe of St Peter in Rome; but the prophet can smell idolatry as surely as Dr Paisley, the Ulster prophet, can smell Popery.[1]

Why are the images *of their silver* when the central tradition speaks so often of a *golden calf*? Perhaps the gold has been melted down and taken to adorn a temple in Nineveh. *And now they...have made them* suggests a recent innovation; *of their silver* may reflect that silver is all they have left, like Rehoboam's brass replacements for Solomon's golden shields (1 Kgs 14.25-28). What is implied by *the sacrificers of men*? Ps. 68.19 also speaks of God receiving מתנות באדם, human sacrifices; the rebel leaders who process in David's victory parade, before being ceremonially put to death (cf. p. 136). Hosea's זבחי אדם probably implies a similar national occasion; though H.W. Wolff (*Hosea*, p. 225) thinks the images are small figurines, and the sacrifices are of Israelite first-born children.

The kissing of silver calves in Hosea sounds like the more respectable 'O come, let us worship and bow down; Let us kneel before the LORD our Maker' of Ps. 95.6. Indeed the collection in Book IV (90–106) offers a number of parallels to Psalm 80. The next verse, Ps. 95.7, runs, 'For

1. Northern Ireland politician; Protestant and Loyalist.

he is our God, And we are the people of *his pasture and the flock* of his hand' (עם מרעיתו וצאן ידו). Psalm 99 opens, 'The LORD reigneth; let the peoples tremble: *He sitteth upon* the *cherubim*' (ישב כרובים, 99.1). Ps. 96.6 speaks of the four 'virtues' symbolized above the ark and in his throne: 'Honour and majesty are before him: Strength and beauty are in his sanctuary' (cf. Exod. 25.10-22). Ps. 94.1 appeals, 'Thou God to whom vengeance belongeth, *shine forth* (הופיע).'

All this suggests a ritual background for Psalm 80. It involves a procession of the king, the chief priests and other notables into the shrine itself. There they prostrate themselves before the throne of mercy, *bowing down and kneeling*, and no doubt *kissing* the bull-figures at the foot of the throne—once independent subordinate gods in a Canaanite pantheon, now extensions of the one God of Israel in his invisible majestic presence (Goulder, *Korah*, pp. 112-14). We may think, following Hosea, that the ruin of Psalms 74 and 79 has been repaired, and that a silver replacement has been made for the earlier golden throne. The ark at Shiloh, borne forth to battle, was spoken of as 'the ark of the covenant of the LORD of hosts who sits upon the cherubim' (יהוה צבאות ישב הכרבים, 1 Sam. 4.4); David brings the ark into Jerusalem, 'the ark of God whereupon is called the Name, even the name of the LORD of hosts who sits upon the cherubim' (2 Sam. 6.2); and in the hour of national military crisis Hezekiah turns to pray to the 'LORD of hosts, the God of Israel, that sittest upon the cherubim' (Isa. 37.16). So יהוה/אלהים צבאות is understood as the title of Yahweh as an 'ancient war-god' (Gunkel), seated upon his cherubic throne. צבאות was taken to mean *armies*, Israelite and angelic; but it was in fact an ancient *name* of God, a plural of pantheon like אלהים—hence the 'impossible' אלהים צבאות (Gunkel).

God is prayed to *shine forth* (הופיעה), to *cause his face to shine* (האר פניך). This is sometimes understood to stand for a miraculous, or perhaps subjective, 'theophany' in the Temple, an omen of the coming deliverance. This cannot be excluded, for the Korahite psalmists spoke of going to 'see the face of God' (Pss. 42.3; 84.8), and of processing 'in the light of thy countenance' (Ps. 89.16). But Deut. 33.2 speaks of Yahweh *shining forth* from Mount Paran in a storm, and in the Asaphite Ps. 50.2-3. God *shines forth* with a fire before him and a tempest round about him; and the same is implied in Ps. 94.1 as Yahweh comes to judge the earth. So it is likely that this is the central force of the expressions in Ps. 80.2-4 also. God is to *stir up* his *might*, as he 'awaked as one out of sleep, Like a mighty man that shouteth by reason of wine' in

Ps. 78.65. He is to *shine forth* and *cause his face to shine* in the lightning, as he comes to judge the earth; and so *we shall be saved*. That will be more like a real theophany.

Tate adduces Ugaritic evidence for the use of *y-p-ʿ* for divine assistance in battle.

80.5	O LORD God of hosts,
	How long wilt thou be angry against the prayer of thy people?
6	Thou hast fed them with the bread of tears,
	And given them tears to drink in large measure.
7	Thou makest us a strife unto our neighbours:
	And our enemies laugh among themselves.
8	Turn us again, O God of hosts;
	And cause thy face to shine, and we shall be saved.

The prayer of vv. 2-4 now turns to a lament. The cry goes up, *How long?* The Hebrew עשנת means *have you been angry and continue so to be?*; the root is associated with *smoke*, but the frequent translation *fume* is quite inadequate. *Against* is perhaps too strong: ב merely implies *at* the prayer. *Tears*, a diet of disaster, impoverishment and misery, have indeed been Israel's destiny since 732: God has ladled it out by the quart, as we would say, שליש, a *third*, perhaps of an ephah. The hateful *neighbours* once more rub salt in the wounds: they not only *laugh among themselves*, but they make Israel מדון, *an object of contention*—they quarrel among themselves over the division of the spoil. We have here a further hint of the alliance of client peoples which the Assyrians have got together, and whose names appear in Ps. 83.6-8.

The recurrence of the 'refrain' verse in vv. 4, 8, 20 has suggested (for example to Eaton) some form of congregational response. The first colon of the verses varies a little, perhaps to form a climax: *O God* (v. 4), *O God Zebaʾot* (v. 8), *O Yahweh God Zebaʾot* (v. 20). Maybe the מנצח, who is there in the Heading but without a Selah passage to cantillate, has something to do with it.

80.9	Thou broughtest a vine out of Egypt:
	Thou didst drive out the nations, and plantedst it.
10	Thou preparedst *room* before it,
	And it took deep root, and filled the land.
11	The mountains were covered with the shadow of it,
	And the cedars of God with the boughs thereof.
12	She sent out her branches unto the sea,
	And her shoots unto the River.
13	Why hast thou broken down her fences,
	So that all they which pass by the way do pluck her?

80.14 The boar out of the wood doth ravage it,
And the wild beasts of the field feed on it.

15 Turn again, we beseech thee, O God of hosts:
Look down from heaven, and behold, and visit this vine,

16 And protect that which thy right hand hath planted,
And the son that thou madest strong for thyself.

17 It is burned with fire, it is cut down:
They perish at the rebuke of thy countenance.

18 Let thy hand be upon the man of thy right hand,
Upon the son of man whom thou madest strong for thyself.

19 So shall we not go back from thee:
Quicken thou us, and we will call upon thy name.

20 Turn us again, O LORD God of hosts:
Cause thy face to shine, and we shall be saved.

80.9-12. The vine symbolized Joseph from early times: 'Joseph is the son (בֵּן) of a fruitful tree, the son of a fruitful tree by a fountain; Its branches (בָּנוֹת) run over the wall' (Gen. 49.22). Hosea spoke of Israel/ 'Ephraim' as 'a luxuriant vine which putteth forth his fruit' (Hos. 10.1); God will 'cast forth his roots as Lebanon. His branches shall spread... they that dwell under his shadow shall return; they shall revive *as* the corn, and blossom as the vine' (Hos. 14.5-7). The psalmist exploits the traditional image to pathetic effect. Joseph was *a vine* transplanted from *Egypt*—as in Psalms 77, 78 and 81 the beginning of the *Heilsgeschichte*. *The nations* were *driven* from the land as in Exod. 15.14-16, to enable it to be *planted* in, נטע, as in Exod. 15.17. God carefully *prepared* space for it and *it took deep root*. The image is allowed full play: the vine-*boughs* covered *the mountains* of Lebanon *with its shadow*, and *the cedars of God* that grow there. The reference is to David's exaction of tribute from Hamath in Lebanon (2 Sam. 8.9-11), and the more recent conquest of the city by Jeroboam II (2 Kgs 14.28): the traditional northern boundary of Israel was the pass of Hamath (1 Kgs 8.65). The *branches* extended *to the* Mediterranean *Sea* on the one side, and the Euphrates *River* on the other, as in 1 Kgs 5.1-4 and other triumphalist texts.

Deut. 11.24 sets the boundaries as 'from the wilderness and Lebanon, from the river, the river Euphrates unto the western sea', and Delitzsch and others interpret Ps. 80.11 as similarly covering the four points of the compass; but *the mountains* naturally refer to the 10,000 ft range to the north, with *the cedars of God* in parallel, not to the southern *wilderness*. The Asaphite liking for a play on words is again in evidence in v. 10, פָּנִיתָ לְפָנֶיהָ—cf. below on v. 18, אִישׁ יְמִינֶךָ.

80.13-17. The psalmist now turns to draw a moving contrast between the greatness of Israel's past and her present evil condition. God has *broken down her fences*, the walls or thorn-hedges with which the Israelite farmer protected his vineyard (Isa. 5.5; Lk. 14.23); the tramps and thieves can walk along, *pass by*, and help themselves, *pluck it*. Israel's enemies are once more portrayed as wild animals (Pss. 74.19; 76.5; 79.7), *the* Assyrian *boar from the forest*, and the lesser *wild beasts of the field*. God is prayed to *look down from heaven, to behold* the pathetic sight, and to *visit this vine*, to take prompt action. *The son that thou madest strong for thyself* is correctly understood by RV text as *the branch*: the Joseph text cited above from Gen. 49.22 spoke of the tribe as a בֵּן of a fruit-plant whose בָּנוֹת climb over the wall—the 'son' is the main shoot and the 'daughters' are the side-branches. The first half of the verse is more problematic, but the general meaning is not in dispute.

The opening word כַּנָּה is a hapax. The Syriac and Vulgate take it as a noun, a *stock, root*, as does the Targum (כבא), and this is accepted by Anderson and Tate (*nursery stock*). Gunkel and Kraus render *its garden*, reading גנה. Delitzsch and a majority of commentators understand it as the imperative of a presumed כנן, and translate *And protect that which...*; this was the interpretation of LXX, and of RV mg.

זיז שׂדי in v. 14 has been variously understood. Tate cites translations *the leader boar* and some form of *insect* predator; but the phrase recurs in the (Asaphite) Ps. 50.11, where the sense is most naturally *the wild animals of the countryside*.

80.18-20. It is not only the *people*, Joseph, the 'son' of the vine, that God has *strengthened for himself*; it is also *the man of his right hand, the son of man*, the king Hoshea, whom he has empowered for the same end. God's purpose has been evident from the beginning, the establishment of his vine to fill his land: he declared it in his covenant (Ps. 81.11-16), and he brought it to pass in history (Pss. 78.65-66, 70-72; 80.9-12). It is *for himself* that God has made his people formidable; and the harassed king's wisdom and leadership have seen them through some troubled years and still inspire confidence.

There is so little that a people facing extinction has to offer its God in exchange for its deliverance. The psalmist promises faithfulness and worship: *we shall not go back from thee, we shall call upon thy name*. But nowhere in the Asaph corpus is it suggested that there has been worship of any other god, and king and people have called on Yahweh's name repeatedly; it is less than a decade since the fellow-priest at Dan was boldly maintaining, 'Our heart is not turned back (לֹא־נָסוֹג again), Neither have our steps declined from thy way' (Ps. 44.19; Goulder, *Korah,* pp. 85-98). The bankrupt has nothing to pledge but his good intentions. Or he may try one last repeated appeal of faith: *Restore us, Yahweh, God of* the invincible heavenly *hosts*; Cease your incomprehensible anger, *Cause your face to shine*—that is all you have to do, and *we shall be saved.*

Delitzsch and Gunkel favour seeing a link between איש ימינך in v. 18 and בנימן in v. 3, *Benjamin, the son of the right hand*; and reference is made to Genesis 48, where Jacob's right hand is laid on Ephraim, in symbol of the highest blessing. Kraus is wise to be sceptical here: if the psalmist had intended the play on words, he could have written בן ימינך. The *right hand* of the Most High came also at Ps. 77.11.

The Liturgical Theory

It is obvious that both 79 and 80 are public psalms, both of them national laments. I have argued that the setting of Psalm 80 can be defined more exactly. It is an עדות, a ritual psalm whose enactment was a *testimony* to Israel. It was chanted *at the Lilies*, in the courtyard of the Bethel temple, whose porticoes were ornamented with carved lily-work on the capitals. The ritual involved the prostration of king and priests before Yahweh 'Elohim Zeba'oth, whose invisible presence was understood as *seated upon the* winged-bull *cherubim*-throne within the temple. Such an action was the climax of a series of appeals made under threat of national catastrophe—Psalms 73, 74, 77, 79, 80; the workers' leader may begin with words from a distance, but the ultimate step must be to call on the Managing Director in person in his or her office. It may be that a personal request from a humble delegation will yet move the Board to withdraw the dismissal.

It is not difficult to see, then, why Psalm 80 comes as the climax to the Asaph laments; or why laments form so large a proportion of the series. Priest and king are standing on the verge of the unthinkable. Faith may from time to time raise its diffident head (Pss. 73.17-29; 74.12-17; 77.11-21), but reality presses in relentlessly—the slaughter of the army, the devastation of every shrine in the land, the desecration and burning of the national temple, the arrogant imposition of harsh terms, the erection of heathen images, the derision of neighbouring peoples.

It is this crisis which has brought about the need for new psalms, and for a modification of the traditional festal ritual as we find it in the Korah sequences. We still have a pilgrimage psalm to open the season (Ps. 50, 'Gather my devoted ones together unto me'); a day of pre-festival lamentation (73, 74); the consecration of the king for war (75); the celebration of God's power in battle (76). So far the Asaph series follows the Korah sequences step by step, as I have argued above. But thereafter the pattern of worship has been adjusted to meet the needs of the hour. The king's night of meditation (77) comes earlier in the week than did the Korah night of desolation (88). The recalling of God's wondrous works in Psalm 78 is of far different length and emphasis than the same theme in Psalm 47. There is no celebration of the inviolability of God's city (48, 87): how could there be after the events referred to in Psalm 79? The prostration of the national leaders before the divine throne in Psalm 80 has some echoes of the carrying of the ephod in procession in Psalm 47, but there are much closer parallels in Book IV.

The plausibility of the liturgical theory for the Asaph psalms rests in part on the sequential similarity with the Korah series, but partly also on particular features—the gathering in the opening psalm, 50; the references to the festival in 81; the climax in the judgment of the gods in 82; the possibility of explaining the collection as a whole. It does not count against the hypothesis that it does not follow the Korah pattern step by step without alteration; if it had been acceptable to do so, there would have been no need to compose a new psalmody. New liturgies are devised to meet new needs, and it is their nature to build in part, but only in part, on earlier worship patterns: Cranmer's Holy Communion follows the mediaeval Latin Mass much of the way, but changes have been made in favour of the thought of Bucer and the piety of Osiander. So it may well be that the Asaph series provided psalms for the autumn festal week at Bethel, rather than the occasional *Bussfeier* supposed by Mowinckel; that Psalm 79 was chanted on the 18th Bul and Psalm 80 on the 19th, in the last years of Hoshea's reign. We shall see reasons for siting Psalm 81 on 20th and Psalm 82 on 21st.

Chapter 6

THE NEW YEAR CELEBRATIONS

Psalm 81

81.1   For the Chief Musician; at the Gittite *quarter* (עַל־הַגִּתִּית).
       A Psalm of Asaph.
2   Sing aloud unto God our strength:
       Make a joyful noise unto the God of Jacob.
3   Take up the psalm, and strike the timbrel,
       The pleasant harp with the psaltery.
4   Blow up the trumpet in the new season (בַחֹדֶשׁ),
       At the full moon, for (לְ) our solemn feast day.
5   For it is a statute for Israel,
       An ordinance of the God of Jacob.
6   He appointed it in Joseph for a testimony,
       When he went out over the land of Egypt.

After so many laments, Psalm 81 opens with a marked change of tone: there is celebration, joy and the sounding of music. But the psalm divides into two parts, so sharply differentiated that earlier commentators, such as Olshausen and Duhm, saw them as two distinct psalms. The summons to festal rejoicing lasts for only five verses, and then gives way to a further homily, not unlike Psalm 78 in impact. God calls his people to hear, and to obey; he delivered them in Egypt and gave them his law; but they did not hearken, and he gave them up; if only they had listened, all would have been well. The festival has all the jollity of Christmas in a nineteenth-century orphanage.

Although the opening tone is so different from Psalms 77, 78, 79 and 80, the historical sermonizing is very similar. The preacher begins from the oppression in Egypt, as in Psalm 78, from the Exodus as in Psalms 77, 78 and 80. He stresses the disobedience of the wilderness, again as in Psalm 78; and concludes, as there, that further deliverance is still possible. The call, 'Hear, O my people', with its prophetic-sounding challenge, is reminiscent of the similar charge in Psalm 50. So Psalm 81 belongs securely with the Asaph collection; and this is confirmed by its use of *Joseph* for the people in v. 6, as in Pss. 77.16, 78.67 and 80.2. The historical situation which we have found to underlie the remainder of the collection will then suggest an explanation for the form of Psalm 81 too. It is the time of the big day of the festival, יום חגנו, and on this day the custom, the חק לישראל, was music and dancing, blowing the שופר and singing. But the rejoicing is rather muted, with the land in devastation, and annihilation staring the community in the face. So the best thing is to keep singing, but to repent at the same time. Hence the combination of a short hymn and a longer historical homily.

The mention of Joseph (actually יהוסף) in v. 6 as the name of the people seemed to Gunkel to indicate a Northern Israelite locus for the psalm; and also the prophetic tone of the second section, reminiscent of Hosea (wilderness) and Amos (condemnation of vacuous festivals). He is followed by Mowinckel (*Psalms*, II, p. 95; though cf. p. 72n), Weiser and Dahood. Other commentators—Delitzsch, Kirkpatrick, Anderson, Jacquet—think of Josiah's reign, in view of the Deuteronomic language; but there is another explanation for this, and Josiah's hope of regaining northern territory does not adequately account for *in Joseph* (v. 6).

The heading note על־הגתית is obscure. 81 was a festival psalm (v. 4), and is likely to have been used later at the Jerusalem autumn festival with a procession of the ark (1 Kgs 8.1-2; Kraus, *Worship*, pp. 183-88). The original form of this procession is said to have begun from the house of Obed–Edom the Gittite (2 Sam. 6.10-12). We might think then that whereas the other Asaph psalms, apart from Psalm 80, have no note of location (על־), and were chanted in the Temple enclosure when taken over in Jerusalem, Psalm 81 was in use at the beginning of the procession, and was sung *at the Gittite quarter*. The same note occurs at the head of Psalms 8 and 84; 84 is also a processional psalm at the beginning of a festal series (cf. Mowinckel, *Psalms*, II, p. 215; Goulder, *Korah*, p. 41).

The psalmist calls for the expression of national rejoicing. The whole people can join in the chanting (הרנינו) and joyful crying (הריעו); but the hidden agenda is not too far to seek. The singing and shouting are *to God our strength*, that is *our defence* in the present hour of peril. The musicians are to *take up the rhythm*, זמרה, the music, as in Amos 5.22. The *timbrel*, or tambourine, is to be *struck* by the women (Exod. 15.20; Ps. 68.26). Temple musicians must play the *pleasant lyre*, and the *psaltery* or zither. The *blowing of the* great horn *trumpet* was the prerogative of the priests (Josh. 6.1-21). So the whole community is charged to join in, each according to his or her status and skill. Such a united display of loyalty should please the divine protector.

There is general agreement that *our feast* is the autumn festival, *the* feast (1 Kgs 8.2), the feast of Yahweh (Hos. 9.5; Judg. 21.19; Lev. 23.39; against Delitzsch and Gunkel, who favoured Passover); but two points are unclear. (1) Which day of the feast is *the day*? (2) Do the two halves of the verse refer to the same occasion, or two separate ones?

(1) The autumn festival was in early times called חג האסיף, the Feast of Ingathering. It is the last of the three great festivals in the early calendars (Exod. 23.14-16; 34.18-23), and is, following its name, a thanksgiving for the year's harvest; the threshing-floor and wine-press are mentioned in Deut. 16.13. However, the close of the old year was also seen as the beginning of the new one: Exod. 34.22 says it is to be celebrated *at the turn* (תקופת) *of the year*, and Exod. 23.16 *at the going forth* (בצאת) *of the year*.

The beginning of New Year will therefore have been originally reckoned as the *end* of the week's festival of Ingathering, that is 21st Bul in Northern Israel, where Bul (= harvest) was the festal month (Ethanim = Tishri, a month earlier, in Jerusalem). With time New Year, ראש השנה, was felt to belong at *the beginning* of the feast which was now called Tabernacles, and given a spurious connection with the so-called dwelling in booths in the wilderness (Lev. 23.43). In Ezek. 40.1 the 10th Tishri has become New Year; in Lev. 23.23-25 the 1st Tishri has become an independent feast, and in Num. 29.1 'it is a day of blowing of trumpets'. But in early times New Year was part of, and in some sense the climax of, the autumn festival—when the year 'turned', and 'went forth'.

With the transfer of New Year to an independent day, the importance of the last day of the feast lapsed, and there is no significant ritual appointed for it in the mishnaic tractate Sukkah. Its position was however retained in folk memory, and we find reference in John's Gospel to 'the last day, the great day of the feast [of Tabernacles]' (Jn 7.37). The words of Jesus in the following discourse, 'If any man thirst, let him come unto me, and drink... I am the light of the world' (Jn 7.38; 8.12) are often understood to reflect the contemporary use of the last day of the feast: it was *especially* the day of the drawing of water, and of the towers of illumination (*m. Suk.* 4.1; 5.2-4). These rituals were in any case forward-looking: Tabernacles closed the long summer, and there was need to pray for the autumn rains, and (primitively) for the perseverance of light through the winter. Nor is it believable that a

festival lasting a week should lack a climax. So the most natural understanding of *the day of our feast* seems to be the last day, 'the great day',
21st Bul. A relic of this thinking in fact survives into modern Jewish
liturgy: the cycle of Torah readings begins on the last day of Tabernacles
(now 22nd Tishri, עצרת), and terminates on the same day in the following year.

A similar pattern of worship seemed to underlie Psalm 89, the last
psalm in Book III, whose first, hymnic section formed the conclusion of
the old Korah psalmody (Goulder, *Korah*, pp. 211-28). Ps. 89.16-17
describe a march past the shrine ('They process [יהלכון] in the light
of thy countenance') with the impressive, synchronized shout ('Blessed
is the people that know the תרועה'), and the repeated chanting of
hallelujahs ('In thy name do they rejoice all the day'). The same features
are implied in Ps. 81.1-6. The people are urged to *sing aloud to God*
(הרנינו); but the people do not know the words of Psalm 81, they can
but chant God's name. They are to shout (הריעו), and what they shout
will be the תרועה. The music made so explicit in Ps. 81.3-4 is implied in
the 'rejoicing' of Ps. 89.17. Both festal series ended with a bang.

Such a conclusion is not contradicted by Ps. 81.4, *Blow up the* שופר...
At the full moon (בכסה) *for the day of our feast.* Two of the Israelite
pilgrim-festivals were at full moon, and lasted the week of full moon,
Unleavened Bread, 15-21 Abib/Nisan, and Tabernacles, 15-21 Bul (in
Northern Israel). כסה occurs only once elsewhere in the Old Testament,
in the form כסא: 'He will come home for the day of full moon'
(Prov. 7.20, ליום הכסא). *Full moon* is thought of like our Christmas: it is
both a day (15th) and a season, a week. A modern family may visit the
grandparents at Christmas, that is, either on Christmas Day or during
Christmastide; the over-trustful Israelite husband is returning with his
bag of money *for the day of full moon*, in time for 15th, but the festival
continues through *full moon*, for the whole of the week 15th-21st. So
here the *blowing of the shofar* is commanded בכסה, *in full moon*, that
is, during the full moon week, ליום חגנו, *for the day of our feast*, for the
climactic day, that is, 21st. In the Mishnah the trumpet is blown every
day in the festival (*m. Suk.* 5.5).

We do not know at what time of day our psalms may have been
chanted; Ps. 42.9 says, 'And in the night his song shall be with me', and
Isa. 30.29 speaks of 'a song as in the night when a holy feast is kept', so
we may think perhaps of them as being rendered in the evening. Since
any shouting, singing, timbrel- and lyre-playing, trumpet-blowing, and so

forth will certainly have been in the morning, it would be appropriate for
Psalm 81 to be sung in the evening of 20th, and this would then give
force to the Hebrew ל, *for* the day of our feast, rather than ב, *on* the
day; though this would not be necessary, and the ל might be merely for
variety.

(2) This leaves the problem of בהדשׁ in v. 4a unresolved. The root חדשׁ
means *new*, and it would be attractive to suppose it meant *In the new
[year]*, even though it is widely used, especially in later texts, for *new
[moon]*. This would then give good sense, since *the New [Year]* would
be identical with *the day of our feast*, viz. 21st Bul; it would explain the
absence of any ו linking *in the new [moon]* with *At the full moon*; and it
would avoid the surprising charge to sound the trumpet a fortnight ago.
I should prefer this option; there is no parallel for such a use, but then
New Year is not otherwise referred to in early texts, and in later ones it
has developed the independent title ראשׁ השׁנה. If the standard *in the
new moon* is preferred, we might think that kings of Israel summoned
their people to the festival at New Moon each autumn with the שׁופר:
'till tower and town and hamlet have heard the trumpet's blast'. The
two trumpet-soundings might then be aligned in the psalmist's thought;
as we would put it, 'as in the new moon, so at full moon'. But we have
no evidence of any trumpet-blowing on 1st Tishri in monarchical times,
and the syntax is strained.

The חדשׁ/כסה problem has produced only speculative and implausible solutions.
Kraus, in his commentary, infers a 'fourteen-day festival' from 1st to 15th Tishri (at
Jerusalem); this then has to be in the time of the later calendars in Leviticus 23 and
Numbers 29 which mention 1st; and *Joseph* has to be the name of Israel as a whole
when in Egypt. But even the first part of this structure does not follow the texts. *The
feast of the Lord* in Lev. 23.39 is from 15th-21st, with an extra day on 22nd, and 1st
is another of 'the set feasts' (v. 37). He omits to discuss the question in *Worship in
Israel*. Tate thinks of the possibility of months being counted from full moon.
Mowinckel at first thought a reference to trumpet-blowing on two days to be acceptable (*Psalmenstudien*, II, pp. 81-89), but later havered between the two days, either
1st or 15th (*Psalms*, I, p. 124). The 15th has been generally favoured as *the day of
our feast* simply on the basis of בכסה, understood as *[the day of] full moon*; there is
no other evidence for 15th as *the day* of the festival.

81.5-6b. The psalmist is to give the second two-thirds of his piece to the
importance of Israel's *hearkening*, and *walking in God's ways*; and he
hastens to ground his call for public rejoicing in the *ordinance* God laid
down. It was in fact *appointed in Joseph for a testimony*, that is a rite

which should stand as a witness to God's power to deliver (cf. Ps. 80.1); in the days when God *went out* (בצאתו) *upon the land of Egypt.* In Exod. 11.4 Yahweh says, 'About midnight will I go out (יוצא) into the midst of Egypt'; the synchronization is not intended to be exact—the statute was given shortly after the Exodus, at Meribah. The reference is probably to the משפטים which we have in Exod. 20-23, 34, which include the חג at the going forth of the year (23.16; 34.22); no rejoicing is mentioned in this Book of the Covenant, but that may be assumed, and it is stated in Deut. 16.14.

The tribes which actually came out of Egypt were the *Joseph*-tribes, perhaps with the addition of Benjamin (Ps. 80.2); it is for this reason, and no other, that God is said to have appointed the ordinance *in Joseph.* However, the unification of Israel depended upon the sense of a *shared history*, and we have seen the move to this end in Ps. 77.16, 'Thou hast with thine arm redeemed thy people, *The sons of Jacob and Joseph.*' The Jacob tribes (Reuben, Levi, Zebulun, Issachar, [Judah and Simeon]), and the northern immigrants (Naphtali, Dan, Asher, Gad) needed to be assimilated to the Joseph Exodus experience. So here too it is emphasized as a *national* statute: it is *for Israel*, not just for Joseph, and it was ordained not by the God of Joseph but by *the God of Jacob.* We have the trace of a later attempt to take the history over too. The name is spelt, uniquely, not יוסף but יהוסף. This looks like the attempt of a Judahite editor to alter the text to יהודה, which has been resisted, and the original partly reinstated. We have good cause to be grateful to the obstinate conservative who did this.

P.A.H. de Boer ('Psalm 81.6a') renders, 'It was in (the territory) of Joseph that he instituted it as a testimony; because of his [Joseph's] rising over the land of Egypt' (pp. 76, 73). The lexical analysis is done with all de Boer's learning and care, but the proposed flow of the psalmist's thought seems obscure.

81.6c	I will hearken to a lip that I did not acknowledge (שפת לא־ידעתי אשמע):
7	'I removed his shoulder from the burden: His hands were freed from the basket.
8	Thou calledst in trouble, and I delivered thee; I answered thee in the secret place of thunder: I proved thee at the waters of Meribah (Selah
9	Hear, O my people, and I will testify unto thee: O Israel, if thou wouldest hearken unto me!
10	There shall no strange god be in thee; Neither shalt thou worship any alien (נכר) god.

81.11   I am the LORD thy God,
        Which brought thee up out of the land of Egypt:
        Open thy mouth wide, and I will fill it.

12   But my people hearkened not to my voice;
        And Israel would none of me.

13   So I let them go after the stubbornness of their heart,
        That they might walk in their own counsels.

14   Oh that my people would hearken unto me,
        That Israel would walk in my ways!

15   I should soon subdue their enemies,
        And turn my hand against their adversaries.

16   The haters of the LORD should shrink before him (יכחשו לו):
        And their humiliation (עתם) should endure for ever.

17   But he should feed him (ויאכילהו) also with the fat of wheat:
        And with honey out of the rock should I satisfy thee.'

81.6c. The divine speech which follows in vv. 7-17 is concerned with Israel's failure to *hearken* (שמע) to God: *Hearken, O my people* (v. 9a); *if thou wouldest hearken unto me* (v. 9b); *but my people hearkened not to my voice* (v. 12); *Oh that my people would hearken unto me* (v. 14). שמע is used four times here to emphasize that the disasters which have befallen Israel have come because they *did not hearken* to God, and to urge them to do so in future. The same word אשמע has the same meaning in v. 6c. The speaker, representing the whole people, confesses that he *did not acknowledge* God's commands in the past (לא־ידעתי, I ignored them), but he signifies his intention to *hearken* to them (אשמע) in the future. The divine ways do not burst upon him by a secret revelation: he will hearken *to a lip* (שׂפת) which he had not before acknowledged. God does not have a lip, and it is difficult to find unmediated parallels for שׂפה meaning *speech*. The *lip* is rather that of the מנצח who is about to recite the Selah after v. 8, a passage which there is little problem in identifying. The revelation is no new thing. God delivered it at Meribah centuries ago; it has been regularly recited at the public festival, and as regularly bypassed.

A number of different interpretations have been proposed for v. 6c, for which see Tate; but modern commentators, Tate himself included, go for the 'cultic prophet' interpretation (cf. especially Mowinckel, *Psalmenstudien*, III; Johnson, *Cultic Prophet*). According to this view the psalmist is a prophet on the Temple staff. Mowinckel translates, 'I hear a voice that I know not. "I took the burden from thy back..."'; and comments, 'What will the mystic have heard that the others cannot hear? Suddenly he knows. The unknown voice becomes clear words, these form sentences—and now he tells the people what he has heard' (pp. 38-39).

This interpretation is beset with difficulties. (i) The Hebrew has *I removed his shoulder...* their *hands were freed* (LXX, Syriac: his *hands*). This requires an antecedent for *his, their*, which appears conveniently in v. 6 as *Joseph*. Mowinckel requires a second person for a divine address, and emends the text to *thy... thy*. Johnson (p. 8) and others (*BHS*) propose transferring v. 11b, *Open thy mouth...*, to improve the text still further. (ii) The cultic prophet is *ex hypothesi* a professional, used to hearing and declaring, *Thus says Yahweh...* How then is he supposed to *hear a voice which he has not known [before]*? (iii) To speak of *hearing the lip* of God would be an anthropomorphism of unparalleled crudity. We may contrast the nearest approximation, 'words proceeding from the mouth of God', where the revelation is the *words*, and the anthropomorphism is less shocking. The regular translation of שׂפה as *voice* is forced.

81.7-8. God has spoken at every festival in memory through the *lip* of his tradent, the מנצח, telling the story of the deliverance of Joseph from Egypt, *removing the burden* of bricks *from his shoulder, freeing their hands from the basket* of slavery. We again see the speaker's embarrassment in his attempt to incorporate all Israel in the Exodus experience. Actually, as everyone knew, it was only *Joseph* who had been in slavery on the Egyptian building-sites, so the oppression is spoken of in the third person, *his...his/their*. But the aim is to make everyone feel involved, in the deliverance, in the law-giving and in the disobedience: so in v. 8 the psalmist changes without explanation to the second person, *Thou...thee*, and has God address the people, *O my people...O Israel*. Such subtle incorporation has been practised widely. Lincoln spoke of 'our fathers' at Gettysburg to an audience most of whose fathers had been at the time in Europe, and St Paul used the same words to a mainly Gentile church at Corinth; it is not often that we catch the rhetorician at work between third person and second.

The *burdens* (סבלות) are a regular feature of the Exodus oppression story (Exod. 1.11-14; 5.4; 6.6-7), and the calling to God in trouble is told in Exod. 2.23-25. The Asaph psalmist knows about the plagues (Pss. 78.42-51; 81.6b), and the Exodus (Pss. 78.13, 52; 81.8a), but he proceeds straight to the revelation in the desert, where God *answered thee from the secret place of thunder*, and *proved thee at the waters of Meribah*. Here is a crucial element in the old tradition: the great encounter with God took place not at Sinai but at Meribah, near the southwestern border of modern Israel with Egypt. There is no mention of Sinai (or of a mountain) in any Asaph psalm: Sinai belongs with another tradition (see below, p. 278). I have already suggested that

Ps. 78.41, 'they provoked the Holy One of Israel', was to be explained as a reference to the rebellion at Kadesh/Meribah, where Yahweh 'shewed himself holy (יִקְדַּשׁ) among them' (Num. 20.13). We have an echo of Ps. 81.8bc in the אֱלֹהִים passages in Exodus 19–20. At Exod. 19.19 God *answered* Moses in thunder, and at 20.20 Moses says, 'God has come to test you'. There is a similar reminiscence in the Blessing of Moses, 'with whom thou didst strive at the waters of Meribah' (Deut. 33.8); though here Meribah has been assimilated to Massah, as in the later Ps. 95.8, and Exod. 17.7.

The dominant metre of Psalm 81 is 3:3, and this is broken by the three cola of v. 8. The first, *Thou calledst...*refers to the Exodus. The second two, *I answered thee...I proved thee*, are in parallel and concern a separate event, the *proving at Meribah*. This then leads straight into a Selah. It acts thus as an introduction to a recitation of a part of the wilderness tradition. The rest of the psalm is a homiletic exposition of this recitation, so we are not in doubt as to its theme: it is that God gave the people his covenant at Meribah, and they did not *hearken*. At first blush this might allow for many possibilities, but here we may reflect reassuringly that hitherto we have usually found considerable verbal echoes in the Asaph psalms with clusters of phrases in our Pentateuch; and these might then plausibly be taken to be the core of the relevant Selah. Thus the Selah at Ps. 77.10 followed a series of rhetorical questions, each of which contained wording in common with Exod. 34.6-7; that at Ps. 77.16 followed a sequence of phrases recalling Exodus 15. We may therefore expect a similar habit of writing in Psalm 81: as we go through the remainder of the psalm we may note any Pentateuchal echoes, and if there should be any marked cluster of such, take that as an indication of the Selah passage recited after v. 8.

81.9-11. How then did God *prove* Israel *at the waters of Meribah?* There is no suggestion of any murmuring, or requiring of water, or of water from a rock: the event takes place *at the waters* of Meribah because Meribah was an oasis, and the Josephites had settled by an oasis. This is not Israel testing (נִסָּה) God, but God proving (בָּחַן) Israel. No: rather it was at Meribah/Kadesh, that the Josephites met the challenge (אֲבַחֶנְךָ), *I, Yahweh, am thy God, Which brought thee up out of the land of Egypt.* By the 720s, and for many years before, it had been accepted that the God who brought Israel up out of Egypt was Yahweh; but it is likely that the worship of Yahweh was introduced not by Joseph and

Benjamin, but by Moses and the Levites, from Jethro his priest in
Midian (Exod. 2–3). The God whom the Josephites had come to worship at Kadesh was 'El: his priest was called Reuel (רעואל, 'El is my
kin), and the people was called Israel, like other southern tribes, Ishmael
and Jerahmeel; their shrine was called Bethel, and they still had, in the
eighth century, a preference for speaking of God as אל. It was only after
the covenant at Shechem that their leader Hoshea took the name
Yehoshea, Joshua, and it was agreed that אל was a word for God, and
יהוה was his name. But the people had not been worshippers of 'El in
Egypt, and it is normal for a change of religious allegiance to be resisted
by conservatives: so God's *proving* of Israel, and the people's failure to
hearken, will be echoes of tensions and rebellions long ago, now buried
under the parallel story of the Golden Calf. For a fuller discussion see
Chapters 11–13.

The challenge was also a promise, *Open thy mouth wide, and I will
fill it.* Yahweh was the God who had brought about the deliverance
from Egypt, and Yahweh would provide for them in plenty. For those
who live by oases on the margin of the desert of rock and sand, such a
promise is vital; and it was not less welcome as an assurance at harvest-
time each year when incursions of enemy soldiers had brought
widespread pillage and vandalism, and starvation was again a threat.

Attempts to spiritualize these words (Gunkel, Weiser, Tate) should be resisted. The
literal meaning is the natural reading, and is borne out by v. 17: suggestions that *thy
mouth* is that of 'the prophet', and that it is to be filled with the word of the Lord,
and that the verse would go better after v. 6c, are all part of the misguided 'cultic
prophet' theory.

81.9, Hear, O my people, and I will testify unto thee; O Israel... closely
echoes Ps. 50.7, 'Hear, O my people, and I will speak; O Israel, and I
will testify unto thee'. Both verses follow a Selah; both speak in the
name of God; both continue with the divine self-proclamation—'I am
God, thy God' (Ps. 50.7), *I am Yahweh thy God* (Ps. 81.11). Both then
lead into homiletic rebukes for faithlessness, and calls for obedience in
future. It is likely to be the same writer at work. In Ps. 81.10 Yahweh's
claim to be Israel's *sole* God is stressed: there is to be *no strange god*
(אל נכר, אל זר) in Israel, and no doubt this was the condition insisted
upon by Reuel, and the one which caused the contention (מריבה);
because God declared himself holy among them (יקדש בם), he required
their undivided loyalty (Num. 20.13).

Several Pentateuchal passages beside Numbers 20 are recalled by these verses. '*I am Yahweh thy God* who brought thee forth *from the land of Egypt... There shall not be* for *you* other gods before my face' (Exod. 20.2-3) is clearly related. '*He that brought thee up* (המעלך)' comes in Deut. 20.1; to *testify unto* (העיר ב) comes in Deut. 5.1, 6.4, 8.19; there was no אל נכר with Israel in Deut. 32.12, but they provoked Yahweh with זרים in 32.16.

T. Booij ('Background') traces a regular pattern through a series of texts, Deuteronomistic, prophetic and Priestly, in which Yahweh (i) recalls the deliverance from Egypt, (ii) restates the giving of his commandments, especially the worship of him alone. and (iii) rebukes Israel for disobedience. This is helpful, but Psalm 81 leaves it vague in what way Israel has disobeyed, not *walking in* God's *ways*. The similar reproach in Psalm 50 does not suggest any worship of other gods, but the desertion of Yahweh's *moral* commands.

81.12-17. The national defeat, and the peril of worse to come, are indicated by vv. 15-16, *I should soon subdue their enemies...their adversaries...the haters of Yahweh.* Their obsessive presence is a clear indication of Yahweh's wrath (Ps. 79.5, etc.), and of the sin which must have been committed to incur such a punishment. Like other preachers, the psalmist is wise enough not to be too specific in his denunciation: *my people did not hearken to my voice, they would none of me, they would not walk in my ways.* When he homed in on particular sins in Ps. 50.18-20, it was not too impressive; but neither passage mentions idolatry, the central target of later critics.

As in the later D-theology, however, the divine promises are seen as conditional. If only God's *people had hearkened*, he would not have *let them go after the stubbornness of their heart* (Deut. 29.19; Jer. 7.24); he would have *turned his hand against their adversaries*. They would *soon have been subdued*, and come *shrinking* (יכחשו) to him, Yahweh; *but their humiliation should endure for ever.* The days of devastation and hunger would be over for good, as God fulfilled the promise of v. 11, *Open thy mouth wide...: He should feed them also with the fat of wheat; And*—miraculously—*with honey out of the rock* (says God) *should I satisfy thee.*

The Hebrew of the last two verses has raised some problems. כהש has often been taken to mean *feign submission*, but Eaton ('Notes') has argued for a basic sense of *shrink*, which I have accepted. Verse 16b is ambiguous in that עתם would naturally refer to *the haters of Yahweh*; Eaton suggests a meaning *their humiliation*, rather than the normal, surprising *their time*, with a derivation of עת from ענה. This seems convincing (cf. Tate); the object in v. 17 is singular (הו־), and will refer smoothly to the singular *Israel* in v. 14 (cf. *thee*, v. 17b). The psalmist has written himself into a muddle over his persons in another way. God is supposed to be the speaker from v. 7, and *I* = God runs from there to v. 15; but in v. 16 he drops into the third person, *The haters of Yahweh should shrink before him*. This then leads into difficulty in v. 17: at first he sticks with his third person, *He should feed him...*, but then goes back to his original first person, *should I satisfy thee*. Tidy-minded critics (Delitzsch, Gunkel, Kraus) would like to put him straight with emendations; Tate is right to resist them.

Verse 17 gives a double echo of Deut. 32.13-14: '[God] made [Israel] suck *honey out of the* crag (דבש מסלע) and oil out of the flinty *rock* (צור)' recalls v. 17b, מצור דבש; and 'With the *fat of* kidneys of *wheat* (עם־חלב כליות חטה)' recalls v. 17a, מחלב חטה. This crowns a formidable parallel between Psalm 81 and Deuteronomy 32, especially 32.12-16. (i) Like Ps. 81.7-17, Deuteronomy 32 is a proclamation of Yahweh's grace and a rebuke of Israel's faithlessness. (ii) The story is taken up from when '[God] found [Israel] in a desert land' (Deut. 32.10), as Ps. 81.8 moves from the proving at Meribah. Deuteronomy 32 does not refer to Egypt, perhaps because the Egyptian deliverance was not yet accepted as the experience of all Israelites. (iii) 'Yahweh alone did lead him, And there was no *strange god* with him' (Deut. 32.12) is soon contrasted with 'They moved him to jealousy with *alien* gods' (32.16); this language is repeated in Ps. 81.10. (iv) 'He made him to suck *honey out of* the crag and oil out of the flinty *rock*... With *the fat of* kidneys of *wheat*' (32.13-14) is echoed in 81.17. (v) 'He forsook God which made him, And lightly esteemed the Rock of his salvation' (32.15) is the same charge as 81.12, where Israel would not hearken to Yahweh and would none of him. It seems very likely therefore that the Selah after v. 8, *I proved thee at the waters of Meribah*, consisted of Deuteronomy 32, or part of it. The concentration of verbal echoes in five verses, Deut. 32.12-16, and their absence otherwise from a 43-verse poem, suggests that the Selah was brief, perhaps Deut. 32.10-21.

The Liturgical Theory

It is widely conceded that 81 is a psalm for the autumn festival: I have mentioned above the difficulty of interpreting v. 4 to give the exact temporal setting, some critics favouring 1st *and* 15th, others 15th only, others again a presumed festival *from* 1st *to* 15th. I have offered reasons for thinking that *the day of our feast* is in fact the climactic day, 'the last day, the great day of the feast'; and that בחדש should be rendered *in the new season*, viz. New Year, 21st; the month being Bul, the festal month in (Northern) Israel. If Psalm 81 were chanted in the evening, as we have evidence for thinking, and was giving instruction for joyful music on the following morning, it would be in use for 20th. This would be very convenient for the liturgical hypothesis I am proposing, since the last chapter placed Psalm 79 on 18th and Psalm 80 on 19th.

Psalm 82

82.1   A Psalm of Asaph.
         God standeth in the divine congregation (בעדת־אל);
         He judgeth among the gods:

2   'How long will ye judge unjustly,
         And respect the persons of the wicked?   (Selah

3   Judge the weak and fatherless:
         Do justice to the afflicted and destitute.

4   Rescue the weak and needy:
         Deliver them out of the hand of the wicked.

5   They know not, neither do they understand;
         They walk to and fro in darkness:
         All the foundations of the earth are moved.

6   I said, Ye are gods,
         And all of you sons of the Most High.

7   Nevertheless ye shall die like men,
         And fall like any (וכאחד) prince.'

8   Arise, O God, judge the earth:
         For thou shalt inherit all the nations.

Psalm 82 features a long speech by God, like the Asaph psalms 50 and 81; it sounds the note of judgment, like 50; and God is seen as the judge of Israel's oppressors, as in Pss. 75.8-9, and 76. Of the language, *All the foundations of the earth are moved* recalls Ps. 75.4, 'The earth and all the inhabitants thereof are dissolved: I have proportioned the pillars of it'. The picture of God dominating the lesser gods recalls Ps. 77.14, 'Who is a great god like God?' The final prayer to him to *Arise* and act is as in Ps. 74.23, or, in different words, in Pss. 79.8-13, 80.19.

Psalm 82 is the climax of the Asaph psalm-series. Psalm 50 gathered God's people for the divine judgment; and judgment should begin with the household of God. Psalms 73–80 consisted almost entirely of open or veiled appeals to God to take action against the arrogant invaders—

Psalms 73, 74, 79 and 80 offering moving accounts of the nation's plight; Psalms 50, 78 and 81 explaining it as due to failure to keep the covenant; Psalms 75, 76 and 77 trying to believe that despite all God would bring Israel to victory. Psalm 82 carries the mood of these last three psalms to the ultimate. Judgment Day, it is imagined, has now arrived. The invaders, *the wicked* of vv. 2, 4, are able to wreak their havoc only because of heavenly powers unseen, *gods, sons of the Most High,* who are sitting there in *the divine congregation.* It is they who have conspired to bring about Israel's ruin, as may be seen from the *fatherless and destitute* who are visible in every village. It is they who have put the invaders up to all this iniquity, *judging unjustly*; and God will now *stand in the divine* assembly and deliver his judgment upon them, a judgment of death. The hopeful scene is painted in with the Asaph psalmist's characteristic vigour; but the weakness of his situation in reality comes through in the last verse, *Arise, O God.* Things are desperate: it is time for God to get up off his throne.

Mowinckel saw that the principal theme of the autumn festival was God's coming to judgment. The great sequence of psalms in the 90s announced God's kingship as a reality; and that reality was to take shape in his coming to judge the wicked of the world, and rebellious nature besides (Pss. 93–99). Book IV comes from Jerusalem, perhaps from Josiah's time: there is a king still (91), but the ambitions of empire have receded. Psalm 82 is written in an earlier generation, when the heathen gods are still a reality and monotheism lies in the future. The shadow of the Ugaritic pantheon covers nascent Yahwism: the *gods* are *all sons of the Most High,* who is not Yahweh. The *congregation of El,* עדת־אל, I have rendered as *the divine congregation,* like ארזי־אל in Ps. 80.11, *the cedars of El, the divine cedars*; Israelites did not believe in an old god El, whose throne was disputed by his sons Baal, Yam and Mot, so *the congregation of El* would be a mistranslation. But El was the Most High, the father of the gods, at Ugarit, and this Canaanite mythology is still powerfully in the background. There is still belief in a divine assembly where Yahweh (spoken of as אלהים) is only *primus inter pares.* There are (sixty-nine) independent gods with real authority over other countries, and it is to their malign influence that Israel's ills are to be traced.

Mowinckel saw the cult to be the resolution of the tensions of real life. Psalm 82 was not a prophetic vision of a judgment to come; it was the piercing of the veil between earth and heaven to behold the scene behind the scene here below. God was even now pronouncing the fate of the rebel gods. Faith can discern this truth, for faith knows where the ultimate power resides, and that present evils cannot be conformed with Israel's covenant, and that God is not mocked. Each year the turn of the seasons marks his resuming of his kingdom; the new year means that the Great King is taking up his rule, in the Israelite idiom *judging*; and kings like David and Solomon began their rule by judging their enemies to death. So faith knows that all is well in heaven; all that is needed now is that God should *arise* and *judge the earth.* Perhaps we make too great a difference between Israelite worship and that of a modern Christian congregation. The liturgy provides, 'Christ has died; Christ is risen; Christ will come again'. In the car going home the worshipper believes the first; in church, in the dignity and music and warmth of common devotion, he or she may accept the second and hope the third. So with the ancient Israelite: Psalm 81 tells us of the music and the united conviction of the community; 82 sees his faith transcending the firmament to the world of ultimate reality; Psalm 83 shows us the view he saw going home.

Psalm 81 called for rejoicing, for singing and sounding the שׁוֹפָר, for shouting the תרועה (81.2 הריעו) on 'the day of our feast', the climactic day, the 21st; for it is then that God will enact his judgment. We have the same images transmuted in the Apocalypse of St John the Divine. The first two Woes are past (Rev. 11.14), with the trampling of Jerusalem by the nations (11.2) and the martyrdom of the saints (11.7): 'And the seventh angel sounded [the שׁוֹפָר], and there followed great voices [הריעו] in heaven, and they said, The kingdom of the world has become the kingdom of our Lord and of his Christ: and he shall reign for ever and ever [ויהי עתם לעולם]. And the four and twenty elders...worshipped God saying... The nations were wroth, and thy wrath came, and the time of the dead to be judged' (11.15-18). It is not for nothing that commentators have associated this passage with New Year.

It was Mowinckel who recognized decisively that the עדת־אל consisted not of Israelite judges or angels but of *gods* (*Psalmenstudien*, II, pp. 65-77). The unhappy history of attempts to evade the plain meaning of the text is told by R.B. Salters ('Ps. 82, 1'); the impossible translation of אלהים as *judges* is still maintained by Jacquet. There is a good discussion of the relevant texts in Cooke ('Sons'). Salters (and other critics) follow the Greek and Latin translators in supposing a Hebrew *Vorlage* עדת־אלים.

Gonzalez ('Psaume LXXXII') and Niehr ('Götter') present similar arguments for having it both ways: the language of vv. 2-4 is the prophets' social critique of the wealthy in Israel, and the אלהים are their divine sponsors. For Niehr the oppressors are in some way Canaanite officers misjudging in Israel, and their gods will be punished for it; for Gonzalez the polytheistic Canaanite background has faded, under which the gods were protectors of the nations. But we have no evidence for either Canaanite judges in Israel or for gods of the nations as part of the prophetic critique. The אלהים are gods of other peoples, and their unjust rule ('judging') is at Israel's expense through their protegés' wicked incursions.

Mowinckel's discussion of the liturgical setting of the psalm is in *Psalmenstudien* (II, pp. 65-71). He stresses that the judgment of the gods is an alternative image in worship to the victory over the sea-monster: the *Chaoskampf* logically precedes Yahweh's enthronement, whereas the judgment scene follows it. Mowinckel did not see the significance of Psalms 82 and 89A (where there is a similar scene) both coming at the end of their respective series.

Where Mowinckel offered a clear setting for Psalm 82, other commentators have found the psalm a puzzle. Delitzsch attributed it to Asaph in David's time, and Kraus and Dahood take it to be old; Gunkel thought it was a late prophetic imitation, and Anderson and Tate put it late. The latter view takes the *gods* to be domesticated 'intermediaries' in a way that fits uncomfortably with the implied background mythology. Classifications of Psalm 82 as a prophetic liturgy, or references to vv. 2-7 as an oracle, are not very helpful; we need some suggestion of the occasion when such a liturgy could be in regular use.

The association of Rev. 11.15-19 with New Year is made by A.M. Farrer (*Rebirth*; *Revelation of St John*), and in my 'Apocalypse'.

82.1. Belief in other gods alongside Israel's God became politically incorrect, and its evidences are not widespread. Deut. 32.8 (in the LXX/Qumran form of the text, 'according to the number of the sons of God') and Exod. 15.11 are contemporary; Isa. 24.21-24 ('the host of the height') is a late survival. Warnings against such heresy are indirect evidence, like Deut. 4.19. However, the gods survive thinly disguised as angels in Ps. 89.6ff., 'the assembly of the holy ones...the sons of the אלים...the council of the holy ones'; and the problem of theodicy requires that they remain independent and self-willed angels, 'princes' of the nations, Persia, Greece, and so forth, down to the time of Daniel (10.13, 21). Nor would God have dignity as the King of the Universe without his angelic court, or *congregation*, and his cabinet or 'council', which are often spoken of (Isa. 14.13; 1 Kgs 22.16-17; Job 1.6-7; 15.8; Jer. 23.18).

An English judge sits to pronounce sentence; Israelite judges stood: Isa. 3.13, 'The LORD standeth up (נצב) to plead, and standeth to judge the peoples'; Ps. 76.10, 'When God arose to judgment'. So here, God has had enough. His formidable rising recalls Cromwell with the Rump Parliament; or Stalin with the Politburo, perhaps, his pen poised to sign 'Death to the Traitors'.

82.2-5. The divine onslaught opens with a rhetorical 'How long?'; the psalmist anticipates Cicero's 'Quousque tandem, Catalina...?' by many centuries. The guilt of the gods is patent in that they have betrayed the primary trust God puts in judges: that they should judge righteously (Ps. 58.2 מישרים תשפטו), and that they should not 'lift the face of the wicked' (פני רשעים תשאו), that is, favour them. This principle formed the basis of early Israelite law, and is sometimes thought to have constituted the original ten commandments: 'Ye shall not afflict any widow or father- less child (יתום)... Thou shalt not follow a multitude to do evil; neither shalt thou speak in a cause to wrest judgment; neither shalt thou favour a weak man (דל) in his cause... I will not justify the wicked (לא־אצדיק רשע). Thou shalt not wrest the judgment of the poor (משפט אביון) in his cause... And thou shalt take no gift' (Exod. 22.22; 23.2-3, 6-8). The psalm verse ends with a Selah: Ps. 82.3-4 run, *Judge the weak and fatherless* (שפטו־דל ויתום), *Justify* (הצדיקו) *the afflicted and destitute, Rescue the weak and poor* (אביון), *Deliver them from the hand of the wicked* (רשעים). Such a cluster of similar language may incline us to think that the opening verses of Exodus 23, or some similar text under- lying our Book of the Covenant, constituted the Selah of the psalm. Here was God's fundamental provision for justice upon earth; and it was being openly defied by Nisroch the god of Assyria.

For suggestions that a version of Exod. 23.1-8 was originally a law for local judges, and constituted a Decalogue, see McKay, 'Decalogue'; Blenkinsopp, *The Pentateuch*, pp. 199-200.

The *weak, fatherless, afflicted* (עני), *destitute* (רש) and *needy* are not the submerged tenth in Nineveh, for whom the psalmist had little con- cern; they are the wretched of the earth in Israel. A decade of repeated invasions, battles, sieges and devastations has left the smiling country in ruins. The menfolk dead, enslaved or under arms, the land is often untilled, or its harvests stolen or burned; starving orphans and pathetic old women scavenge for what they may. Civilized people of the 1990s are scandalized to hear of the atrocities wrought by the Serbs in the Bosnian civil war: Amos tells of the Syrians threshing Israel with thresh- ing instruments of iron, and of the Ammonites who ripped up the women with child in Gilead, and he did not live to mention the horrors dreamed up by the Assyrians. It is small wonder that the psalmist felt God's patience must be exhausted.

God's speech is addressed to the gods, who are spoken to in the second person in vv. 2, 3, 4, 6, 7; the lapse into the third person in v. 5 is not due to his turning away in despair, but to a different subject. The *They* of v. 5 are the רשעים, the *wicked* of v. 4, who *know not, neither do they understand,* but *walk to and fro in darkness*. The same lack of understanding (לא יבין) is predicated of the invader in Ps. 49.21: what they do not understand is that this is God's land, and he will have the last word—death shall be their shepherd, they will be like the beasts that perish. They *go to and fro* (יתהלכו) in the meantime, marching up and down in Israel's sacred territory. Such ignorance is not to be attributed to the gods in any case (nor any walking to and fro); the gods know what is what, and therefore have the greater guilt.

All the foundations of the earth are moved (ימוטו): the same verb is used similarly at Ps. 46.7, 'The nations raged, the kingdoms were moved (מטו).' Nations are thought of as like mountains being moved (במוט, Ps. 46.3), tottering under the impact of the rebel waters swelling beneath them; Ps. 11.3 speaks similarly of lawlessness as a sign that 'the foundations are destroyed', and Ps. 96.10 rejoices that with Yahweh's reign 'the world is stablished that it cannot be moved'. As Mowinckel says (*Psalmenstudien*, III, p. 46) injustice in heaven threatens a return to primal chaos.

Kraus argues that the gods are still the subject of v. 5, being testified as blind and ignorant in Isa. 44.9, 18 and other texts; this is a false inference—Deutero-Isaiah is a monotheist deriding idols, and his comments do not apply to the polytheist assumptions of two centuries earlier. Most commentators fail to make it clear that the *wicked* are *foreign invaders*; Tate, for example, thinks in terms of the hoary figure of the wealthy Israelite oppressor. But *the gods* are elsewhere gods in charge of the affairs of foreign countries, and their authority can be seen as extending only to their own nationals.

The word דל, *weak*, is repeated from v. 3 to v. 4 in a way alien to Hebrew poetry. Gunkel emends to דך, but we may think the repetition is due to an intentional echo of דל in the Selah passage from Exodus 23.

82.6-7. God *said, Ye are gods*; that is, he had accepted that they were divine, with the normal privilege of divinity, immortality. Budde ('Ps. 82.6f.') argued from parallel uses of אני אמרתי for a translation *I thought*; but this then implies fallibility in God. Nor can *I said* mean *I decreed* ('a definitive statement', Tate, *Psalms*, p. 330); it is true that God might have decided to make them gods, but he could hardly have decided to make *all of them sons of the Most High*. Rather he had conceded their divine status, but now that they have betrayed their trust so disgracefully, he pronounces their sentence. They are to be stripped of their divine privilege. They will *die like men, And fall like any prince*. God is seen as judging like a king in his earthly court, where kings may have their courtiers executed for rebellion, as Elizabeth executed Essex. The gods sit trembling in his court, as disloyal princes (שׂרים) fear the axe, or worse, in an earthly court.

The language is carried over from Canaanite mythology, half accepted, half outgrown. In the Ugaritic tablets El was the Most High, and all the gods gathered in the assembly at his court were his sons; the three most powerful, Baal, Yam and Mot strove for the mastery, and each obtained it in turn, putting his predecessor to death. Most of this structure of thought has survived into Psalm 82. *All the gods* are *sons of the Most High*, who is not Yahweh; they are gathered in an assembly, court or *congregation of El*. Yahweh is the master, whose word is law, and before whom the others tremble and are silent. They are condemned to mortality, though not perhaps to instant death. But the psalmist does not take most of this too literally. He has spoken elsewhere repeatedly of Yahweh as El, and as the Most High; and although he thinks gods may die, he is probably rather sceptical about their coming to life again. We are not perhaps so different. Popes and Archbishops proclaim their belief that Christ descended into hell, although none of them thinks there to be a place of punishment under our feet. Religious myths are sometimes said to function as rhetoric to evoke appropriate responses; or, as Dr Goebbels put it, poetic truth.

82.8. Israel's leaders and people know that their God is in ultimate power in heaven; and that New Year is the season when his reign is reestablished, and judgment is given. So the scene just described is not so much a prophecy as an inference; as the rabbis in Auschwitz knew that God would see justice, seem things what they might. All that remains is for God to take action that brings his judgment into effect here below; for him to *Arise* and *judge the earth*. The contemporary Deut. 32.8, like Psalm 82, retains something of the old Canaanite myth: 'When the Most High gave to the nations their inheritance, When he separated the children of men, He set the bounds of the peoples

According to the number of the sons of God' (Qumran; cf. LXX). The Most High separated the peoples into seventy nations, the number of the sons of God. The following verse runs, 'For the LORD's portion is his people; Jacob is the lot of his inheritance'; Yahweh was awarded Israel, and the other gods took each his own people. The confidence of the psalmist is that that arrangement is now at an end. The gods have abused their position, and will be deprived of it: Yahweh will take over all their portfolios, he will *inherit in all the nations*, as the Israelite army, under his aegis, wins an empire the size of Alexander's, from the Strymon to the Indus.

Psalm 83

83.1	A Song. A Psalm of Asaph
2	O God, keep not thou silence:
	Hold not thy peace, and be not still, O God.
3	For, lo, thine enemies make a tumult:
	And they that hate thee have lifted up the head.
4	They take crafty counsel against thy people,
	And consult together against thy hidden ones.
5	They have said, Come, and let us cut them off from being a nation;
	That the name of Israel may be no more in remembrance.
6	The tents of Edom and the Ishmaelites;
	Moab and the Hagrites;
7	Gebal, and Ammon, and Amalek;
	Philistia, with the inhabitants of Tyre:
8	Assyria also is joined with them;
	They have been an arm to the children of Lot. (Selah

Psalm 82 saw God beyond the screen of the heavens condemning the lesser gods for the abuse of their powers; they had sanctioned the ruin of his afflicted people, who called on him to put his judgment into effect on earth. Psalm 83 now reveals the real situation facing Israel, their sense of encirclement by plotting tribes and nations, their fear of being *cut off from being a nation*, that *the pastures of God* may be *taken in possession*. In Ps. 82.8 the concluding prayer was that God, the Most High, would arise and judge the earth: now it is that God *whose name is Yahweh* may make himself known as *the Most High over all the earth* (v. 19). We have met a similar plot for Israel's destruction at Ps. 74.8; and of the language נוה, *pasture* (v. 13), in Ps. 79.7 (and Exod. 15.13), and God's *enemies/ those that hate him* (v. 3) in Ps. 81.15-16.

Psalm 83 is thus a natural successor to Psalm 82, and a completion of the whole Asaph series. Gunkel correctly called it a *Volksklagelied*, but, as so often, his classifications hide as much as they reveal. The Hebrew tradition calls it a שִׁיר, *a Song*, and the tone is not plaintive, like Psalms 74 and 79, but aggressive. Verses 10-19 are a row of full-blooded curses; the comparatively mild imprecations of Ps. 79.10, 12 are transformed into a spiritual heavy bombardment, praying destruction, storm, fire, terror and confounding on the enemy conspiracy. Like Admiral Benbow, the psalmist means to fight, and if necessary to go down fighting.

The real situation is not easily distinguished from the psalmist's imaginings; for no doubt he is laying it on thick if he is to move his *silent* God to action. Verse 9 shows who the front line aggressors are: *the children of Lot*, Moab and Ammon, with the backing of *Assyria*. It may be that the impressive alliance pictured in vv. 7-9 is a reality; that the hyenas are closing in on the stricken zebra. But they do seem to consist of all Israel's neighbours apart from Judah, and to include some rather distant and uncooperative desert tribes. The *Hagrites* lived in the steppe 'throughout all the land east of Gilead' (1 Chron. 5.10). *Gebal* here will be a tribe known later as living southeast of the Dead Sea near Petra, spoken of by Josephus as Gobolitis, and by Pliny the Elder as Gebelene; not the better known Gebal = Byblos, north of Tyre. The *Ishmaelites* and *Amalek* are also nomads from the southern desert regions. The implacable hatred felt towards Amalek, both in the D-tradition (Deut. 25.17-19) and by P (Exod. 17.8-14), testifies to the existence and effectiveness of the tribe in our period.

The key to a historical understanding of the psalm is the mention of Asshur, אַשּׁוּר. We may leave aside suggestions that the term stands for Syria, or Samaria, which are forced interpretations to support *partis pris*. But Gunkel has argued more reasonably that what is intended is an obscure desert tribe mentioned in Gen. 25.3 among the descendants of Keturah, 'And the sons of Dedan were Asshurim.' The גַם, *also*, suggests that Asshur was a marginal contribution to the alliance, added on as an afterthought, *an arm*, lending a hand, as we would say: not the kind of language in which an Israelite poet would have spoken of the dreaded armies of Shalmaneser. However the Hebrew הָיוּ זְרוֹעַ לְ does not at all imply marginal assistance. In Isa. 33.2 the prophet prays to Yahweh, 'Be thou their arm (הֱיֵה זְרֹעָם) every morning', and Jer. 17.5 reads, 'Cursed is the man that trusteth in man, and maketh flesh his arm (זְרֹעוֹ)': to *be an arm to* means to be the mainstay. Asshur's position at the end, and the □ם, rendered by Kraus *sogar*, most naturally form a climax to the list of enemies.

We may also consider the Assyrian position in the 720s. Tiglath-Pileser had campaigned every year from 745 to his death in 727 and had conquered enormous areas on every side of his home base, Babylon, Urartu, Syria, Israel, Gath. He could hardly expect trouble-free tribute from all these proud and independent peoples, to be able to send his full forces west every year. Restiveness, disaffection and punitive expeditions are part of this way of life. Besides, he had defeated Israel in 732 and annexed half its territory: there was no need of further offensives, and after his death it might take Shalmaneser a little time to take over the reins. So inevitably there will have been some years, indeed most years in the early 720s, when no Assyrian army attacked Israel. But in that people's weakened state, their armies decimated, their cities burned, their God insulted, their provinces lost, this must have seemed a golden opportunity to their long-oppressed neighbours; rather as June, 1940, seemed a good moment to Mussolini to declare war on France and Britain. Hitler was certainly *an arm to* him.

But would Israel's neighbours have felt like this in the eighth century? Indeed they would. In the early decades of the century Jeroboam II established an empire on the lines of Solomon's: 'He restored the border of Israel from the entering in of Hamath unto the sea of the Arabah...he warred, and he recovered Damascus and Hamath' (2 Kgs 14.25, 28). In his last years the peoples he had defeated raised their heads in rebellion. Amos 1–2 delivers a series of punitive oracles, roared by Yahweh from Zion: on Damascus, Gaza, Tyre, Edom, Ammon, Moab—these are the peoples surrounding Israel, northeast, southwest, northwest, southeast, ending with Edom, Ammon, Moab on the east. The list is remarkably close to that in Psalm 83: Edom, Moab, Ammon, Philistia (= Gaza), Tyre, with the desert tribes besides; and Psalm 83 seems to subsume the desert groups with their settled neighbours, the Ishmaelites with Edom, the Hagrites with Moab, Gebal and Amalek with Ammon, to describe a counter-clockwise circle from southeast to southwest. There is one notable change. Damascus is missing, and has been replaced by Asshur: but then Assyria captured and annexed Damascus in 733, twenty years or so after Amos's prophecy.

83.2-6. The Amos prophecy contrasts sharply with God's *silence, holding his peace.* When God roars, the hyenas know that the lion is coming; at his rebuke the chariot and horse will fall (Ps. 76.7). If enemies are at liberty to scheme, to murmur (יהמיון) and to plot Israel's extirpation, it is because *God* is *silent* and *inactive* (שקט). The psalmist addresses him as both אלהים and אל, as in earlier Asaph psalms (cf. Ps. 50.1), and he will make himself known as עליון in v. 19.

The psalmist seeks to involve God's feelings from the beginning; the enemy are *thine enemies, they that hate thee,* conspiring against *thy people, thy hidden ones,* over whom God has cast his protective cloak, *making a covenant against thee.* They are seen as arrogantly *lifting up the head, taking crafty counsel, consulting together with one consent.* How does he know all this? It is paranoia. But the defenceless do well to be paranoid: even if only some of these peoples send independent raiding parties, it will be hard to repel them; nor, as Jeremiah is to warn, will blessing attend him that trusteth in flesh. And should Assyria decide indeed to *be an arm to the children of Lot,* Israel will without doubt be *cut off from being a nation,* unless God can be brought to break his mysterious silence.

There is an Asaphic play on words נשאו/נשא in *they that hate thee/have lifted* (Tate).

It is remarkable how hard commentators have found it to accept what seems to be the face value of *Assyria* in v. 9, and settle for a setting in Northern Israel in the 720s. Five main lines have been tried to fix the historical background. (i) Delitzsch and Kirkpatrick opted for a campaign of Ammon, Moab, Edom and other tribes against Jehoshaphat in 2 Chronicles 20 (see below). (ii) At the turn of the century Maccabaean times were a favourite, Asshur being understood as a code for Syria; Gunkel destroyed this option by pointing out the absence of (a) any Maccabaean triumphalism, and (b) any reference to Antiochus. (iii) Gunkel himself, who generally favours post-exilic dates, thought of an attack in the fourth century, otherwise unknown. This was dependent on his understanding of Asshur as the little-known desert tribe of Genesis 25; but he was effectively criticized by Kraus (see above), and hardly anyone has been willing to follow this proposal.

(iv) Kraus saw clearly that Asshur means the world-power Assyria, but he thought that the list of enemies was too numerous to be realistic. He was followed in this by Weiser, who said that the list consisted of enemies past and present. Kraus therefore dissolved the historical reality into a mythical attack of the nations against Jerusalem, such as he found in Psalms 46 and 48; there will be some pre-exilic invasion (Weiser: between the ninth and seventh centuries), but the detail is valueless. No doubt Kraus and Weiser are right to see the shadow of the mythical *Völkersturm* across the page; but their denial of the realism of vv. 7-9 is surprising. All the major enemies are well known to have been active in the eighth century (Amos 1–2), and Arab tribes are a military force in Assyrian records from Qarqar (854) onwards. If all the nations of the world are supposed to be joining in the eschatological onslaught, should we not expect something a bit more impressive, Magog, perhaps, or Egypt?

(v) Tate and others note that in Ezra 6.22 Assyria is spoken of where *Persia* is meant; and he suggests that Assyria was used a 'an *example*' of a hostile world power, citing Lam. 5.6; Isa. 11.11; 19.23-25; 27.13; Zech. 10.10-11—all passages from after Assyria's eclipse in 612. Further, almost all the enemies are clustered round Judah in the south, rather than Israel; so it is natural to think of a late date (in line with two indications of late language), and a southern locus. It is difficult to accept this. 'Assyria' is always used for a *Mesopotamian* great power, in the way that British people used to speak of the Soviet Union as 'Russia', and after 587 Babylon and Persia were suzerains over Judah, and not at all likely to be an arm to local enemies. Amos 1–2 is firm evidence that Northern Israel was also threatened by Moab and Edom. For the language see below, v. 13.

Delitzsch and Kirkpatrick were able minds, even if more credence was given to the Chroniclers' historicity then than now. 2 Kings 3 describes a campaign of Israel, Judah and Edom against Moab, and this is transformed in 2 Chronicles 20 into an attack on Jehoshaphat, only, by Moab, Ammon and 'with them some of the Ammonites'. The last are clearly an error (cf. LXX ἐκ τῶν Μιναίων) and are taken by *BHS* as מעונים, an Arab tribe referred to in 2 Chron. 26.7; in 20.10, 22-23 the invaders are said to come from Ammon, Moab and Mt Seir, that is, Edom. Whereas Elisha's prophecy had been determinative in 2 Kings 3, on this occasion the Spirit of the LORD comes upon Jahaziel of the sons of Asaph, who speaks stirring prophetic words. The battle is then won as the Korahite Levites sing and praise God; and the army returns in triumph with psalteries and harps and trumpets (בנבלים ובכנרות ובחצצרות, 2 Chron. 20.28).

The nineteenth-century savants were not wrong to see a connection with our psalm, but they did not see enough connection, and they saw it in reverse. The Chroniclers wished to write Northern Israel out of the script, and to give glory to King Jehoshaphat of Judah, so they 'interpreted' the 2 Kings 3 story with the aid of the Asaph psalms. The Asaphite Psalm 82 spoke of God pronouncing judgment (שפט) upon Israel's enemies, and those enemies turned out to be Edom, Moab, Ammon and a variety of desert tribes in Psalm 83, backed by Assyria. Their conspiracy to *take in possession the pastures of God* comes through in 2 Chron. 20.11 as 'coming to cast us out of thy possession'. The Asaphites reveal their method of praising God in Psalm 81, where they call for the use of the harp, psaltery and trumpet (כנור, נבל, שופר). The link to these psalms was provided by the king's name, Jehoshaphat, *Yahweh judges* (שפט). The (Korahite) Chronicler is thus able to introduce his confrères, the Asaphites, as the heroes of the occasion; though he cannot resist giving credit also to his own clan, who set the praises off 'with an exceeding loud voice' in 2 Chron. 20.19. He makes the enemy alliance vague and enormous, 'a great multitude from beyond the [Dead] sea from Syria', but he specifies the main participants correctly, and he turns the 2 Kings 3 invasion of Moab into their invasion of Judah in line with Psalm 83. It was, like all the Chronicler's work, a remarkably neat job; and a testimony to the understanding of the fourth century that the Asaph psalms were a series, of which 81, 82 and 83 belonged together.

83.10   Do thou unto them as unto Midian;
         As to Sisera, as to Jabin at the river Kishon:
11   Which perished at En-dor;
         They became as dung for the earth.
12   Make their nobles like Oreb and Zeeb;
         Yea, all their princes like Zebah and Zalmunna:
13   Who said, Let us take to ourselves in possession
         The pastures of God.
14   O my God, make them like the whirling dust;
         As stubble before the wind.
15   As the fire that burneth the forest,
         And as the flame that setteth the mountains on fire;
16   So pursue them with thy tempest,
         And terrify them with thy storm.
17   Fill their faces with confusion;
         That they may seek thy face, O LORD.
18   Let them be ashamed and dismayed for ever;
         Yea, let them be confounded and perish:
19   That they may know that thou alone, whose name is YHWH,
         Art the Most High over all the earth.

83.10-13. Verse 9 was followed by a Selah, and vv. 10-13 make reference to three famous victories which God had granted Israel in earlier times: the Selah marks an intermission, in which will have been chanted some account of the exploits of Deborah, Jael and Gideon. It is the presence of so many desert tribes among the invaders which especially distinguishes the imagined confederacy of vv. 6-9; and this then suggests the precedent of the Midianite invasions in the days of the Judges. In Judg. 8.24 Ishmaelites and Midianites are taken to be identical, and the same view must have been held by the redactor of Gen. 37.25-36. So Midian is mentioned first; and 'the day of Midian' seems to have been a familiar theme (Isa. 9.3; 10.26).

However, the peril is dire, and the need for divine action is extreme, and the thought of massacred enemies leads on from one set of historic interpositions to another—*Do to them like Midian, like Sisera, like Jabin*; the sequence of כְּ's piles up like the vacuous rhetoric of a modern politician. Sisera and Jabin are more to the point, in fact, for it was God's action which turned the day *at the river Kishon*: 'The river Kishon swept them away, That ancient river, the river Kishon. O my soul, thou hast trodden down strength' (Judg. 5.21). On two matters our psalmist knows a tradition which has not come down to us. He sites the death of the two Canaanites at En-dor, which is indeed not far from Taanach and Megiddo (Judg. 5.19), but which is not mentioned in Judges 4–5; and he includes Jabin among the fatal casualties. Jabin is not mentioned in the Song of Deborah, and he has become a shadowy and unreal figure in Judges 4—'Jabin king of Canaan', 'Jabin king of Hazor', 'the hand of the children of Israel prevailed more and more against Jabin the king of Canaan, until they had destroyed Jabin king of Canaan' (4.24). But there never was such an office.

On the other hand Oreb and Zeeb are a pair in Judges 7, spoken of as 'princes', שָׂרִים, and Zeba and Zalmunna a second pair in Judges 8, spoken of as kings. The 'slaughter of Midian at the rock of Oreb' was probably familiar to Isaiah (Isa. 10.26), so we may think that the Selah concentrated on parts of our Judges 7–8, which are reproduced accurately in the eighth-century psalm and prophecy, and that the Sisera/Jabin theme was drawn in by association. It is unclear whether it is the Midianite leaders of old (Tate) or the present confederates (Anderson) who are supposed to be intending to occupy God's land; no doubt both would be in mind.

Gunkel, followed by many, proposed a series of emendations to these verses. (i) *as to Midian* seemed out of place with Sisera and Jabin, and to belong better with v. 11. (ii) The Midianites were actually attacked by Gideon at 'the spring of Harod' (Judg. 7.1, עֵין־חֲרֹד), which might then have been corrupted to עֵין־דֹּר, and thence to עֵין־דֹּאר. (iii) Verse 12 is overladen, *Make them, their nobles, like Oreb and like Zeeb and like Zebah and like Zalmunna their chieftains*; a more regular rhythm would be *Make their nobles like Oreb: and their chieftains like Zeeb*, the second couple being introduced from Judges 8. We do well, with Tate, to be wary of so much neatness. Midian comes suitably first in view of the number of desert tribes in vv. 7-9; we should avoid any attempt to reconcile a variant form of the tradition with the Deuteronomistic account; and the overloading may come from the psychological pressure. Our psalmist is like a frightened medicine man, repeatedly stabbing the effigy of his foe.

Tate notes the presence in v. 13 of two prosaic expressions, אֲשֶׁר and אֵת preceding an object, and argues that these are signs of a late date. This is a slim basis for such a conclusion: אֲשֶׁר occurs in pre-exilic poetry in Pss. 94.12; 95.11; Obad. 20 and other passages; אֵת in Pss. 47.5; 92.7; and Obad.19. In Ps. 45.7 as in Ps. 83.13 אֵת follows לָנוּ.

83.14-19. O my God reveals the speaker once more as the national leader, probably the king (Eaton, *Kingship*, p. 61; Tate). The cursing petitions rise to a climax: God is to be like the desert wind which raises great spirals of *whirling dust* (גַּלְגַּל, against many commentators who favour a dry wheel-shaped plant); like the *wind* at harvest time which blows away the *stubble/chaff*; like *the fire* which rages through the tinder-dry *forest*, or the *flame* driving up the side of the *mountains* (as in Deut. 32.22). This is the God of direct action. As the rebel confederates turn and run, he is to *pursue them with his tempest, and terrify them with his storm*: the wind and fire of the similes are realities in the lightning and thunderbolts with which the divine avenger comes after them.

The overthrow of the enemy army is seen as with massive slaughter, *confounded and perishing*; their unburied bodies will, like ancient Midian, be *dung for the earth*. This edifying picture is not, however, the end of the matter. The few survivors, and the wicked who sent them, will have *their faces filled with confusion*; they will *be ashamed and dismayed for ever*. But the consequence of this will ultimately be satisfactory. Defeat in ancient war entailed the bringing of tribute in subsequent years to the festival of the victor's gods; and serious defeat entailed the attendance of the worsted king at those occasions. Jehu went to pay Israel's tribute at Nineveh before the days of sprung motor cars; and Ps. 47.10 sees the princes of the peoples gathered together as the people of the God of Abraham, for the celebration of Ingathering at ninth-century Dan (Goulder, *Korah*, pp. 157-59). So now the defeated enemy will *seek thy name, O Yahweh*; they will confess (יָדְעוּ) that *thou alone, whose name is Yahweh, art the Most High over all the earth*. Many of these peoples have been worshipping עֶלְיוֹן, *the Most High*; henceforth they will recognize that it is Yahweh alone to whom this title belongs, and will be attending his feast each year in Bethel. So Greater Israel will become coterminous with the inhabited world, and everyone will live happily for ever after.

The Liturgical Theory

Book III of the Psalter closes with Psalm 89, which stands at the end of the Korah psalm-series. The psalm consists of two parts, identified by Gunkel as a hymn (vv. 2-3, 6-19), and a national lament (vv. 4-5, 20-53); the two parts differ also in metre, subject and tone, as well as raising syntactical problems at the joins. I have supported Gunkel in arguing for two distinct settings for the two parts; in my case for a ninth-century climax to the Dan festival for the former section, and a long appendix added at Jerusalem in the 590s for the latter (*Korah*, pp. 211-38).

The first part of the psalm (89A) is a celebration of Yahweh's power, and his faithfulness to his people. The image developed is of his domination of the heavenly council: 'The heavens shall praise thy wonders, O LORD; Thy faithfulness also in the assembly of the holy ones. For who in the skies can be compared unto the LORD? Who among the sons of the gods is like unto the LORD, A God very terrible in the council of the holy ones, And to be feared of all them that are round about him? O LORD God of hosts, who is a mighty one like unto thee, O LORD?' (89.6-9). The psalm goes on to celebrate Yahweh's power over the sea, his victory over Rahab, his creation of heaven and earth, and the blessedness of his people.

The verses which I have cited recall Psalm 82: these are in fact the only two passages of this kind in the Bible. God is seen *in the assembly of the holy ones* (בקהל קדשים) as in 82.2 he stands up *in the congregation of [the] god[s]* (בעדת־אל]ים[). The underlying theology is polytheistic: *the holy ones* (קדשים) of Psalm 89 are spoken of also as *sons of the gods* (בני אלים), as in Psalm 82 they are *gods* and *sons of the Most High* (אלהים, בני עליון). The mood in the heavenly assembly is of sullen rebellion suppressed by terror: in Psalm 89 *A God very terrible in the council of the holy ones, And to be feared above all them that are round about him*; in Psalm 82 *ye shall die like men, And fall like any prince.* In both psalms Yahweh totally dominates the assembly.

In *Psalms of the Sons of Korah* I explained the position of 89A as reflecting the climax of the Dan festival, the ritual of the 21st Bul. There were references to a day-long ceremony: 'In thy name do they rejoice all the day long' (89.17). This was expressed in the mass, synchronized shout, 'Blessed is the people that know the תרועה' (89.16a), and in a march past, 'They walk, O LORD, in the light of thy countenance'. The last phrase may suggest an exposition of the ephod, or of the Urim and

Thummim. A similar setting, though with a markedly less triumphalist tone, would make sense for Psalm 82. The last day of the festival is traditionally the day of Yahweh's triumph, as he takes up his reign in the New Year. There is music, trumpets, shouting, rejoicing (Ps. 81.2-4). The age-old image is celebrated of the national God dominating and terrifying the lesser divinities. Only Psalm 82 lets slip the ruin the latter have wrought on orphaned, impoverished Israel.

Triumphalism is always a mistake, because human success is never permanent. The jingoist mood which seemed natural in Ahab's Israel jarred increasingly when the psalm was used in late seventh-century Judah: with the capture of Jerusalem in 597 ('Thou hast profaned his crown to the ground'), and the deportation of Jehoiachin ('thine enemies have reproached the heels [עקבות] of thine anointed'), it was necessary to draw Yahweh's attention to reality. Hence the addition of the long appendix, 89B: Yahweh is top God in the heavenly council—why does he not do something then about King Nebuchadnezzar?

The addition of Psalm 89B to the earlier hymn suggests a rationale for Psalm 83. Perhaps we should think of Psalm 82 as the celebratory hymn, sung in the morning, and Psalm 83 as the added lament chanted before sundown on 21st; but such detail must exceed our knowledge. What would seem more certain is that no community standing on the verge of the unthinkable could have borne to go home in the forced optimism of Psalm 82. God's reign of terror in the heavenly assembly was theology. Reality was the devastations, defeats, massacres and starvation of the last few years, the expectation of an Ammonite–Moabite invasion, the threat of semi-savages from the desert periphery, the long shadow of Shalmaneser. One should surely end with prayer for God's destruction of these wicked men, and for their confession of his supremacy.

So the Asaph psalms end as they began, with the suggestion of a psalmody for a week of festal worship. Psalm 50 saw the people called to gather for the feast, and rebuked for their sins. Psalms 73 and 74 were laments led by the king over the national ruin, before the festival began. Psalm 75 accompanied the royal reconsecration for the nation's defence, and Psalm 76 celebrated God's power in battle. Thus far the psalmody followed the same pattern as the Korah psalms. Thereafter the present crisis asserted itself in a sequence of less triumphal psalms. Psalm 77 reveals an all-night vigil for the king, in which he found a religious solution to the present trials in the Exodus story, and he expounds this to the people, with suitable admonitions, in Psalm 78. Psalms 79 and 80 urge God to act before it is too late. With Psalm 81 we turn to the traditional rejoicing for New Year, but the gladness is pathetically forced. Psalm 81 itself breaks down into a rebuke for past faithlessness; Psalm 82 is a blustering removal from the harshness of the present to the imagined reversals of eternity; Psalm 83 shows us finally exactly who was involved, and when and where. We cannot but pay a tribute of admiration to the faith and courage of the Asaph psalmist who has produced such a psalm cycle. His poetry heartened his successors in Jerusalem, who amended his text for the Babylonian crisis; and the Maccabaeans who cited it; and the oppressed of the Holocaust who found comfort in it; and Christian sufferers in many generations.

Chapter 7

A BRIEF HISTORY OF THE PSALTER

The psalms are arranged in three different ways which cut across each other and require explanation. There are six collections: three for David (3–41, 51–72, 138–45), one each for the sons of Korah and for Asaph, and the Songs of Ascents. There are the five Books (1–41, 42–72, 73–89, 90–106, 107–150). There are the genre differences: hymns, public laments, and so forth. There must be some reason for these three overlapping and contradictory arrangements: to name but a single instance, why of the Psalms of Asaph Psalm 50 has been separated and finds itself in Book II, while 73–83 open Book III which is completed with alien (and heterogeneous) psalms.

I have argued in this book and elsewhere that a *liturgical* explanation is primary. It is not a problem that the different genres are represented in an apparently haphazard way: if a set of psalms were being provided for a national festival, we should expect it to begin with a pilgrimage psalm, to continue with an opening act of penitence, with a series of hymns and other varied material for the celebration, in the light of contemporary crises. We should think it singular if a liturgical scholar collected all the confessions, canticles, intercessions, and so forth in the Prayer Book, and did not mention that their present arrangement was to provide balanced services of worship. But the way in which the collections and the Books in part coincide and in part go against one another is a problem. I have tried in a number of publications to argue a case why this should be so; but it may be helpful to set out my conclusions in brief here, referring the reader to the discussions.

The earliest collection of psalms which has been preserved to us in approximately its pristine form is the second 'for David' collection, referred to at Ps. 72.20 as the Prayers of David (51–72). They were composed around 970, and were for the most part (Pss. 52–68) responses to the situations in which David's loyalists found themselves between the start of Absalom's rebellion and the victory march into Jerusalem when it had been put down. The considerable details, especially in Psalms 60 and 68, can be given good sense from this context. The rebellion was understood, as in 2 Samuel 11–20 and 1 Kings 1, as God's punishment of David for the murder of Uriah. Psalm 51 was prefaced to the series as David's psalm of penitence after his denunciation by Nathan, and this was understood in Jewish tradition (cf. the heading). Psalm 69 was added as a response to Sheba's rebellion, Psalms 70–71 as a response to Adonijah's attempt to seize the throne, and Psalm 72 ('For Solomon', heading) as a celebration of Solomon's accession.

The whole sequence had theological meaning as a fulfilment of Nathan's prophecy, 'Now therefore the sword shall never depart from thine house...' (2 Sam. 12.10). David had sinned, and God had punished him for it, but God had been true to his word, and had not taken the throne away from him as he had from Saul; and he had been succeeded by his favoured son, whose reign was to be a golden age. Such a story was a paradigm of Israel's annual experience. Each year king and people must fall short of God's demands, and each year will bring its recompense in drought or locusts or national defeats; but God is true, and each new year will bring expectation of better things, justice, and peace, and the tribute of conquered enemies.

The headings in Psalms 51–72 not only supply the linking words 'for David', and 'historical' notes, which are later guesses, almost all wrong; they also give occasional notes of location (על): at Mahalath, the Dove of the Far Terebinths, the Lily of Testimony. These are indications that the psalms were chanted in the course of a procession; and just as 2 Samuel 6 is often (and correctly) understood to echo an annual procession of the ark to the Jerusalem Temple, so the account of David's ascent of the Mount of Olives in 2 Samuel 15 should be understood as the pattern of an annual mourning procession. Participation in ritual enrols the new generation as among the loyal people of God and the Davidic king. The nation thus trod in the steps of David and his faithful followers, and heard the psalms chanted at the stations marked in the Samuel story. As memories blurred it became necessary not only to sing, but also to tell the tale; and the Selahs in the psalm text provided breaks in which our Succession Narrative (2 Sam. 11–20; 1 Kgs 1) could be recited. I have set out a full account of these psalms and the ritual accompanying them in *The Prayers of David*.

There is a brief critique of the book in M. Millard's *Komposition* (pp. 42-43) but it is unfortunately not very accurate. Millard says (1) that the book treats the heading

לדויד historically, but none of the 'historical' heading notes; and thus comments not on the text but on a postulated earlier version; (2) that if the postulated processional use were so, the redactors were either ignorant of it or ignored it; (3) that the book ignores the heading element ממכתם, and is not consistent in treating סלה as a division marker within the text. In fact the historical notes in the book are accepted in the case of Psalms 51 and 72: the others are explained in each case as the guesses of later scribes who knew that there had been a relation to Samuel–Kings but who made false inferences from the psalm-text. To explain our present text as the accretion of time ('eine von [Goulder] postulierte Vorform') is not a disreputable evasion but the necessary resource of every critic: Millard does it himself all the time. The suggestion that a processional use had been forgotten in the redaction is far from implausible: processions at Jerusalem were suspended during the Exile, at least. The Gospels were used processionally in Egeria's time, but such a use has fallen away. The term ממכתם is explained in *Prayers of David* (p. 111) and in the comments on subsequent psalms; and סלה is understood consistently, both in *Prayers of David* and in *Psalms of the Sons of Korah*, not as a simple divider in the text, but as the occasion for a cantillation of the relevant part of the story-tradition.

The procession, and the recital and chanting that went with it, took a day; but the autumn festival was a week's celebration, and there must have been psalms sung on the other days too. These have not survived as a distinct collection, but there can be no doubt that some of them have survived individually, and that we have such among the psalms in Book I (1–41). The 'royal' psalms are heavily concentrated in Book I, and we may think especially of Psalms 2, 18, 20, 21, 22 and 24; Eaton and others have included 19 and 23 as among royal psalms, and we might suspect that 18–24 was an early core to the present first 'for David' collection (3–41). It was David who chose Jerusalem as the site of the national Temple, and Solomon who (re-)built the Temple, so naturally royal concerns were more to the fore there than in the ancient priestly foundations in the north. Psalm 18 gives an account of God's coming in the storm to rescue 'David and his seed': rather like the opening of Psalm 50, but the tone is much more positive. Psalms 20 and 21 are blessings on the king in battle, not dissimilar to the opening of Psalm 45 and to Psalm 75. Psalm 22 marks the passion of the apparently royal speaker. Psalm 24 accompanies the procession of the ark into the Temple, and is comparable to Psalm 47, when God 'went up with a merry noise'. We seem to have here the bones of a royal Jerusalem festival psalmody from the monarchy, perhaps from the early monarchy. I have yet to expound this hypothesis.

About 930 the Solomonic kingdom divided. The main part of the people, Israel, separated from Judah, whose king retained the Davidic descent and legitimation. Jeroboam had to choose a new religious centre from among the old northern shrines. Shechem had been pre-eminent (1 Kgs 12), but lay in ruins (12.25), while Dan had seemed to the author of Psalm 68 to offer the sole remaining challenge to Jerusalem (68.16-17). Dan was in any case a wise choice, since Jeroboam was an Ephraimite, and Israel needed a national centre away from Ephraim. The priests at Dan were the family of Korah, and once their shrine became the centre for the national festival, they developed a set of psalms suited to the occasion. We have these psalms in two collections, 42–49 and 84–85, 87–88 (with the first part of 89).

There are two sequences because there were two editions of the Dan psalms, one from the high days of the Omrids in the ninth century, the other from the time of the Assyrian invasions of the 730s. There was a psalm for each day of the festival, often describing or implying the day's ritual. Both the main sequence (42–49) and the supplement (84, etc.) begin with a pilgrimage psalm. The earlier one, Psalm 84, speaks of the pilgrimage with joy ('How amiable are thy tabernacles...'); the later one, Psalm 42, is also bound for 'the land of Jordan, and the Hermons, the little hill' of Dan, but the priest conducting it goes mourning because of the oppression of the enemy. Both series preface the feast with a day of lamentation; but whereas Psalm 85, the earlier one, is concerned for a good harvest from the crops, Psalm 44 describes a bitter scene of military defeat, enslavement, ruin and national disgrace, the handiwork of Tiglath-Pileser.

I have referred above to the rites of the festival itself. On 15th Bul the king was re-consecrated, riding out in his armour, enthroned to administer divine law, married to a new wife to sire princes who will govern his empire (Ps. 45). On 16th God's victory over the waters, and over his earthly enemies, was celebrated with a great bonfire (Ps. 46). On 17th the ephod was carried in procession into the Dan temple (Ps. 47). On 18th was the celebration of God's inviolable city, Dan, with a circumambulation of the city (first with Ps. 87, later with Ps. 48). On 19th a dire warning was issued to Israel's enemies (Ps. 49). On 20th a representative priest was beaten and let down into an underground chamber, 'cast away among the dead', there to pray in the dark and terror for God's mercy on his people (Ps. 88). Finally, on 21st there was a triumphal march past, with shouting of the תרועה and Hallelujahs; God triumphed over Rahab in creation and he dominates the other gods—he will see his people to success in the coming year (Ps. 89.2-3, 6-19).

The Korahites were happy with their older psalmody through the comparatively easy times of Jeroboam II. It was the destruction of so many fine cities in Galilee that led them to substitute Psalms 42–43 and 44 for 84–85, and the more comprehensible, and nervous, Psalm 48 for the obscure and triumphalist Psalm 87. But the new psalm sequence was not in use for many years: Dan was lost, and the Korahites moved south, first no doubt to Bethel, but soon to a permanent home in Jerusalem. I have written an account of their varied fortunes in Chapter 3 of *The Psalms of the Sons of Korah*, and a full exposition of their psalms in the same book. The present book has offered an account of the history and psalmody of the shrine at Bethel in the 720s, which I will not summarize.

Millard comments briefly on *Psalms of the Sons of Korah* in his *Komposition* (pp. 41-42). He accepts my paralleling of the two Korah series, but declines further engagement because the final version of the collection speaks of Zion/Jerusalem, not Dan. This then leaves him with the problem of the reference to Jordan, Hermon, and so forth in Ps. 42.7, which he regards as 'schwierig' (p. 65); and there is more 'difficulty' with Ps. 48.2. There is an unresolved discrepancy in Millard's writing: he will not discuss other proposals of diachronic development, while pressing his own.

The Jerusalem Temple had its own psalmody, as I have indicated; and although Judah was never imperialist as Israel had been, the authority of the Davidic monarchy was so strong that little pressure was felt to alter the long-established, royal-centred festal liturgy. The change came with the arrival of Sennacherib's army at the gates of Jerusalem, and of the Korahite priesthood within. It was seen that the northerners had brought with them not only a beautiful psalmody, but also a much humbler one, suited to the situation of national peril. But at the same time Hezekiah was unwilling to let go the long association with the history of David, and a compromise was adopted. The Korahite psalms, 42–49, were taken over and used for the opening of the Jerusalem festival, down to 19th (of Ziv/Tishri, the southern festal month); but for 20th/21st the old Davidic cycle was retained, 51–72, with the Olivet procession. Thus was formed the outline of our Book II of the Psalter, 42–72. One or two glosses were necessary, especially in Psalm 48, so as to make clear that Jerusalem was the city of God, and Zion, not Hermon, his mountain. But the Korahites came to accept that: as they were later to put it, 'the dew of Hermon fell upon the hill of Zion' (Ps. 133.3). Only Psalm 50 was missing from our present Book II: but the feast was still a seven-day affair—the eighth day was not added till after the Exile.

The Deuteronomic revolution brought the need for further changes. In part these were political. It had seemed proper in the tenth century to speak of the Davidic king breaking his enemies with a rod of iron, and dashing them in pieces like a potter's vessel; in the age of Asshurbanipal and Nebuchadnezzar such language appeared less realistic. In part the changes were theological. Kings should no longer multiply wives unto themselves, nor greatly multiply to themselves silver and gold, but humbly write out copies of the Deuteronomic code; Israel should in principle be a theocracy. But they were also liturgical: the old practice of the daily morning sacrifice had become elaborated into an offering morning and evening.

The result of these pressures was a new psalmody, Psalms 90–104, the basis of our Book IV. A special providence is still promised to the king ('he shall give his angels charge over thee', Ps. 91), but the old belligerence is gone. It is, as is often repeated, the LORD who has taken up his reign; and instead of subduing the nations under us and the peoples under our feet, the psalmist bids merely to tell it out among the nations that Yahweh is king. But the most important innovation is the element of alternation. The psalms that begin 'Yahweh has taken up his reign' are 93, 97 and 99, and Ps. 95.3 proclaims, 'For Yahweh is a great God, And a great king above all gods'. The verses calling on the sea and the natural world to rejoice at Yahweh's coming judgment are repeated from Psalms 96 to 98, both of which begin 'O sing unto the LORD a new song'. The odd numbers announce God's awesome reign; the even numbers call upon the world to rejoice at it.

Our Book IV comprises seventeen psalms (90–106), and it will hardly be an accident that the Psalter contains two further units of seventeen psalms, Book III (73–89) and the Great Hallel (120–36). The latter bears a striking similarity to Book IV in that both conclude with a pair of psalms giving an outline of sacred history (105–106, 135–36). A plausible explanation of these features, and of the alternations in Psalms 93–99, arises from Ps. 92.1-2, 'It is a good thing to give thanks unto the LORD... To shew forth thy lovingkindness *in the morning*, And thy faithfulness *every night*'. The liturgy was a twice-daily affair, morning and evening. The festival began on the evening of the first day (15th Tishri) and, in the seventh century, closed on the evening of the seventh day (21st): so there were fifteen liturgical occasions. When an eighth day was added (22nd) after the Exile, two further services were needed, with two extra psalms. 106 is visibly a psalm from the exilic/post-exilic period ('Save us, O LORD our God, And gather us from among the nations', 106.47). A limited confirmation of this may be found in the occasional hints of the time of day implied by particular psalms; for on this hypothesis the even-numbered psalms from both sequences would fall in the evening, and the odd-numbered in the morning. 95, 101 and 121 are usually understood as morning psalms, 134 as a night psalm. I have set out the argument for Book IV with some detail in an article ('Fourth Book').

There is a short critique of this article by G.H. Wilson in J.C. McCann's collection of essays (*Shape*, pp. 45-51). Wilson notes that the liturgical explanation was based on Mowinckel's autumn festival hypothesis, for which the evidence was centrally the psalms in the 90s; the argument is therefore circular, as is the argument for alternating worship. Wilson is right about this; but it is a mistake to think that circularity destroys an argument. It is a policy of despair to require external evidence (e.g. about patterns of pre-exilic Israelite worship) when none exists. In biblical scholarship, as in many other areas, we have to be content with plausibility, not proof.

There had been Bethel priests in Jerusalem from after the demise of the Northern Kingdom, and their psalms with them; but with the close of the seventh century the situation of Judah came increasingly to resemble that for which the Asaph cycle had been composed. None of the three psalm sequences in use in Jerusalem (the core of Book I, Book II less Psalm 50, and Psalms 90–104) was suited to the dire situation of the period after 597, and in particular in the early Exile; whereas the Asaph sequence had been composed for just such a time of crisis. The sense of impending disaster, and of disaster arrived, which pervades the series fitted exactly with the situation now facing the southerners. At all events the Asaph psalms were welcomed, and were in use in the 590s. They did not need much adaptation. Ps. 74.5-7, 'And now all the carved work [of thy temple] they break down with hatchets and hammers' could be glossed as at 'mount Zion, wherein thou hast dwelt' (Ps. 74.2). Ps. 79.1, 'O God, the nations are come into thine inheritance; Thy holy temple have they defiled' can similarly be clarified with a third colon, 'They have laid Jerusalem in heaps'. The great account of Israel's history in Psalm 78 concentrates excessively on northern traditions and ignores Jerusalem completely; but this can be rectified with one or two references to the cowardice of 'the children of Ephraim' (Ps. 78.9), and God's preference for Zion over 'the tent of Joseph' (Ps. 78.67-69).

These, and a few further innocent touches, have been sufficient to persuade the learned of two and a half millennia that the Asaph psalms originated in Jerusalem.

There were only twelve Asaph psalms, and this was insufficient for the new twice-daily festal liturgy. The sequence was accordingly amplified from the unused resources of their Korahite allies. The latter had kept alive the tradition of their displaced psalms, 84 and 85, 87 and 88, and the first part of 89; and these five psalms were now drafted in to fill the gap. Psalms 85 and 88 were indeed laments suited to the pathos of the national situation. Only Psalm 89 offended by its triumphalism, and this was amended by a massive expansion, from 16 to 52 verses (adding vv. 4-5, 20-53): the divine promise to David through Nathan was set out in all its fulness (vv. 20-38), and contrasted with the pitiful reality, as God's enemies 'reproach the footsteps of thine anointed' on his way to Babylon (vv. 39-52).

It must seem very probable that Book III at first consisted of the Asaph psalms, 50, 73–83, with the reserve Korah psalms, 84–85, 87–89, seventeen in all: two each for the eight days of the feast, plus the final evening. But with time, and perhaps with the return of some from the East, the older, more popular, less depressed Book II resumed its ascendancy. True, it provided only for morning psalms, but this could be overlooked. What could not be bypassed was the fact that the eighth day was now established. So a psalm was needed before the final day's liturgy, marked by the ancient Davidic collection, 51–72. Psalm 51 proclaimed the spiritual message which the destruction of the Temple had enforced, 'Thou delightest not in sacrifice that I should give it: Thou hast no pleasure in burnt offering. The sacrifices of God are a broken spirit...' (Ps. 51.17-18); and a very similar theme seemed to dominate Psalm 50, the first of the Asaph collection, 'I will take no bullock out of thy house, Nor he-goats out of thy folds...'

But if Peter is thus robbed to pay Paul, who shall pay Peter? Times of peril were never far away, and the new Book III did not lose its relevance. So, with Psalm 50 lost to it, a new psalm was drafted in as no. 86. As with Book II, the new insertion was made not at the end but before the liturgy for the final day, 86–87 preceding 88–89. The psalm was something of a compound of themes from earlier 'for David' psalms, 31, 40, 11, 25, and so forth; its prayer for mercy, forgiveness and the end of God's anger in the day of trouble follows the theme of the preceding 85.

In this way Books II and III have reached their final form. The evening–morning alternations have been imposed artificially on a compound Book III not designed for such a purpose, and it is only the significant seventeen in the collection, achieved by the insertion of the alien Psalm 86, which suggests such a festal use. Again we are able to trace the Book's history only because of the enduring rivalry of the singing guilds in the Second Temple. The Asaph guild, the old Bethel priesthood, made sure that their name stood at the head of Psalms 73–83; the Korah guild, the better established and more influential ex-Danites, claimed their own Psalms 84–85 and 87–88. The old Jerusalem psalmists, who had been anonymous and had merely composed 'for David', now took the name of Ethan and laid claim to Psalm 89 by virtue of their large expansion of it. But Psalm 86 was just another David psalm, and was left as such. The power struggle between the guilds emerges in the form of genealogies in 1 Chron. 6.33-47 and elsewhere (see my *Korah*, pp. 77-79).

Thus it is possible to set out a scenario for the history of our Psalter which takes account of both the headings and the Book divisions, in line with the conclusions of my three *Studies in the Psalter*. It would be possible to carry the story on further, with the expansion of Book I and the creation of Book V; but, as Sheherazade said to the Sultan, that is a tale for another night. The reader should not think the less of it because it is only a scenario. There is much argument in the *Studies* and in the 1975 article which undergirds such a picture; and it may claim to present a much more detailed and more plausible account of the history of the Psalter than either the classic accounts of Gunkel and Mowinckel or the more contemporary outlines of Gerald Wilson and Millard. For so remote a period our evidence will always be limited, and we must hypothesize; but, as Bishop Berkeley might say today, plausibility is the guide of life.

The above account is a more worked out version of the basic theory proposed by J.P. Peters (*Psalms as Liturgies*; on this see above p. 16). Until recently it has been the only horse running in the race. Delitzsch attempted to suggest verbal links between one psalm and the next; for instance 'Oh that I had wings like a dove!' (Ps. 55.7) led on to Ps. 56.1, 'The dove of the distant terebinths'. But generally commentators were interested in the psalms, not in the Psalter; and even Mowinckel in *Psalmenstudien VI* does not offer an explanation of the grouping and ordering of our present Book.

The last decade has seen a new interest in the Psalter, especially in America, but it has been mainly concerned with the *editing* of the book. Gerald Wilson (*Editing of the Hebrew Psalter*), compares the editing at Qumran, and notes the use of *Hallelujah*, הודו, the absence of a heading (as in 43), and certain themes, which bind groups of psalms together in a way that notes of author and genre do not always do: for instance Psalms 65–68 are hymns of praise in a sea of (mainly) laments, Psalms 51–72, and 93, 96–99 are enthronement psalms. In more recent articles (especially 'Royal Psalms'), Wilson has argued that the overall structure of the Psalter is significant (McCann, *Shape*, pp. 72–82): the first two books celebrate the kingdom of David, but this is despaired of in Book III, and a turn is made to the Kingdom of God in Books IV and V. There are significant points here, though the argument depends in part on alleged royal psalms at the end of the Psalter Books ('Royal Psalms'), of which Psalm 41 is questionable.

Others have seen broad theological interests at work among the editors of the Psalter. Walter Brueggemann ('Obedience and Praise'; McCann, *Shape*, pp. 29–41) sees a movement from obedience in Psalm 1 via despair in Psalm 73 to praise in Psalms 145–50. James Mays has pointed to Psalms 1, 19 and 119, the three 'Torah-psalms', as a key to understanding the whole book ('Torah-psalms'), and notes ways in which psalms were reinterpreted by the editors of the Psalter (McCann, *Shape*, pp. 14-20): a personal thanksgiving, Psalm 30, is taken to be a public psalm for the dedication of the Temple (heading), or psalms like 33 and 24 which had once accompanied ritual become catechesis. There is a collection of similar suggestions in McCann's book (*Shape*), but the horizon is limited to features of the editing and later use of psalms: there is no general theory to account for the detail of the Psalter.

The only other attempt to provide such a comprehensive account of the Psalter is Matthias Millard's recent *Komposition*. Millard takes Gunkel's *Gattungen* as his basis, and tries to outline a *formgeschichtlich* account of the ordering of the psalms, as they now stand, headings and all. For instance, he begins from the Korah psalms, and notes that both the first (42–49) and second (84–85, 87–88) series begin with pilgrimage psalms (42–43, 84), proceed to a lament (44, 85), then a royal psalm (45, the inserted David psalm 86), then *Zionslieder* (46–48, 87) and finally a wisdom psalm (49, 88). As 42–43 are also laments, the series shows the same structure as a number of individual psalms (e.g. Ps. 22), beginning with a lament and turning to a hymn. The turning point is seen as a supposed oracle: an oracle is often thought of at Pss. 85.9 and 46.11-12, and 85 and 46 are the psalms where mourning turns to praise. Millard's book is full of suggestions for the location of individual psalms. For example, Psalms 49 and 73, taken by most commentators as two wisdom psalms reflecting on human fate, are seen as placed at either end of the second David collection (51–72), expanded by 51's twin, 50; or the pilgrimage series 120-134 has been extended by the double historical praises, 135–36, answering the call to 'bless the LORD' in Ps. 134.2, and then the related Psalm 137, the song of the exiles who will not forget Jerusalem.

Millard's book is to be welcomed, not only as a serious attempt to explain the hitherto mysterious structure of the Psalter, but as offering many insights. He is certainly right in pointing to the clustering of psalms of a similar type (e.g. the laments of 137–144 and the hymns of 145–50), and in noting the recurring sequence lament–hymn. But two general criticisms may be made of his scheme.

1. His patterns are often neater than the texts allow. If the oracle were the turning point of a series, and one comes at the turning point of the lament 85, we should expect a parallel oracle at the end of the lament 44, not of the hymn 46. But is not Ps. 45.2 the claim to be delivering a royal oracle? 45 does not fit the claimed sequence, and is treated as an insertion; and 86, although *for David*, is actually a further lament. 46, 48 and 87 are indeed celebrations of God's city: but 47 is not on this theme—why has the more general hymn been inserted between the two Zion hymns? The description of 49 as a wisdom psalm is only possible at the cost of considerable emendation of the text (cf. Goulder, *Korah*, pp. 181-95); nor is it clear why, if one is moving from lament to praise, one should wish to close on such a supposed low note.

2. Although he offers answers to many features of the Psalter, Millard leaves other matters surprisingly open. There is an 'Elohistic' psalter, 42–83, but why is the name אלהים preferred in these psalms?—at least the 'Elohistic redactor' is dispensed with, but there is no alternative explanation. Why do the two Korah series begin with pilgrimage psalms? Does this not suggest a festal setting for the whole, elsewhere described as 'very questionable'? The Asaph series also has a lament near the beginning, Psalm 74, but the hymn-like 75 and 76 are then succeeded by further laments 77, 79 and 80—why is this? Why did an editor think it suitable to detach 50 and place it next to the 'twin' 51 while leaving the rest of the series intact? Millard may reasonably reply that he has set out a proposal for the entire Psalter in 250 pages, where I have covered only 47 psalms in three volumes: but then the subject really requires a more detailed exegesis than he has yet been able to devote to it.

Part II

E, D, J, P

Chapter 8

THE PRIMACY OF THE ASAPH TRADITIONS

This book began as a study of the Psalms of Asaph. It revealed the collection as a unity, composed in Bethel, the national sanctuary of (Northern) Israel, in the 720s. It showed the response of the Israelite leadership to the threat of extinction by the Assyrian armies, the waverings between faith and realism, between hope and depression; and many of the details of life in that terrible decade—the images of enemy gods set up as insults in the sanctuaries of Yahweh, the wrecking of his shrines, the gathering of smaller peoples to settle old scores. It also seemed to show indications, more speculatively, of a pattern of festal worship shared with the Korahite psalms at Dan.

The instructed reader will, however, have been aware that something much more significant has emerged from this study. As we have sifted through these ancient prayers, a golden key has fallen into our lap: we have, for the first time, independent, datable evidence of the earliest form of Israelite historical traditions.[1] We have the means to reconstruct a history of the Pentateuch starting from the beginning. For the story of the Exodus and wilderness is the experience of the Asaph/Joseph community, and of it alone. There is not a reference to the Exodus in either the Korah psalms from Dan or the Prayers of David (51–72) from Jerusalem. Our psalms, *per contra*, speak of the Exodus as God's action *in Joseph* (Ps. 81.6), as the leading of *Joseph* (Ps. 80.2); and *Jacob* is included with *Joseph* in Ps. 77.16 only for the sake of national unity.

A history of the Pentateuch has been the holy grail quested by Old Testament scholars for nearly a quarter of a millennium, and it has been frustrated by the lack of non-Pentateuchal evidence. All that could be done was to isolate striking features in the text, and to erect them as criteria. God is spoken of sometimes as יהוה, sometimes as אלהים;

---

1.   I have set out a provisional sketch of these traditions in 'Asaph's *History of Israel* (Elohist Press, Bethel 725 BCE)', *JSOT* 65 (1995), pp. 71-81.

sometimes Israel is addressed in the second person singular, sometimes in the second person plural; the key might lie in the primitive *Credo* in Deuteronomy 26; Deuteronomic language extends from Deuteronomy 1 to 2 Kings 25; an author with priestly interests seems to have had the last say. All of these criteria have been used to propose histories of the Pentateuch, and all are partly true. The present state of division and aporia among scholars arises from a lack of datable, external evidence for the pre-exilic period; and this our study has been able to supply.

The major source which has appeared is the historical traditions in the Psalms of Asaph. These I will set out in outline in the first section of this chapter. They are derived from two elements in the Asaph corpus: (i) the actual wording of the psalms, and (ii), slightly more speculatively, from the passages in the Pentateuch and elsewhere which the psalm-texts seem to imply as Selahs. But there is also a minor source, the Psalms of the Sons of Korah. My earlier book of that title (1982) showed a similar awareness of national/tribal history in wording and Selah, and I give a short recapitulation of results in a second section. Then, finally, I shall offer an assessment of some of the leading Pentateuchal theories in the light of this new evidence.

The reader will notice one further important difference between the present theory and its major competitors. Their hypothetical sources/ authors/tradents are known by sigla, J, E, D, P; J^1, J^2, L, Dtr, etc. These shadowy figures are the creation of modern scholarship, and are not normally identified with groups or individuals mentioned in Scripture. It must, for example, be a curiosity that for many modern critics the last hand in the Pentateuch is P, a *priestly* school, whereas the heroes of the Chroniclers' work, which presumably overlaps with the Pentateuchal redaction, are not priests but *Levites*. A strength of the present hypothesis, *per contra*, is that it is rooted in the biblical tradition. It begins from evidence that there were two groups of northern tradents at the two main northern shrines, Dan and Bethel: the Korahites and the Asaphites. It ends with the three groups of tradents who stand behind the Chroniclers' work, the Korahites, the Asaphites and the Merarites. Family traditions were strong in the ancient world. The two old northern clans held their own across four centuries of catastrophe; in time they grudgingly permitted the Jerusalem Merari men their half-place in the sun.

The Asaph Traditions

The following traditions were familiar to the Asaphites before 722:

1. *Creation* was supposed to have taken place in a battle between God and the sea and its dragons, together with the river-monster Leviathan (Euphrates). The account is in Ps. 74.13-14, and corresponds with texts in Job, Isaiah and elsewhere, but not Genesis. There are in fact no Genesis traditions in the Asaph collection; but we may infer familiarity with the legend of Lot's daughters from Ps. 83.9, 'They have been an arm to the children of Lot.'

2. *The oppression in Egypt* comes in Ps. 81.6-8, '[God] appointed [festal celebrations] in Joseph for a testimony. When he went out against the land of Egypt...I removed his shoulder from the burden: His hands were freed from the basket. Thou calledst in trouble...' The language recalls Exodus 1–2. Psalm 77 also is a meditation on the troubles leading up to the deliverance from Egypt, and of the three Selahs the first seemed to echo the crying to Yahweh of Exod. 2.23.

3. *God's self-revelation.* Ps. 77.8-10 led up to a second Selah, and the wording of these verses was full of echoes of God's revelation of his name and character in Exod. 34.6-7. This would constitute a difference from the Exodus order, but there are similar revelations of God's name and being in Exodus 3 and 6.

4. *The Plagues of Egypt* are described in Ps. 78.43-51. The poetic form makes categorization difficult, but the list of plagues seems to comprise (i) the turning of rivers to blood, (ii) the attack by flies and frogs on the Egyptians, (iii) their plants devastated by two kinds of locust, (iv) their cattle destroyed by hail and thunderbolts, (v) a pestilence which killed their first-born. This account is much elaborated in Exodus 7–12.

5. *The Exodus* is presented in two forms. (i) In the older form God terrifies the waters with the voice of his thunder, the whirlwind and lightning; his way is in the sea, and he leads his people there like a flock by the hand of Moses and Aaron (Ps. 77.17-21). Although the account has much in common with the old creation myth, there is a clear Exodus foundation here as the people escape Egypt (*thine arm redeemed thy people, The sons of Jacob and Joseph*). There is no mention of the Egyptian army; and I have argued (p. 106) that both *Jacob* and *Moses* had been introduced into *Joseph/Aaron* traditions for nation-building motives. (ii) A more developed form of the story comes in

Ps. 78.12-13, 53: the sea is cloven, the waters stand as a heap, and they overwhelm the Egyptian enemy. The second version is closely similar to the Song of the Sea in Exodus 15, and there were sufficient echoes of this Song in Ps. 77.11-16 to suggest that it formed the third Selah there.

6. *Cloud and fire* were provided to lead Israel on by day and by night (78.14, 52): in the latter verse from Egypt itself, in the former from the Sea. These symbols of divine guidance have become pillars in Exod. 13.21-22, 14.19-20.

7. *Water is provided from the rock* yielding abundance for the people to drink. It is a sheer gift of God. There is no tempting of God by the people as in Exodus 17, nor contention as in Numbers 20, and Moses does not strike any rock. There are twelve springs at Elim in Exod. 15.27, and the bitter waters of Marah are miraculously sweetened in Exod. 15.22-26 (after some murmuring); but neither event corresponds closely with Ps. 78.15-16.

8. The people tempt God by doubting his ability to provide bread and flesh. God rains down manna and winged fowl as the sand of the seas; but as they eat for their lust, his anger smites down the flower of the people (Ps. 78.17-31). The story is similar to that in Exodus 16 (murmuring, quails, manna), but much more similar to that in Numbers 11 (murmuring, quails in volume, God's anger smites with plague as the flesh is between their teeth, the Graves of Lusting).

9. *Lack of faith leads to wasted years in the desert*: 'they believed not in his wondrous works. Therefore their days did he consume in vanity, And their years in terror' (Ps. 78.32-33). This recalls Israel's failure to believe (Joshua and) Caleb's good report of the land, and God's punishment of a generation in the wilderness (Num. 13–14).

10. *The covenant* was concluded at Meribah, where God answered Israel from the secret place of thunder (Ps. 81.8), and it is implied in Ps. 78.34-37: 'When he had slain them, then they inquired after him, And they returned and sought after God earnestly... But they flattered him... Neither were they faithful in his *covenant*'. The covenant came after the death of the faithless generation. It provided for monolatry on Israel's side, and providence on God's: an outline was probably recited as the Selah after Ps. 81.8. This is soon succeeded by the words, 'There shall no strange god be in thee; Neither shalt thou worship any strange god... I am the LORD thy God, Which brought thee up out of the land of Egypt: Open thy mouth and I will fill it' (Ps. 81.10-11). There are some similar words in Ps. 50.7. All this bears a marked relation to the

אלהים-passages in the Sinai covenant story of Exodus 20–24. Israel camps at the oasis at Meribah in Numbers 20.

11. A part of the covenant was the requirement to give *justice to the weak* of society, the poor, orphaned, and so forth. There seems to be an echo of this in God's rebuke to the gods of the nations in Psalm 82, 'How long will you judge unjustly and show partiality to the wicked?... Give justice to the weak and the orphan... Rescue the weak and the needy'. The wording of these verses flanking the Selah are close to the laws of Exod. 23.1-8.

12. *The covenant was quickly broken by Israel, but God forgave the sin*: 'But they flattered him with their mouth, And lied unto him with their tongue. For their heart was not right with him, Neither were they faithful in his covenant. But he, being full of compassion, forgave their iniquity, and destroyed them not' (Ps. 78.36-38). Ps. 81.12 similarly says, 'But my people hearkened not to my voice; And Israel would none of me', though there is no mention of the forgiveness. The 'flattering', and so forth, means that Israel soon fell back to worshipping other gods, as in Exodus 32; the forgiveness recalls Moses' intercession in Exodus 33–34. The last verses of Psalm 81 echo a number of phrases in Deut. 32.13-18, which is likely to have been familiar.

13. *The Settlement* is described in Ps. 78.54-55: 'And he brought them to his holy border, To his mountainous land which his right hand had purchased. He drove out the nations also before them, And allotted them for an inheritance by line, And made the tribes of Israel to dwell in their tents'. Similarly in Ps. 80.9-10, 'Thou broughtest a vine out of Egypt: Thou didst drive out the nations, and plantedst it, And it took deep root and filled the land'. Again the wording is similar to Exod. 15.17-18, and the story covers the period of Joshua–Judges.

14. *The battles of the Judges period* are known in some detail: 'Do thou to them as unto Midian; As to Sisera, as to Jabin at the river Kishon: Which perished at En-dor; They became as dung for the earth. Make their nobles like Oreb and Zeeb; Yea, all their princes like Zebah and Zalmunna' (Ps. 83.10-12). This covers much of the same ground as the stories of Deborah and Gideon in Judges 4–8, though with some notable differences.

15. This extends to *the loss of the Ark at Shiloh*. God 'forsook the tabernacle of Shiloh, The tent which he placed among men; And delivered his strength into captivity, And his glory into the adversary's hand. He gave his people over also unto the sword... Fire devoured their

young men; And their maidens had no marriage-song. Their priests fell by the sword; and their widows made no lamentation' (Ps. 78.59-64). The psalmist knows about the *death of Hophni and Phinehas*, and the primary concern of the latter's *widow* for the Ark rather than her husband; he also knows that the Philistines took Shiloh, a fact suppressed in 1 Samuel 1–4.

16. *David's rise from being a shepherd to being a king, and his victories over the Philistines* close Psalm 78 (65-66, 70-72). God 'smote his adversaries backward: he put them to a perpetual reproach. He chose David also his servant, And took him from the sheepfolds... To feed Jacob his people, and Israel his inheritance. So he fed them according to the integrity of his heart; And guided them by the skilfulness of his hands'. This is the outline of the story of 1 Samuel 16–1 Kings 1.

17. *The Davidic–Solomonic empire* is celebrated in the vine image of Ps. 80.11-12: 'The mountains were covered with the shadow of it, The cedars of God with the boughs thereof. She sent out her branches unto the sea, And her shoots unto the River.' The boundaries of Greater Israel are understood to be the Euphrates and the Mediterranean as in 1 Kgs 5.1 (EVV 4.21), and to include South Lebanon as in 2 Sam. 8.9-11.

So the Asaph community were familiar with the history of Israel in outline from Exodus 1 to 1 Kings 5 in our Bible; and if they chanted their psalms and Selahs at national festivals each year, the people of Ephraim, Benjamin and Manasseh would have been familiar with them too. There are many gaps in the outline, for some of which there may have been traditions, and others no doubt not.

The Korah Traditions

In contrast with the rich historical traditions underlying the Asaph psalms, the Korah traditions are thin; but even their thinness and negativeness may be significant. We may notice first two marked absences: there is no mention of, or indirect reference to, the Exodus; and the people of God is always referred to as Jacob, never Israel. I list the references to the people as named. (In some cases the reference may be to the patriarch rather than the people, but the text is ambiguous.)

44.5   Command victories for Jacob
46.8, 12   The God of Jacob is our high tower
47.4   He chooseth our inheritance... The excellency of Jacob

84.9	Give ear, O God of Jacob
85.2	Thou hast brought back the captivity of Jacob
87.2	The LORD loveth the gates of Zion
	More than all the dwellings of Jacob.

At least in Psalms 44, 47, 85 and 87 *Jacob* has to be the people, and it may be in all seven cases. Although the number of references is not large enough to be conclusive, the absence of *Israel* is noticeable. The Asaph psalms have *Israel* 15 times to *Jacob*'s seven; here *Jacob* never stands clearly for the people on its own—it appears twice as 'the God of Jacob', four times in parallel to *Israel*, and once as *the sons of Jacob and Joseph.*

For Ps. 48.12, 'Let the daughters of *Judah* rejoice', as a gloss for Jerusalem use, see my *Korah*, pp. 167-68.

Although there was no open reference in the Korah psalms to any event in Israelite history except the Settlement (Ps. 44.2-9), in *The Psalms of the Sons of Korah* I examined the language of the passages leading up to the Selahs, and was able to suggest a number of possible historical echoes. In some cases these are irrelevant for our purposes: for example, Ps. 87.2, 'Glorious things are spoken of thee, O city of God (Selah', looked like the occasion for reciting the foundation legend of the shrine at Dan. In others they were too speculative to bear the weight of the present argument; but two passages seemed probable, Pss. 44.2-9 and 85.2-9.

Psalm 44 is a national lament accompanied by ritual prostrations (v. 26), and repeated cries of Hallelujah ('In God we have made our boast, הללנו, all the day long', v. 9). It begins, 'We have heard with our ears, O God, our fathers have told us, What work thou didst in their days, in the days of old' (v. 2); this recalls the recital of the Torah 'before all Israel, in their ears' by the priests and elders in Deut. 31.10-11; 27.9. We have an instance of such a recital by Joshua in Joshua 24, where the wording is close to phrases in Psalm 44:

Josh. 24.2	Your fathers dwelt...
Josh. 24.17	us and our fathers
Ps. 44.2	our fathers have told us
Josh. 24.8	ye possessed their land (ותירשו)
Ps. 44.3	they gat the land in possession (ירשו)
Josh. 24.12	he drave the peoples out from before you
Ps. 44.2	Thou didst drive out the nations

Josh. 24.12	not with thy sword nor with thy bow
Ps. 44.6	For I will not trust in my bow, Neither shall my sword save me
Josh. 24.20	If ye forsake the LORD, and serve strange gods...
Josh. 24.23	Now therefore put away the strange gods which are among you, and incline your heart unto the LORD
Ps. 44.18	Our heart is not turned back, Neither have our steps inclined from thy way
Ps. 44.23	If we have... spread forth our hands to any strange god

So insistent a coincidence of language suggests that the Selah at Ps. 44.9 was some recital underlying part of our Joshua 24.

The situation of the Selah at Ps. 85.3 is similar, but more complex. Ps. 85.9 reads אשמעה מה־ידבר האל יהוה כי ידבר שלום, which may be rendered, 'I will hearken to what the God Yahweh speaks, for he speaks peace...'; the divine message is that which has just been recited in the Selah. The psalm opened, 'LORD, thou wast favourable unto thy land: Thou didst return to the captivity of Jacob. Thou didst forgive the iniquity of thy people, Thou didst cover all their sin. (Selah.) Thou didst take away all thy wrath: Thou didst turn from the fierceness of thine anger. Turn us...' The psalm is again a national lament. It begins with a reference to some previous classic occasion in which God remitted his anger and forgave the nation's sin, and prays that he will do the same again now: Weiser interprets this (though without reference to the Selah) as pointing to the *Heilsgeschichte* which he sees as being recited in the festal cult.

Now the Danite priesthood were Levites, and descended from Jonathan b. Gershom b. Moses (Judg. 18.30); and Deut. 33.8-9 records a northern tradition that the Levites had earned their priesthood by their loyalty to Yahweh at Massah, where they massacred their apostate fellow-tribesmen. This story, which is also the core of Exodus 32, in vv. 25-29, is important because it legitimates the Danite priesthood (the sons of Korah), and Moses their leader and ancestor, as having divine authority: 'Thy Thummim and thy Urim are with him whom thou lovest, Whom thou didst prove at Massah...' The Exodus story contains a number of phrases echoed in Psalm 85:

Exod. 32.12	Turn from the fierceness of thine anger
Ps. 85.3	Thou didst turn from the fierceness of thine anger
Exod. 32.32	Yet now, if thou wilt forgive their sin
Exod. 34.7	forgiving iniquity and transgression and sin
Ps. 85.2	Thou didst forgive the iniquity of thy people, Thou didst cover all their sin.

Exod. 34.6	Yahweh, Yahweh, a God (אל)
Ps. 85.9	I will hearken to what the God (האל) Yahweh speaks
Exod. 34.6	plenteous in mercy and truth
Ps. 85.11	Mercy and truth are met together
Exod. 32.34	Behold, my angel shall go before thee
Ps. 85.14	Righteousness shall go before him

With the accumulation of language in common, it seems probable that the forgiveness appealed to was forgiveness for the apostasy at Massah, and that this story was recited in the Selah, in a form underlying parts of our Exodus 32–34.

For a fuller exposition of the passage, with a review of alternative explanations of the term Selah, and of the 'prophetic' interpretation of Ps. 85.9, see my *Korah*, pp. 102–11.

A third, less clear possibility is suggested by the sudden change to the divine first person singular in Ps. 46.11, 'Desist, and know that I am God', coupled with Selahs following Ps. 46.8, 12, 'Yahweh of hosts is with us; The God of Jacob is our high tower.' In the story of Jacob's vision at Bethel (familiar in Hos. 12.4), God says, 'I am Yahweh the God of Abraham... And behold, I am with thee' (Gen. 28.13-15). Cf. my *Korah*, pp. 147-48.

So the Korahites' traditions of pre-settlement events were not impressive. What does impress is their confidence. The Asaph tradents at Bethel needed to be ingratiating: the God *of Jacob*, the sons of *Jacob and* Joseph, Israel/*Jacob*, the hand of *Moses and* Aaron. The sons of Korah had presided at Dan when the Asaphites were heathens in Egypt. They had acknowledged Yahweh before Joshua was heard of. Their priesthood went back to Moses. The new invaders, Joseph and Benjamin, were welcome to accede to the union if they wished, and join the nation's worship at their shrine. But it was not for them to refer to God's people by the name *Israel*, by which only the combined tribes of Ephraim, Manasseh and Benjamin called themselves, or to mention the Exodus, which only these groups had experienced. There is something breathtaking in this aristocratic arrogance which draws our reluctant admiration; but then pride comes before a fall, and they certainly had a fall in 732.

Our Fathers Have Told Us

The appearance of so much evidence of eighth-century historical tradition gives a new perspective on the Pentateuchal problem; and it may be convenient at this point to comment briefly on some of the major theo-ries of the last hundred years in its light. I cannot provide a new history of Pentateuchal study—two excellent outlines have been published recently, Joseph Blenkinsopp's *The Pentateuch* (1992), and Cees Houtman's *Der Pentateuch* (1994)—but the reader may find it helpful to contrast the picture emerging from the Bethel and Dan psalms with the views of well-known critics.

(1) We may begin from the classic Documentary Hypothesis as out-lined by Julius Wellhausen, first in his *Die Composition des Hexateuchs und der historischen Bücher des ATs* (which appeared originally in article form in 1876–77), and then in his *Prolegomena to the History of Israel* (first German edition 1878). Wellhausen was the heir to a tradi-tion—de Wette, Vatke, Hupfeld, Nöldeke, Kuenen, Graf—opposing the idea of a basic priestly *Grundschrift* to the Hexateuch. On the contrary the priestly tradition was the last of three sources to be incorporated. It was preceded by the work of the Deuteronomist, and before him by the work of JE. The *Prolegomena* is a devastating book, and it is not sur-prising that it turned the tide and swept all before it. In field after field—the Place of Worship, Sacrifice, the Sacred Feasts, the Priests and Levites, the Endowment of the Clergy—Wellhausen was able to show a three-stage movement. JE showed a family-based, agricultural, natural, spiritual religion. D witnessed to the influence of the prophets, but with the coming of the law book in Josiah's reign, institutionalism, Levitical priests, Jerusalem worship and tithe-taxes have begun to take over. P (or its four-covenant alter ego Q) is the codification and formalizing of reli-gion: all is centred on the priests and the Tabernacle, an invention of post-exilic times, and the genuine religion of earlier Israelite farmers is swamped by historicizing fictions. The three-phase story, so widely sup-ported, was the more persuasive because it chimed in with the anti-Semitism of the times. Prophetic Israelite religion was the forerunner of the faith of Jesus: the priestly debasement was the beginning of Judaism, and of the institutional Church. Behind Wellhausen's faceless Q stand the sinister figures of Wagner's Nibelungen, and the giants Fafner and Fasolt.

Hupfeld had convinced Wellhausen that the northern E was a source independent of the earlier J, but he followed Nöldeke in thinking that J and E had been combined before 722 (*Prolegomena*, pp. 6-9). Thus Wellhausen saw the biblical story from Genesis to 2 Kings as the combi-nation of four documentary sources: two eighth-century sources, J and

E, using יהוה and אלהים respectively, which were soon combined to cover our books of Genesis, Exodus and Numbers; a seventh-century law corpus, D, with an extensive history from Joshua to 2 Kings, which was completed in the Exile; and a fourth, priestly source, P, from the time of the Exile, which provided much of the genealogical and ritual material in Genesis–Numbers and Joshua.

More than a century has passed since Wellhausen's two books, and many of his conclusions have been disputed; but their central thesis, shorn of its anti-institutionalism, seems unassailable. The Old Testament does reveal a development in Israelite religious thinking. The last hand in this is the priestly school, whose spokesman is Ezra. Before that stands the work of a Deuteronomic school which produced both the law book, Deuteronomy 12–26 (or something like it), and then the D-history. Earlier still there is plentiful evidence of a less organized, more direct religion. What is not so certain is his conclusion that these three phases are represented by four parallel documentary sources, with redactors to edit them together.

The weakest point in Wellhausen's majestic structure is, by common consent, his E source. But it is here that the evidence from the two psalm collections ratifies his conclusion: there really was a set of historical traditions in the eighth century in Northern Israel, the Asaph psalm tradition, and it really did use אלהים as its normal term for God. Since this has been so widely discredited, it is both surprising and reassuring to find it confirmed. However, there are rather severe limits to the confirmation. Wellhausen's E was particularly important in Genesis, and we have found no Genesis elements in the Asaph psalms. The collection uses יהוה as well as אלהים, so the latter name is not determinative. Many of the passages attributed to E by Wellhausen do not concur with our psalm evidence. More significant still, the E source is earlier than any J source for the Exodus–wilderness narrative: it is the Asaph/Joseph tribes which experienced the Exodus and wanderings, and their tradition has only been marginally adjusted to include the traditions of other northern (Jacob/Korah) groups. Any southern contributions are secondary. Nor was the E tradition limited to the Pentateuch: it included elements from our Judges and Samuel, and extended at least as far as the Solomonic empire. Finally, E was not a document: it was a body of oral tradition, recited at festal worship, originally as Selahs, background stories to expound the psalms, and to ensure that further generations forget not the works of God but keep his commandments.

In time I shall suggest reasons for thinking that Wellhausen's picture of J, D and P as independent documentary sources requires restatement. He was mistaken in thinking of independent documents and of redactors; the truth lies rather in an incremental model and a setting in recital at worship, with first the Dan Korah tradents taking the recital over, and in exile the Jerusalem sons of Merari. But these are only amendments to a theory that has stood the test of time. I have nothing but admiration for the amazing achievement of Wellhausen's two great books. *Scribamus spoliis, Ille magister erat.*

(2) Wellhausen's E was criticized in 1933 by W. Rudolph and Paul Volz in *Der Elohist als Erzähler: Ein Irrweg der Pentateuchkritik?* Their critique was confined to Genesis, Volz covering Genesis 15–36 and Rudolph the Joseph story; Rudolph later extended the argument in *Der 'Elohist' von Exodus bis Joshua* (1938). Volz exposed the difficulties of constructing a coherent duplicate narrative to be ascribed to E: it was all very well to attribute to J and E one version apiece of a duplicate story like the passing off of a patriarch's wife as his sister, but E required a credible cycle of stories. Nor did the אלהים/יהוה, אמה/שׁפחה, Canaanite/Amorite, Jacob/Israel divisions fit the stories exactly: if the criteria were to be applied rigorously, essential sentences would have to be excised from what were clearly literary units. Hence Volz refused the view of E as an independent continuous source, and envisaged him as a re-editor (*Neuherausgeber*) of the J narrative. The false trail of the parallel E-source had been started by Hupfeld when he broke up the אלהים material into the later P and the earlier E. The parallel source problem is especially acute with the Joseph story, as Rudolph argued, since it runs as a single coherent tale in a flowing style, and the claimed doubled narratives with Ishmaelites and Midianites, or two words for the brothers' sacks, are patient of more straightforward explanations. The style was, however, noticeably different from the J of Volz's chapters, and must be credited to a different author.

The criticisms of Volz and Rudolph have established themselves, and have been elaborated by Frederick Winnett ('Re-examining the Foundations') and others. Volz was in fact only partly right. His picture of a single original continuous story which underwent later editing is correct: but he was insufficiently radical, and his clinging to the priority of J was an error. Both the Abraham and the Jacob cycles give prominence to Shechem and Bethel, the Asaph sanctuaries; the whole Joseph story glorifies Joseph (and Benjamin), the Asaph heroes; and the whole

Exodus complex is Asaphite. So in making 'E' the re-editor of J, Volz was mistaken: 'E' is primary throughout. He was right in attacking the idea of two parallel sources, and right in disputing the יהוה/אלהים criterion; so we could concede him total victory of a paradoxical kind. He thought there was one central narrative written by the Yahwist and edited by the Elohist (and later P): there was in fact one central narrative handed down by the Elohist and then adapted by the Yahwist, and later P. Rudolph's arguments were more questionable, and I return to them in Chapter 9.

Rudolph was right, however, in the important comment that the style of the Joseph story is different from the rest of Genesis; but the same is true of the great stories in Genesis 20–22. Here the name for God is preponderantly אלהים, in contradistinction to a hitherto dominant יהוה, and there must be some reason for this. In addition Abraham is a different man in these tales, a more moral, humane and noble figure; the narrative is more measured, and the emotional tension higher. We have a different author here too. So Astruc's יהוה/אלהים distinction was not entirely mistaken; and we shall find it useful in the exegesis of Exodus 19–24 also.

(3) A new dimension to Pentateuchal criticism was introduced by the soaring imagination of Gerhard von Rad, in particular with his celebrated essay, 'The Form-Critical Problem of the Hexateuch' (1938). Von Rad noted that outline versions of the whole Hexateuch story were present in a number of liturgical passages; in particular the short 'Credo', 'An Aramaean ready to perish was my father...' (Deut. 26.5-9), the father's answer to his son's question in Deut. 6.20-24, Joshua's covenant speech at Shechem (Josh. 24), and in Psalms 78, 105, 135, 136. So the narrative had its ultimate origin in the liturgy. However, it was noticeable that none of these liturgical pieces contained any reference to the law-giving at Sinai: so it was likely that the Patriarchs–Exodus–Settlement story belongs in one liturgical context, while the Sinai covenant belongs in another. We have three pilgrim-festivals in early Israelite tradition, and a number of sanctuaries. Von Rad sited the main narrative at Gilgal for the Feast of Weeks, and the law-covenant tradition at Shechem for Tabernacles. These cultic recitals were established in the period of the Judges. The creative theological development of them, and their reduction to writing, we owed to the Yahwist, who lived in tenth-century Jerusalem, during the 'Solomonic Enlightenment'.

This brilliant reconstruction is almost totally wrong; but like other flights of the imagination it contains some liberating insights. The three Hexateuch passages are now widely agreed to be heavily overwritten by the Deuteronomists, and there is no evidence that the Deuteronomy 26 'creed' is early; some of the psalms, especially 135, 136, are very late; the Solomonic Enlightenment is unevidenced, and probably wishful thinking. Gilgal, according to Kraus, is to be associated with Unleavened Bread/Passover rather than Weeks (*Worship*, pp. 152-65); and Weeks is more likely to be the feast for the renewal of the covenant (2 Chron. 15.9-15; *Worship*, pp. 58-61), and originally associated with Beersheba, the Well of Oaths/Seven.

So much realism is in danger of reducing von Rad to a student's Aunt Sally; his was the baseless fabric of a vision, but it it was a vision nonetheless. (i) He saw correctly that the great narrative had its genesis in the liturgy, and that meant the liturgy of the pilgrim-festivals. He was not the first to suggest that, for it had been proposed for the Decalogue by Mowinckel (*Le Décalogue*, 1927) and Alt ('The Origins of Israelite Law' [1934], in *Essays*), and by Johannes Pedersen ('Passahfest und Passahlegende', 1934) for various Passover traditions; but von Rad made a total scenario which carried initial conviction. We have seen in fact that he was not wrong in picking out Psalm 78 as evidence of an early form of what he called the Hexateuchal narrative: 78 begins from Exodus and goes through to 2 Samuel, rather than from Genesis to Joshua, but it is an early (eighth century) form of the overall story.

Von Rad deserves credit for seeing the genesis of the Hexateuch in the liturgy of the festivals; but he has been criticized (Blenkinsopp, *Pentateuch*, p. 17) for not specifying the link between cult and narrative. This omission has been repaired in our own psalms study; for it has repeatedly appeared that the Selahs in the text of Books II and III—the Prayers of David as well as the Asaph and Korah psalms—stand for breaks in the psalm-chant for a cantillation of the relevant narrative. Sometimes, as with Psalm 78, the psalm itself reveals the content of the community's historical tradition. More often, as with Psalm 77, the text hints at the assumed narrative, and its clustering of echoes from our Pentateuch enables us to descry with some confidence the underlying story. So although von Rad did not see this important pointer, his instinct was sound: the matrix of the Pentateuch was indeed the festal liturgy.

(ii) Von Rad noticed a second crucial feature, the absence of the Sinai story from the early 'creeds'. Here we may gloss the crude statement with some provisos. The father is to answer his son in Deut. 6.20-24 with an outline history which does not mention Sinai: but it concludes, 'And the LORD commanded us to do all these statutes...', which implies some giving of the covenant. Psalm 78 refers twice explicitly to the covenant (78.10, 37), and to the law (vv. 5, 10), testimonies (vv. 5, 56), and commandments (v. 7). So the giving of a covenant is a part of the Exodus–wilderness narrative from early (eighth century) times. Nevertheless the absence of the name Sinai—and for that matter Horeb—from the early tradition is striking and significant. The old tradition knew the locus of the covenant as Kadesh/Meribah. Sinai was a later intrusion brought in by the Jerusalem tradents, whose Judahite ancestors had come from the Sinai peninsula.

(4) Even more influential was Martin Noth, who, like von Rad, wished to bypass the Wellhausen source documents and concentrate on the earliest oral forms of the tradition. His two monumental studies are *Überlieferungsgeschichtliche Studien* (1943), which considers the Deuteronomic corpus from Deuteronomy to 2 Kings, the Chronicler's work and that of the priestly author; and *Überlieferungsgeschichte des Pentateuch* (1948), an examination of the traditions behind Genesis–Numbers. Whereas von Rad (following Wellhausen and a long tradition) had spoken of the Hexateuch and drawn a firm line after Joshua 24, Noth spoke of the Tetrateuch, and drew the line after Numbers 36.

Fundamental to this dichotomy is the consensus of the time that there is no D-material before Deuteronomy and no P-material after Numbers, apart from Joshua and a few verses of Deuteronomy. Noth was faced with the question why this was so, and answered that Deuteronomy was put in its present form (apart from some late additions in Deut. 31–34) as an introduction to the D-history; it is substantially a literary work of the sixth century, with its historical framework in Deuteronomy 1–3 a foreshadowing of the Joshua–Kings history to follow. Its laws, and the traditions incorporated into the history books, are of greater antiquity. Similarly, we have the literary deposit of J, E and P in the Tetrateuch, a late composition; but between Genesis 12 and Numbers lie the nuggets of many ancient oral traditions. These were recited in pre-monarchic festivals at different sanctuaries, and came to coalesce under five central topics: the Exodus, the Settlement, the Promises, the Wilderness and Sinai. With the formation of a tribal amphictyony with a cultic centre at Shechem, the way was open for development of a single continuous narrative. This was already a unity, whether in oral or written form, in

the Judges period; and the achievement of J, E and P is limited to
retelling it in slightly variant forms, prefixing to it the creation and flood
stories, and inserting the genealogies.

As with von Rad, much of this enormous theory is mistaken, but
important parts of it were dramatic advances. It certainly is the case that
Dtr, the school which composed the Deuteronomic history, prefaced
Deuteronomy 1–3 to the corpus; that there was no doubled J/E tradition
running through the history; and that the speeches and authors' comments at various critical points indicate a single hand from Deuteronomy
1 to 2 Kings 25 (with some later glosses, naturally). But just as Noth
argues that Joshua's entry from the east requires the explanation of why
the invasion was not made from the south, given in Deuteronomy 2, so
does the whole narrative presuppose knowledge of the Exodus, and
even occasionally of Abraham, Isaac and Jacob (who, like everything
else, can always be attributed to a later gloss). The Asaph psalms show
that in fact there was from the eighth century a continuous historical
tradition in the hands of Deuteronomist-type tradents, running from the
oppression in Egypt to Solomon's time, and no doubt beyond: so
Deuteronomy 1–3 is not so much a *preface* to the D-corpus as a *link*
between the Exodus–Numbers story and the D-work. Such evidence
confirms the modern feeling that D's hand is not entirely absent from
the Tetrateuch, and may be seen in such passages as Genesis 15; and
that there is a single coherent theme from Genesis 12 to 2 Kings 25, the
promise of the land to the multiplied seed of the patriarchs under the
provident hand of God (Clines, *Theme*).

Noth's reconstruction of the oral tradition behind the Tetrateuch is
similarly patchy. There were indeed Settlement traditions at Dan (Ps. 44)
and Bethel, and no doubt other sanctuaries from early times. But the
Exodus–southern wilderness–Meribah covenant traditions belonged to
Bethel, and to Bethel only down to the 720s. There were other wilder-
ness traditions at Dan with Moses and the Levites, and at Jerusalem with
Sinai, but none of these were fused at Shechem in the Judges period.
Nor were the patriarchs a part of the official tradition at any of the three
main sanctuaries: the name of Jacob is known, and that of Abraham, at
Dan (Ps. 47), but we have narrative traditions only of Jacob from Hosea.

So Noth's scenario is not wrong, but it is badly out of focus. There
were indeed oral traditions celebrated in different local sanctuaries from
the Judges period, but these continued independently for centuries
longer than he supposed. The 'main' tradition, of the Exodus, wilderness

and covenant, belonged to the Joseph–Benjamin tribes, and had its locus in Bethel. Perhaps it was earlier celebrated by the same tribes in Shechem, before the repeated destruction of the latter; but insofar as Shechem was the early centre of the Israelite 'amphictyony', it was the place where the new central tribes accepted the worship of Yahweh, and the covenant of alliance with the older settlers: in 730 the Korah priesthood at Dan knows nothing of the Exodus or Meribah. The fusion of northern traditions does not take place until Dan's loss in the late eighth century; and Sinai comes in in Jerusalem a century later. For this part of his great scheme Noth was out by half a millennium.

(5) Von Rad and Noth dominated the early post-war years; but there was a restiveness which in time produced Rolf Rendtorff's *Die Über-lieferungsgeschichtliche Problem des Pentateuch* (1977). Rendtorff began with the smallest units of the tradition, the individual stories, and argued that they had passed through a series of redactions. The larger complexes sometimes showed no awareness of other such complexes: Exodus may present the land as inhabited by foreigners, for example, without any suggestion that it had been promised to the patriarchs repeatedly. The so-called documentary sources explain nothing. There are no linguistic, stylistic or theological grounds for maintaining *continuous parallel* documentary sources. J is a fiction. Initially there were the individual stories and legal units, which were from the eighth century edited by proto-Deuteronomic 'circles' into the larger complexes, and then later by a priestly school, which supplied half a dozen narrative units and much legal matter. There were no independent redactors either. The whole thing grew by constant re-touching into its present whole.

Rendtorff's book is a fine instance of radical common sense, and a great deal of it is right. What he has not allowed for is the early stage at which the basic units have been gathered into a continuous narrative. We have them so in Bethel in the 720s, and the running story must have been proclaimed there from generation to generation for many years before (Ps. 78.3, 'Which we have heard and known, And our fathers have told us'). But that central point apart, he has shown a masterly sense for the truth. There were no parallel sources. The Pentateuch has grown by constant redaction, and the redaction was in process from the eighth century by proto-Deuteronomic tradents. The Genesis complexes were added after the main Exodus–Settlement–[Solomon] story had been put together, and that is why the latter sometimes ignores the promises in the former. The main hands in the accumulation of the units have indeed been Deuteronomic and priestly; we have no need of independent redactors. So much innovative insight deserves high acclaim.

In one respect Rendtorff represents a step backwards, however: he, and many of his generation, withdrew from the liturgical matrix in which Mowinckel, Pedersen, von Rad and Noth had seen the origin of the Pentateuch. In its place we have 'Deuteronomic circles' and constant redactions, which are not too exactly described. Are we to think of groups of influential Israelites gathered in committee to re-do the tradition, on the lines of modern Bible translators? Or was the master-text kept in the Temple archives, with individuals just copying it out once every twenty-five years, and making what improvements seemed good to them? Was some of this work done, as is often supposed, in exile? If so, did Nebuzaradan give special permission for the official version of the Torah to be carried to Babylon?

The Asaph psalms confirm the liturgical view: the national story was told by 'our fathers' from generation to generation; it was recited by the מנצח in the Selah intervals, and echoed in the psalms themselves, not least in Psalm 78. Each autumn the appointed tradent would retell the tale; each year he would add a suitable gloss to match current needs; with time many of the glosses would become traditional; new tradents would introduce new ideas, perhaps new theologies; in the seventh century the dominant tradents were northern—that is Korahite and Asaphite—and so Deuteronomic; in the sixth and fifth centuries the Jerusalem priesthood—the Merarites—gained a stronger voice. So despite himself Rendtorff's study speaks for a liturgical setting for his *Überlieferungsgeschichte*. Constant redaction is only plausible with repeated *oral narration*; and that is testified in our psalms as taking place at the full moon of New Year (Ps. 81.4-5).

(6) Confidence in the early date of J was ebbing in the 1970s. John Van Seters published *Abraham in History and Tradition* in 1975. The first part of the book effectively overthrew any claims of a patriarchal age in the second millennium. The patriarchs had camels, which were not domesticated till the first millennium, and they circulated among Aramaeans, Arabs and Chaldaeans who are first found in the first millennium; no argument from names, customs or archaeology is valid for a second millennium date. Then the Abraham stories are analysed, and are found to be substantially *literary* reworkings by a single Yahwist author, to be dated around the Exile. He had a few oral traditions like the wife-as-sister story of Genesis 12, and these had sometimes been already

re-worked by a more thoughtful pre-Yahwist, as with the similar story in
Genesis 20; but the Abraham cycle was essentially the literary work of J,
later supplemented by P. Van Seters gave no credence to the traditional
יהוה/אלהים criterion for distinguishing sources.

Van Seters went on to publish a whole series of books: *In Search of
History* (1983), *Prologue to History: The Yahwist as Historian in
Genesis* (1992), *The Life of Moses: The Yahwist as Historian in
Exodus–Numbers* (1994). In these he argues two less plausible theses.
First, he draws parallels between the Pentateuch narrative and history-
writing in Mesopotamia and (more especially) Greece: a late date for J,
in the Exile, would place him not much before early Greek historians
like Herodotus, with whom a number of points of contact are alleged.
Thus J's purpose is seen to be the writing of an early kind of history,
with a strong divine element. Secondly, the Exodus–Numbers narrative
is dated late, and this involves seeing it as dependent on Deuteronomy. I
have countered the latter claim for a number of the stories below in
Chapters 11–13; but I think that the many differences from Herodotus
and Thucydides make unconvincing the idea that the Yahwist was a kind
of Greek historian. In any case 'J'—the Korahite expansion of the
Asaph traditions—belongs comfortably, with its frequent D-phrasing, in
the reign of King Josiah.

Van Seters's Abraham was soon succeeded by Hans Heinrich
Schmid's unpretentious but significant *Der sogenannte Jahwist* (1976).
Schmid showed that many of the stories in Exodus–Numbers which had
been attributed to the Yahwist in fact contained strong signs of
Deuteronom(ist)ic language, and that their form often presupposed the
form of prophetic oracles, especially in Isaiah and Jeremiah. Moses' call,
for instance, seemed to be an echo of Jeremiah's, or of Gideon's and
Saul's in Dtr; or the hardening of Pharaoh's heart, and the demand for
Israel's faith in God, seemed to be a reminiscence of the hardening and
faith themes in Isaiah 6–7. Schmid also drew on Lothar Perlitt's
Bundestheologie im Alten Testament (1969) for arguments that Genesis
15, a 'covenant' passage attributed widely to J or E, was in fact nothing
but Deuteronomic. In other words, according to Schmid, J = D. Van
Seters's Deuteronomic period Yahwist is an unnecessary hypothesis, and
due for Occam's razor.

It will be seen that all these authors are in line with Rendtorff, and
similar remarks apply to them. It is singular that Perlitt's study of the
history of the ברית concept should have so totally ignored the uses of

the term in the Asaph psalms, and Schmid has worked on the theory that there was no E, and therefore a late J = D brings the whole Tetrateuch down to Josiah's time or later. In fact the Asaph community gave a central place to the covenant, and Psalm 81 shows it to be a covenant with two sides to it, God's provision as well as Israel's monolatry; and the Exodus–Numbers history extracted in the first part of this chapter provided the thread on which Schmid's J = D could base his embroiderings. Nonetheless all three authors are substantially right. There was no early Yahwist in King Solomon's court. The great creative theologian of von Rad was a humble exiled Asaphite, not I think in Babylon, but at the court of King Josiah.

(7) Within the present decade, two further proposals have been made, both involving late dating, and both dispensing with the now dubious 'J'. Norman Whybray rejects both the documentary and the 'supplementary' hypotheses in *The Making of the Pentateuch* (1987). With a firm grip on Occam's razor, he settles for a single author of the Pentateuch from exilic times, who has inherited a large number of 'fragments', the narratives and short legal pieces. These may go back a long way, though studies of folklore have been inconclusive for claims of oral tradition. They have passed through some Deuteronomic editing, but there is nothing to show that there was ever a Deuteronomic J in the form proposed by Schmid; indeed Genesis–Numbers would be incomplete without an account of the Settlement. Nor need the P traditions be as late as is often supposed: the work of M. Haran suggests rather that the P legal traditions went back to pre-exilic Jerusalem. Whybray is impressed by the studies of Robert Alter and others on the literary achievement of the Pentateuch, and takes this to be an indication of the work of a single author to the whole Pentateuch.

Only slightly less radical is Erhard Blum, who has two 'layers' of composition in his *Studien zur Komposition des Pentateuch* (1990), which succeeds an equally massive *Die Komposition der Vätergeschichte* (1984). Blum predicates two blocks of early tradition, one a patriarchal history and the other a Mosaic narrative. The patriarchal history tradition was first formed in the late pre-exilic period, and was re-edited in a second version during the Exile. The Mosaic narrative was put together earlier, some time after the fall of the Northern Kingdom in 722. The two were put together in a Deuteronomic Composition (K^D) around 500. A second written version, the Priestly Composition (K^P), was an expanded form of K^D, and was made in the fifth century.

Blum expounds carefully the numerous Deuteronomistic elements in Genesis, Exodus and Numbers, and his late datings are a function of this study.

It will be seen how close Blum is to the conclusions I have drawn from the psalm evidence. His Mosaic narrative from the post-722 period is my Asaph Exodus–Numbers tradition, which continues, however, into the later history. His *Vätergeschichte I* is my Asaphite Genesis, prefixed to the Exodus–wilderness story during the seventh century. His *Vätergeschichte II* is my Korahite re-edition of the Asaphic Genesis, put by me at around 600. My Asaphic psalms showed a strong tendency to Deuteronomic language already in the eighth century, so I could date K^D, that is my Korahite expansion of the whole Asaph tradition, to Josiah's reign; and since Psalm 78 showed a D-history already forming *in nuce*, I was not forced into Blum's general late dating scheme. I am less close to Whybray. My psalms give me a continuous, not a fragmentary source from at least the eighth century; and a corollary of this is a full Genesis–Kings narrative a century later. But I am with Whybray in denying an early written form to these traditions: he is right in thinking of a single writing author, from exilic times, who has formed the (approximate) final form of the Pentateuch.

The scholars I have so briefly discussed are of course but a selection of many who have ventured hypotheses; and it is easy to regard their endeavour as a pathetic form of blind man's buff, where there are no satisfactory criteria, and shadowy authors, or circles, or redactors, come and go by fashion, and dating may vary by many centuries. But I hope that the present study may yield a better confidence. The Asaph psalms tell us what traditions were available in Bethel in the 720s, and their many discrepancies from the Pentateuchal and D-history narratives suggest that in them we have the earliest form of the story. Since we also have a number of traditions from the Korahite sanctuary at Dan, we should be in a position to form an outline history of the Pentateuch, told from the beginning. The analysis of these two psalm collections should mean that we can take off the blindfold.

Chapter 9

JACOB AND JOSEPH

The historical traditions traceable in the Asaph and Korah psalms showed at least one surprising feature: although there was a rich consciousness of the Exodus, wilderness and covenant stories in Bethel, there were nothing more than indirect hints of our Genesis. There was appeal to the contest between God and the water-monsters in creation, which does not appear in Genesis; Yahweh was spoken of as 'the God of Abraham' at Dan (Ps. 47.10), and as 'the God of Jacob' in both series; and there was mention of 'the children of Lot' (Ps. 83.9). This raises the question whether the stories in our Genesis may not be substantially later than those in our Exodus–Numbers; for while the argument from silence is always perilous, we cannot defend the claim that any of our Genesis stories was part of the *official liturgy* in the northern sanctuaries.

The absence of Genesis stories from the two psalm cycles does not of course imply that something related to them was unknown. We have echoes of some patriarchal narratives in other early traditions, and I consider these in the present chapters. It will be convenient to begin with Jacob, and then to take Joseph; and in a following chapter to work back to the Creation.

Jacob

We have three pre-722 texts outside the Genesis narrative which imply traditions related to Jacob: Hos. 12.4-5, 13, and the two 'blessings' of Genesis 49 and Deuteronomy 33. Of these the Hosea passage is markedly the most informative, and most commentators agree in attributing it to the original prophet.

An exception is Blenkinsopp, who takes the Hosea verses to be a later gloss (*Pentateuch*, pp. 113-14); but it would be a problem then to explain Jacob's weeping and supplicating, which are absent from Genesis 32. Critics are not agreed however on the purport of the passage. According to Wolff (*Hosea*, pp. 211-12) the chapter coheres around the theme of *deceit* (מרמה, 12.1-2; cf. 8-9), and the attitude to Jacob is negative—'Jacob was a deceiver from the beginning, and so is his people'. P.R. Ackroyd, however ('Hosea'), took a more positive view—'The success of your father Jacob was due to divine favour, and the same blessing is available for his people'. This is supported by Grace Emmerson (*Hosea*, pp. 128-38). Ackroyd limits his exegesis to the narrow context, while Wolff's attempt to see the verses in the light of the whole chapter is impressive.

Hosea seems familiar with five stories about Jacob, each of which is related to the Genesis Jacob cycle; the latter in general presents a kindlier image of the patriarch:

(1) Hos. 12.4, 'In the womb he tricked (עָקַב) his brother.' The 'trickery' is hard to imagine if it does not consist in taking Esau's heel, as in Genesis 25; for Esau is the first-born, and other pre-natal trickery is difficult to imagine. So Hosea sounds rather pejorative. The version in Gen. 25.19-26 is more complimentary. The struggle in Rebekah's womb was, as the oracle showed, a sign that Esau the elder should serve Jacob the younger; and Jacob's name is derived not from any trickery, but from his having emerged with his hand gripping Esau's *heel* (עָקֵב).

The translation *tricked* is from Wolff (*Hosea*, pp. 211-12); RV's *took his brother by the heel* is an assimilation to Genesis. NRSV *tried to supplant* is closer to the sense.

(2) Hos. 12.5, 'At Bethel [God] found him, and there he spake with us.' The story in Gen. 28.10-22 gives a more positive and characterful view of Jacob. It is not just that God 'finds' him, but that he finds the stone of destiny, the gate of heaven, and expresses a proper religious awe at his experience.

Emmerson (*Hosea*, p. 129) takes Jacob to be the subject of 'found', with a change of subject in the second half of the sentence. Graham Davies (*Hosea*, pp. 70-77) suggests that Hosea is familiar with the Bethel liturgy, and in particular with the Genesis 28 story as the foundation legend of the sanctuary, and with Psalms 80 and 81; he credits the psalms to Bethel on grounds similar to those I advocated in Chapter 1. He is thus able to retain MT's 'us': God revealed himself to Jacob at Bethel, and he teaches 'us' there standards of חסד and משפט (12.7), which 'we' contemporary Israelites have deserted. With the full Asaph psalmody, Davies could have cited Ps. 50.5 for Israel as a people of חסד, and Ps. 82 for God's demand for משפט.

Westermann (*Genesis*, II, pp. 450-60) attributes the key promise of Gen. 28.15 to 'J' (as opposed to the later vv. 13-14); it is v. 15, '...I will bring you back to this land', which answers the theological anxiety posed by 722.

(3) Hos. 12.13, 'Jacob fled to the land of Aram' presupposes a reason for his flight, presumably his continuing to trick Esau, and the latter's resentment. Gen. 25.27-34 and 27.1-45 alike put an acceptable face on Jacob's fast work. It was Esau's *impatient greed* which was the cause of his first fall. Jacob did not cheat him in any way: he merely offered to purchase the birthright, as any sensible brother might, and Esau *despised his birthright*. In ch. 27 there really was deception over Isaac's blessing, but this was not Jacob's doing. It was his mother who put him up to it, cooked the meat, put the goatskins on his arms and neck and clothed him in Esau's festal garments; Jacob was really only behaving properly in 'obeying his mother's word' (27.13), and he did raise an objection, as was only right (27.11-12), and his mother accepted full responsibility. We find exactly the same method of exculpation with Matthew's rehandling of the Sons of Zebedee story (Mt. 20.20-28).

Westermann (II, pp. 434-44) dates Isaac's actual blessings late: 'that Yahweh has blessed', and the pair עבד/שחה are Deuteronomic, and עמים/לאמים is common in the later prophets. He thinks that the blessings are independent of the oral form of the story: the 'primitive' concept of an irrevocable blessing, and the fact that the story involves a succession of two-character dialogues, suggest that it should be divided into 'J' narrative and Deuteronomic blessings. We may accept Westermann's points, but think rather that a traditional story has been retold here by a single author, as is argued by Van Seters (*Prologue, passim*); the earlier shameless glorying in successful deceit (Gen. 12.10-20; 38; 48, etc.), reproved by Hosea, is now replaced by a subtle shifting of the blame. (Ackroyd cites these passages as evidence that pride in cleverness was a regular Israelite characteristic.) The end of Esau's blessing, 'when you break loose, you shall break his yoke from your neck', would be at home any time after the late ninth century (2 Kgs 8.20, 22).

(4) Hos. 12.13, 'there Israel served for a wife, and for a wife he watched (שמר)'. Jacob's flight to Aram, Israel's serving (עבד) Laban, and watching, are paralleled in 12.14, 'By a prophet the LORD brought Israel up from Egypt, and by a prophet he was watched over (נשמר)'. Jacob's flight and servitude are foreshadowings of his people's trials in Egypt; God was keeping watch over the watcher. The repeated באשה is unclear; it may well stand for Jacob's two wives. The patriarch's hard life, so described, is filled out in his dramatic reproach of Laban in Genesis: 'the frost [consumed me] by night; and my sleep fled from my eyes... I served thee (עבדתיך) fourteen years' (Gen. 31.40-41).

This understanding is close to Ackroyd. Wolff understands the verse as a reflection on foreign marriages, which end in sexual rites and non-Yahwistic worship, a recurring emphasis in his commentary. Ackroyd is justly critical of this.

(5) Hos. 12.4-5, 'and in his strength he strove with God. He strove with the angel and prevailed, he wept and sought his favour' (MT). The text is difficult: one would have thought that if Jacob prevailed in the striving, there would be no further need of tears and supplication, nor is there in the story in Genesis 32.

Ackroyd justifies MT on the ground that weeping is found alongside triumph in Psalm 57 and (less obviously) at Mal. 2.13; but the change of mood in the psalm may be due to other things (Goulder, *Korah*, pp. 116-23). Wolff (*Hosea*, p. 212) proposes a rather plausible change to the text, giving a translation, 'In his wealth he strove with God. He [God] strove with him and prevailed; he [Jacob] wept and sought his favour.' With so much uncertainty it is best to leave the question open.

It must suffice to be confident that the tradition is older than Hosea, for his God/angel is more developed than the river-spirit of Genesis 32, who must win the contest before dawn, or it will be too late. Besides, the problem of the people's name must have been resolved long before. The older settlers, with their centre at Dan, knew themselves as Jacob, as we see from the Korah psalms; the Joseph/Benjamin group, with their reverence for 'El and their centre at Beth-el, brought the name Isra-el with them. When it came to be accepted that they were one people, there had to be a solution to the nation's name, and it is this story which provided it. The patriarch was called Jacob *at first*, but 'he strove with God (שרה את־אלהים), and he strove (וישר) with the angel' (Hos. 12.4-5), and so *God gave him the name* Israel (Gen. 32.28), saying in Hosea-like words שרית עם־אלהים.

So we have a complex development. The old story was about the river-god who opposed Jacob's crossing of the Jabbok, and Jacob *wrestled* with him (יאבק, Gen. 32.25); he was a night-spirit, and Jacob won by 'touching his thigh', grasping his testicles. Hosea knows a more orthodox and decent form of the story: Jacob was striving with God, or his angel, and it was from this striving that he got his change of name. The Genesis author(s) have added aetiologies for Penuel and the forbidden thigh-meat, and other matters.

Westermann (II, pp. 512-21) shows how complex is the history of the story, and successfully isolates the earliest form. The dating of the later additions is perilous.

We have access to three further matters from Jacob's life, all from the Blessing of Jacob in Genesis 49.

(6) Gen. 49.5-7, 'Simeon and Levi are brethren; Weapons of violence are their swords...in their anger they slew men, and in their selfwill they houghed oxen. Cursed be their anger, for it was fierce; And their wrath for it was cruel: I will divide them in Jacob, And scatter them in Israel.' It is certainly true that Simeon and Levi failed to establish themselves as independent land-owning tribes. Genesis 49 seems unaware of Levi's second career in the priesthood, which has suggested a setting for Genesis 49 in Jerusalem where the Zadokite priesthood was not Levitical in origin. The offence for which this 'scattering' is the punishment is that they combined to murder a number of men, and deliberately lamed oxen (presumably belonging to surviving members of the same community). This was done in a fit of unbridled anger.

The Genesis author tells a related story in Genesis 34, but the relation has become distant, and markedly more positive. The incident arose, we now see, not from some act of unprovoked temper but from the fact that Dinah, Jacob's only daughter, had been raped by a dreadful Canaanite called Shechem (34.2). Jacob's sons were naturally very upset about this (34.7); and further, Hamor, Shechem's father, tried to lure Jacob into a mixed marriage (34.8-12). The boys served Shechem and his people out with a clever trick: they persuaded them to be circumcised, and then, when they were sore, they would fall on them and kill them (34.13-24). The deed was actually done by Simeon and Levi, who deserve the highest credit for avenging their sister's honour; but all the boys joined in, taking the animals and booty, and enslaving the women and children (34.25-29). Jacob himself panicked a little at the thought of setting up a feud, but Simeon and Levi correctly said they had acted on principle, 'Should he deal with our sister as with an harlot?' (34.30-31). The Genesis author comes a long time after the 'Blessing of Jacob'. The motive for the action has become honourable, the responsibility is with all the family, Simeon and Levi are now not villains but heroes. The author is not likely to be interested in exculpating the long-disappeared Simeon, but if he were a northerner he would be keen to do his best for Levi; and the fear of mixed marriages is a topic important to the Deuteronomists (Deut. 7.3-4).

Westermann (II, pp. 532-45) separates out three strands: A, the old patriarchal (Shechem) story; B, the tribal (Hamor) version from the Settlement period, when Israel settled peaceably alongside the Canaanite town-dwellers; C, a late (exilic) version, with several echoes of Deuteronomy, especially the prohibition of intermarriage in Deut. 7. We are concerned with version C. But the mixed marriage question, which surfaces in our literature in Ezra–Nehemiah, will also have been urgent in the occupied lands of the north after 722.

(7) 'Reuben, thou art my first-born... Unstable as water, have not thou the excellency; Because thou wentest up to thy father's bed; Then defiledst thou it; he went up to my couch' (Gen. 49.3-4). Implied is some incident of sexual licence resembling Gen. 35.22; presumably, as there, Reuben slept with one of his father's concubines, not his mother or stepmother.

(8) We have four lists of the tribes of Israel in our early documents: an open list of tribes in Deborah's Song, some of which fought and others not; and three lists of tribes as sons of Jacob, in Genesis 49, Deuteronomy 33, and Genesis 29–35. I give the names in their respective orders:

Judges 5	Genesis 49	Deuteronomy 33	Genesis 29–31
Ephraim	Reuben	Reuben	Reuben
Benjamin	Simeon	Judah	Simeon
Machir	Levi	Levi	Levi
Zebulun	Judah	Benjamin	Judah
Issachar	Zebulun	Joseph (= Ephraim	Dan
Naphtali	Issachar	+ Manasseh)	Naphtali
—	Dan	Zebulun	Gad
Reuben	Gad	Issachar	Asher
Gilead	Asher	Gad	Issachar
Dan	Naphtali	Dan	Zebulun
Asher	Joseph	Naphtali	Joseph
	Benjamin	Asher	Benjamin

Westermann (III, pp. 215-44) offers an account of the growth of the tribal tradition, which we may accept and amplify. Judges 5 mirrors the tribal situation at the time of Deborah's battle. 'Israel' is seen as consisting of ten tribes, six of whom fought, and four are reproached for not fighting. The leading tribes are Ephraim, Benjamin and Machir; it is noticeable that this is close to the order of Ps. 80.3, 'Before Ephraim and Benjamin and Manasseh...' As these tribes are foremost, it is not surprising that 'Israel' is used for the people. Genesis 49 was a similar secular list from the Judges period, according to Westermann, with nine tribes in the third person. Three failed tribes, Reuben, Simeon and Levi, have been prefixed to the list with 'blessings' in the first person; and the successful tribes, Judah and Joseph, have had their oracles added to. The failure of the first three tribes is accounted for in line with their moral lapses, now expanded in Genesis 34–35. Judah was originally saluted as militarily successful (like a lion); the third oracle is an (ex post facto?) prophecy of the Davidic–Solomonic kingdom. The twelvefoldness is independent of the original form.

Deuteronomy 33 is a later development of the genre, now with a cultic setting. The big figures are now Levi and Joseph, and Judah is isolated—'O LORD, give heed to Judah, and bring him to his people' (33.7). Simeon has been forgotten, his place among the twelve being taken by the doubling of Joseph to Ephraim and Manasseh. Deuteronomy 33 stems from days when Joseph ruled in (Northern) Israel, Levi presided over Urim and law, and Judah was separated, that is, the ninth–eighth centuries.

Barnabas Lindars (*Judges 1–5*, pp. 209-96) gives a comprehensive discussion of Deborah's Song, which he takes to have been written well after the battle; but the presence of Machir and Gilead as variants from the later Manasseh and Gad mean that the Song is older than the two Blessings (pp. 212-22).

The two 'Blessings' are evidence of early attempts to rationalize the varying success of the tribal units in the form of legends, and to relate the tribes to the people in the form of a genealogy. In Judges 5 the tribes were just tribes; with Genesis 49 they have become descendants of eponymous patriarchs, with Jacob as their father. The six 'Leah' tribes are taken first, and have more considerable sayings than the following 'handmaid' tribes, though there is no suggestion at all of different mothers; Joseph and Benjamin are appended at the end. This arrangement corresponds with the pattern of settlement revealed by archaeology, and by the tribal map. The main concentration of Israelite villages in the twelfth century was between the Jordan and the central Palestinian ridge, south of the Plain of Esdraelon: here were the tribes of Reuben, Simeon, Levi and Judah, now pushed east and south, and Issachar and Zebulun, now pushed north. There was a smaller concentration north of the Plain of Esdraelon, later the territory of Naphtali, Dan and Asher, with Gad moved into Transjordan. Joseph and Benjamin were a later wave of settlement, so they belong last; but they have done well for themselves, and have taken the best land in the centre of the country.

The pattern of Israelite settlements in the twelfth and eleventh centuries is set out in Israel Finkelstein's *The Archaeology of the Israelite Settlement*. His maps show the division of Israelite villages south and north of the Plain of Esdraelon; the alignment of them with the Leah and the handmaid tribes is my own suggestion. Finkelstein accepts that there was a later arrival of Israelites from Egypt, but he minimizes it. Noth (*History*, pp. 68-109) explains the final pattern of tribal settlement as a function of earlier (Leah) tribes being pushed east, south and north, by a later wave of Joseph/Benjamin invaders.

The Deuteronomy 33 list is a northern modification of the Genesis 49 list. Reuben still remains first, but Simeon is dropped to make space for Joseph as Ephraim-and-Manasseh. Judah comes next, now among the disappointments, while Levi, in his priestly garb, is now the first of the successes: he and the now promoted Benjamin and Joseph are the backbone of Israel. There is a general south-to-north movement, with Benjamin before Joseph, and a southeast to northwest conclusion with Gad, Dan, Naphtali and Asher to end. Gad and Asher, the two sons of Zilpah according to Gen. 30.9-13, are separated.

So although the Bethel psalmody gave us no hint of any stories about Jacob, it becomes clear that its repeated phrase 'the God of Jacob' (Pss. 76.7; 81.2, 5) was not empty. The official liturgy celebrated a *Heilsgeschichte* which began with the oppression in Egypt; but there was also a familiar cycle of stories about the people's ancestor, which was not quite on a par with the Exodus–wilderness–covenant tradition, but was still honoured. This story followed the outline of the Genesis Jacob cycle, with some variation; and it also followed the general three-phase pattern of a folklore legend, (i) the hero's predicament, (ii) its resolution, (iii) a permanent settlement. Thus (i) Jacob tricked his brother Esau from the womb on, and was forced to flee (his vengeance) to Aram (cf. Gen. 25.19–28.9); (ii) God found him at Bethel, and watched over him as he served (Laban) night and day for his two wives, by whom he had numerous children, eponyms of the tribes (cf. Gen. 28.10–32.3); (iii) he returned to Palestine, where he 'strove' with the angel, and was given the name Israel; (he made peace with Esau) and settled, despite his elder sons causing trouble by their lust, and the violence at Shechem (cf. Gen. 32.4–35.27).

We may now enquire into the likely setting of our Genesis version of the Jacob story, abstracting from it the limited priestly expansions, mainly 27.46–28.9 (a nicer reason for Jacob's going to Aram) and most of 35 (Jacob's second vision at Bethel, genealogy, and so forth). Is it probable that a full 'J' version was already known to Hosea and the authors of Genesis 49 and Deuteronomy 33? Should we think rather, with Schmid,

Van Seters, Blum and others, of a 'late' Genesis version, written in the Exile, or even later? Or is there some middle position? I shall argue for the last, with the main outline of the story settled in the seventh century in Jerusalem.

(1) We may notice first a paradox in the story of Genesis 29–30 (35). *The order of births* in these chapters is similar to that in the old Jerusalem version in Genesis 49; but the story-teller is unquestionably a northerner, from Ephraim, and in fact from Bethel. Jacob's journey to Aram begins with the revelation and promise at Bethel in Genesis 28, and it ends with his return to Bethel in Genesis 35. He has adventures at Mahanaim, Penuel and Shechem, all of them shrines in Josephite territory. He has a favourite wife, Rachel, who is the mother of Joseph and Benjamin, the Asaphite tribes. She was beautiful, where Leah was plain, and he loved her from the beginning, but was cheated of her on his wedding-night; she was unhappily barren for a long time, but in the end God blessed her with the birth of Joseph; she it was who behaved with resource and courage over the theft of the teraphim; and she died tragically giving birth to Benjamin. The two children whose coming was so long delayed are, like other such births in the Bible, the true children of destiny.

The man who told these stories was from the tribes of Joseph, from Bethel; he was an Asaphite. But why then has he deserted the northern tribal sequence of Deuteronomy 33, and followed the outline of Genesis 49? We should have an answer to this if the Genesis story were elaborated in Jerusalem in the seventh century. It would be necessary to accommodate Judaean feelings, so the Leah sons should be given pride of place. The Rachel tribes may accept their Judaean place at the end of the register, on the understanding that their eponyms' births were delayed by providence, in view of their higher destiny. Rachel's long barrenness suggests the sub-plot of the two concubines, and the two successful northern tribes, Dan and Naphtali, are now grouped together and ascribed to Bilhah, Rachel's maid, while Leah's maid Zilpah is credited with the marginal Gad and Asher. The sub-plot is allowed to divide Leah's pregnancies, and Issachar's name is explained by the story of the mandrakes, giving him promotion over Zebulun. So the Judahite listener is happy that his tradition is given the priority; and the northern listener is happier, because the tale is slanted in favour of his ancestress.

(2) A central theme of the Jacob narrative, and one which it shares with the patriarchal story more generally, is the divine *promise of the*

land: it is indeed in large measure the promises of land, progeny and divine protection which give the Pentateuch its theme, and link Genesis on to the later books. However, there is here a second paradox. The later books seem hardly to be aware of this momentous word of God, so often repeated. Hosea does not associate it with Jacob in his mentions of the latter; the covenant is rather with the people, and their election took place not in the patriarchal period but in Egypt (Hos. 2.15; 11.1; 13.4). It is the Egyptian experience which dominates the oracles of Jeremiah (2.4-8; 11.3-5), and even Ezekiel, in ch. 20, views the promise (oath) of God as having taken place at Israel's election in Egypt (20.5-6). In the pre-priestly passages in Exodus, Numbers and Deuteronomy the promise of the land—so central, especially in the last—is normally seen as given to 'your fathers', presumably in the Exodus period. In Exod. 3.8 the land is spoken of as inhabited by Canaanites and others, without any reference to the patriarchal promises. It is not till a further half-century on, till Deutero-Isaiah, that the promise is understood to have been made to the patriarchs (41.8-10; 51.1-3; 54.1-3).

The paradox was first expounded by K. Galling, *Die Erwählungstraditionen Israels* (1928): Galling supposed that the Egypt election tradition was primary and the patriarchal tradition secondary, but both went back to early sources. J. Hoftijzer (*Die Verheissungen an die drei Erzväter*, 1956) took a more logical approach: the Egypt tradition was original, and the patriarchal promises were all inserted by late redactors, some priestly, some Deuteronomistic. His conclusions were largely supported by J.A. Emerton ('Promises'), who put the insertions in Josiah's reign; he excepted three possible texts as more original, two of them in the Jacob Bethel story (Gen. 28.13,15). Van Seters (*Prologue*, pp. 215-45) attributes the whole patriarchal promise tradition to a Deuteronomistic school in the exilic period.

However, despite this general picture, there is an awareness of the patriarchs by the late seventh century. Three times the Deuteronomic paraenesis speaks of the patriarchs as 'your fathers' (Deut. 8.3, 16; 10.22); and the common phrase 'the land which the LORD swore to our fathers to give us' (Deut. 26.3, etc.) may have the same meaning. The trio, Abraham, Isaac and Jacob, occurs at Deut. 6.10, 9.5, 27; and Joshua's great rehearsal of the *Heilsgeschichte* begins with Terah and Abraham, Isaac, Jacob and Esau (Josh. 24.2-4). Jer. 11.3-5 does indeed speak of God's covenant made when he brought the people out of Egypt, but he said to them, 'that I may establish the oath which I sware *unto your fathers* to give them the land'. So it would seem that the patriarchal story, and with it the promise of the land to Abraham, Isaac and Jacob, was gaining acceptance before the Exile.

Van Seters stressed Jer. 11.3-5, and believed that 'our fathers' in Deuteronomy always meant the Egypt/wilderness generations ('Reformulation', pp. 448-59), but he was mistaken in both points, and also, according to Blenkinsopp (*Pentateuch*, p. 113) on Ezekiel 20. Blenkinsopp (*Pentateuch*, pp. 117-18) concludes, 'By... 598/597 BC there existed, at least in outline, a consecutive history from entry into Canaan to descent into Egypt, with the three great ancestors in... genealogical sequence'.

It has seemed to be a difficulty that the language in which the patriarchal covenant is expressed is often noticeably Deuteronom(ist)ic. Gen. 15.7, for example, 'I am the LORD that brought thee out of Ur of the Chaldees, to give thee this land to inherit it', sounds very like the similar formula '...that brought thee out of the land of Egypt...'; and the promised extent of the land from the Sea to the River Euphrates (Gen. 15.18) is Deuteronomic (Deut. 1.7; 11.24; Josh. 1.4). There is Deuteronomic language similarly in the promise to Jacob, Gen. 28.15. The conclusion has often seemed to follow that the promise theme—and with it much of the Genesis story—is exilic, or later. There has, however, been a reaction against the long-held view that the Deuteronomists had no hand in Genesis, Exodus and Numbers; and the considerable amount of Deuteronomic language in the Asaph psalms confirms this. Ps. 80.12 says '[Israel] sent out her branches unto the sea, And her shoots unto the River'. So it seems likely that the patriarchal material was at the least re-written by the [Asaphite] Deuteronomists in the seventh century; and quite possibly that it was composed by them.

For the reaction against excluding D from Genesis–Exodus–Numbers, see H.H. Schmid, Van Seters and Blum (who think the latter books are post-Deuteronomistic), Blenkinsopp (who inclines to the view that the Deuteronomists wrote them [as I do]), and M. Vervenne ('Question') who keeps an open mind.

These considerations tell against the older hypothesis of an early 'J', since such an author would have been more consistent in carrying the patriarchal covenant over into Exodus–Numbers, and it would have been familiar to the early prophets. But the tendency to see the land-promises as a function of the loss of the land in the Exile should be resisted. The Deuteronomic laws and paraenesis stress the land-promise because four-fifths of the land had been lost in 732–722. Hosea saw the loss of that land as the corollary of (Northern) Israel's disobedience to the covenant (Hos. 9.1-6). It was a natural move to project the land-promise back on to the patriarchs as their story was developed in the seventh century. It is the refugees from Bethel (and points north) who are in mind when God says to Jacob there, 'And, behold, I am with thee, and will keep thee whithersoever thou goest, and will bring thee again into this land: for I will not leave thee, until I have done that which I have spoken to thee of' (Gen. 28.15).

(3) *The positive form of the Genesis Jacob tradition* tends to the same conclusion. It may be (with Wolff) that Hosea was being pejorative about the patriarch, but in any case the Jacob who strives with the 'man' at the Jabbok in Genesis 32 cuts a better figure than the weeping, beseeching Jacob of Hosea 12. The Shechem incident as told in Genesis 34 is more creditable all round than the few harsh words of Gen. 49.5-7. More generally we have the impression of a developing, embroidering, ameliorating tradition. It was not that Jacob tricked his brother and so had to flee Esau; it was Esau's crassness and Rebekah's scheming which were the real factors. The handmaid tribes of Genesis 49 (if such they are) are sorted into pairs, with the more important pair assigned to Bilhah, maid to Rachel, the tradents' ancestress. There are etymologies for the twelve boys, and Issachar has been moved up a place to fit the plot of Leah's 'hire' of Jacob with the mandrakes. Judah's name no longer means 'thee shall thy brethren praise' (Gen. 49.8), but 'This time I will praise the LORD' (Gen. 29.35), as befits a democratic northern tradent. There are many details in the Laban narrative which read like developments, without any secure evidence.

(4) We may note finally the story-teller's attitude to *Esau*. Esau is a rough, stupid, impulsive, unpleasant man, who marries unpleasant women and intends to murder his brother; but by ch. 33 he has estab-lished himself with a large private army, and he treats the suppliant Jacob with magnanimity and kindness. Gen. 27.40 prophesies Edom's 'breaking loose' from servitude to Israel, and this happened under Joram king of Judah in the ninth century (2 Kgs 8.20-22). Edom is among the enemies of Israel in the eighth century (Amos 2.10-12; Ps. 83.7), but we do not hear of it as a threat to Judah in Isa. 13-27, and it is not mentioned as among those who attacked Judah in 2 Kgs 24.1-3, in 598. It is not until the fall of Jerusalem in 587 that Edom becomes execrated in perpetuity with Ps. 137.7-9. It is difficult to reconcile the generous Esau of Genesis 33 with the hatred of Psalm 137 and Obadiah;

it belongs more comfortably in the seventh century.

So all the factors point to, or can be reconciled with, a single solution. The Jacob story already existed as a continuous three-part folklore tale before Hosea: the patriarch's predicament with Esau, his flight to Aram where he gained flocks, wives and children, and his return and settlement in the land. This basic story was told in an expanded form by Asaphite tradents in seventh-century Jerusalem. The main motive behind the new composition was the promise of the land: most of the land of Israel had just been lost, and the Jacob story made it clear that from the beginning God had destined the land to the people in perpetuity, and if they should have to leave it temporarily, God would be with them and bring them back. The story provides a reconciliation between Judahite ideas of Jacob's family and Josephite pretensions; it puts a favourable gloss on the character of the patriarch; and it paints Esau in colours suited to a rough but irenic neighbour. The language and ideas of the cycle are often Deuteronomic, and this is because the Bethel tradition was (proto-)Deuteronomic, as may be seen from Psalm 78 and other Asaph psalms. There is sufficient evidence from Jeremiah and elsewhere that the three-patriarch story, with its promise of the land, was familiar before 598.

Joseph

There is an obvious difference between the Jacob and the Joseph narratives. The former is episodic, with several different themes strung on to a rough plot, the journey to and from Aram; the latter is to a single theme, how the Israelites came to go down to Egypt, and how Joseph rose to be the Pharaoh's chief minister, and so place them favourably. There is an equally obvious reason for this.

There were a variety of old traditions about Jacob, legends which already, by Hosea's time, presupposed the Aramaean journey in something like the Pentateuchal form. We have no similar echoes from early times of Joseph legends. The Asaph psalm references, the Deuteronomy references, and those in the early prophets are alike in beginning the history of Israel from the Exodus: even Ezekiel opens the *Heilsgeschichte* there (ch. 20), with a bow to earlier ancestors (20.4, 42). Psalm 105, usually dated after the Exile (L.C. Allen, *Psalms*, pp. 40-44), is the first mention of Joseph's career outside Genesis; and there is an implied reference in Joshua 24. The smoothness of the story, combined with this silence, suggests that the Joseph narrative is a new creation, with its birth in Jerusalem in the seventh century.

While the festival was celebrated at Bethel, it was enough for Israel's history to begin with the oppression in Egypt (Ps. 81), and to allow the Jacob legends to float informally. But with the catastrophe of 722 celebrations ceased at Bethel. Judah was the surviving remnant of Israel, and if the old national salvation story was to continue its unifying and edifying power, it must be given its place in the celebrations at Jerusalem. It must be accepted that the people's relation with God was not just through David, the founder and hero of the Jerusalem cult, but back to Jacob/Israel, the father of *all* the tribes; and in particular that the *whole* people had been down to Egypt, and had been thence delivered by God's outstretched arm. We have seen the first steps in this direction, extending the people in Egypt from two to twelve tribes, in Ps. 77.15, 'Thou hast with thine arm redeemed thy people, The sons of *Jacob and Joseph*', and Ps. 77.21, 'Thou leddest thy people like a flock, By the hand of *Moses and* Aaron'. So here lay the puzzle: if Jacob/Israel had fathered twelve sons and brought them up to be an incipient clan in Canaan, how had they come to be settled in Egypt, in numbers sufficient to be a people?

In one respect the northern exiles were well placed. For two centuries Judah had been a backwater, conscious of belonging to a greater entity, Jacob/Israel, often domineered by its more powerful kings or attacked by them. Now the proud northerners were their suppliants; any claims to their throne or a superior priesthood had lapsed, and they were offering treasures without money and without price—treasures of law, of psalmody, and above all of national myth. These could be accepted with alacrity, and we may think that not only Hezekiah and Josiah welcomed them, but that in the long half-century between their reigns Yahwist priests in Jerusalem found the Danite and Bethelite exiles redoubtable allies against King Manasseh. These stories enabled Jerusalem to become the sole symbolic head of a notional twelve-tribe people: all could trace their ancestry to one patriarch, all had gone down to Egypt, all had been delivered, all had been given one covenant, and the promise of the land, from Dan to Beersheba, and perhaps from the Sea to the River. Our Old Testament is evidence that the southern authorities accepted the offer with both hands.

But the northerners had a second, more subtle advantage. The story, especially the great Exodus–wilderness story, was *their* story, and the

Bethel clergy, the Asaphites, were its tradents. It did not at first occur to the southerners that those who tell the story have the privilege of slanting it to their own benefit; though in time this became painfully obvious, and steps were taken to redress the position. But, as with most of the Jacob cycle, it is obvious that the basic Joseph narrative has been composed by and for the sons of Asaph. The hero of the story is Joseph, their patriarch. The only brother not implicated in the plot against him is Benjamin, their fellow-tribesman, and it is Benjamin who takes the second highest profile in the later part of the story. Joseph is awarded a double place in the allocation of tribal lands by his dying father; so his two sons, Manasseh and Ephraim, gain parity with the others, as in Deut. 33.17. Of the two, Jacob gives the higher blessing to the younger Ephraim; so we may be confident that the story-teller is an Ephraimite—and Ephraimite story-tellers held office at Bethel, as Asaphites.

It is usually thought (Westermann, III, pp. 178-94; Redford, *Joseph*, pp. 20-21) that Jacob's blessing of Ephraim and Manasseh was not part of the original Joseph story; but its point, the hegemony of Ephraim, is only a more specific statement of the interest of the whole Joseph narrative, the hegemony of the Joseph tribes. It is part of the creative tradition of the same community.

There is a notorious series of dissonances in the narrative, especially in the second half of ch. 37, for which a wide spectrum of explanations has been offered. The perspective of the present essay suggests that Donald Redford's solution (*Joseph*, 1970), is the closest to being right. The Asaphites had long been on terms with the Korahites from Dan, and in the 720s had accepted them as (junior) colleagues at Bethel. They wished accordingly to accommodate the feelings of their fellow-exiles, which could be done by exonerating their leading eponyms. So 'the brothers' conspire to kill Joseph, but *Reuben*, the senior Leah/Jacob patriarch, persuades them to spare his life. Joseph is stripped and thrown into a dry pit, from which Reuben plans to rescue him and restore him to his father; but Midianite traders passing by find him and sell him as a slave in Egypt. When in due course the brothers come down to Egypt to buy corn, Joseph exacts a hostage against their return, and this is the second senior Leah/Jacob patriarch, *Simeon*. When the brothers reach home, *Reuben* asks Jacob to let him take Benjamin to Egypt so as to redeem Simeon (Gen. 42.35-38); and no doubt it was Reuben who was the family's spokesman on their second, fateful Egyptian expedition. So the sympathies of the listener are engaged in favour of Joseph (of course), and against the anonymous 'brothers', but with a soft spot for Reuben and Simeon, the senior two of the old Leah/Jacob tribes.

With time, however, this cosy northern monopoly is disturbed. The feelings of the Jerusalem hosts have to be more closely considered: was Judah, eponym of the remnant survivor tribe which had so kindly welcomed the exiles, implicated in the original plot? So Judah comes to take a more central place in the story. Joseph has been thrown into the pit, and the brothers are eating when some Ishmaelite traders are sighted. Judah seconds Reuben's proposal to spare Joseph's life, and proposes selling him to the Ishmaelites. Ishmaelites and Midianites are elsewhere interchangeable (Judg. 8.22-24), so the redaction is less clumsy and scandalous than has sometimes appeared. The Midianite traders lift Joseph from the pit, and (the brothers) sell him to (these) Ishmaelites. Later in the story Judah appears in his true colours as spokesman for the family, referred to as 'Judah and his brothers' (Gen. 44.14). His name is substituted for Reuben's in chs. 43–44, and he makes a most moving speech (Gen. 44.18-34), and offers himself in perpetual slavery in order to release Benjamin (Gen. 44.33).

Redford's analysis is cogent in pointing to two features: (i) the whole narrative depends on the dreams in ch. 37, whose fulfilment is told in the rest of the story—so the narrative is a fundamental unity, and cannot be split into two *parallel* sources, J and E (*Joseph*, pp. 68-69); (ii) the Judah-version in Gen. 37.26-27 is familiar with the Reuben-version in Gen. 37.22, and is therefore an embroidery upon it (*Joseph*, pp. 139-41). Redford traces this embroidery through numerous discrepancies, and provides a table of the two versions, with further glosses and the contributions of the (P) editor of Genesis, on pp. 182-86.

Hans-Christoph Schmitt (*Die nichtpriesterliche Josephgeschichte*, 1980), argues that the Judah-version is primary, with the Reuben-version a theological and ethical improvement on it. Reuben's offer of his sons as surety for Benjamin is never carried through, and has been inserted (with a higher pledge!) to outbid Judah. Judah proposed *selling* Joseph in ch. 37, whereas Reuben acted from good-heartedness. Judah never admits guilt as Reuben does in Gen. 42.22. So Reuben is the more ideal brother (*Josephgeschichte*, pp. 17-20); but also the Judah story is concerned with the self-preservation of the brothers, while the Reuben story centres on God's direction of history (Gen. 42.21-22; 45.5-8). These arguments are not strong. The Reuben-version fades out at 42.38, and it is natural to think, with Redford, that he was spokesman and surety in chs. 43–44, but his name was suppressed in favour of the later Judah. There is no suggestion in the story that Judah's motives were less noble than Reuben's: both with the pit and with the pledging he is simply practical. And the divine direction of the story is implicit in both versions, since the (divinely inspired) dreams dominate the whole narrative.

These alterations are a testimony to the shifting balance of forces in Jerusalem in the later seventh century. At first the Asaphite מנצח has it all his own way. He is telling the story which will enable all Israel to share in the Exodus myth, and his audience accept his creation with gratitude and humility. But with time, as I suggested in the last chapter, Jerusalem tradents make their presence felt. We seem to sense strong representations being made behind the scenes, and the Asaphite story-teller has then introduced Judah as sub-hero the following year. In time Jerusalem story-tellers would be taking over the tradition and adapting it to their own advantage. 1 Chronicles 6 sets out three families of Levites, those of Asaph, Korah and Merari; in their capacity as 'singers' the three guilds competed for the spotlight of national tradent-in-chief, and each has materially affected the continuing redaction of the tradition. Merari, the Jerusalem tradents, were the last in the field, but the Judah-redaction of the Joseph narrative is a testimony to their early and effective interposition.

Redford takes the (Reuben-)narrative to be the *creation* of the author ('writer'), drawing on a number of themes which we know of from both Israelite and Egyptian sources—the youngest son who is triumphant over his elder brothers, the truth of dreams, the power of the wise man to save the community, the promotion to vizier under the king, and so forth. He takes ch. 39, Potiphar's wife, to be an insertion, but it again draws on a common folklore theme, the spurned wife. He notes the masterly hand of the author in the irony and pathos of the story, his ability to raise the tension by repetitions which slow its pace, and by embellishments. All this I find convincing. What is less convincing is his claim that the Reuben-version was originally just a tale told for enjoyment about a boy whose dreams came true; it was the Judah-version, in his view, that bridged the gap and brought the sons of Israel to Egypt (*Joseph*, pp. 250-51). This is dependent on the 'possibility' (p. 160) that in the Reuben-version Jacob came to Egypt only for the five years of famine, and died in Palestine.

The story of Judah and Tamar in Genesis 38 is a similarly ambiguous witness to the struggle behind the scenes. We are left in two minds as to the sympathies of the narrator. On the one hand, the story elevates Judah. It tells how his progeny came to birth, as one more pair of brothers, of whom the divine destiny of the younger was to triumph. Judah is the only patriarch, other than Joseph himself, to be dignified with a story describing the providential continuance of his family, after hope had nearly been extinguished. On the other hand Judah is a disgrace. He breaks his promise to marry Shelah to Tamar; he gets drunk; he sleeps, as he supposes, with a prostitute; he is content to have his daughter-in-law burned alive without enquiry; and he ends with the reluctant and humiliating confession, 'She is more righteous than I'. Such ambivalence is a sure sign of two tradents at work: an old Judahite story of the marvellous birth of Perez has been retold with less sympathy by a northerner as the adventure of dirty old Judah.

Emerton ('Tamar', p. 411) cites from an essay by B. Lüthi in 1906: 'The attitude to Judah is not that of a member of the tribe, but of a non-Judahite who is kindly disposed to Judah, but also thinks he should give him some fatherly advice.' Emerton thinks the (pre-Pentateuchal) story comes from Canaanites in the Adullam area who meet these criteria. Redford (*Joseph*, pp. 16) thinks the story was told (i) to stress the duty of Levirate marriage, and (ii) for the aetiologies of Perez, Zerah, etc. But its inclusion in Genesis is surely to dignify Judah's descendants as on a par with Joseph's; and the tale of his line's near extinction and marvellous preservation in conception and birth puts it on a level with those of Abraham and Isaac. So the story comes from Judah; but it is difficult to think that the Judahites painted their forefather in such disreputable colours.

The Joseph- and Jacob-cycles are similar pieces of high artistry. In part this is shown by the parallel development of the plot, which keeps the hearer on the edge of the chair to the end—even in the overlong later expansions. Joseph, like Jacob, has a three-part story: his predicament (Gen. 37, 39–40); his triumph over adversity (41.1–44.17); his recognition and reconciliation with his brothers, and the family's transfer to Egypt (44.18–47.27). The two stories have been formed in the same community, but the character of the heroes is different, and suggests a different composer. Jacob is throughout *artful*, and the narrator values artfulness. He has his hand on Esau's heel from the start; he cheats him of his birthright, and of his blessing; he deceives his father; he escapes to Haran in time; he is cleverer than even the artful Laban, and makes himself owner of huge flocks; he marries both Laban's daughters, and escapes with his teraphim; he pacifies the angry father and comes safely to Canaan; he pacifies his angry brother with gifts, and settles peaceably; he pacifies the angry river-god, and extracts his blessing. Joseph is clever too, but he is not deceitful: he is virtuous, wise and magnanimous. He works his way into Potiphar's favour, resists his wife's temptations; works his way into the gaoler's favour, interprets everyone's dreams correctly, including his own; he shows Pharaoh how to run the country, he serves his brothers out with a fright but no worse, and ensures a happy ending with tears and forgiveness all round. This is a different character from that of Jacob, and the dream theme is new also.

There are other differences too. Whereas the Jacob cycle normally speaks of God as Yahweh, the Joseph narrative always uses אלהים (the only apparent exceptions falling in the later inserted ch. 39). The promises of the land, of progeny, and of the divine presence, so persistent in the earlier patriarchal stories, are totally absent. Indeed, God never speaks directly to anyone at all in the Joseph story. The defensive attitude of Genesis 12–36 is gone too. Where the greatest pains are taken to ensure that Isaac and Jacob marry inside the family, Joseph marries an Egyptian girl, the daughter of an idolatrous high priest. He moves at ease among Egyptian notables, and we never hear of his observing sabbath or insisting on *kashrut*. It is not believable that such a story was created in the siege atmosphere of the Exile, when the prophets derided idolatry, and preserved their national identity with the sabbath and food-laws, and forbade inter-marriage. It breathes the fresh air of Josiah's reign, when confidence was rising. There is reflection too: the name Yahweh was not revealed till the Exodus (Ps. 81.11): he should rather be spoken of as אלהים. We find the same practice (and very likely the same author) in Genesis 20–22, and in Exodus 18–24.

The attitude of the narrator to Egypt is of naive admiration, reminiscent of Herodotus two centuries later. On the whole Israel had enjoyed friendly relations with Egypt from Solomon's days on, during the 22nd–25th Dynasties (927–c. 725). It was a different feeling from the menace of Assyria, and it was only because of the relative weakness and non-imperial policy of Egypt that the Israelite monarchies were able to flourish for four centuries. Perhaps so friendly a picture would be less sustainable after Pharaoh Necho killed Josiah at Megiddo in 609, but the Joseph story could have been composed at any time in the decades before that. Egypt is seen as a potential worshipper at Israelite festivals in Ps. 68.32 (tenth century) and Ps. 87.5 (ninth century), and a possible ally in Isa. 31.1 (eighth century): it is not till later that Egypt is synonymous with hostility to Israel, as in the Wisdom of Solomon.

Wellhausen did not find compelling evidence for parallel J and E sources in the text of Genesis 37–50, but inferred them from their supposed presence elsewhere in Genesis (*Composition*, p. 52). Rudolph showed that the parallel source hypothesis was unsupported: even the dissonance in 37.18-28 could be explained as the work of a single author. A single basic plot was indeed required by the dreams in ch. 37, but, as Redford and Schmitt argued, a single author was not plausible. Redford saw the Reuben–Midianite story as primary, being composed and then expanded by the

Judah–Ishmaelite additions in 625–450. Schmitt took the two versions in the reverse order, the Judah form going back to the United Kingdom of the tenth century. Redford seems to be right: the narrator is from Joseph, indeed from Ephraim, and the Asaph and Korah psalms reveal a situation in the eighth century in which only Joseph and Benjamin had been in Egypt, and other tribes are ignorant of the tradition.

Redford favours a late date, even for the Reuben-version, partly on the grounds of vocabulary, partly of Egyptian parallels. Both of these considerations are disputed by Schmitt (*Josephgeschichte*, pp. 130-49), and he sometimes (slave-trading) has a point. But the balance of evidence makes a tenth-century date for the basic story unlikely. The Egyptian parallels suggest to Redford a date in the Saite period (from 625), and he includes in his 'late' sources for comparison Deuteronomy, Jeremiah and Ezekiel. I am quite content with the early end of his proposed span, and the more general evidence cited above suggests 640–610.

Noth comments, '[The story] has at its basis the question: "Jacob and his sons went down to Egypt (Josh. 24.4): how might that have come about?"' (*Pentateuch*, p. 209). This is clearly the central theme of the chapters: a divine providence, known from the beginning in Joseph's dreams, works even through the brothers' malice (Gen. 45.5). Joseph, through divine inspiration, wins favour on all sides by interpreting the dreams of prisoners and of Pharaoh. His rise enables his family to escape the great famine, and positions them to prosper and multiply: so will they be ready for the next phase of their destiny, the Exodus. His character—trustworthiness, probity, far-sightedness, administrative ability—no less than his interpretative powers, is seen as evidence of the action of God (Gen. 45.4-8).

The centrality of this *Heilsgeschichte* theme puts other proposals in the shadow:

1. Westermann (III, pp. 24-25) sees Gen. 37.8 as a key text: 'May and ought a brother to rule over his brothers?' This would then be a reflection on the debate whether Israel should be a monarchy or a theocracy, and would site the narrative in the tenth century or so. He also mentions 'the obvious proximity to the patriarchal stories into which it was inserted'. Both arguments seem dubious. The narrator seems in no doubt that Joseph had been chosen by God to rule over his brothers, to their great blessing in Egypt; and very likely, in his view, to their blessing in eighth-century Israel. The 'obvious proximity' argument cuts both ways: I have suggested that the Jacob stories were also put together in the seventh century.

2. Von Rad, in the epilogue to his *Genesis* commentary, and in *Wisdom in Israel* (pp. 46-47, 199-200), suggested that the Joseph story should be categorized with Wisdom literature: it described a prudent, pious young man, who stands out against the invitations of a temptress, is blessed by God, and succeeds at court—the parallel with many texts in Proverbs is obvious. The thesis has been criticized, especially by J.L. Crenshaw ('Method') and Redford (*Joseph*, pp. 100-105). Joseph's behaviour in boasting to his older

brothers is not at all what is recommended in Proverbs; nor is Potiphar's wife merely a temptress, but a woman scorned. Nonetheless, von Rad's proposal has a certain force; we may think that the Proverbs tradition was in part a reflection on the Joseph narrative.

3.   Commentators from Gunkel on have spoken of the chapters as a *Novelle*, and have compared it to Ruth, Esther, Tobit and other 'short stories'. There is truth in this, and Joseph is clearly based on the Cinderella-type folk-tale in which the spurned younger sibling outdoes its elders and ends up in the palace. But there is the important difference that Joseph provides the indispensable link from Jacob in Canaan to Israel in Egypt. He is the key figure who sets the national Exodus myth on its way.

4.   Westermann correctly notes that the Joseph story is confined to Genesis 37, 39–45: 46–50 are the conclusion of the Jacob story. He also isolates chs. 39–41 as a political unit set inside a family story, chs. 37, 42-45. The second point is not really significant: Cinderella has to do with her fairy godmother, the coach and the prince, and these scenes fall within two passages with her sisters: but, as with Joseph, the central scenes are necessary to resolve the family problems. Nor is Joseph absent from chs. 46–50, especially in ch. 48, the blessing of his sons: see the next chapter, the excursus on P's expansions in Genesis.

Chapter 10

ABRAHAM, CREATION AND THE SONS OF MERARI

Abraham

The composition of the Joseph story solved some problems, but it raised others. The Exodus–Numbers narrative was now carried back with a continuous national history to Jacob/Israel, the father of the whole people; but if Joseph was the father of the Joseph tribes, and Jacob of the Jacob tribes, where did Abraham and Isaac come into the story? For the God of Abraham was honoured in eighth-century Dan (Ps. 47.10), and the whole country could still be referred to as Isaac at the same period (Amos 7.9, 16). Sooner or later the genealogical solution was bound to occur to the thoughtful. Abraham, Isaac and Jacob were not the names of independent early leaders of the Settlement: they were all the same family. As Joseph was the *son* of Jacob, so Jacob was of Isaac, and Isaac of Abraham. Perhaps this solution was in the air for many years, perhaps it became official no earlier than the seventh century: we first meet it outside Genesis in Deut. 6.10, 9.5, 27. Of the two earlier patriarchs it is clear that Abraham commanded the wider loyalty.

Apart from these passages, there is no pre-exilic reference to Abraham or Isaac outside Genesis: so we know of their presence in tradition, but we know of no story connected with them. It has been widely speculated that Abraham traditions (at least) go back to the second millennium, and Westermann can assert confidently that this is so, and that there is no possibility of stories being invented (II, pp. 29, 34); but Van Seters (*Abraham*) sees a date around 600 as the period of the tradition's genesis, and for a number of reasons considered below, that seems more likely.

There is a major difference between the Joseph and the Abraham sagas, the former being a single elaborate plot, while the latter is an accumulation of small blocks. But this should not be used as an argument to imply a development over centuries: two or three generations would be sufficient—compare the development of the Gospel traditions. Nor should the word 'invent' be allowed in the discussion. Religious tradents apply traditional forms, they elaborate and infer: 'invention' implies *mauvaise foi*. Redford proposed that the whole Joseph story was composed from standard folklore themes (youngest son triumphs, spurned wife, etc.), and Westermann himself (II, pp. 420-30) allows that much of the Isaac story in Genesis 26 has been similarly created (out of Gen. 12, 20–21). The first indication outside Genesis that we have of stories of the patriarchs is in Psalm 105, where the account is close to Genesis and is probably derived from it, after the Exile.

The basic structure of the Abraham saga was given in the fact that he had only one 'son', Isaac, whereas Jacob, his competitor as father of the nation, had twelve. Two patterns of divine blessing were available in tradition: straightforward fruitfulness, such as with Jacob, or Job, or Israel in Egypt; and miraculous, delayed fruitfulness, as with Rebekah, or Rachel, or Hannah, or Elizabeth. If Abraham had only one son, Isaac, by his wife, she may be inferred to have been in the latter category, an ageing woman whose womb the Lord had closed, only to open it wonderfully at a late stage; and it will have been wonderful indeed, since the whole existence of the people hung on this providential conception.

So the Abraham drama is in three acts, like the Jacob and Joseph dramas. Jacob was in peril of his life from Esau, Joseph from his brothers, and the Egyptian authorities, Abraham from his inability to father a son. God saved Jacob's life and gave him wealth, women and sons in Aram; he saved Joseph's life and gave him wealth, power and sons in Egypt; he saved Abraham by the miraculous conception of his single son. Jacob returned to the land, made peace with Esau, and settled; Joseph made peace with the brothers, and settled the family in Goshen; Abraham settled, buried his wife in the land, and saw Isaac married.

The core of the Abraham complex is thus given in Gen. 15.1-6, 18.1-15, 21.1-3, Abraham's plight, the annunciation of Isaac's conception, and his birth. But so bald a tale lacks light and shade, and tradition provided a second folklore motif in the mockery of the loved-but-barren wife of destiny by the unloved-but-fruitful wife of convenience. We meet this motif again with Rachel's envy of Leah in 30.1-21, and with Hannah's provocation by Peninnah in 1 Samuel 1. Abraham's migration was remembered as in association with other tribes, including the Ishmaelites; Ishmael had settled in 'the wilderness of Paran' in the Negev (Gen. 21.21; cf. 16.14), as did Abraham (12.9; 20.1). In the time of the Asaphite psalms, in the eighth century, Ishmaelites were associated with Hagarenes (Ps. 83.7), so the way was open to a 'stock' elaboration. Abraham had an ageing wife, Sarah, Princess; but as she could not conceive, she gave him her slave-woman, Hagar, who bore him a bastard son, Ishmael—as Jacob's slave-women Bilhah and Zilpah stood in for his wives Rachel and Leah. However, just as Peninnah riled and provoked the barren Hannah, so did the upstart Hagar despise her mistress once she had conceived. When Sarah was strict with her, she ran away, and was found by the angel of Yahweh by a spring in the southern steppe; she received an oracle of her son's destiny (16.11-12), and he grew up as an archer in the wilderness of Paran (21.20-21). So the core story grows to consist of Genesis 15–16, God's promise of a son and the birth of Ishmael; Gen.18.1-15, the annunciation of Isaac's conception; and Gen. 21.1-3, the birth of Isaac.

It is a cardinal point that the central core of the Abraham cycle includes Gen. 15.1-6; for there is general agreement that these verses are 'Deuteronomic'. Thus 'The word of Yahweh came to...' is frequent in Jeremiah; descendants 'numerous as the stars in heaven' recur in Deut. 1.10; 10.22; 28.62; the address אדני יהוה is unique in Genesis to 15.2, 8, but comes also in Deut. 3.24; 9.26; faith, belief in Yahweh's action, is a key concept in early prophetic times, for example, Isa. 7.1-9; 37.1-38; the phrase 'it was reckoned to him as righteousness' recurs in Deut. 24.13; Ps. 106.31. Westermann (II, p. 230) suggests that the earlier form of the story promised a son only, while the present version promises son and descendants; this could be so, but is a speculation—the story as we have it is steeped in the language of Asaph–Deuteronomy.

   The second Ishmael story, Gen. 21.8-19, is a composition later than that in Genesis 16; it uses אלהים not יהוה, and is formed on the basis of the Genesis 16 story, as the second wife-as-sister tale is formed on the basis of Gen. 12.10-20. The oracle in 16.11-12 makes no reference to Hagar's returning home, and the repeated 'And the angel of the LORD said unto her' (16.9, 10) suggests an interpolation made when the second story of 21.8-19 was required (see further below, pp. 239-40).

A third folklore theme was at hand to lend drama to the tale: the patriarch whose life is imperilled by the beauty of his wife. Three times we meet this situation in Genesis, twice with Abraham, once with Isaac. In each case the prudent patriarch passes his wife off as his sister, and twice the neighbouring potentate takes her into his harem; but God ensures no undesired consequences. In the earliest form, Gen. 12.10-20, the Asaphite author has transferred to the story the circumstances of his own myth. Abraham thus becomes a type of his descendants' future: driven from the land by famine, he goes down to Egypt, where he falls into the power of Pharaoh; Yahweh afflicts Pharaoh with plagues, and Abraham escapes, loaded with the spoil of the Egyptians.

The argument of this book is that the Exodus story was the tradition of the Joseph–Benjamin tribes only, and was handed on at Bethel by the Asaphite clergy in the most primitive form that we have. There is no reference to Abraham in the Asaph psalms, despite their interest in the national history: so any transference of the story to Abraham is likely to have been made after 722 in Jerusalem, by the same Asaph tradents. For the priority of the Genesis 12 version over Genesis 20, 26, see Van Seters, *Abraham*, pp. 167-91; Westermann II, p. 161, 'The question can now be considered as settled.' Thompson (*Origin*, pp. 51-59) is not so certain.

A further theme lay to hand with the names of Lot, and of Sodom and Gomorrah. Abraham's settlement had been part of a movement of peoples, not only Ishmaelites but Moabites and Ammonites, referred to in Ps. 83.9 as 'the children of Lot'; they had settled in Transjordan when Abraham and Ishmael had arrived in the south. The presence of the Dead Sea between the two had long been explained by the legend of the wicked cities of Sodom and Gomorrah, already a stock item in Isa. 1.10. So it became convenient to amplify the Abraham cycle further. Lot had been an associate of Abraham, his nephew. As they both prospered, the land (of Palestine) became too small for the two of them—Abraham had over three hundred men in his clan!—so they divided it between them, and Lot chose the fertile valley area (Gen. 13). He was corrupted by the easy life there, and was nearly destroyed in the overthrow of Sodom and Gomorrah (18.16–19.29). The origin of the peoples of Moab and Ammon lay in the well-known scandalous incestuous union of Lot with his daughters which then followed (19.30-38).

Gen. 18.22-33, Abraham's intercession with God for the cities of the plain, is a classic instance of the holy man as intercessor. The theme goes back to Amos (7.1-6), but the closest parallel is Ezekiel 14, where God says, 'Son of man, when a land sinneth against me...though these three men, Noah, Daniel, and Job, were in it, they should deliver but their own souls by their righteousness' (14.13-14; cf. 19). If the Sodom story were an established part of the national tradition, we should have expected Ezekiel to mention Abraham.

The Lot theme was valuable to the narrators because it involved the divine right to the land: Abraham needs to be shown not merely as the fathei of the people, but as the first patriarch to whom the land was promised. Indeed, now that the greater part of the land has been occupied by the Assyrians, God is portrayed as making a 'covenant', that is an oath (ברית), that despite a present intermission, the land will be Abraham's descendants' for ever (Gen. 15.18). The oath was made because Abraham believed God's word over his descendants. Once more the suggested context is the seventh century, the time when Isaiah

had expected Ahaz to believe God's word (Isa. 7.9), and Hezekiah did
believe and was justified (Isa. 37). Abraham asks for a sign of Yahweh's
promise, and is rewarded with the vision of his presence between the
divided animals; as Ahaz was bidden to ask for a sign in Isa. 7.10-14,
and unwisely declined. For Abraham there was a delay till the fourth
generation, when the iniquity of the Amorites would be complete (Gen.
15.16); for the narrator the fourth generation may well be at hand since
the disaster of 722—the iniquity of the Assyrians was certainly no less.

The second half of Genesis 15 is as 'Deuteronomic' as the first. 'I am Yahweh who
brought you...' comes also in Deut. 5.6; Lev. 25.38; 'to give you this land to
possess' recurs at Deut. 3.18; 9.6; 12.1, etc.; the address אדני יהוה follows 15.2;
Deut. 3.24; 9.26; the enactment of an oath by passing between the halves of divided
animals is found also in Jer. 34.18-20 (only); the prophesied oppression in Egypt is
an Asaphite theme, as in Gen. 12.10-20; the destruction of the native inhabitants for
their wickedness comes also in Deut. 9.4-5; the River Euphrates as the border of
Israel is found also at Deut. 11.24, Josh. 1.4, as well as in the Asaphite Ps. 80.12.

For ברית as an oath see Perlitt (*Bundestheologie*, pp. 72-76), Westermann (II,
pp. 215, 228-29). Van Seters (*Abraham*, pp. 263-78) infers an exilic setting from
'from Ur of the Chaldees', and the oppression prophecy: the former is likely to be a
later gloss, fitting the P introduction in Gen. 11.31.

Although Abraham lives in the Negev, he is portrayed as travelling up
and down Palestine. In Genesis 12 he arrives from Haran and builds
altars, first at Shechem, at the (sacred) מקום by the oracular terebinth
(12.6-7), and then between Bethel and Ai (12.8), before journeying on to
the south. He thus legitimates the earlier and the later sanctuaries which
had been served by the Asaphite clergy, his narrators. The time is far
away and long ago, when 'the Canaanites were in the land'; Canaanites
were thought of as a distinct community in the days of the Judges, but
had been assimilated long before the seventh century. In 12.1-3 Yahweh
promises to make of Abraham a great nation, and a source of blessing to
all humanity; and in 12.7 his offspring is promised the land. In Genesis
13 he returns to the sanctuary-site between Bethel and Ai, where he and
Lot divide the land; and again Yahweh promises him the land, north,
south, east and west from Bethel, for ever; and offspring like the dust of
the earth (13.14-16). He is to rise up and go through the length and
breadth of the land (13.17); and this he does, beginning from his settlement at Hebron in the south (13.18, Beersheba at 22.19), and going as
far as Dan in the north, in pursuit of the kings of Shinar, Ellasar, Elam
and the Nations (14.1-16). So he foreshadows the future not only in

moving at ease through the whole land, but also in defeating the kings of the southern Euphrates region who will be a peril to Judah in the late 600s.

Thus the twin promises of progeny and of the land are set out and foreshadowed in Genesis 12–21; but they must be seen as settled on a more permanent basis before narrator and listener can rest. So the final act of the Abraham drama, as of the Jacob and Joseph tales, is of settlement. Abraham has been promised the land, but he owns not a metre of it: however, Sarah's death means that he needs a burial place, and the Hittites sell him the Machpelah cave by Hebron. He has been promised descendants, but his precious Isaac is unmarried, and a prey to the daughters of the land, those sirens of religious corruption so feared by the Deuteronomists; however his trusted servant is despatched to his old family in Aram, and under divine guidance brings back the (apparently) biddable and modest Rebekah. So the first steps can be seen to have been taken towards the permanent fulfilment of Yahweh's word.

The themes of Abraham as international general defeating the Mesopotamian kings, and of the purchase of the burial-site, belong after the period of Asaphite ascendancy, and are to be ascribed to the Merarites ('P') in the exile. The Machpelah story in particular should be our warning not to think of them as a single person, only interested in sabbath and circumcision and the tabernacle, and forever telling how the whole congregation fell on its face before the glory of the LORD: Genesis 23 is a tale told with artistry, and others beside Asaph tradents could narrate with skill.

There is, however, a further group of Abraham stories which should be credited to one of the Asaphite story-tellers: the second version of Sarah being passed off as Abraham's sister (Gen. 20), the second Hagar–Ishmael story (21.8-21), and the binding of Isaac (22.1-14). These masterpieces are probably from the same mouth as the Joseph narrative, for not only do they regularly use אלהים for the deity, but they show the same high narrative technique—the power of pathos and irony, the restraint which leaves the listener to infer the full truth, the ability to slow the pace of the story with repetitions so as to heighten the tension.

Two features of the Genesis 20–22 stories have been noticed for many years. (i) Whereas Genesis 12–16, 18–19, 24 use יהוה for God, either predominantly or exclusively, Genesis 20–22 uses אלהים similarly. (ii) Genesis 20 is a 'duplicate' of Gen. 12.10-20, and Gen. 21.8-19 of Genesis 16. The classic solution, a continuous 'E' narrative parallel to an earlier 'J' story, is no longer viable. The author(s) of

Genesis 20–21 are familiar with Genesis 12, 16; and both our eighth-century traditions, the Korah and Asaph psalms, use both יהוה and אלהים. We should rather think
of a series of Asaphite tradents in seventh-century Jerusalem, passing the high office
of מזכיר from father to son (see below, Chapters 14–15): a later tradent will improve
on his predecessor. Genesis 20 is an advance on Gen. 12.10-20, as is Gen. 21.8-19
on Genesis 16. The use of אלהים is an indication of growing reflection. We shall find
an Asaphite author using אלהים in Exodus, up to the moment of revelation at Meribah
(Ps. 81.11), and the same thought is at work here and in the Joseph story—how can
one speak of יהוה before he has revealed himself? It is often asked why an improving
author should have left the first (scandalizing) wife-as-sister story in place if he dis-
approved of it, and not simply replaced it with Genesis 20; but the question presupposes a writing 'redactor' who may do as he pleases with his 'text'. With the
hypothesis of a recital of tradition at worship, the tradent has licence to elaborate but
not to delete.

For the later Asaphite narrator, the tension of Abraham's peril may
be increased if the wife-as-sister story is taken not only at the beginning
of the cycle, when Sarah was (young and) beautiful, but *after* the
promise that she would conceive; so he sites it in Genesis 20, after the
angelic visitation to Abraham and Lot. It had seemed as if the bitterness
of childlessness was past; but now Sarah is seen disappearing into
Abimelech's seraglio, whence she can only emerge defiled for ever.
However all things are possible with God, and with him there is no
shadow of turning. The new tradent is further concerned to portray
Abraham as a more moral man. We now learn that Sarah really was
Abraham's (half-)sister, so he was not telling a lie (Gen. 20.12); he used
the same device regularly (20.13-14); it was justified because of the
godlessness of the district (20.11). Abimelech was not visited with unde-
served plagues as Pharaoh had been, but warned by God in a dream
(20.3-7; God reserved direct speech for his own people, cf. Gen. 31.24
[Laban]; Num. 22.20 [Balaam]); the divine visitation was limited to
temporary barrenness all round (20.17). Abimelech gave Abraham
slaves, cattle and money freely, after learning of the deception, not
before, like Pharaoh (20.14-16); and Abraham is a prophet, whose effec-
tual, fervent prayer is able to bring healing to the king (20.7, 17). So the
patriarch is transformed from the deceitful and cruel sharpster of
Gen. 12.10-20 into an honest, reasonable and spiritual figure, worthy to
be father of his people.

Westermann (II, pp. 316-29) stresses that the text declares Abimelech and not
Abraham to have acted in the integrity of his heart; and concludes that the narrator is
concerned with the problem of the Gerar king's morality. Surely this goes too far: the

narrator sees that Pharaoh was treated scandalously in Genesis 12, and he justifies everybody. But Westermann notes properly that he presupposes Genesis 12 (especially in 20.2); and that Abimelech is a non-Israelite treated with sympathy, a feature not much in evidence in early texts. Here again we have a parallel in the Joseph narrative: when the community has space to breathe, Gentile kings no longer have to be bogeys, but may seem more *sympathique*.

We find the same motives at work in Gen. 21.8-19. The new tradent decided to retell the tale after Ishmael's birth, the further to heighten the tension. We had supposed that Abraham's lineage was half-safe with the birth of Ishmael: but now the child seems certain to perish of thirst in the wilderness of Beersheba. We were introduced to the same anxiety with Sarah's peril in Genesis 20. In order to achieve this effect, the narrator sends Hagar back to Sarah by glossing in a command of the angel in 16.8-9, and the child is born not in the Negev but in Abraham's household. Thus the scene is set for a second cliff-hanger.

Everyone behaves badly in Genesis 16, and this, as in Gen. 12.10-20, is an embarrassment to the more sensitive story-teller. There Hagar had been insolent to her mistress (the Hagarenes had shared in the downfall of Samaria, Ps. 83.7); now the girl is without fault, and the cause of her expulsion is that her son, less than a year old (Gen. 21.14, 15), is playing with her master's heir. In 16.5-6 Sarah is jealous and petulant with her husband, and cruel to her maid; in 21.10 she merely insists that the son of Abraham's wife be brought up as his sole heir, without competition. In 16.6 Abraham hands his concubine over to his wife's whip without a pang. In 21.11 Sarah's demand 'was very grievous in Abraham's sight on account of his son', and in v. 12 even the bondwoman is remembered. He agrees to her dismissal only on God's assurance that he will provide for them; and he generously looks after their future with some bread and a skin of water, which he himself puts on the young mother's shoulder (21.14). Finally, in 16.11-12 all that the angel will foretell is that Ishmael will be a wild ass of a man, the enemy of all; in 21.13, 18 God undertakes to make a great nation of him. As with Genesis 20 we notice a surprising sympathy with the non-Israelite Hagar in the later account. In early times Gentiles were almost always bad; it is later that we meet fine, religious Gentiles like Abimelech of Gerar, or Joseph's Pharaoh, or Job, or Cornelius. By the time the second Hagar story was told, Hagarenes and Ishmaelites are distanced figures in a far-off desert, like Tartars and Cossacks to a modern Westerner, well after the death of Timur Leng.

The tale of Ishmael's peril is told with an artistry that parallels that of Isaac's peril in Genesis 22; and it is in the latter story that the tension reaches breaking point. Sarah almost became an alien's concubine, Ishmael almost died of thirst, and now Isaac, in the face of all the divine promises, is bound on the altar with his father's knife raised. The threat of death to the two boys runs a similar course. In both God commands Abraham to take the fateful, seemingly fatal decision. In both he rises early, before dawn, and sets the heavy journey on its way. In both he lays the burden on the victim—bread and water on the girl's shoulder, wood on the boy's. The pathos is not lost on the listener in either case: the water, as he knows, is soon gone in the desert; the wood raises Isaac's innocent question, 'But where is the lamb?' The narrator knows how to deepen the emotion by artful repetition. Hagar 'went and sat her down over against him... And she sat over against him': Abraham and Isaac 'went both of them together...so they went both of them together', 'Here am I... Here am I... Here am I'. He knows the pull of a parent's heart—'Let me not look on the death of the child', 'Take now thy son, thy only son'—and of the cry of the innocent—'she lift up her voice and wept', 'My father! Behold the wood...' The victims lie to await their death, Ishmael under the bush, Isaac on the wood. They are saved by the call of the angel of God/Yahweh at the moment of crisis. God opens Hagar's eyes and she sees a well of water; Abraham lifts up his eyes and looks, and behold a ram caught in a thicket. God will make Ishmael a great nation; and through Isaac Abraham's seed will be multiplied as the stars of heaven, and in him shall all nations bless themselves.

It is the later Asaphite story-teller who has made of Abraham the majestic, spiritual figure who dignifies the three religions of Judaism, Christianity and Islam. Jacob is guileful and Joseph is priggish; and the earlier Abraham was much in his grandson's image—travelling between Palestine and the River, a successful deceiver (of Pharaoh), blessed by divine providence, hen-pecked by an unpleasant wife, procreating from concubines, concerned for a marriage within the family. He rises momentarily above this level with Lot, offering him his choice of the land, and bargaining with God for the cities of the plain. But it is the later tradent who has made Abraham a man of God. He rescues his reputation with some pains in Genesis 20; he makes him obey God in the face of a terrible end to half his hopes in Genesis 21; and obedience reaches to nobility in Genesis 22. This is what Paul Tillich called

Abrahamic religion. General Montgomery liked to read the lesson in services during the desert campaigns of 1942–43; and whatever the passage set, he would always read Genesis 22, 'the soldier's lesson', the acceptance of total sacrifice.

Westermann (II, p. 344) following Gunkel, suggests that God's promise of a great future for Isaac and Ishmael in Gen. 21.12bß-13 is a later insertion: if so the Hagar story approaches the Isaac story in impact, for the listener is left in anxiety for the outcome in both. The two stories are likely to come from the same teller. Westermann pleads against this that 21.17 speaks of the angel of God and 22.11 of the angel of Yahweh; but the latter may be in imitation of Gen. 16.7, 9, 10, which he was rewriting in Genesis 21. He takes the Ishmael story to go back to an oral form in the patriarchal period, against Van Seters (*Abraham*, pp. 35, 310)—and Van Seters is more willing than many to allow arguments for orality. Westermann concedes that the Genesis 22 story is 'relatively late' (II, p. 355), that is, for him, the later period of the monarchy, when the putting to the test of an individual by God came more to the fore. But the most obvious examples of such testing elsewhere in the Old Testament are Job and Daniel, figures first mentioned in Ezekiel 14.

Creation, the Flood and the Work of P

The late eighth century brought to Palestine first Assyrian armies and then an Assyrian administration and foreign settlers; and so contact with Mesopotamian culture, with all its impressive wealth and success. If Ahaz king of Judah was so struck by the altar in Damascus at his meeting with Tiglath-Pileser (2 Kgs 16.10-18), we may easily imagine the effect of a more subtle, more permanent intercourse. One such influence was the realization that the old monster-battle creation myth was *passé*. More sophisticated alternatives were available, and these would enable the Exodus–Joseph–Jacob–Isaac–Abraham story to be continued backwards, and so linked up with creation itself.

The *Atraḥasis* myth, put together from Akkadian fragments from the seventeenth to the sixth centuries, was such an alternative. Humans were created to offer sacrifices for the high gods, such as the lower divine beings were unwilling to perform. They were formed by mixing the body of a dead god with clay, his spirit (it seems) remaining to animate the first seven pairs of men and women. Their multiplication, however, caused excessive noise, and it was decided to cull them by means of a deluge: Atraḥasis the sage is warned, however, to build a boat, and to take on animals and birds. The deluge lasts seven days and nights, and he then offers sacrifice on the purified earth. Mami, the mother-goddess, produces an object of lapis lazuli to remind her that no such deluge should recur.

The standard edition of *Atra-Ḥasis* is by W.G. Lambert and A.R. Millard (1969); there is a discussion in Van Seters (*Prologue*, pp. 47-77) who broadly accepts their understanding of the text.

The creation/flood story occurs in other forms which are in part closer to our Genesis: we may think of the story of Ut-Napishtim in the *Gilgamesh* epic, which has more detailed parallels with Noah, or the expulsion from the garden of Eden theme which is reflected in Ezekiel 28. The latter are known to us from seventh- and sixth-century sources. But the combination of creation and flood is found in *Atraḥasis*.

The seventh-century northerners accordingly adapted the new myth to Yahwist theology and melancholy experience. Man had been created from clay, and the God Yahweh had breathed into him the spirit of life. Adam and Eve had been set in the happy garden as Israel had been given the land. God Yahweh had warned them not to touch the tree of knowledge, as he had commanded Israel to keep his law. The woman had tempted the man at the behest of the snake, as the daughters of the Canaanites were to tempt Israel to the worship of snakes and other idols. The couple had disobeyed God as Israel had disobeyed the terms of the covenant; and they had been expelled from Eden as now Israel had been expelled from (most of) the land. The world of Sennacherib and Ashurbanipal was a world of thorns and thistles and birth-pangs; a world in which innocent shepherd-people were murdered by their fellow-men, a degenerating world of blood-feud and vengefulness, where the inclination of the thoughts of men's hearts was only evil continually.

The combination יהוה אלהים in the Paradise story remains a puzzle; understood here as the self-conscious domestication of a pagan myth—it was not some Mesopotamian deity who presided over Eden, but God Yahweh. The political sub-text of the story is expounded by Blenkinsopp (*Pentateuch*, pp. 63-71) and goes back to Norbert Lohfink's essay, 'Die Erzählung vom Sündenfall' (1965), with some foreshadowing in von Rad, *Genesis*, Section 2.

Of such a situation Yahweh could not but repent; as the gods blotted out tumultuous humankind in *Atraḥasis*, so will Yahweh have blotted out the corrupt world with a 40-day rain-deluge; and so will he blot out the evil Assyrians. Noah, the righteous and blameless man of his generation who found favour in the eyes of Yahweh, is a figure for Israel,

Yahweh's elect, now dedicated to Deuteronomic obedience and a new righteousness. Israel will survive the coming destruction, and will sacrifice to Yahweh on an earth no longer under curse, where the seasons come round under his guarantee, and there will be catastrophes no more. There will still be wicked men like Ham/Canaan who take advantage of their innocent fathers' mishaps, but they can expect the curse of servitude, which Israel will obediently enforce.

Blenkinsopp (*Pentateuch*, pp. 77-97) follows Westermann (I, pp. 396-97) in seeing the P version of the Flood narrative as primary, and the 'J' version as a supplement; and draws the economical conclusion that the 'J' version is later than P. Westermann himself believed in an early J, so he implies a post-P redaction (Blenkinsopp, *Pentateuch*, p. 97 n. 21). I am following Westermann's general scenario, but with a seventh-century 'J'. It is difficult to believe that a supplementing editor would *de novo* repeatedly speak of a 40-day rainstorm when glossing P's account of a 150-day global upheaval; the clumsy combination of two existing accounts, with suppression of some 'J' overlaps, is a more believable hypothesis. We may compare the unhappy combination of Mark's and Luke's stories of the anointing of Jesus in Jn 12.1-8.

So the old creation myth of the destruction of the water-monster, which was still orthodoxy in Psalm 74 and survived into later texts in Job and Isaiah, was replaced by something less crude which we have in Genesis 2–11; the paradisal beginning and its sad end, the struggle of the pastoral with the agricultural way of life, the descent into technology, the water catastrophe and the new beginning, leading up to Abraham. The Yahweh-Elohim tradents, still the old northerners in Jerusalem, formed their pre-Abraham tale into two complexes, each of which they sealed with a genealogy: a primaeval complex, Gen. 2.4b–4.26, and a Flood complex, assorted passages in Genesis 6–10, with an appendix in the Babel story, Gen. 11.1-9. An important character in the Genesis 10 genealogy is Nimrod, who began in Babel and ended by founding Nineveh and other great cities of Assyria (Gen. 10.8-12). The scattering of the world's peoples is ascribed to the arrogance of the people of Babel, whose tower reaching heaven is likely to be based on the vast ziggurat Etemenanki, raised in Babylon in the early seventh century. Thus the whole complex can be comfortably sited towards 600. We have no direct indication of how these narratives were used. We may simply speculate that they formed part of a public recital of sacred traditions at the annual festivals, especially at Tabernacles.

According to Van Seters (*Prologue*, pp. 182-84) Etemenanki is likely to have been first built in the eighth century, being first mentioned c. 765. It was destroyed by Sennacherib, but rebuilt by Esar-Haddon, who made it the largest building in the Near East. It was again destroyed by Ashurbanipal, and rebuilt under Nabonidus and Nebuchadnezzar. It might thus have inspired the Tower of Babel story in either the seventh or the sixth century.

The story is complicated by an evident second voice in the telling of the Genesis stories. For Genesis 1–11 it has been plausible to conjecture *an alternative version* of the tradition. For famously the P creation narrative in Gen. 1.1–2.4a is different from the Adam-and-Eve creation story, the P genealogy in Genesis 5 differs from the JE genealogy in Genesis 4, a P Flood story has been interwoven with a J Flood story, and so on. However, when we come to the patriarchal narrative, it is now increasingly agreed that there is no continuous P account of Abraham, Jacob or Joseph. For Abraham, the Merarites have contributed the circumcision covenant in Genesis 17, the burial of Sarah in Genesis 23 and the genealogy in Genesis 25, and a few verses here and there, but nothing continuous. For Jacob there are P elements in Genesis 28 and 34–36; and much of Genesis 46–50 is from P; but these cannot be made into a continuous Jacob narrative. Hence a long-standing malaise. Are we to think that P took over the JE(D) narrative and added to it substantially; and if so how are we to think of P's position that he was able to do this? Or are we to think of a once fuller P narrative, which a redactor has fused with JE, scaling down the P elements after Genesis 12? Or were the P elements merely fragments, which the redactor could handle more easily? The position is made the more complex in that whereas in the patriarchal stories the P-elements are superimposed on a continuous Asaphite narrative, in the Flood story (at least) the continuous narrative is P's, and the 'J' elements have been added.

A continuous P-narrative through Genesis is still defended by Emerton ('Priestly Writer'), but he has to concede P's familiarity with the 'JE' story: he does not make it clear what use his P-narrative was intended to fulfil, and it sounds as if it was read privately in the Temple. Blenkinsopp's bold view of 'J' as a late supplement to P in Genesis 1–11 (*Pentateuch*, pp. 93-94) also evades the question of these writers' *Sitz im Leben*; and one is uncomfortable with Yahweh's walking in the garden in the cool of the day, or smelling the sweet odour of the sacrifice, or coming down to see the tower, in a post-P (? fifth century) redaction. Van Seters (*Prologue*, pp. 160-73) argues for the transfer of certain verses in the Flood story to J, so giving him a continuous coherent narrative; but he has to ignore the יהוה/אלהים distinction which is so important elsewhere in the story.

The last problem may be taken first. The Merarites ('P') are best understood as handling the tradition in Babylonia, in the Exile. There for the first time Israelites found themselves among predominantly uncircumcised people, so circumcision (Gen. 17) became a badge of identity. There annual festivals were no longer practicable, but sabbath was observable, and this too became a badge of Israelite identity. Psalm 104 had described creation in poetry: Yahweh decked in *light* (vv. 1-2), his rebuke of the *waters,* with his chambers set on those above, and those below confined in the seas and the springs (vv. 3-13), the *vegetation* on the earth to feed man and beast (vv. 14-18), the *moon and sun* (vv. 19-23), the *fish* and Leviathan (vv. 24-26), the animals and man—God feeds them all, and takes away their breath in time (vv. 29-31). The Merarites told this story in august prose, and styled the features into six days, with a sabbath of divine rest (Gen. 1.1–2.4a). So history was set on its way with a legitimation in eternity of Israel's weekly symbol of religious devotion.

The new creation narrative could be prefixed to the J tales of Eden, Cain and Lamech, setting out an ideal, vegetarian world of peace, very good, from which the progressive 'J' degenerations could lead naturally into the Flood. The second genealogy (ch. 5), the line of Seth this time, serves the Merarites' purpose of a theological chronology; but its only hint of degeneration is the comment on Enoch, the virtuous seventh in the line of ten, who lives briefly enough to escape the Deluge. But whereas the older primal narrative could be fitted into the new Merarite picture, the 'J' Flood story was another matter. Its climax was Noah's sacrifice (Gen. 8.20-22), and its distinction of clean and unclean animals (7.1-5) was made with this in mind. Sacrifice on Gentile soil was blasphemy to priestly exiles who daily witnessed idolatrous sacrifices in Babylonia. So the whole older Flood narrative was suppressed, and replaced with the continuous 'P' narrative which survives in our Gen. 6.9–9.17: the Merarites could offer a longer flood, 150 days, with a whole year in the ark, and a more dramatic deluge stemming from the fountains of the great deep, and so forth.

The Merarites might do as they pleased in Babylonia, and Ezra might bring their polished Pentateuch back to Jerusalem with authority; but the long-established Jerusalem tradition did not easily die the death. There were Korahite and Asaphite tradents to contend with, and in the end there was compromise. The simple consistent P-version was overlaid with clumsy additions from the familiar J-form; so now the flood is

150 days, now 40; the clean animals are now pairs, now sevens; the climax is now Yahweh's smelling of the sacrifice, now God's covenant of the rainbow. Most great human enterprises end sadly in compromise and muddle.

The key to the setting of the Asaph + Merari Genesis is the structure of the overall story which has emerged in the last two chapters. There are two preliminary sections, the primaeval and the Flood sections. Each of them is clearly marked off by its two concluding genealogies. The JE primaeval section ended with a genealogy (with minimal appended narrative, 6.1-8) in Gen. 4.17-26. The present completed form ends with the fuller P genealogy which comprises Genesis 5. Similarly the J Flood section ended with the genealogy of Noah in Genesis 10, with the Babel appendix in 11.1-9; and it now ends with the P genealogy of the line of Shem in 11.10-29.

These two preliminary sections are then succeeded by the three patriarchal sagas, those of Abraham, Jacob and Joseph; but the Joseph saga proper ends in Genesis 47, and the last chapters are an additional part of the Jacob cycle, the old man's settling in Egypt, his blessing of his grandsons and his sons, and his death and burial. The three sagas are of similar length: Abraham 22 pages of *BHS*, Jacob 21 pages, Joseph (37.1–47.27) 18 pages. I have noted the way in which they follow the traditional folklore pattern: Act 1, Cinderella in the Kitchen; Act 2, Cinderella at the Ball; Act 3, Prince Charming's Visit to Hardup Hall. This subdivision—predicament, resolution, settlement—is marked in the text by the presence of suitable signals, usually genealogies, as with Sections (1) and (2), but sometimes with other considerable additions of P material, as also with (1) and (2).

Thus the Abraham cycle falls into three sections: (3) Gen. 11.31–17.27, Abraham's childlessness, and God's promise; (4) Genesis 18–22, the conception and birth of Isaac, the end of the threat of extinction; (5) Gen. 23–25.18, the settlement; the purchase of Sarah's burial site, the marriage of Isaac, and the progeny of Abraham's three wives. All three of these sections are signalled in the ways I have mentioned. Although there has been minimal P matter in Genesis 12–16, P has contributed the whole of Genesis 17 to round off Section (3). Section (4), Genesis 18–22, ends with the genealogy of Nahor, 22.20-24, whose descendants include Rebekah, to feature in later chapters. Section (5), Gen. 23–25.18, closes with the list of Abraham's descendants through Hagar and Keturah, 25.1-18; the tale of his true-born family from his wife Sarah will take longer to recount. Thus the three phases of the Abraham saga are signed off in the text, either by a major P element (ch. 17), or by a genealogy.

The same is true of the Jacob saga. The story falls convincingly into three: (6) Gen. 25.19–28.9, Jacob under threat; Esau is his elder brother with birthright and expected blessing from his father, but by artfulness he wins both birthright and blessing, and escapes Esau's murderous intentions; (7) Gen. 28.10–32.3, Jacob in Aram; he becomes wealthy, the husband of four women and father of twelve sons, and escapes Laban's wrath; (8) Gen. 32.4–36.43, Jacob's return; he settles in the land, placates Esau, and escapes the anger of the Shechemites. Section (6) ends with P's only considerable contribution, 27.46–28.9. Instead of Jacob fleeing to Haran in the face of Esau's anger, his father sends him to 'Paddan-Aram' in quest of a suitable wife. Section (7) is without either P addition or genealogy. The treaty with Laban at Mizpah is already a legal closure, and after the list of births in 29–30 no further genealogy was appropriate. P has, however, made up for this in Section (8). Westermann finds numerous traces of P's style in the Shechem incident in Genesis 34; P has provided Jacob's return visit to Bethel and the theophany there, 35.(1-)9-13, and the closing genealogy, 35.22-29. Someone has appended the long genealogy of Esau in ch. 36, which in some sense rounds off the whole Jacob saga. So, with the understandable exception of Section (8) we have the familiar markers of the story-divisions, either considerable P elements, or genealogies, or both.

There is not so much P in the Joseph story. Section (9), Genesis 37–40, describes Joseph in a series of perils: murder in Dothan, slavery in Egypt, false accusation by Potiphar's wife, oblivion in prison. With Section (10), Gen. 41–44.17, these perils are at an end: his interpretation of Pharaoh's dreams leads to his promotion, and he is able both to aid and to confuse his erring brothers in their need. The reconciliation comes with Section (11), Gen. 44.18–47.27, as Judah appeals to Joseph in true humility, and the latter's heart is moved to forgiveness, and to the reunification of the family in Egypt. P has taken the opportunity to close the passage with a list of the seventy Israelites who went down to Egypt, and with a fulsome account of the arrival of 'Israel' (46.8–47.27). Only Joseph's buying up of the whole country is thought to be a further non-P appendage.

It is for the most part P who has completed the book of Genesis. The old poem was available to him which we know as Jacob's Blessing

(Gen. 49.1-28), and the legend of the blessing of Ephraim over Manasseh (ch. 48), and other elements; but the framework of the story, Israel's seventeen years in Egypt (47.28-31), his death (49.29-33) and burial (50.12-13), with the constant reference to his approaching demise, are all from the Priestly author. The remainder of ch. 50 is an epilogue consisting mostly of repetitions from earlier chapters (Westermann, III, p. 210).

Now two features of this division of the Genesis text will have already struck the reader: the likelihood that the division is the work of P himself, and the relation to the traditional lectionary pattern in synagogue worship. In nine of the twelve sections the end is marked either by a genealogy or a considerable P-passage, all except (7), (9) and (10), for which reasons could be adduced. P provided the conclusion to (1) and (2), genealogies; to (3) the circumcision covenant and (5), a genealogy; to (6), Isaac's despatch of Jacob to Laban, and (8) several features including a genealogy; to (11), a genealogy and other matter, and (12) the death and burial of Israel. The coincidence of so many of P's contributions with the end of a content-section—and also the beginning of a content-section, 1.1–2.4a opening (1), 23 opening (5), 47.28-31 opening (12)—can hardly be fortuitous. P's work was not a continuous Genesis-story parallel to the earlier tradition: only his Flood narrative was independent and parallel, and for the patriarchs he was adding to the established account. It is P who has divided the earlier tradition, and has added the terminal and opening paragraphs himself.

Equally significant is the correspondence between P's twelvefold division of Genesis and the traditional Jewish lectionary cycle, still observed to this day. The cycle provides 54 divisions of the Torah for use round the year, the last ones being short. There are 50 or 51 sabbaths in the lunisolar year (twelve moons of either 29 or 30 days, 354 days in all), and the 54 provide for the extra month, Second Adar, which makes up the backlog to the solar year, roughly every third year. Some such dividing system must have been in operation for as long as the annual reading cycle has been practised. Now of the 54 sections twelve comprise the book of Genesis, and they are virtually the same as those which I have just argued to be implicit in the text.

Content Divisions	Conclusions (g = genealogy)	Traditional Parashot
(1) 1.1–6.8 Creation	5.1-32 (P, g)	1.1–6.8 בראשית
(2) 6.9–11.30 Flood	11.10-30 (P, g)	6.9–11.31 נח
(3) 11.31–17.27 Abraham I	17.1-27 (P)	12.1–17.27 לך לך
(4) 18–22 Abraham II	22.20-24 (g)	18–22 וירא
(5) 23.1–25.18 Abraham III	25.1-18 (P, g)	23.1–25.18 חיי שרה
(6) 25.19–28.9 Jacob I	27.46–28.9 (P)	25.19–28.9 תולדת
(7) 28.10–32.3 Jacob II	–	28.10–32.3 ויצא
(8) 32.4–36.42 Jacob III	35–36 (P, g)	32.4–36.42 וישלח
(9) 37–40 Joseph I	–	37–40 וישב
(10) 41.1–44.17 Joseph II	–	41.1–44.17 מקץ
(11) 44.18–47.27 Joseph III	46.8–47.27 (g, P)	44.18–47.27 ויגש
(12) 47.28–50.26 Jacob IV	49.29–50.13 (P)	47.28–50.26 ויהי

The sections are almost identical. The few verses at the end of (1), Gen. 6.1-8, are seen by Blenkinsopp (*Pentateuch*, pp. 74-76) as closing the tale of degeneration in 1.1–6.8; in (2), 11.31-32, Terah's move to Haran, may be seen as belonging either with Abraham's migration or as a preparation for it; 32.2-3, Jacob's coming to Mahanaim, is treated more naturally as a contrast with Laban's departure (32.1) than as the beginning of his settlement in Palestine.

A regular cycle of readings has been in place in Judaism since at least the time of the Mishnah: *m. Meg.* 3.4 prescribes the special readings for the four special sabbaths (in Adar) and continues, 'On the fifth the regular order is resumed.' The Gemara on this passage in the Babylonian Talmud discusses two possible special readings for sabbath Sheqalim in the third century, one of which began, 'When thou takest...' (Exod. 30.12); a tradition is cited that the same passage is repeated, and this is said to favour Exod. 30.12ff. as the reading 'because [the regular portion containing this passage] falls about that time.' M. Simon comments, 'The portion *Ki Thisa* in which this passage occurs usually falls on a sabbath about the beginning of Adar' (*b. Meg.* 29b, Soncino translation and note, p. 180): כי תשא is read on the 20th or 21st sabbath of the traditional cycle, which begins after Tabernacles; sabbath Sheqalim is about the 18th sabbath in the normal cycle, or 22nd in leap years. R. Marcus notes that the six books of Philo's *Questions on Genesis* correspond closely with the first six lections in the traditional synagogue lectionary, and that the same seems to be true for his *Questions on Exodus* (Loeb edition, viii-x). If this is so, the traditional cycle can be traced back to the first century. For further discussion see I. Elbogen, *Gottesdienst*, pp. 155-74.

The establishment of this twelvefold division of Genesis from the beginning suggests a solution to the development of the Pentateuch. The earlier [JE/D] form of the Pentateuch was shaped in the seventh century by the Asaphite (and Korahite) clergy in Jerusalem. The fuller form, amplified by P, was developed in the sixth and fifth centuries in Babylon. The earlier form is likely to have been recited at festivals, especially Tabernacles (Deut. 31.10-11). Mass attendance at festivals was impracticable in the Exile, and sabbath became increasingly important. The practice arose of reciting a part of the Torah each sabbath, and with time an annual cycle of recitals was established. With the absence of the northern Levites, a new stress and a different theology could be incorporated.

Such a conclusion would find both support and tension with modern thought on P. For P the sabbath is a central feature, incorporated even into creation, foreshadowed in the manna story, instituted in pride of place at Exod. 31.12-18, the first ritual and the last command ordained in the initial Sinai section. It was not till the Exile that Israelites found themselves among an overwhelmingly uncircumcised community, so that circumcision became a crucial badge of national and religious identity. The lengthy accounts of the Tabernacle, with idealistic arrangements following Ezekiel in many respects, suggest an origin in Babylon when the Temple needed to be rebuilt. Abraham's journey from Ur via Haran to the land could well represent an aspiration to follow the same route (Ezra 7.7). Ezra on his return proclaims a law which contains provisions from Leviticus 23, and which seem to approximate to our Pentateuch, even if not wholly identical. In all these respects an origin for P in Babylonia, perhaps 'at the place called Casiphia' (Ezra 8.17) commends itself.

For an account of P on these lines, cf. Blenkinsopp, *Pentateuch*, pp. 238-39. However, Blenkinsopp's more general account of the structure of Genesis under P is based on the occurrence of the word תולדות, which comes ten times in the book, and is said to indicate five chiastic 'panels' in Genesis 1–11, and five in the patriarchal story. This is not very persuasive. The first occurrence, in 2.4a, refers, as Blenkinsopp says (*Pentateuch*, p. 60) to the preceding 'generation' of heaven and earth, and the second (5.1) covers the second 'panel' (p. 59), so 2.4b–4.26 are apparently not included. Also the phrase '*the book of* the generations of Adam' is unexplained; and the panels are very irregular in length (and interest). But above all such elaborate chiasms can only be noticed by study of a written text, an unlikely setting for the original Genesis. Such chiasms have been a distraction in modern literary criticism, as in Thompson, *Origin*, and Fokkelman, 'Genesis'. The true structure of the book is to be seen by analysing the narrative, not by selection of an individual word. The Merarite author does in fact use תולדות as an indicator at the beginning and end of some of his sections, but it is not to be treated as an infallible key to his thinking.

On the other hand there are some obvious tensions. Noth's theory of an independent P narrative running through the Tetrateuch has been widely approved; but the twelvefold division of our Genesis, as set up by P for liturgical recital/reading, suggests that P edited and rewrote a version of the whole Pentateuch, including Deuteronomy. What then is to be made of the close parallel between Num. 27.12-14, where Moses is sent up Mt Abarim to view the land and die, and Deut. 32.48-52, 34.1, 7-9, where the same command is given and Moses actually dies? What also of Josh. 18.1 and 19.51, where the distribution of the land is 'completed' in P-like formulae?

The Asaph psalms have already put these questions in a different perspective. In the eighth century in Bethel there was consciousness of a continuous *Heilsgeschichte*, running from creation (the killing of Leviathan) to the empire of David and Solomon. The story is told as a continuity from the oppression in Egypt to the rise of David in Psalm 78; but the Exodus–wilderness story has a special status. It was then that God 'acquired his congregation long ago, and redeemed it to be the tribe of his heritage' (Ps. 74.3). The king resolves his comfortless trouble by 'calling to mind the deeds of Yahweh', when 'with his strong arm he redeemed his people, the sons of Jacob and Joseph', and 'led his people like a flock by the hand of Moses and Aaron' (Ps. 77.12-21). Psalm 81 is given entirely to the Exodus–wilderness story as the pattern of God's deliverance and Israel's disobedience.

So the whole notion of a D-corpus, a history of Israel from Joshua to Jehoiachin, prefaced by the Deuteronomic laws and a historical introduction, is undermined. The Asaphites brought to Jerusalem a two-part historical canon: the classic Exodus–wilderness story, and its continuation from the Settlement to modern times. They and their Korahite co-Levites had been in Jerusalem for over a century, in which they developed the Exodus–wilderness saga, prefaced it with the patriarchal and creation/Flood narratives, and terminated it with a fuller version of the law, presented as Moses' last words. So the core of our Pentateuch was already in place by 600.

These elements will have become familiar by recital at the feast, and will have been carried in the memory to Babylon. There they were taken over by new tradents with a loyalty to the Jerusalem priesthood (and a resistance to Korahite pretensions—Num. 16!). They were interested in the primal period and materially altered Genesis 1–11, but in other ways they mostly left Genesis alone; chronological ordering, the circumcision covenant, the first ownership of the land, periodic genealogies, were their main additions. The Exodus and wilderness stories interested them more, and they expanded and reordered these considerably. They added a mass of cultic and other provisions between Exodus 25 and Numbers 10. They naturally still retained Deuteronomy as a time-honoured divinely ordained code; and they closed it with their own account of Moses' death (Deut. 32.48-52; 34.1, 7-9, now separated by the insertion of the long poem, Deut. 33). Moses was implicated in the sin at Meribah, and Aaron had died soon afterwards on Mt Hor, so Moses gets a preliminary warning in Numbers 27; but he still has the Midianites to fight (Num. 31 P), and his final 'Words' to deliver.

The national history from Joshua on was important too, and the P tradents inserted the passages on the distribution of the land into its early chapters. However, rewriting the whole thing was a task for someone else, and this was in time accomplished by the Chroniclers. But the Chroniclers started again, and wrote a second history, effectively from the death of Saul to Ezra. So this leaves the D-corpus, Deuteronomy 1–2 Kings 25, as an apparently complete work of the Deuteronomists, prefixed by Genesis–Numbers, an apparently complete work of the priestly authors; so as to deceive even the wise heart of Noth.

So the priestly version of the Pentateuch, effectively the final version, was formed by the need for a weekly sabbath recital in the sixth century, in worship by the waters of Babylon. We can tell that this was so from a double coincidence. The twelve divisions of Genesis in the traditional lectionary coincide with the structure of the book: two preliminary sections, the primal and the Flood stories; three patriarchal sagas, each dividing into three, predicament, resolution, settlement; and a closing section, Israel's coming to Egypt. But these twelve divisions are also signalled by a regular pattern of closures, often genealogies, often P additions, sometimes both. It is a pity that we cannot look for such indications in the remaining books. In many cases there is no such clear division of the text into natural units; there is little call for genealogies; and the story often advances in large monolithic blocks, Exodus 35–Numbers 10 being exclusively P for example, most of Deuteronomy being D. Nevertheless the establishment of the first twelve lectionary units as virtually identical with the twelve divisions of Genesis is enough. In the beginning was the מקרא.

Chapter 11

THE EXODUS

It may be helpful to the reader if I recapitulate the arguments scattered in the book which concern the history, and the history of traditions, underlying our books of Exodus and Numbers.

1. Whereas there is no mention, nor echo, of the Exodus story in the Korah psalms, nor in the Prayers of David, there are numerous references and allusions in the Asaph psalms—74, 77, 78, 80, 81. It is also these psalms which alone refer to God's people as Joseph—in 77, 78, 80, 81—and once as the specific tribes of Ephraim, Benjamin and Manasseh (80). It would seem likely therefore that the Asaph/Joseph community, the tribes of Ephraim, Manasseh and Benjamin, were the Israelites who had experienced the oppression and deliverance in Egypt, the Exodus—or at least that they believed themselves so to have done. This is made the more likely by the probable association of the Asaph psalms with Bethel in Ephraim: they belong in the last years of (Northern) Israel, and in that decade Bethel was the surviving national religious centre. Furthermore the story represents Joseph as the hero of the descent into Egypt, with Benjamin as his favoured brother: this would be well explained if the original tribes (supposedly) redeemed from Egypt were Joseph and Benjamin.

2. The Korah psalms are associated with Dan by a number of geographical hints: the land of Jordan, the Hermons, the 'little hill', the waterfalls (42), the river of God (46), the mountain noble in height in the far north (48)—though the collection had naturally to be adapted later for use in Jerusalem (48, 84, 87). The foundation of Dan is described by the D-historians with many scurrilous libels in Judges 17–18, but two important details emerge which are much to the shrine's credit, and therefore probably historical: its priesthood were Levites; and the founding priest was called Jonathan b. Gershom b. Moses. It would be

hard to name a more distinguished pedigree: Moses is the most famous of all Israelites, and Gershom was his older son.

3. Psalm 85 opens with an appeal to God's having forgiven the people's sins in the past, and the language showed repeated similarity to that of the Golden Calf story in Exodus 32 (pp. 197-98). In the core verses 32.25-29, and also in the early account in Deut. 33.8-9, the Levites' willingness to slaughter their fellow-tribesmen on this occasion is presented as the legitimation of their priesthood. We may think therefore that this story was in use at Dan as part of the *hieros logos* of the shrine: it justified the priesthood there as being Levitical, and in particular as tracing its descent to Moses. The Levites had at first settled in the south (Num. 26.58a), but had later migrated to Dan (Judg. 17.7–18.20).

4. The Korah psalms regularly speak of the people as Jacob, and never as Israel, whereas the Asaph collection normally uses Israel, and Jacob and Joseph occasionally. This is most easily explained if the main settlement which took place in the Ephraim–Manasseh hill country in the twelfth century was of people speaking of themselves as Jacob; and if the later, Joseph–Benjamin (Caleb, etc.) immigrants described themselves as Israel. As later arrivals they were more willing to compromise than the Korahite priests at Dan: they sometimes used the name of their central group, Joseph, but they could bracket on 'the sons of *Jacob and Joseph*' (77), or speak of 'the God of Jacob' (75, 76, 81). Israel would be a suitable name for a people emerging from the Negev, after the Exodus: like Ishmael or Jerahmeel. The paradox of one people having two different names was resolved by the Jabbok story, where the patriarch had at first been called Jacob but was now renamed Israel.

5. Moses' grandson, the founder of the sanctuary at Dan, was called Jonathan, יהונתן; so his father Gershom was a worshipper of Yahweh. Exod. 2.22 represents the birth of Gershom as taking place before the revelation at the burning bush; so we may credit the tradition that Moses himself was a Yahwist, even if his own children do not bear Yahweh-compounded names, and was the leader who introduced the worship of Yahweh. It is improbable that the Joseph/Benjamin (Israel) tribes should independently have become Yahweh worshippers. Rather, their name suggests that they were (? became) worshippers of El. This would be in line with the use of El as the name of God 19 times in the Asaph psalms, the name occurring in nine of the twelve poems. There are also theophoric El-names from the wilderness story, like Eleazar and Bezaleel; and their religious centre was renamed Beth-el.

6. We should then have the question, How did the worship of El and of Yahweh come to be reconciled? A suggestion of how this might have happened arises from Num. 13.8, 16, where the Ephraimite who spies out the land (and later occupies it) is at first called Hoshea, הושע, but Moses changes his name to Joshua, יהושע. It is Joshua who in the end gathered 'all the tribes of Israel' to Shechem, and 'made a covenant with the people that day' that they should worship Yahweh alone (Josh. 24.25). We may infer that Hoshea, leader of the Israelite (Joseph–Benjamin) immigration, made a treaty of union with the earlier Jacobite settlers at Shechem; the national God was to be recognized as Yahweh (though the name El would still be accepted); and this was symbolized by the changing of the leader's name to Joshua, *Yahweh is saviour*.

7. The site of the Levite massacre, which achieved the first acceptance of Yahweh under Moses, is given under two names: 'whom you tested at Massah, with whom you contended at the waters of Meribah' (Deut. 33.8, and other passages). But Meribah is the site of the covenant God made with Joseph/Israel in Psalm 81, and has nothing to do with the acceptance of Yahweh by the Levites/Jacob/Moses. We should think therefore that the Levite/Moses incident took place at Massah (where no waters are mentioned in Deut. 33), while the oasis ('waters') of Meribah was the site of a religious crisis for the Joseph/Israel group. As geographical moves in the period were often associated with changes of religion (1 Sam. 26.19), it is quite likely that the introduction of El-worship at Meribah caused similar contention to that at Massah; displaced priesthoods are rarely complaisant.

8. If Moses was the leader of a Levite/Jacobite tribe whose crisis took place at Massah, and if his grandson's community at Dan never speaks of the people as Israel and never refers to the Exodus, Moses plainly had nothing to do with the Egyptian experience. Tradition supplies the name of an alternative leader, Aaron, Moses' 'brother', and it seems likely that he was historically the leader of the Exodus. Psalm 77 brackets the two leaders, as it brackets the two settlements, in the interests of national unity: 'Thou leddest thy people like a flock By the hand of *Moses and* Aaron'; compare 'Thou hast with thine arm redeemed thy people, the sons of *Jacob and* Joseph'. Our Exodus/Numbers story is the result of generations of Korahite and Asaphite tradents combining to unify the national myth. The story is, in the last resort, the Israel/Joseph story as we have it in the Asaph psalms; but the hero has become Moses, the

leader of Levites, revered for so long by the sons of Korah, and the people of Jacob.

9. While archaeology has built up a reliable picture of the pattern of Israelite settlement (pp. 217-18), it has produced few relevant second millennium inscriptions: the most significant being the Merenptah stele. Usually dated in the last twenty years of the thirteenth century, this claims a victory over a group of people called Israel somewhere in Palestine. We should then suppose that the Joseph/Israel clans, whom tradition claimed to have escaped from Egypt, made at first for the less arid areas of South Palestine, but were driven from there by an Egyptian army, and settled for a generation or more round Meribah in the southern steppes. During this time they could have increased from some hundreds to some thousands, and so become an effective force in the Settlement.

10. During the seventh century the task of telling the national story was accepted as belonging to the old northern tradents, the families of Asaph and Korah. With the Exile such a tradition was broken, and the ex-Jerusalem authorities in the settlements by the Euphrates found the opportunity to assert themselves. One obvious instance of this is the claim of the Korahites to priestly privilege in Numbers 16, and their subsequent discomfiture; another is the arrangement of the Genesis story into twelve sections for sabbath reading (pp. 245-52). It is normal, and not misleading, to speak of these new tradents by the symbol P. We shall find reasons, however, for giving them a more human face. 1 Chron. 5.27–6.15 lists three supposedly 'Levite' families, those of Gershon, of Kohath, and of Merari. In the following chapters I will argue that the senior, Gershon-line comprise the Asaphites; the most numerous, Kohath-line are the Korahites; and the last and weakest, Merari-line are the Jerusalem, priestly P-school. They are the last major group to undertake the telling of the national tale; but their influence has not been inconsiderable.

11. The Merarites had Judah traditions of their own, to which they wished to give priority: not only in the interest of chronology, or of cultic matters like the construction of the tabernacle, or the circumcision covenant, or the Holiness code, but also in some narrative matters. They had a tradition of having settled around Mt Sinai before their move north, and this has required a massive upheaval in the wilderness story. The original Asaph account sited the earlier settlement at Meribah, by Mt Hor. This was adjusted by the Korahites to square with their

Moses/Levite tradition that the mountain was Horeb, which has come to dominate the account in Deuteronomy. But the Merarites insisted on their own Mt Sinai. They accepted Moses as the leader, so Horeb is quietly identified with Sinai, and given pride of place in the Exodus account; Meribah and Mt Hor and Aaron are postponed to a subsidiary position in Numbers.

These eleven theses offer effective criteria for discriminating between three families of tradents whose interaction may account for the growth of the national story, from its first evidences in the eighth-century Asaph psalms to its 'final' form in the fourth century—for our rough purposes the Massoretic Text. The interaction is continuous over the four centuries: Asaphites and Korahites in seventh-century Jerusalem, Merarites with the now established version in sixth- and fifth-century Babylon, Korahites and Asaphites with the returned Merarites after Ezra in Jerusalem. In particular the theses enable a resolution of the duplications and contradictions which have constituted the Pentateuchal problem. It may be convenient to set the differences between the three schools in a table:

	Asaph	*Korah*	*Merari*
Sanctuary of Origin	Bethel	Dan	Jerusalem
Name of People	Israel	Jacob	Israel
Principal Tribe	Joseph	Levi	Judah
Name of God	'El	Yahweh	Yahweh
Leader in Desert	Aaron	Moses	Moses
Tribes in Exodus	Joseph/Benjamin	All	All
Site of Crisis	Meribah	Massah	Massah/Meribah
Site of Revelation	Meribah	Horeb	Sinai

The Asaph psalms sketched a continuous account of the national history, of which we may distinguish a series of phases which are covered in our Exodus–Numbers: the oppression, the plagues, the Red Sea, the wilderness rebellions, the covenant, the apostasy. I shall comment on these narratives in turn.

The Oppression in Egypt: Exodus 1.1–7.13

Psalm 81 speaks of this: 'He appointed [the festival] in Joseph for a testimony, When he went out over the land of Egypt... I removed his shoulder from the burden: his hands were freed from the basket. Thou calledst in trouble, and I delivered thee' (81.6-8). The *burden*, סֵבֶל, recurs frequently in the early chapters of Exodus as סבלות (1.11-14; 5.4; 6.6), and the children of Israel cried, and their cry came up unto God, in

Exod. 3.7, 9 (2.23P). So the basis of the oppression is set from the beginning: a motive is supplied for it in Israel's multiplying and Pharaoh's envious fear, and the story is linked on to Genesis with the succession of the Pharaoh who knew not Joseph.

A major break at Exod. 7.13 is justified by Houtman (*Exodus*, pp. 494-95) who closes the first volume of his commentary at this verse. The plagues narrative opens at 7.14. The only verses in Exod. 1–5 commonly attributed to P are 1.1-5, 7, the 'Names' and numbers of the families migrating into Egypt; and 2.23aß-25, God's hearing of Israel's groaning. The latter theme was already present in Psalm 81, but was displaced by the Korahites' elevation of Moses. In Exod. 3–4 it is God who takes the initiative, and there is no place for intercession: but he twice refers to the cry of the sons of Israel in 3.7-9.

The Korahite tradents must now attempt to fuse their Moses-saga with the Asaphite story, or they will be too late; and a fine job they have made of it. Moses is to be Aaron's brother and partner in the face of Pharaoh, and he cannot be introduced too soon. The legend of the birth of Sargon, familiar perhaps from increased contact with Mesopotamia, offers an attractive opening. The newborn Sargon was laid in a papyrus box rendered waterproof with bitumen, and placed by his priestess-mother among the reeds of the Euphrates; carried down the river he was rescued by a water-drawer; he became the lover of the goddess Ishtar, and rose to the throne. The tale can be adapted to present needs. Pharaoh had decreed that all Hebrew boys should be killed as part of the oppression (though had that been done the damage would have been unthinkable; so the tale of the two clever midwives is brought in to save the occasion). That would be why Moses' mother put the little lad in the ark among the reeds. That in turn can lead on to his being found by Pharaoh's daughter, and brought up as an Egyptian prince, his own mother being paid to nurse him. The simple tale is a masterpiece: Moses' high destiny is implied from his infancy. All Israelites can rejoice in the outwitting of the wicked Egyptians by divine providence and Israelite determination; and for the Korahites, their Moses has left the Asaphite Aaron standing at the starting gate.

Brian Lewis (*The Sargon Legend*) offers a new version of the Sargon text, with a full discussion and a list of similar legends of heroes exposed in infancy. The text was in the library of Ashurbanipal, and so was known in the seventh century; Lewis derives the Moses version from a common ancestor. Moses was originally unrelated to Aaron: see below on Exod. 15.20, 18.12, pp. 273, 276.

The Korahites are not free simply to compose on a *tabula rasa*: they have their own Moses traditions which must be patched on to the Egypt narrative. Moses and his Levites had been settled in Midian, where his father-in-law, Jethro, had been priest of Yahweh, and (as is commonly and plausibly supposed) had introduced him to Yahweh-worship. The holy mountain revered as Yahweh's abode by these Midianites was Mt Horeb. An ingenious twist to the tale enables these elements to be incorporated. Moses champions one of his abused fellow-Israelites and, being a man of spirit, kills the Egyptian bully; but his quarrelling countrymen turn against him, and he has to flee. It is accordingly to Midian that he goes, where he meets his future bride by the well—like Eliezer and Jacob before him. He is welcomed by the girl's father Jethro and marries her, fathering two sons. He drives the family sheep further than usual, and coming to 'Horeb, the mountain of God', receives his commission. Yahweh (the name interpreted to mean 'I am') is the God who appeared to Abraham, Isaac and Jacob, and the ever-burning bush is the sign of his abode; Moses is commanded to return to Egypt and organize the Exodus.

Midian is regularly represented in the Pentateuch as being east of the Arabah, south of Moab (Num. 22, 25, 31; Judg. 7–8); in Gen. 25.4 as extending into northern Arabia, on the east side of the Gulf of Aqaba. This area is favoured by modern commentators, following Josephus, *Ant.* 2.257, and Ptolemaeus, *Geographia* 6.7.27 (Noth, *Exodus*, p. 31; Houtman, *Exodus*, p. 113). There is a mountain range in this district called in modern times *Jebel Harb*, just south of the 28th parallel (McNeile, *Exodus*, pp. cv-cvi), but there are suitable peaks also further north. We may conclude that the early Moses–Levite area of settlement was in this district then. Jebel Harb is over two hundred miles from Kadesh/Meribah, which are southwest of Jerusalem, and so would approximate to the eleven days' journey 'by the way of Mount Seir', specified in Deut. 1.2. 'Mount Seir' is the mountainous country normally east of the Arabah, so it would be on the way in a dogleg journey skirting the Gulf of Aqaba. A day's journey in ancient times is reckoned at about twenty miles (G.I. Davies, *Way*, p. 23, n. 23; but Davies allows only ten miles a day, or perhaps even six, for a large nomad group with animals [p 111, n. 32], which may be implied in Deut. 1.2). Of course this is a long way from the traditional Sinai: it is small wonder that those who have identified the two sites as one have found themselves perplexed. It did not trouble the Korahite tradents that Moses was supposed to have walked more than two hundred miles alone through waterless desert from Egypt to Horeb: with God all things are possible.

There is the further complication that sometimes 'the mountain of God' seems to be quite near Egypt: in Exod. 3.12, 18 it is only three days' journey, and at 4.27 Moses returning from Horeb meets Aaron there. This suggests that there is a third

The Psalms of Asaph and the Pentateuch

mountain in the tradition. The place where *Aaron* received his commission in the old Asaphite tradition was a nameless 'mountain of God' in northwest Sinai; the place where *Moses* received his revelation in the Korahite tradition was Mt Horeb, east of the Gulf of Aqaba. The Merarites had their roots in the south of the Sinai peninsula. Davies (*Way*, pp. 67-69) distinguishes a northwest Sinai 'mountain of God' from Horeb/Sinai, which leaves him with some problems, especially with Deut. 1.2.

The commission scene in Exod. 3.7-16 has presented problems which perplexed even the skilled Korahite. His own tradition told him that Moses had received a revelation at Mt Horeb that the future God of his people was called Yahweh; but this was in no way related to Egypt or any Exodus. The Asaphite narrative, however, to which he was assimilating, told him that, following the Exodus, God had said to Israel, 'I, Yahweh, am your God, who brought you up out of the land of Egypt' (Ps. 81.11). So he tries to combine the (Korahite) revelation of Yahweh's name with the (Asaphite) out-of-Egypt theme, but he has not been very successful. Moses asks for a sign so that he may be trusted, and is helpfully told that the sign will be Israel's arrival at Mt Horeb. He then asks for Yahweh's name, and is told it; but if the people knew it already (as in most of Genesis), it is surprising that Moses does not know it, and if they do not know it, he could apparently have given the name Baal and got away with it.

Cf. Childs, *Exodus*, p. 61, 'Have the people forgotten the name of their God, or was the God of the Fathers nameless?...' Childs's lengthy discussions (pp. 53-79) of how the sign can be made sense of, why Moses asks for the name of God, the meaning of the Tetragrammaton, and so forth, are a sad dignifying of an ancient muddle, arising from the fusion of two traditions. The אהיה derivation is one more false etymology, and lacks any theological profundity.

So Moses is set to return to Egypt, with the convenient death of the old Pharaoh and all who remembered him: but now there is the problem of fitting Moses in with Aaron. Here the Korahites had a more difficult task, for they had Asaphite feelings to soothe: Aaron must be given his place, but at the same time that must be a lower place than Moses'. Two devices are tried by which Aaron can be allowed something of his old position, but in both Moses virtually elbows him out.

In the old Bethel tradition Aaron must have established his leadership, no doubt with a call from God; but the story has been so totally retold in Moses' favour that the traces of this Aaron-story are too faint to make a reconstruction. Noth (*Exodus*, pp. 27–47) notes a series of duplications and inconsistencies which he aligns with J and E narratives, of which the latter is only partially preserved. But he regards all the Aaron references, 4.13-16, 27-29, and other mentions in ch. 5, as later glosses (pp. 46, 51), as do many critics (cf. Blum, *Pentateuch*, p. 27 n. 92). Blum himself, however, points to the weakness of this hypothesis (pp. 27-28). It lacks literary justification as 4.13ff. fit neatly on to 4.10-12. At 3.18 Moses was told that he and the elders were to go to Pharaoh, and at 5.1 it is Moses and Aaron who go; but Aaron has spoken to the elders at 4.29, and it is inconceivable that he should not at least represent them at 5.1. Nor is there any obvious motive for a pre-P (Noth, *Exodus*, pp. 61-62) introduction of Aaron. Aaron, as ancestor of the Jerusalem priesthood, is hero to P; but no one suggests the hand of P in 4.13–5.21.

In the first scheme, Aaron actually roused the people (as he must have done in the Asaph tradition), but Moses told him what to say. We have this in Moses' pathetic objection that he is slow of speech (Exod. 4.10) and afraid (4.13); God appoints Aaron his brother to do the speaking— he will be god, and Aaron will be his mouth (spokesman, 4.14-16). This picture is carried through in 4.29-30; and perhaps this was tried in some earlier lost version of the plagues story, but it has left no trace upon them now. Aaron does speak for Moses to the people, and so gains their confidence in him (4.30); but this does not apply to the negotiations with Pharaoh. Moses-and-Aaron go in to see Pharaoh together, but the talking is invariably done by Moses, who has got over his modesty, and appears to be pretty articulate.

A second element from the Asaph tradition was Aaron's rod, and this has withstood Korahite pressure slightly better. In the old story the magic rod with which the plagues were invoked was Aaron's rod, and for the first three plagues Moses is still commanded, 'Say to Aaron, Take your rod...' (7.19; 8.5, 16); but thereafter the rod is forgotten for a while, and to bring on the hail and the locusts Moses stretches out *his* rod to heaven (9.23; 10.13). This rod the Korahites supplied in Exodus 4, and made it a magic rod indeed. Moses is hesitant whether the people will believe him, so Yahweh bids him to throw his rod on the ground, and it becomes a snake (4.1-5). It is perhaps unclear how this portent in Midian will lend credence to Moses' coming mission in Egypt; but it provides their hero with a rod of his own with which to outclass Aaron. At 4.17 he is told, 'And thou shalt take in thy hand this rod', and at 4.20 it is 'the rod of God'.

H.H. Schmid (*Jahwist*, pp. 46-48) notes parallels between the early chapters of Exodus and eighth-/seventh-century prophets. Moses' hesitations at his call are similar to those in Jeremiah 1, and the call of Isaiah is to deliver God's word to a hardened people (כבד, hiph.), for whom signs should lead to trust, and do not (Isa. 6–7). He also points to a notable amount of Deuteronomic phrasing in the narrative: a land flowing with milk and honey, Canaanites, Hittites, Amorites, etc. (3.8). All this would suggest a seventh-century date for the Exodus story also.

The argument has been refined by Blum (*Pentateuch*, pp. 20-43). Exod. 3.1–4.18 are an insertion into the main narrative, with a clear 'seam' at 4.19, and Jethro as the father-in-law, as against Reuel in 2.18 (cf. Noth, *Exodus*, pp. 30-33). In 3.12 Moses is to offer the Israelites, as guarantee of his bona fides, a prophecy which they can only verify later—like Deut. 18.21-22; and there are parallels between Exod. 14.13-14, 30-31 and 1 Samuel 12 and other Deuteronomic texts. But the D-parallels are limited to 3.1–4.18, 11.1-3, 12.21-27, 13.3-16, 14; Blum infers that these passages were a late Deuteronomistic composition elaborating an earlier account.

The late date apart, I agree with Blum's general picture (his K^D = my Korahites). But his analysis is too demanding: when speaking of midwives or bulrushes or plagues, one cannot expect the mention of Canaanites and Hittites, or a land flowing with milk and honey. There are many references to 3.1–4.18 material in the narrative following, for example 4.20, 21, 28; and for Reuel/Jethro see below, p. 276. Childs (*Exodus*, pp. 144-49) points to a series of similarities between Moses' confrontations with Pharaoh and the legend of Elijah and Ahab, and others. The whole pre-P narrative is by the same (Korahite, D-type) hand: in this Schmid is nearer the truth.

It is in ch. 5 that the older pre-Korahite story most clearly shows through. Elsewhere throughout Exod. 5.1–12.32 negotiations with Pharaoh are conducted by Moses-and-Aaron, or at least by Moses: at 5.10-21 the negotiators are the Israelite 'foremen', and Moses and Aaron cool their heels outside, waiting to hear the result. Even here a reconstruction of the Asaph/Aaron version would be a speculation, but Noth is surely justified in seeing an earlier tradition underlying our text.

Noth (*Exodus*, pp. 53-56) perhaps overplays his case by stressing the 'us' in 5.3: God had revealed himself to Moses, but in 5.3 Moses and Aaron say, '... has revealed himself to us'. Childs (*Exodus*, p. 95) is justified in criticizing this, but not, I think, in imputing Noth's suggestion to his desire to minimize Moses in the early tradition.

The greater part of Exod. 1.8–6.1 is commonly credited to the older tradents. The Merarites/P have completed the oppression section, as they completed the sections in Genesis, partly with a piece of their own theology (6.2-13; 6.28–7.13), and partly with their usual genealogy (6.14-27). In the first they try to clear up the muddle which their predecessors had left over the worship of Yahweh. Often it had seemed with the northern tradents as if the patriarchs worshipped Yahweh; but in fact Yahweh-worship had been no older than the wilderness period, as even the burning bush story implied. The matter is therefore set out clearly in 6.2-8. God had been worshipped by the patriarchs indeed, but he had been known only as El Shaddai. It is by his proper name Yahweh that he is now to be known, but he is the same God whom they served. The unconditional covenant which God made with the patriarchs is now to be fulfilled. Thus the Merarites append their own version of the revelation to Moses at the bush; and they also extend the Moses/Aaron::God/prophet relationship to the coming negotiations with Pharaoh. This, however, is less successful, as in the following chapters Moses does all the talking, and Aaron never opens his mouth.

Ezek. 20.5, 'making myself known to them in the land of Egypt', is often, and reasonably, thought to underlie P's revelation in Egypt: but then where did Ezekiel get it from? It is likely that he knew the older Asaph/Aaron version with a revelation in Egypt, and that the Korahite burning bush was a Johnny-come-lately.

It has often seemed a problem how P (or the redactor who included both passages) reconciled 6.2-8 with 3.1-15. In view of the many points of contact between 6.2–7.13 and the earlier chapters, Noth (*Exodus*, pp. 61-62) maintains that P is familiar with the JE account (and its Aaron-based expansions): while Childs (*Exodus*, pp. 111-12) takes them to be independent versions of long oral tradition. Blum (*Pentateuch*, pp. 231-41) attempts a middle course: we have to do neither with a source nor a redaction but a conception independent of K^D. Noth seems to make a strong case; and the 'problem' is one which meets us repeatedly—in Genesis 12/20, 16/21, 1/2–3. When a story has been recited in liturgy for a century, no tradent is in a position to suppress it, unless (like the Leviathan creation myth) it is widely felt to be *tramontato*. He may add his own second version, but he may not omit the first. Experience shows that most of those present are not paying close enough attention to notice the discrepancies; and those who are soon exercise their ingenuity in reconciling them.

The genealogy is (as so often) no innocent table of names, but a part of the on-going struggle for the leadership. The Korahites had no doubt that Moses was the first-born son of Amram (Exod. 2.1), though they have slipped their guard by having his elder sister around to watch over the ark. But in time, being the old priesthood at Dan, they were to aspire to a share in the Jerusalem hierarchy, an ambition which came to grief (Num. 16). Now the Zion priests were in some difficulty, since their line went back in fact to Zadok, who was not even an Israelite; so a genealogy was needed which could not only make them respectable, but enable them to outdo the Mosaic line from Dan (Judg. 18.30). This was achieved by turning Aaron's family into the original priesthood, and ancestors of Zadok (1 Chron. 6.35-38), and by promoting Aaron to be

Moses' *elder* brother, 83 when he was 80 (Exod. 6.20; 7.7). They have furthered the same interest by adding the paragraph Exod. 7.8-13, in which Aaron's rod outdoes that of Moses in Exod. 4.1-5: it not only becomes a snake, as his had, but it eats up all the snakes into which Pharaoh's magicians had turned their rods. A man who can do that must deserve to be the father of God's true priesthood.

The Merarites could develop the story as they pleased in Babylon, but when they brought it back to Jerusalem (Ezra 8), it was open to further amendment. The genealogy is not limited to establishing Aaron's position, but in 6.21, 24 we learn the names of the family of Korah: there are no prizes for guessing who had the final hand in the tradition.

I have offered a fuller account of the Korahites' struggle with the Zadokites in *Korah*, pp. 65-84. The present genealogy is singular in giving the descendants of Reuben, Simeon and Levi only: the Merarites were only interested in the Levites, and forgot about the later tribes. Childs (*Exodus*, p. 132) suggests that 'the redactor' ended the section with the genealogy, and began the plagues from 6.28: this is plausible, and if so the Merarites will have added an opening (1.1-5, 7) and a closure (6.2-27) to the oppression story, and an opening (6.28–7.13) to the plagues.

The Plagues: Exodus 7.14–13.16

I have argued above (pp. 120-24) that the Bethel priesthood knew not only that God had 'gone out against Egypt' (Ps. 81.6), but that he had taken action in a series of specific plagues (Ps. 78.42-51): these had then been developed during the seventh century into the seven plagues of Ps. 105.26-38, and in time into the ten plagues of Exodus 7–12. I refer the reader to that discussion for the earlier steps in that development: the analysis results in the following table:

Psalm 78 (Asaph)	Psalm 105 (Korah)	Exodus 7–12
(1) Rivers to blood	(1) Waters to blood	(1) Waters to blood
(2) Flies & frogs	(2) Frogs	(2) Frogs
	(3) Flies & gnats	(3) Gnats
		(4) Flies
		(5) Cattle plague
		(6) Boils
(3) Caterpillar & locusts	(4) Hail & Lightning	(7) Hail
(4) Hail & frost	(5) Locusts	(8) Locusts
[(5) Hail & thunder]		
		(9) Darkness
(6) First-born	(6) First-born	(10) First-born

Psalm 105 displays the labours of the seventh century. Abraham (with Isaac and Jacob) has by now received the promise of the land; Joseph has been in prison in Egypt (with some pre-Pentateuchal fetters and an iron collar), and elevated to power; the wonders in Egypt are now performed by God's 'servant Moses, and Aaron whom he had chosen'. The plagues of Psalm 78 are slightly reordered for clarity. Thus the flies and frogs are plainly different afflictions, and become plagues (3) and (2)—the frogs are thought of as prior, since they must have left the blood-river of the Nile. Psalm 78 has apparently two different hail plagues, the first with hailstones/frost on the vines and sycamores, the second with thunderbolts on the cattle. Psalm 105 takes these as a single event, hail and lightning on the vines and fig-trees—the cattle are omitted. Further, since locusts strip the trees as well as the crops, Psalm 105 takes the tree-plague before the crop-plague. If, as we may suspect, he is working to a scheme of seven, the seventh wonder in the land of Ham will be the Exodus: 'Then he brought them out with silver and gold...'

Our Exodus version shows the fuller development of the Korahite story, upon which some further elaboration has been superimposed by the Merarites (P): the latter have introduced three further plagues, the gnats (3), now divided from the flies (4), the boils (6), and the darkness (9). The Korahites worked to a formula: (i) Moses is sent to negotiate with Pharaoh, who refuses him (vv. 1, 2, 4, 5, 7, 8); (ii) he has been sent by 'the God of the Hebrews' (1, 5, 7, 8); (iii) he is accompanied by Aaron (1, 2, 4, 7, 8); (iv) the plague is set off by various means—Aaron's rod (1, 2), Moses' hand/rod (7, 8), Yahweh direct (4, 5); (v) the plague is called off in further negotiation (2, 4, 7, 8); (vi) Pharaoh's heart is hardened.

This division of the plagues between J(E) and P is that of Noth, which is accepted by Blum (*Pentateuch*, p. 13) and Van Seters. There is an alternative (more elaborate) three-way split between J, E and P in Childs (*Exodus*, pp. 130-77) following Wellhausen. But the latter is more speculative, while Noth's analysis corresponds happily with the evidence from Psalm 105, which dovetails impressively with his J without his being aware of the fact.

Van Seters (*Moses*, pp. 80-81) dates the 'J' plagues in the Exile on the ground that they are unknown to Deuteronomy. This is not convincing. Deuteronomy has frequent references to Yahweh's 'signs and wonders against Egypt' (Deut. 6.22; 7.19; 11.3; 26.8; 29.2-3), the very phrase that is used of the plagues in Ps. 78.43. Deut. 7.15 speaks of 'all the evil diseases of Egypt which thou knowest', clearly by observation; and 28.60 of 'all the diseases of Egypt which thou wast afraid of'. The plagues were familiar in Bethel in the 720s, and were an accepted tradition in Jerusalem during the next century.

The Merarites wanted to extend the miseries of the Egyptians, but they did not want to take too long over it. They suppressed all preliminary negotiation with Pharaoh (i), and mention of 'the God of the Hebrews' (ii); the plagues are twice initiated with natural means, dust for the flies (3), ashes for the boils (6) (iv); the troubles also cease without further negotiation (v). So the P plagues are briefer than those of the earlier version. Aaron retains his position in (3) and (6), as ancestor of the priesthood (even his rod is still used in (3)). The Merarites also enjoyed the discomfiture of the magicians, who are present in (3) and (6), as in (1) and (2), and are smitten by the boils in (6).

Van Seters (*Moses*, p. 80) suggests that the magicians, who are such a feature of P in 7.1-13 and plagues (3) and (6), may have been introduced by P also in plagues (1) and (2). This is entirely plausible.

The P expansion is rationally based. Gnats (כנים) are not the same as flies (teeming insects, ערב), so the flies-and-gnats of Psalm 105 become two distinct plagues. The hail and lightning of Psalm 105 spared the cattle, so boils are introduced on man and beast as plague (6), and the hail hit them further in (7). Psalm 105 also introduced the plague-sequence with the mysterious verse, 'He sent darkness, and made it dark; And they rebelled not against his words' (v. 28). The 'they' is naturally Moses and Aaron of v. 26, and the 'rebelled not' will mean that they accepted their difficult mission to Pharaoh: the darkness will then be the storm cloud that so often shrouds Yahweh as he comes to deliver his own (Ps. 18.12-13, etc.)—dark is his path on the wings of the storm. The Merarites have, however, interpreted the darkness differently, and it has now become the ninth plague, the presage of the ultimate disaster.

The only plague which is apparently not derived from the account in Psalm 105 is (5) the cattle plague or murrain (דבר), and the story is problematic. Not only is the tale short (Exod. 9.1-7), with the omission of Aaron, and of the second interview to bring the plague to a halt; it results in the death of all the Egyptians' cattle (9.6), which leaves the reader perplexed when he finds their cattle further smitten first with boils and then with hail. It seems best to see (5) therefore as a later insertion. Ps. 78.48 reads, 'He gave over also their cattle to the hail (ברד)', but two MSS read דבר, pestilence, murrain, and the reading is at least as old as Symmachus. We may think therefore that a fifth-century Asaphite has introduced the cattle murrain as plague (5), in deference to

11. *The Exodus* 267

a traditional v. l. in his psalm collection. This would have the further
advantage of bringing the total to a round figure of ten plagues.

Noth attributes (1), (2), (4), (7), (8) and (10) to J, and this corresponds closely to
the plagues in Psalm 105, which I have traced to the Korahites' elaboration of Psalm
78. He attributes (3) and (6) wholly to P, as I have, and the beginning and climax of
(9), 10.21-23, 27; I doubt the subdivision—the Merarites knew how to imitate the
content of the earlier tradition (Aaron's rod and the magicians in (3), for example),
and were capable of adding the conclusion, whereby Pharaoh and Moses see the last
of one another. He points out the difficulties over (5), and credits the intrusion to a
late hand in J.

The death of the Egyptian first-born was already the climax of the
plagues in Psalm 78, and so the trigger for the Exodus. The event is
seen as in part natural: God 'made a path for his anger; He spared not
their soul from death, But gave their life over to the pestilence; And
smote all the firstborn in Egypt, The beginning of their strength in the
tents of Ham' (Ps. 78.50-51). The death was caused by a *pestilence*
(דבר), brought about by divine wrath at the hand of a band of angels
(v. 49). Psalm 105 omits the pestilence, and introduces the gloating elaboration of the spoiling of the Egyptians: '*He smote* also *all the firstborn
in* their land, *The beginning* to all their *strength*. And he brought them
forth with silver and gold: And there was not one feeble person among
their tribes' (105.36-37). The wording of Ps. 78.51 is almost retained;
but (as with the Red Sea) the providentialist element is heightened by
omitting the pestilence, a natural (and common) event. But Psalm 105
knows about the pestilence, because it says that no Israelite was כושל,
ailing: as with the flies and the hail, God has made a distinction between
the Egyptians and the Israelites (expressly so, Exod. 12.7).

Psalm 105 does not hint how the Israelites came by the silver and
gold: perhaps the Egyptians bribed them to leave. But by the time the
Korahites have developed the story in Exod. 11.1-3, 12.35-36, Pharaoh
drives Israel *out* in panic, and the people have extorted the jewellery and
valuables as a kind of export subsidy. The colours of the great deliverance are painted in by loving hands: *every* first-born child dies, from
Pharaoh's first-born to the first-born of the mill-slave, and the animals
too (cp. 9.6 again!); the unparalleled loud cry, the dogs which growl not
at the Israelites, the humiliation of the Egyptian officials and of Pharaoh
himself (Exod. 11.1-8; 12.28-39).

A bitter anti-Egyptian feeling is evident in Psalm 105 and the Korahite
expansion in Exodus, and calls for an explanation. On the whole Israel

enjoyed peaceful relations with Egypt during the ninth and eighth centuries, and after 600 the enemy was in Babylon. But at the end of the
seventh century Egypt adopted an aggressive policy. 'Pharaoh Neco'
invaded Judah and killed King Josiah in 609, imprisoned Jehoahaz, made
Jehoiakim king and imposed an enormous tribute of silver and gold
(2 Kgs 23.29-35). It would be unsurprising if this policy raised strong
feelings of resentment in Jerusalem; and if the tradents have taken their
psychological revenge by heightening the plagues, and by introducing
the spoiling motif—'he brought them forth with *silver and gold*'. There
is a further heightening of Egyptian agonies in the Wisdom of Solomon,
a work often thought to have been composed in the second century
BCE, under Egyptian taxation.

It has long been noticed that the early calendars in Exodus 23 and 34
prescribe a spring festival of Unleavened Bread, not of Passover;
although there is reference to 'the blood of the pilgrimage feast of
Passover' at Exod. 34.25. We have therefore to posit the spring celebration of the Jacob tribes from early times as being the agricultural festival
of המצות but to suppose that the Israel (Joseph–Benjamin) tribes had
their own spring celebration of הפסח, which was celebrated at Bethel,
the Exodus 34 calendar being that in use in that sanctuary. It will then
be unsurprising that King Josiah inaugurated the Passover ritual in
Jerusalem in 2 Kgs 23.21-23. During the previous century the Exodus
story has been adopted in Jerusalem as the experience of the nation, and
its culmination is the Passover, celebrated by long traditional rites in
Bethel, but now in the new national centre. These are then set out by the
Asaphites in Exod. 12.21-27, with further provisions on the consecration
of the first-born (13.1-2, 11-16), and on the eating of unleavened bread,
now explained as a reminder of the haste in leaving Egypt (13.3-10). It is
noticeable that both these last paragraphs are full of Deuteronomic language, but it is quite unnecessary to posit a later Dtr redactor.
Deuteronomic language was evident in Psalm 78 and other Asaphic
psalms, and the Deuteronomists are simply the (great-)grandsons of the
Bethel tradents.

The Passover ritual is set out in its traditional form in Exod. 12.21-27,
with the sacrifice of the lamb and apotropaic rites with its blood; there is
no mention of unleavened bread. This is added and historicized in 13.3-
10, and the two themes are combined in Deut. 16.1-8, with the old tradition that the meat should be 'seethed' (בשׁל). But with time this
seemed dangerous in view of the prohibition on seething a kid in its

mother's milk, and the Merarites inserted a detailed prescription for the sacrifice, which must now be roast (Exod. 12.9). They are also introducing the Mesopotamian calendar with Abib/Nisan as the first month, against the old Israelite autumn new year, and canonizing various other practices (12.1-20, 40-51). Their calendar is a further indication that their recension of the Torah was made in Babylonia. Also Deuteronomy 16 required the Paschal animal to be sacrificed and eaten in Jerusalem, whereas the Merarite Exod. 12.1-13 speaks merely of 'in the houses where you live', as would be necessary in Babylon.

Thus the opening two sections of the Exodus story follow a comparatively simple pattern. The basic story is the old Joseph- Benjamin/Israel story, the oppression in Egypt and the plagues, culminating in the pestilence which killed the Egyptian first-born. We have this story in Psalms 81 and 78, and can fix it to Bethel in the 720s. Already, as Psalm 77 shows, the Bethel clergy had included the Jacob tribes with Joseph, and Moses with their own leader Aaron; the price of extending the tribal myth to be a national myth was the fusion of the Jacobite legend of Moses and the Levites. This was accepted, but it was not perhaps at first realized how high the price was to be. Moses in time not only shared the leadership with Aaron but usurped it almost exclusively. The Korahites knew how to drive a hard bargain.

For Exod. 1.1–13.16 there was not much Korahite tradition to intrude into the established Asaphite story. Moses' marriage to the daughter of the Midianite priest Jethro, and his initiation into the worship of Yahweh, could be conveniently inserted into the oppression narrative. For the rest it was a matter of giving colour and definition to the Asaph story: sometimes with the importation of Mesopotamian legend (Sargon), sometimes with contemporary theological themes (signs as a basis for trust, popular rejection of God's word, a prophet's hesitation), sometimes with Deuteronomic language, sometimes with the ferocity of anti-Egyptian sentiment. All these features tend to suggest a date of composition in the last years of the seventh century.

As in Genesis, the Merarites tended to add their expansions at the beginning and end of a unit. For the oppression they left the established story virtually untouched, adding merely a linking preface (Exod. 1.1-7) and an extended appendix (6.1–7.13)—the P revelation to Moses, the genealogy, Aaron's position as spokesman, the competition with the magicians turning rods into snakes. The plagues have been a little different,

since they rise to a climax, and the insertion of the gnats, boils and
darkness needed to be made at suitable points. Nevertheless the major P
insertions have been made at the end of the unit, with more than 30
verses in 12.1-20, 41-52, dovetailing with (and taking precedence over)
the older ritual prescriptions in 12.21-27, 13.1-16. But this time the neat
topical pattern, with the P additions concentrated at the end of each
topic, is not reflected in the traditional reading cycle. Where it has
seemed natural to divide the text into (A) the oppression, Exod. 1.1–
7.13, (B) the plagues, 7.14–13.16, the cycle has (13) Exod. 1.1–6.1,
שמות, 'The Names', (14) 6.2–9.35, וארא, 'And I appeared', (15) 10.1–
13.16, בא, 'Go'. The two topics have been divided somewhat artificially
into three, with the plagues taken as seven-plus-three. No doubt this is
because of a need for more, shorter lections with time. Perhaps the old P
cycle included Joshua; but there might be many possibilities.

Chapter 12

THE WILDERNESS

The Crossing of the Sea

The Sea-crossing, the climax of the deliverance from Egypt, had already
a long history before the Asaph psalms were written. In the tradition
behind Psalm 77, the Israelites escaped Egypt in an impressive thunderstorm: there was no mention of pursuing cavalry, or miraculous parting
of the waters, or the overwhelming of the enemy (77.17-21). But
already the great experience of the Joseph and Benjamin tribesmen has
been adapted for the inclusion of the whole nation: those redeemed were
'the sons of *Jacob and* Joseph', and God led them 'by the hand of
Moses and Aaron' (77.16, 21). Furthermore the Asaph psalmist implies
a knowledge of our Song of the Sea (Exod. 15.1b-18), since phrases
from the latter come with some frequency in the psalm, and sections of
it are likely to have been used for the Selahs (pp. 103-104). With the
Song and the fuller statement in Psalm 78, we are able to make out the
state of the tradition as celebrated at Bethel in the 720s.

G.W. Coats ('Reed Sea'), argued that the Sea-crossing opened the wilderness narrative, rather than closing the Exodus; citing the prominence of the cloud and fire, and
the 'murmuring' of 14.11-12. He is supported by the traditional lectionary cycle,
where the 16th lection runs from Exod. 13.17 to 17.16.

The Sea-crossing marks the beginning of the trials of the wilderness:
he 'clave the sea, and caused [Israel] to pass through; He made the
waters to stand as an heap' (Ps. 78.13); thereafter 'In the daytime also
he led them with a cloud, And all the night with a light of fire' (v. 14).
Later in the psalm, 'he led them safely, so that they feared not: But the
sea overwhelmed their enemies' (v. 53); but this leading seems to cover
the whole wilderness period—'he led forth his own people like sheep,
And guided them in the wilderness like a flock' (v. 54). More detail is
available in the Song. 'With the blast of thy nostrils the waters were

piled up: The floods stood upright as an heap: The deeps were con-
gealed in the heart of the sea. The enemy said, I will pursue, I will overtake, I will divide the spoil... I will draw my sword, my hand shall
destroy them. Thou didst blow with thy wind, the sea covered them;
They sank as lead in the mighty waters' (Exod. 15.8-10). So were the
horse and rider thrown into the sea, Pharaoh's chariots and his host
down into the depths like a stone (vv. 1, 4-5, 21).

Noth (*Exodus*, p. 124) sees a combination of ideas in the Song, in one of which the
Egyptian army is 'covered' by the returning waters, and in the other is 'sunk' (15.5,
10). This seems prosaic: the covering and the sinking are paralleled in both verses,
and were understood by the poet as the same thing.

In the course of the next century the Asaph and Korah tradents retold
and clarified the story. It needs to be explained why the escapers did not
make straight for the land of Israel: this was because the fear of fighting
the Philistines (!) might have discouraged them (Exod. 13.17-19). The
'leading' of 78.53 has now been naturally interpreted as with the cloud
and fire of Ps. 78.14, and reflection has suggested that these will have
been *pillars of* cloud and fire—otherwise how could they have acted as
guides? (Exod. 13.21-22). Furthermore, a new function occurs for the
cloud and fire which heightens the suspense. The Israelites are on foot,
and are blocked by the Red Sea; the Egyptians are on horses, and by
Exod. 14.9 are about to overtake them. The angel of God therefore
manoeuvres the pillars to between the two armies, and prevents any
Egyptian attack in the night (14.19-20). The question must also have
arisen as to what was the precise route taken by the people, and the
answer is supplied: Succoth (12.17), Etham, on the edge of the wilderness (13.20), the sea of reeds (understood to be the Red Sea), the
wilderness of Shur (15.22). None of these places is known with cer-
tainty, but we may see them as forming an itinerary eastwards, bound
for Kadesh, the oasis of Meribah, and Mt Hor.

For discussions of the geography, see Davies, *Way*, pp. 70-74, 79-84; Houtman,
Exodus, pp. 105, 122, 127. Davies takes seriously the possibility that the Red Sea
extended at least to the Bitter Lakes in the period. Rameses will then be near to Qantir
or Tanis, in the northeast Delta area; Succoth, the Egyptian *Tkw*, will be in the Wadi
Tumilat, thirty miles southeast (some march!); Etham is unknown, perhaps near the
Bitter Lakes or Lake Timsah. In Gen. 16.7 Hagar is found by a spring on 'the road
to Shur', said to be between Kadesh and Bered (16.14). שׁוּר, *a wall*, may refer to the
Egyptian frontier wall. The road is likely to be the central desert track from Palestine
to Egypt, crossing the frontier north of Lake Timsah. But although יַם סוּף probably

meant originally the Sea of Reeds (Exod. 2.3, 5; Isa. 19.6), and so a freshwater lake, the phrase is used plainly to mean the Gulf of Aqaba, and so the Red Sea, at Num. 14.25, Deut. 1.40, 2.1, and this is the regular 'translation' in the LXX. So probably a crossing of the Gulf of Suez (in its present form) is imagined from at least the eighth century (Exod. 15.4), with heroic marches. At Num. 33.36 Israel covers the ninety miles from Ezion-Geber to Kadesh in a day.

The events of the crossing are similarly an interpretation of the earlier tradition. The Song saw the miracle as the effect of God's wrath: 'with the blast of thy nostrils the waters were piled up; The floods stood upright as an heap... Thou didst blow with thy רוח, the sea covered them' (Exod. 15.7-10). But רוח may be a wind as well as God's angry breath, and this becomes 'a strong east wind all night' (14.21), so that the waters are divided, and there is dry ground for Israel to pass over. The Song is already so triumphant over Pharaoh's cavalry that Israel's own deliverance is not actually mentioned: now the hostility to Egypt which has been so evident in the plagues receives added stress. Pharaoh and his officers are portrayed as arrogant in pursuit, and with a powerful army, six hundred chariots strong; at the crucial moment Yahweh returns the sea to normality, and the entire force is drowned, without survivor (14.5-8, 21-31).

The Korahites have been extremely successful in adapting the old Asaph story to their advantage; in a tale of fifteen chapters they have left few inconsistencies to betray the presence of the older tradition. One such is the location of 'the mountain of God' which is in distant Midian at Exod. 3.1, but only three days' journey from Egypt at 3.12, 18. A further one is the comment that Pharaoh saw 'the people were *fled* (ברח)' (14.5), where the new version represents Pharaoh as sending the people out in panic after the last plague (12.31-32), and they go up armed (13.18), and with a high hand (14.8). More significant, the Song is concluded with a short reprise by 'Miriam the prophetess, the sister of Aaron' (15.20). The old story had included the participation of women with timbrels in the triumphal march, as in Ps. 68.26; and their leader was Miriam, *Aaron's sister*. Had the Asaphites known of Moses in early times, she would have been Moses' sister too: this is the first clear sign that Moses had no early connection with the Exodus/Reed Sea narrative.

Schmid (*Jahwist*, pp. 56-60) notes the similarity of form between Moses' speech in 14.13-14, with its corollary in 14.31, and the oracle in Isa. 7.4-9—'Fear not', be still, Yahweh's promise of deliverance, trust; and also the presence of certain Holy War themes. Both of these elements suggest a composition of the 'J' narrative in the seventh century. See also the discussion in Van Seters (*Moses*, pp. 134-39) and in Blum (*Pentateuch*, pp. 17-39).

It is often thought that the shorter song of Miriam is earlier than the longer Song of the Sea, ascribed to the more famous Moses: cf. Childs, *Exodus*, pp. 246-47. But it is easy to suppose that the Israelite tradition of women crowing over the defeat of enemy men (Ps. 68.26; 1 Sam. 18.6-7) has had its effect on the narrative. As with Saul and David there are tambourines, singing and dancing; and Miriam merely repeats her brother's opening words as a refrain.

A century further on, the Merarites were in general content with the story, but added a few flourishes. They reinterpreted 13.17-18, 'God led them not by the way of the land of the Philistines...but God led the people about by the way of the wilderness of the Reed sea': they took this to mean that at first Israel had set out on the coastal road to Philistia, but God had later led them south. As their own tradition was of the Sinai peninsula, diametrically in the opposite direction of the natural approach northwards, this was an appealing exegesis. No doubt they were as ignorant of the location of Succoth and Etham as we are; but they knew that Baal–Zephon and Migdol and (presumably) Pi-hahiroth were on the coastal road where there is a narrow tongue of land between the Mediterranean and Lake Sirbonis, a freshwater lake, and so a natural candidate for the םי ףוס. Here then will have been the site of the miracle. Yahweh has Moses turn the people back (from Etham on the edge of the desert) and encamp at Pi-hahiroth; Pharaoh will think the wilderness has shut them in (perhaps the Egyptian frontier wall is in mind). Pharaoh's heart is hardened, and the Egyptians are to know that 'I am the LORD', in the standard P manner (14.1-4, 15-18). There are one or two more marginal touches: Moses' hand and staff release Yahweh's wind, as with the plagues (14.15, 21a, 26), the Egyptians' wheels are clogged in the (presumed) mud (14.25a), the divided sea is like a wall (14.22).

The most probable sites for Baal-Zephon and Migdol are east of Pelusium by Lake Sirbonis: see Houtman, *Exodus*, pp. 105-106, 112, 124. For the most part the P verses are agreed. Van Seters (*Moses*, pp. 128-34) gives 14.1-4, 8, 9aßb, 15-18, 21aαb, 22b, 25a, 26-27aα, 29; cf. also Childs, *Exodus*, pp. 219-20. Noth (*Exodus*, pp. 102-20) gives rather more, but he is working with the hypothesis of an independent P version. He also ascribes 13.17-19, with its threefold use of םיהלא, and some other elements, to E. 13.19, on the bones of Joseph, must certainly be ascribed to the Asaphites; and they used םיהלא rather than יהוה till Exodus 20, when (for them) Yahweh revealed his identity, as they had through the Joseph story, and in Genesis 20–22. Childs (*Exodus*, p. 220) ascribes 14.5a, where 'the people had fled', to E.

The Wilderness

Hitherto the Asaph tradition has dominated the Exodus narrative. The deliverance from Egypt was the experience of the Israel (Joseph–Benjamin) tribes, and the story was their story, never accepted in Dan, nor in Jerusalem before 722, as a part of the whole people's history. All we have had so far is the grafting in of Moses as the hero of the saga, and a number of minor additions by P. Henceforth, the case will be different. There are three communities behind the Asaph, Korah and Merari tradents, each with its own desert history, and from now on there will be three hands on the tiller.

The old Asaph story, told and implied in Psalms 78 and 81, and in Deuteronomy 32, saw the Israelites as travelling from the Red Sea to Kadesh by the Meribah oasis, a distance of some 120 miles. Four separate incidents are mentioned between the two locations: (i) 'He clave rocks in the wilderness, And gave them drink abundantly' (Ps. 78.15-16); (ii) 'They tempted God by asking meat for their lust', leading God in his anger to rain on them both manna and quails; while the meat was in their mouths, he struck down the flower of the people (78.17-31); (iii) further disbelief in God followed, 'Therefore their days did he consume in vanity, And their years in terror' (78.32-33); (iv) only after all this did they 'seek God earnestly', though even then they were flattering him, and were not faithful to his covenant (78.34-37). Ps. 81.8-15 shows that the last scene takes place at the waters of Meribah, where God proved Israel with the requirement that they worship him only; but they would not hearken to his voice. I have argued above (pp. 115-18) that the second and third points correspond to the manna-and-quails stories in Exodus 16 and Numbers 11, and the wasted generation after Israel's refusal of Joshua and Caleb in Numbers 13–14. The first point has disappeared from the later tradition.

Psalms 78 and 81 are both concerned to move the nation to repentance before it is too late, and the concentration is therefore upon incidents of popular faithlessness followed by divine punishment and forgiveness. But there are two further traditions which have survived in Exodus 17–18. In the first of these Joshua wins a battle against the Amalekites (Exod. 17.8-13); and this must be an Asaphite tradition, since Joshua was an Ephraimite, and the leader of the Israel tribes into the land. Furthermore we should expect some battle. Oases in the desert are the means of life, and are never unoccupied: the Israel tribes could not

have settled at Meribah for a generation without fighting off some previous settlers, and the area is the traditional home of the Amalekites
(Gen. 14.7; 1 Sam. 15.7; 27.8).

The second additional narrative is the scene where Moses greets his
father-in-law Jethro and his family, and Jethro advises him to install tiers
of judges (Exod. 18.1-27). Apparently the story comes from the
Korahites, with Moses, and Jethro, and Moses' children; but a further
slip reveals that all this is a heavy veneer on an earlier tale. Following the
tender reunion, we are told: 'And Jethro, Moses' father-in-law, took a
burnt offering and sacrifices for God: and Aaron came, and all the elders
of Israel, to eat bread with Moses' father-in-law before God' (18.12). No
doubt the Korahite tradents intended it to be assumed that Moses was a
part of the party; but the normal fullness of narration would have mentioned Moses at this point. *Aaron came, and all the elders of Israel*: the
original story told of Aaron and the Joseph and Benjamin leaders joining
in the sacrificial meal; Moses was as yet unheard of, far off in the land of
Midian. We notice too the insistent use of אלהים through the chapter, in
place of the now customary Yahweh. For the Korahites, Yahweh has
revealed himself in Exodus 3, for the Merarites in Exodus 6; the
Asaphites became Yahwists at Shechem (Josh. 24, p. 255), and it was
not until they came to Kadesh that they became worshippers even of El.
So behind Exodus 18 we descry an account of this crucial move. The
priest of El at Kadesh was called Reuel (*El is a companion*, Num.
10.29), and it was at Kadesh by the waters of Meribah that Aaron and
his tribesmen settled, and accepted the God of the local priesthood.

The sacrificial meal is followed ('on the morrow', v. 13) by a scene of
kindly concern for Moses by his father-in-law: he is wearing himself out
by judging every case for the entire people. So the work is delegated,
and judges are instituted for the different levels of case (18.13-27). We
may discern behind this touching tale the pattern of the old Asaphite
covenant narrative. Aaron—now 'Moses'—was initiated by Reuel, his
father-in-law, into 'the statutes of God and his laws' (v. 16). These were
proclaimed by Reuel at a sacrificial banquet attended by the Israelite
leaders; and their acceptance of them was sealed by their 'eating bread
with [Aaron's] father-in-law before God' (v. 12). They agreed thereby
to administer these 'statutes and laws', and were shown 'the way
wherein they must walk' (v. 20). In particular they must 'fear God as
men of truth, hating unjust gain' (v. 21). We have seen the echo of this
in Psalm 82, where the gods of the nations have failed to live up to these

standards: 'How long will ye judge unjustly, and respect the persons of the wicked?'

It may seem implausible to suggest that both Moses and Aaron independently married daughters of desert priests, and in consequence introduced a change of tribal worship; but this seems the most probable reconstruction. Although the Jerusalem priesthood so often spoke of themselves as sons of Aaron, Aaron is not a solo priest in the Pentateuchal tradition: it is regularly 'Aaron and his sons', and on his death Eleazar is instituted in his place (Num. 20). Such a stress upon the *grandson* of the desert priest is what we might expect in such a case; and the continuity of the priesthood is most easily understood if there is a blood connection. Exodus 18 is noticeable both for the repetition of the word *father-in-law* and of אלהים. חתן occurs thirteen times, אלהים ten. Also Aaron's wife is called Elisheba, *My El is fullness* (Exod. 6.23, where she has a respectable Israelite father Amminadab; for the translation cf. Houtman, *Exodus*, p. 90), and his son is called Eleazar, *El has helped*. Even Moses has a second son with the similar name Eliezer, *My El is [my] help* (18.4), also an echo no doubt of the Aaron–Eleazar *Vorlage*.

Thus the desert story which the Asaphites brought to Jerusalem in 722 had substantially five incidents to it. (i) God had miraculously provided water for the tribes as they set out through the desert (Ps. 78.15-16). (ii) The people had been marvellously fed with manna and quails, though this had been followed by plague, interpreted as the wrath of God (78.17-31; Exod. 16; Num. 11). (iii) They had driven the Amalekites away from the oasis of Meribah, Joshua leading the people to victory (Exod. 17.8-16). (iv) They settled for a protracted period (Num. 13–14) by the oasis, at Kadesh, and accepted there a covenant to worship El alone (Ps. 78.32-35; 81.8-15). (v) The covenant was sealed at a holy meal presided over by Reuel, Aaron's father-in-law, the priest of El; and the Israelite elders undertook to administer the 'statutes and laws' of the new religion (Exod. 18).

This basic narrative was to experience two transformations during the following two centuries. For the Korahites, the covenant had been made by Yahweh with Moses at Mt Horeb (Deut., *passim*), east of the Gulf of Aqaba, in Midian. They could not have a prior covenant at Meribah (Ps. 81), and forty years of hanging around at Kadesh before the great revelation at Horeb: so they were compelled to postpone the principal elements of the Asaph story to Numbers 11–20. For the Merarites, the acceptance of the new religion had taken place at Mt Sinai, which is best sited in its traditional location in the south of the Sinai peninsula, Jebel Musa. They achieved this by the simple procedure of systematically altering the name of the 'mountain of God' from Horeb to Sinai throughout the story, and by adding in the names of a few staging posts from their own tradition. As Israelites hearing the tale on the banks of the river Chebar might not be too familiar with the geography of the southern wildernesses, there was little fear of objection; and the resulting equivalence, Sinai = Horeb, is to be found in standard works to this day. We may see the way in which these two re-castings have developed the five points of the Asaph narrative.

Water from the Rock

In Psalm 78 God clave rocks in the wilderness, and gave drink in abundance, without any suggestion of Israel tempting or contending with him (vv. 15-16). Exodus 15 provides two stories of divine provision of water, the second of which is the arrival at the twelve springs of Elim, usually thought to be on the way to Sinai, and inserted by P. The longer narrative is of the 'bitter' waters of Marah which were miraculously 'sweetened' by Moses' throwing a log into the water.

Although Psalm 78 had represented the provision of water as God's gracious gift, the instinct of the seventh-century tradents was to extend the psalm's general message of Israel's faithlessness, and the call to obedience: God *proved* the people in the wilderness (Deut. 8.3), and they were rebellious from the day that he had known them (Deut. 9.24). So the Korahites make Moses the leader once more, and site the water-gift at the significantly named, brackish pool Marah; they style Moses' 'healing' of the water after the Elisha legend of 2 Kgs 2.19-22; they preface this with their stock motif of the people's murmuring; they have Yahweh put them to the test, and deliver a very Deuteronomic charge (15.25b-26). In Josiah's time Israel is still in with a chance.

The syntax in 15.25-26 is clumsy: 'he [Moses] threw it into the water... There he [Yahweh] made for them a statute... and there he put them to the test. He [Moses] said, If you will listen to the voice of Yahweh... I [Yahweh] will bring upon you...' This has led many to posit a Deuteronomistic insertion, but Childs (*Exodus*, pp. 266-67) shows that such havering over the subject is frequent in Deuteronomy (7.4; 11.13; 17.3; 28.20; 29.5). He sees a Deuteronomic writer expanding an earlier J story, where I should speak of Korahites and an Asaphite original.

Childs (*Exodus*, pp. 258-64) discusses the two 'patterns' of murmuring stories, one with punishment and one without. It is the punishment form which is original, since this dominates Psalm 78, in the interests of national devotion. The Korahites have suitably concentrated all the rebellion/punishment stories *after* the (Horeb) revelation, and the more reasonable 'murmurings' form a more venial series in Exodus 14–17.

Although Ps. 78.15-16 imply no fault on Israel's side over the water, the following verse says, 'Yet went they on still to sin against him, To rebel against the Most High in the dry land' (v. 17). עוד ויוסיפו might well be interpreted to suggest that there was sin over the water, and that is how the story has developed, both in Numbers 20, where the event takes place at Meribah, and the name is explained as from the *contending* of the people (20.2, 13), and in Exod. 17.1-7, where the site is called both Massah and Meribah (17.7), and the two names are explained as from the *testing* and the *contending* of the people (vv. 2, 7).

The development here is clearer. The Joseph–Benjamin tribes had settled at Meribah, and the presence of water there flowing from the rock will perhaps underlie the Numbers 20 interpretation; but it is a seventh-century interpretation, with the incident at the end of the sequence of stories instead of the beginning, and the death of Aaron understood as the punishment for the murmuring. Moses and his rod are the agents in bringing the water from the rock. His words, 'Hear now, ye rebels (המרים)' (Num. 20.10) follow Ps. 78.17's למרות; 'the waters came forth abundantly' (Num. 20.11) similarly echoes 78.15. Israel's failure to 'sanctify' (הקדישׁ) Yahweh (v. 12), and Yahweh's 'showing himself holy' (התקדשׁ, v. 13), are interpretations based on the name Kadesh.

The incident in Num. 20.1-13 is heavily scored with P locutions—'the congregation', 'the glory of the LORD appeared', 'they fell on their faces'—and many modern commentators (Noth, Van Seters, Budd) ascribe the whole paragraph to P. But earlier critics had noted some Deuteronomic phrasing: 'It is no place for grain, or figs, or vines, or pomegranates' (20.5; cf. Deut. 8.8), 'the land that I have given them' (20.12; cf. Deut. *passim*). There is no other 'murmuring' story which is ascribed to P alone. Aaron is a hero to P, and could have been killed off in peace and honour like Miriam (20.1). The unique, and morally monstrous, attack on Aaron can only go back to the Korahites, who had no love for either the (Asaphite) leader of the Exodus or the (Merarite) ancestor of the Jerusalem priesthood. The D-language is the visible trace of their earlier version. Van Seters's weak comment is notable: 'Numbers 20:2-13, the only independent P murmuring story, is so obviously an imitation of the J stories...' (*Moses*, p. 188).

Meribah then was the scene both of the Joseph-tribes' acceptance of the new faith, and of their backsliding from it ('contending'); and this is the old Asaph tradition in Ps. 81.8-12, '*I proved thee* at the waters of Meribah... But my people hearkened not to my voice'. There had been a similar acceptance and backsliding by the Levite tribesmen under Moses at Horeb, with far more bloody consequences; and we see the two incidents already fused in Deut. 33.8, '[Levi] Whom thou didst prove at Massah, With whom thou didst strive at the waters of Meribah'. The Levites had been nowhere near Meribah; their celebrated massacre had taken place a hundred miles further east, the site being known as Massah, *testing*. This name has been preserved by their Korahite descendants, and comes twice further in Deuteronomy, at 6.16, 'Ye shall not tempt the LORD your God, as ye tempted him in Massah', and 9.22, where the list of four provocations includes Massah.

Deut. 9.22 runs, 'At Taberah, and at Massah, and at Kibroth- hattaavah, ye pro-voked the LORD to wrath. And when the LORD sent you up from Kadesh-Barnea...'; that is, the fire incident in Num. 11.1-3; Massah; the quails incident in Num. 11.4-15, 31-34; and the spies incident, Numbers 13–14. The D-tradent seems familiar with the order of incidents as we have them in Numbers 11–14, but has inserted the Massah provocation, understood to be the testing of Yahweh for water. Mayes (*Deuteronomy*, pp. 201-202) takes the verse for a late gloss.

This fusing of the two desert rebellions then explains the features of the water incident in Exod. 17.1-7. P opens the story with an itinerary note that Israel is going from the wilderness of Sin (Sinai?), and encamps at Rephidim. But the main narrative is a combination of the Asaph and Korah traditions. The people *strove* (וירב) with Moses, and Moses said, Why *strive ye* (תריבון) with me? Wherefore *do ye tempt* (תנסון) the LORD? (17.2); and Moses calls the name of the place *Massah* and *Meribah* because of the *striving* (ריב)...and because they *tempted* (נסתם) the LORD (17.7). We have thus the clearest evidence of the fusing of the two traditions, with suitable explanations for the two names. *Moses* strikes the rock with *thy rod wherewith thou smotest the river*, recalling the Korahite account of the plagues; *the elders of Israel* are there to witness the wonder, as then; and Yahweh promises, 'Behold, I will stand before thee there upon the rock in *Horeb*' (17.6). Once again the mask slips: behind an apparent *Sinai* narrative there stands an earlier, Korahite account of the event in *Horeb*. The name Horeb, universal in Deuteronomy, has slipped in only three times in Exodus, at 3.1 for

Moses' call, here, and at 33.6. Otherwise the story is the standard form: the people's murmuring, Moses' appeal to Yahweh, Yahweh's action to show his presence. The tradents are decent enough not to have the people punished for what was traditionally (Ps. 78.15-16) and morally a cry in need. For them real sin, punishment and forgiveness begin with the Golden Calf.

Although the sites of most of the staging posts are unknown, a plausible suggestion is that Rephidim is the modern er-Raphid, east of the Gulf of Aqaba (Houtman, *Exodus*, p. 127); and if so part of the earlier Korahite tradition taken over in ignorance by P. Meribah is likely to owe its name to the settling of disputes (ריב) there; cf. the appointment of judges in Exodus 18. Massah (מסה) is less easy to explain; it could conceivably be a corruption of Maśśa' (משא), an Ishmaelite settlement in the Midianite area (Gen. 25.14).

Taberah

In Ps. 78.15-16 God gave Israel streams from the rock, but the following verses show their rebellious heart, for they doubted if he would provide them with food as well as water (78.17-20). 'Therefore the LORD heard and was wroth: And a fire was kindled against Jacob, And anger also went up against Israel; Because they believed not in God, And trusted not in his salvation' (78.21-22). Nevertheless he does supply manna and quails in the verses following; but with a nasty sting in the tail.

In Num. 11.1-3 the people murmur, speaking evil in the ears of the LORD; 'And when *the LORD heard* it, his *anger* was kindled; and the *fire* of the LORD burned among them, and devoured in the uttermost part of the camp'. At Moses' intercession the fire abates, and the place is called Taberah, *burning*. In Num. 11.4-35 God feeds the people with quails.

The Numbers version is an exegesis of Ps. 78.21-22. In the psalm, the burning anger of Yahweh is not an incident distinct from the manna-quails episode; his wrath is to be displayed in the conclusion of the latter story. Nor was the burning anger literal: the fire was only meant symbolically (p. 116). The Pentateuchal author (a Korahite, for Moses, not Aaron is hero) has misunderstood, or reinterpreted the psalm wording. Furthermore, the psalm told the tale at 78.21-22, *before* the covenant in 78.34-35; but the Korahites have postponed the various desert rebellions of the psalm to *after* the covenant. In Exodus 15–18 God is generally gracious and understanding. It is only after he has 'shown his ways', and

Israel has undertaken to observe them, and then has worshipped the Golden Calf, that the atmosphere changes. From Exodus 32 we meet a more severe God who by no means clears the guilty: the tale of disaffections and punishments belongs after Horeb/Sinai, in the book of Numbers.

Budd (*Numbers*, pp. 112-21) notes that the Taberah incident is generally attributed to JE; the presence of the root פלל, *pray*, is a frail reason for assigning it to E rather than J.

Manna

If the revelation was to take place at Horeb, as the Korahites held, the rebellion traditions needed to be postponed to the book of Numbers, as we have seen; and the quails story, which is bracketed with the manna in Ps. 78.17-31, is told there in Numbers 11. But this then raises a further problem: what did the people live on in the pre-Horeb period? The Korahites' solution was to divide the tale, separating the manna from the quails. Israel had manna from early days, and the quails incident arose from a further 'murmuring', as the people grew weary of the heavenly diet. This is how the quails story now begins in Num. 11.4-9.

Childs (*Exodus*, p. 280) supposes that at an early stage the manna and the quails stories circulated independently. But they come together in Ps. 78.19-29, our earliest source: oral traditions before that are speculation.

The elements of the old manna story are present in Exod. 16.4-5, 13b-15, 21b, 27-31, 35aβ (Childs, *Exodus*, p. 274). The people's doubts of Ps. 78.19-20 are now overlaid with a stock P murmuring in 16.1-3. At 16.4-5 Yahweh promises to *rain bread from heaven* for them, as in Ps. 78.24. The dire punishment of Ps. 78.29-31 is no longer apposite, and is postponed to Numbers 11; but *some* edifying tale of disobedience and rebuke is required, surely, if the tradent is to fulfil his paraenetic duty. The old northern law codes at least prohibited work on the sabbath (Exod. 23.12; 34.21): so a specific *test* is provided this time (16.4)—a double portion of manna is to be provided on the sixth day (16.5). Needless to say, some of the people go out to gather on the sabbath, and are suitably reproached by the LORD (16.27-31). But there is manna on the ground each morning, and the people gather as much as they need (16.21); and the provision lasts all their time in the wilderness (16.35).

The Korahite story was about the length of the water story in 17.1-7; and it has been expanded fourfold by the Merarites. There is an itinerary note in v. 1, notes of time and the volume of the manna, the complaining of the people, Moses' appeal to God, the appearing of the glory of the LORD, the laying up of a pot of manna before the Testimony (!), and other interesting detail. They also added in some quails for good measure; they fall in the evening to balance the manna in the morning (v. 13a). The Korahites' invocation of the sabbath theme was quite acceptable to the Merarites: it is true that the commandment has not yet been promulgated (Exod. 20.8-11), but then it was laid down in heaven from Genesis 1, and it is God, not man, who is raining the manna down, and kindly providing a double portion on Fridays.

Some modern critics credit the whole chapter to P, but this leaves 'J' with no manna story, since Numbers 11 limits the manna element to complaints of its sameness. Noth and Van Seters include vestiges of 16.1-3 in their J account. Neither they nor Childs offers an explanation for J's sudden interest in the sabbath. A notorious problem is the inconsequence of vv. 1-12. Yahweh in 16.4-5 makes no response to the people's complaint in 16.2-3 because the latter is the insertion of the later Merarites. But 16.6-12 is all P material, and here Moses and Aaron promise the people meat and bread without any authority in vv. 6-8, while Yahweh actually supplies the undertaking in v. 12. This has a simple explanation in fact: the storyteller's incompetence. When John retells Luke's anointing story, Mary Magdalen ends up with the precious ointment all over her own hair (Jn 12.3). When expanding an earlier story it is quite easy to end up in a muddle. Childs's invocation of the parallel structure of Numbers 14 (*Exodus*, pp. 278-80) is helpful, but only a partial solution.

The Quails

The old Asaph tradition had the manna and quails combined. Ps. 78.23-28 began with God's raining down manna upon the people to eat, and continues: 'He caused to blow (יַסַּע) the east wind in the heaven: And by his power he guided the south wind. He rained flesh also upon them as the dust, And winged fowl as the sand of the seas. He let it fall in the midst of their camp (מחנהו), Round about their habitation.' However, the windfall was no blessing: 'So they did eat and were well filled; And he gave them that they craved (תאותם). They were not estranged from their craving (תאותם), Their meat was yet in their mouths, When the anger of God went up against them, And slew the fattest of them, And smote down the young men of Israel' (78.29-31).

The manna story having been taken in Exodus, it is possible to treat the quails element, with its sin–wrath–punishment–forgiveness theme, with the other tales of disaffection in Numbers. First the 'fire' of divine wrath is isolated at Taberah (Num. 11.1-3); then, with the long gap since Exodus 16, the 'murmuring' can be increased to 'weeping', and attributed to the mixed rabble, and its *craving* (התאוו) for Egyptian melons and garlic, since they are weary of the boring diet God has provided (Num. 11.4-9). Moses complains bitterly, and the *anger* (אף) of Yahweh is kindled (11.10-15). A wind from Yahweh blows (נסע) causing quails to fall about the *camp* (מחנה), two cubits deep and a day's journey around. The people gather the birds, but while the meat was still between their teeth, before it was consumed, the anger of Yahweh struck them with a very great plague. They buried the people who had the *craving* (המתאוים), and the place was called the Graves of *Craving* (קברות התאוה) (11.31-34).

The story has been complicated by the intrusion of the inspiration of the seventy, on which see below (pp. 288-89); but essentially it is just a Korahite (Moses) expansion of the old Asaph story, with some of the language still intact (נסע, תאוה), and a good deal of the meaning (fall of an enormous volume of birds, the flesh in the people's mouths as Yahweh smites).

Budd (*Numbers*, pp. 122-31) says that by common consent there is no P material in the passage. It is in fact substantially the Korahites' rewriting of the old Asaph traditions.

The Spies

Psalm 78 follows the manna-and-quails incident with a less clear reference (78.32-33): 'For all this [divine punishment] they sinned still, And believed not in his wondrous works. Therefore their days did he consume in vanity, And their years in terror'. Since we have the spies narrative in Numbers 13–14, so soon after the quails story in Numbers 11, it seems likely that we should read the psalm verses in its light. In Numbers 13 spies are sent into southern Judah as far as Hebron (13.22), and return with the depressing message that the land is too strongly defended (13.27-29); only Caleb brings a happier picture, and urges advance. But the people refuse, and Yahweh says to Moses, 'How long will this people despise me? And how long will they *not believe in* me, for all the signs that I have wrought among them?' (14.11). In 14.20-25 he decrees that no one from so rebellious a generation shall see the Promised Land, apart from the faithful Caleb. The perseverance in disaffection, the failure to believe in God, the evidence of repeated miracles, the wasting of years, are all in common between psalm and narrative.

Num. 13.17b-20, 22-24, 27-31; 14.11-25, 39-45 are usually taken to constitute the 'J' story. It has its Deuteronomic elements, and is close to Exod. 33–34.6 in 14.13-19, and should be seen as the outworking of the old Bethel tradition by Asaphites and Korahites in the seventh century. The stress on trust in Yahweh, and on the people's unteachable deathwish, bridges the gap between Psalm 78 and Deuteronomy. There is also an important side-effect of the story in explaining how the Calebites alone had invaded Palestine from the south and remained in the Hebron area; the remaining Joseph and Benjamin tribesmen had spent a generation and more around Kadesh, and had finally invaded Palestine from the east. Virtually the same story is told in Deut. 1.19-45: the people are the motivating force in sending the spies, and the Korahite influence has by now moved the incident from before the covenant (Ps. 78) to after it (Num. 13–14). Someone has also noticed by now that Joshua needs to take a stand with Caleb, or he will not be able to lead the people into the land (Deut. 1.38).

To the Merarites in exile, the story had a strong appeal, for they were keen to sponsor a return to the Land of Israel, and were no doubt met with objections that the place was a desert 'that eateth up the inhabitants thereof' (Num. 13.32). It is now Yahweh who takes the initiative in sending the spies (13.1), and suitable names are found for them, including Joshua, of course, under his pre-Yahwist name Hoshea (13.8, 16). The reconnaissance now covers not merely southern Judah but the whole country to the Hamath pass (13.21): sixth-century BCE Zionists want the 'going up' to repopulate the entire Land. The full expansions of both the people's lament and refusal (14.1-10), and of Yahweh's decree of punishment (14.20-35), are a testimony both to the resistance of Israelites comfortably settled in Babylonia, and of the Merarites' skill in the manipulative arts.

Budd (*Numbers*, pp. 140-64) gives a careful justification for the division between 'J' and P, and a plausible account of the motives behind the two versions of the story, and of the version in Deuteronomy 1. Van Seters (*Moses*, pp. 263-82) claims a few more verses for 'J', and derives that from Deuteronomy.

Amalek

With the Ephraimite Joshua as commander, and the Amalekites from the southwestern wilderness as the enemy, the basic story must come from the Asaph traditions; the Korahites have taken it over by introducing Moses and the rod of God to mediate the divine blessing, as in so many other stories. But then no one can expect to keep his hand aloft for the duration of a battle, so his weariness is introduced, with consequent fluctuations in the fighting. This second problem can be resolved by sitting Moses on a stone, with his doughty lieutenants, Aaron and Hur, to hold his hands up for him—his hands now, for the rod has been forgotten. Aaron is, as usual with the Korahites, reduced to being merely Moses' *fidus Achates*, and Hur, as in 24.14, is brought in for the other arm. Moses builds an altar, Yahweh is my standard, since in Israelite campaigns standards were set on hill-tops as rallying points for the troops; and Yahweh has been active with his rod from the hill-top here.

Amalek did not feature in Israel's historical traditions after David's time (1 Sam. 27–30); but the tribe was felt as a menace in the 720s, for Ps. 83.8 speaks of Gebal and Ammon and Amalek as among those who have taken crafty counsel against Israel. The bitterness with which Amalek is viewed in Exod. 17.14-15 is a sure sign that Amalekites formed an important part of the final alliance which brought Israel down, in the same way that Edom did to Judah in 586. It is only Amalek against which Yahweh will have war in perpetuity (17.15); and we have exactly the same implacable vendetta in Deut. 25.17-19, 'thou shalt blot out the remembrance of Amalek from under heaven; thou shalt not forget.' The savage southern tribesmen had inflicted a wound that had gone deep among the exiles in seventh-century Jerusalem.

It is a mistake to emend the text in the hope of connecting נסי, *my standard*, with כס in the phrase יד על־כס יה, *a hand on the [throne] of Yahweh* (Van Seters, *Moses*, pp. 206-208; *contra* Childs, *Exodus*, pp. 311-12). LXX translates כס as κρυφαίᾳ, from כסה, *cover*; and the Samaritan text, and later Jewish exegesis, understand it as כסא, *a throne*. It is best to take the stone on which Moses sat (17.12) as the basis of the altar of 17.15, which is then understood to be Yahweh's throne. Moses' comment, 'A hand on Yahweh's throne', is to recall the power his hand exerted when seated there. Mayes (*Deuteronomy*, pp. 330-31) offers no explanation for the harsh attack on Amalek, merely comparing it with the exclusion of Ammonites and Moabites from the assembly of Israel.

Judges

The old Asaph tradition had Aaron's father-in-law Reuel introduce the Joseph-tribes to the worship of El/'God', and able men, clan leaders, were to administer the laws of the new religion as judges (Exod. 18). 'Aaron came, and all the elders of Israel to eat bread before God' (18.12): Aaron was not a *solus mediator* in the way that Moses was supposed to have been—he was *primus inter pares* in the manner of desert communities, and the whole leadership accepted the new devotion together.

In some ways this suited the Korahites taking the story over. Aaron was new to Kadesh, and will have courted his bride there. Moses is supposed to have been in Horeb before; he had married Zipporah in Exodus 2, and taken her to Egypt (4.20-26), but will have sent her back to Midian (18.2), so a scene in which Moses and Jethro meet once more, and enjoy a sacred meal together, is just what is required. The Korahites paint in the family reunion with loving hands—the bowing and kissing, the kindly enquiries and tales of adventure and blessing; and all is crowned by Jethro's 'confession', his pronouncement that the God who has delivered Israel from Egypt is Yahweh.

Once the story is on the road, the Korahites let it run on. They are not democrats, and are not going to see Aaron and his fellow-elders on a level with Moses; so they picture a touching scene in which poor old Moses is exhausting himself giving judgments all day long, till Jethro advises him to appoint judges for the minor cases. In this way Moses holds the position occupied in the tradents' day by King Josiah, advised by the wise and good high priest Hilkiah. He is the sole mediator between God and men, and the appointer of lesser administrators. The latter are no longer the elders, the clan leaders; they are rulers of thousands, hundreds, fifties and tens, like the officers in Josiah's army (18.21, 25).

This perspective enables many of the 'problems' of Exodus 18 to be resolved: cf. the discussion in R. Knierim, 'Exodus 19'; Childs, *Exodus*, pp. 318-36. Jethro, Moses' father-in-law, is permitted to pronounce Yahweh as Israel's deliverer in Egypt, to bring sacrifices and burnt offerings, and to preside over a religious meal attended by Aaron and the elders: this is because Reuel, Aaron's father-in-law, had been the priest of El at Meribah, and had introduced Aaron and the elders to the worship of El—later understood to be identical with Yahweh (Ps. 81.11). Jethro's 'confession' (18.10-11) is seen as the result of an 'aha-experience': the God who delivered Israel was none other than his God, Yahweh. Ideas of his conversion are later apologetic.

The people come to 'enquire of God' (18.15), but the cases are civil cases. This is because the Meribah covenant laid down a basic divine law, and all later judgments were seen as being based on these 'oracles'. The judges began as able and honest men, and turn out to be colonels and majors in the army. This is because the administration of justice had been in the hands of elders in the wilderness, but in the seventh century it followed military lines, as was argued by Knierim.

This arrangement involves an unfortunate tension: for how are the new judges to be taught the statutes of God and his laws (Exod. 18.20) when Moses has not yet received them? Logic requires that they should rather be appointed *after* the revelation of the covenant. So that is where it is placed in Deut. 1.9-18. Israel has just *left* Horeb (as it has now become), and the first thing Moses does is to take wise and understanding men to be judges; he does so, as in Exodus 18, because the people are too numerous for him to bear the responsibility, and the judges are, also as in Exodus 18, rulers of thousands, and so forth, and as in Exodus 18 they are charged to judge impartially—what is different is that the institution now takes place after the covenant is made.

But changes of story so often involve a tangled web. If the judges have already been appointed in Exodus 18, how is the tradent to deal with their Deuteronomic appointment in the post-Horeb/Sinai story which we now have in Numbers? Most of the old Asaph narrative has been demoted to after the mountain revelation: he cannot have a second institution of judges, since the deed is done already in Exodus 18, but he cannot ignore the post-Horeb institution which his colleagues are enshrining in Deuteronomy 1. The result of this dilemma is the curious hybrid narrative we have in Numbers 11. The main strand is the old Asaph tale of the quails, originally combined with the manna in Ps. 78.17-31, but now separated into (i) manna (Exod. 16), and (ii) quails (Num. 11).

The separation of the two elements suggests a further happy gloss: the people complained of the *sameness* of the manna, but it was really the accompanying *rabble* which started this, not the true Israelites (Num. 11.4-6). The complaining is acute (*weeping*), and Moses is driven to distraction; he is not able to *bear all this people alone* (11.10-15). Yahweh responds by telling him to gather seventy elders to the tent of meeting, and there they will receive of Moses' spirit, 'and they shall bear the burden of the people with thee, that thou bear it not thyself alone' (11.16-17). Moses does so, and the spirit is accordingly given: the seventy prove their new gift by prophesying, and even Eldad and Medad, who had not attended at the tent, prophesy also. In this way important elements of the post-Horeb Deuteronomy 1 story are seen to be post-Horeb: the intolerable strain on Moses, the appointment of a corps of assistants under divine authority to share his burden. But at the same time they are not judges, who had already been installed in Exodus 18. Rather they are prophets, another important institution in seventh-century Judah; and the transfer of the spirit that is on Moses recalls the transfer of Elijah's spirit to Elisha, a story no doubt in circulation by this time.

One last detail comes through from the Numbers narrative. The Israel tribes left Kadesh after some forty years, and the 'J' narrative resumes at Num. 10.29-33: Moses urged Hobab, the son of Reuel the Midianite to accompany them, but he declined. Similarly at Exod. 18.27 Moses let his father-in-law depart, and he went to his own country. In the old Asaph narrative Aaron (and the elders) had been initiated into the new religion by his father-in-law Reuel; but Reuel was a generation older than Aaron, and after forty years not surprisingly he has died. Hence the local priest of El at Kadesh is now his son Hobab, who is also mentioned in Judg. 1.16, 4.11 as a Kenite, and who now accompanies Israel on their way, following the Asaph line; and this is preserved in Numbers 10, at the beginning of a series of old Asaph traditions. Of course his brother-in-law is now Moses, not Aaron; but in Exodus 18 it is Jethro who held the parallel (Korahite) position. He was quickly dismissed before the great revelation was made to Moses and Israel alone.

Chapter 13

THE MOUNTAIN

The Theophany

In the old Asaph tradition, the experience of the great revelation was described thus: 'I answered thee (אֶעֶנְךָ) in the secret place of thunder (רַעַם); I proved thee (אֶבְחָנְךָ) at the waters of Meribah. Hear, O my people, and I will testify unto thee: O Israel, if thou wouldest hearken unto me! There shall no strange god be in thee; Neither shalt thou worship any strange god. I am the LORD thy God, which brought thee up out of the land of Egypt: Open thy mouth wide, and I shall fill it' (Ps. 81.8-11). The following verses go on to imply that Israel did not in fact 'hearken' but failed the 'proving'.

We have a much fuller prose account of the theophany in Exodus 19–20, which is mostly told of the appearance of Yahweh to Moses on the mountain, but is also related in part of אֱלֹהִים, not on a mountain; and significantly, the latter verses give parallels to Psalm 81. 'And Moses [went up] to God (Exod. 19.3a)... And it came to pass [on the third day, when it was morning,] that there were thunders (קֹלֹת) and lightnings and a thick cloud...and the voice of a trumpet exceeding loud; and all the people that were in the camp trembled. And Moses brought forth the people out of the camp to meet God... And when the voice of the trumpet waxed louder and louder, Moses spake, and God answered him (יַעֲנֶנּוּ) by a voice (19.16-17, 19)... And God spake all these words, saying, I am the LORD thy God, which brought thee out of the land of Egypt, out of the house of bondage. Thou shalt have none other gods beside me (20.1-3)... And all the people saw the thunderings (הַקּוֹלֹת), and the lightnings, and the voice of the trumpet...and when the people saw it, they trembled, and stood afar off. And they said unto Moses, Speak thou with us, and we will hear; but let not God speak with us, lest we die. And Moses said unto the people, Fear not: for God is come to prove you (נַסּוֹת), and that his fear may be before you, that ye sin not.

And the people stood afar off, and Moses drew near unto the thick darkness where God was' (20.18-21).

The wording is not always identical, but substantially the two accounts are the same. (i) God *answered* (ענה) Moses; (ii) he did so *from the secret place of thunder*, from the deep darkness from which came 'voices'; (iii) he *proved*/tested Israel; (iv) he announced himself, '*I am the LORD thy God which brought thee* [up] *out of the land of Egypt*'; (v) his command was that he alone should be worshipped. The presence of these five themes in the story, in the very verses where אלהים is the subject, seals the matter. I have already suggested that the Asaphites preferred אלהים, because they did not know the name of their divine deliverer until Meribah/Kadesh: Ps. 81.11 is better translated, 'I, Yahweh, am thy God which brought thee...' They spoke of him earlier as El, and the hero of the narrative at that time will have been Aaron; but by the eighth century Bethel was firmly Yahwist. In the above transcript one or two references to the mountain have been taken out as glosses: in 19.17 the people are simply brought out of the camp to meet God, without any suggestion of an ascent. The whole theophany may be seen as taking place 'by the waters of Meribah'.

The division of the chapter between different sources has been controversial, but the separation defended here is identical to that proposed by Noth (*Exodus*, pp. 151-55); it is similar to analyses by many scholars (see Childs, *Exodus*, pp. 348-49), and is the position taken by Nicholson (*God and his People*). Childs (*Exodus*, p. 349) and Van Seters (*Moses*, pp. 248-52) deny the significance of the Yahweh/God distinction; Van Seters divides the chapters between 'J' and P. Childs criticizes Noth's position on the grounds that (i) 19.9a (Yahweh) foretells the dense cloud of 19.19 (God); (ii) 19.9a is supposed to belong to the volcano-smoke theme, not the storm-cloud anyhow; (iii) 20.18 (God) has not only the thunder, lightning and trumpet (storm-cloud), but also the smoking mountain. The criticism is more telling against Noth's two-source hypothesis than it is against my original Asaphite narrative retold (and inevitably glossed) by Korahites; and I have the earliest form of the Asaph original in Psalm 81, with אלהים, thunder, the covenant and no mountain. Noth (*Exodus*, p. 159) suggests plausibly that the festal trumpet blowing of Psalm 81.4 may be related to the voice of the שפר in the theophany at 19.16.

Such a theophany was an acceptable base on which the Korahites might construct a more adequate narrative: the hero must of course be their Moses, and the site their Mt Horeb. The latter suggested two elaborations: first, the mountain could suitably react to the divine presence in the manner of a volcano, quaking and spewing forth smoke; and secondly, as a holy mountain (Exod. 3.5), it will need protection against invasion by the *profanum vulgus*. The latter element introduces a tension: in the Asaph story, the people stood afar off, trembling in terror at God's thundering voice; for the Korahite adaptation they have to be prevented from crossing the sacred boundary in their enthusiasm. It is the familiar descent from natural awe at the numinous to the defence of priestly prerogative, expounded classically by Wellhausen.

If Rephidim is er-Raphid in Midian, then the Korahites began their tale, 'And when they were departed from Rephidim, they came to the wilderness [of Horeb], and there Israel camped before the Mount' (19.2): the present text is contorted, and Horeb must have been mentioned in the Korah version. Yahweh calls to Moses in good Deuteronomic form, 'now therefore, if ye will obey my voice indeed, and keep my covenant,...ye shall be unto me a kingdom of priests, and an holy nation' (19.3b-6; cf. Deut. 7.6). The Korah expansion thus fits comfortably in the last third of the seventh century. Where in the older tradition Aaron had come, and all the elders of Israel, and Aaron merely acted as their spokesman, Moses is now the sole mediator: he alone receives the conditions, he summons the elders, and gains from the people a promise to do everything that Yahweh commands, which he then reports to Yahweh (19.7-9a). We have moved from oligarchy to hierarchy.

Childs (*Exodus*, pp. 351-60) notes helpfully the difference between 'J' and 'E' over the Mosaic office. In 'J' Moses is often associated with the tent of meeting, and goes alone to see Yahweh, and keeps the people away from the holy mount, and has them consecrate themselves, and finds his face shining with reflected glory; and is thus in many ways a priestly figure. In 'E', however, there is none of this: there is no tent of meeting, the blood-ritual to seal the covenant is not performed by Moses, there is no shining visage. Here Moses is more a prophetic figure, the mediator of the covenant (cf. Deut. 18.18).

The reason for this difference appears from the analysis above. Moses was historically a priest, the leader of the future priestly tribe of Levi, and grandfather of the founder of the Dan priesthood (Judg. 18.30; Exod. 32.25-29): so the priestly image comes through in the Korahite (Dan, Yahwist) expansion. Aaron was the mediator of the Meribah covenant, but he was not historically a priest: he attended sacrifices conducted by his father-in-law Reuel (Exod. 18.12). So the underlying non-priestly story is the work of the Asaph (Joseph/Benjamin, Elohist) tradents.

Hierarchy brings with it the fencing of the holy, and in Exod. 19.10-15 the people are warned of Yahweh's coming: they must consecrate themselves for two days, and wash their clothes, and not go near a woman; and should they touch the fence to be built round Mt Horeb they must surely be put to death. The Asaph theophany merely needs touching up. The people now stand 'at the nether part of the mount', which is 'altogether on smoke, and the smoke ascended as the smoke of a furnace, and the whole mount quaked greatly' (19.17b-18). Moses alone is summoned to the top of the mount, and sent down to warn the people a second time of the mortal danger of touching the holy (19.20-25). For old times'sake he is to bring the ousted Aaron up with him in a second ascent, to receive the conditions of the covenant (19.24).

It is often thought that 19.20-25 are a later expansion (Childs, *Exodus*, pp. 361-64). Aaron's inclusion at 19.24 may be due to Asaphites' disgust at the suppression of their hero.

So impressive a scene needed little amendment by the Merarites. They changed the name of the mountain to their own Sinai, and prefixed a brief note of itinerary, and a date. The latter has been done with finesse. The Korahite story provided for two days of sanctification, 'today and tomorrow' (19.10), and 'on the third day' (19.16) Moses ascends Sinai, a mountain of some 8,000 ft. The Merarites bring the people to the wilderness of Sinai on the third new moon, 1st Sivan, where they camp (for the night) before the mountain (19.2). Moses goes up to God on the 2nd, then, and must be thought to take a full day for such a double journey. He then summons the people, and tells God of their positive response: so the sanctification will be on 3rd and 4th, and the second ascent, before the people, on the 5th. Then the final climb, with Aaron, to receive the Decalogue, will be on 6th Sivan, the fiftieth day after Passover, the Feast of Pentecost. Although the P editors have not noted the coincidence, it cannot be accidental: later interpreters could never have identified the law-giving with the Feast of Pentecost unless they had intended it. Thus the mystery of Moses' repeated ascents of the mountain has its reason.

The Decalogue

It is uncertain how much of the Decalogue was already in the Asaph narrative: I have taken a minimalist position above, limiting it to Exod. 20.1-3, for which there is evidence in Psalm 81, and I shall offer further arguments for that position below. What El required of Israel was *monolatry*, and this was to be expressed in a *calendar* of worship, of which full moon autumnal trumpet-blowing was one of the statutes for

Israel (Ps. 81.4-5). The Decalogue of Exod. 20.2-17 includes the provision for sabbath observance, which is part of the calendar, and the
basic moral ordinances which were certainly known to the Asaphites
(Ps. 50.17-21); but they are likely to have been developments of the
simple basis, No god but me.

The main development in the seventh century is then comprehensible.
Josiah's reformation had focused on the destruction of the Bethel shrine,
which was supposed to have contained a Golden Calf idol (1 Kgs 12.28-
29), and it involved horses dedicated to the sun (2 Kgs. 23.11), Asherim,
and so forth, at Jerusalem. Hence the second Word, 'Thou shalt not
make unto thee a graven image...' The Asaphites knew that no images
had ever been worshipped in their sanctuary, and could happily add the
gloss. The further expansion on Yahweh's jealousy, punishing yet merciful, is a standard Deuteronomic *topos*, recurring in Exod. 34.7, 14; 'the
house of bondage' is also a Deuteronomic phrase (Exod. 13.3, 14). The
'moral' commandments are mostly to be found in Hos. 4.2, 'There is
nought but swearing and breaking faith, and killing and stealing and
committing adultery'; with the exception of the tenth commandment,
coveting, they are exemplified in the 'Book of the Covenant'—respect
for parents (Exod. 21.15, 17), killing (21.12-32), stealing (22.1-15), sex
offences (22.16-19), false witness (23.1-8).

The second commandment contains an ambiguity which may have aided its acceptance. 'Thou shalt not bow down thyself unto them nor serve them' has '*a* graven
image' as the referent for '*them*'; and the two verbs are normally followed by 'other
gods' in the D-corpus. It might thus be taken to concern Asherim, Nehushtan, etc.
But the opening sentence, condemning a פסל in any form, is an attack on images representing Yahweh. The golden bulls of Yahweh's throne at Bethel are not included in
this, as they are not mentioned in Josiah's purge in 2 Kgs 23.15; but we may have
to do with an image at Dan (Ps. 89.16; 42.3; 84.8; repeated references to 'seeing the
face of Yahweh'). Cf. my discussion in *Korah*, pp. 223-28; Childs, *Exodus*,
pp. 404-409.

It is the remaining Words which raise problems, the central one of
which is not often taken seriously. The fourth commandment concerns
the sabbath day; and the sabbath, day, year (and jubilee), is a part of
all the biblical calendar laws (Exod. 23.10-19; 34.18-26; Deut. 16.1-17;
Lev. 23.1-44; Num. 28–29). But the other calendars all give major consideration to the cycle of annual festivals, which were the key element in
Israelite religion. How then is the absence of these feasts to be explained
in the Decalogue?

A possible explanation could be that the fourth commandment was promulgated during the Exile. Pilgrimage feasts to Jerusalem were clearly impracticable for exiles in Babylon; nor was it to be thought that large assemblies of exiled Jews on the feast days would be permitted, or could be organized, on the banks of the Euphrates. But it was possible for Jews in exile, unless enslaved, to cease work on the sabbath, and to spare their families and servants. This could be a continuing badge of Jewishness, and an opportunity indeed for small gatherings for prayer and the recital of Scripture and the singing of the songs of Zion; and it is from the Exile that sabbath begins to take a central place in Jewish consciousness.

Two features of the fourth commandment seem to confirm this suggestion. First, the basis of the commandment is said to be that in six days the LORD made heaven and earth, and rested on the seventh day (Exod. 20.11)—that is, the priestly account of creation is presupposed, from Gen. 1.1–2.4. Secondly, the Word opens, '*Remember* the sabbath day, to keep it holy...': perhaps there is some danger of the sabbath being forgotten, as can easily happen when a people is deported and scattered. Such things do not get forgotten in an established community, and the Deuteronomy 5 parallel merely opens, 'Observe the sabbath day'. The Deuteronomists are also not familiar with P's creation story, and substitute their own more human motivation, 'thou shalt remember that thou wast a slave in the land of Egypt...' (Deut. 5.15). An exilic setting would also give a reason for giving prominence to a short, simple, memorable Table, in apodeictic form: fathers can remember ten commandments and teach them to their children—they are not a handbook for judges.

Alt's celebrated essay of 1934, translated as 'The Origins of Israelite Law', established the apodeictic/casuistic distinction, and claimed that the former had its origin in the liturgy: the principal evidence for this was Deuteronomy 27 and 31.10-12. But Gerstenberger's *Wesen und Herkunft* showed the distinction to be over-simple, as in Leviticus 19 where the two types of law occur side by side. The evidence for a liturgical setting for the first commandment is Ps. 81.9-11; and it would not have been possible to add the third and fourth commandments, and in the Exile, without an authoritative lead in worship somewhere in Babylon. So much of Alt's proposal may be felt still to stand. Perhaps a unified legal system could only be developed through proclamation in the liturgy; but the casuistic material was intended for local elders giving judgments, and the apodeictic rulings for fathers to teach their children.

The exilic situation would then suggest a meaning for the third commandment. 'Taking the name of the LORD thy God in vain' is not likely
to mean perjury, since that is already the ninth Word; and blasphemy,
which would be very rare, is condemned in a different Hebrew phrase
(נקב שם־יהוה) in Lev. 24.16. But Jews in exile might well find themselves expected to recant their faith in Yahweh and praise the gods of
wood and stone, as Daniel and his friends are in Daniel 3, 6. What is
required then is not to apostatize in the moment of challenge, not to take
Yahweh's name לשוא, *for emptiness*. We have the same peril and the
same expectation of faithfulness unto death in Lk. 12.8-12; and Aqiba
and Justin are among the noble army of martyrs who kept the
commandment.

Noth (*Exodus*, p. 163) sees the Word as directed against misuse of the Name for
magic purposes; so also Phillips (*Ancient Israel's Criminal Law*, pp. 53-55), Mayes
(*Deuteronomy*, p. 168). But the Ten Commandments seem at least to open with a
pair (H. Gese, 'Dekalog'), and the pair of commandments on monolatry could well
be followed by a pair on resistance to assimilation in exile.

We have then an outline history of the growth of the Decalogue. The
first commandment goes back to desert times, and is all that is preserved
in the Asaph psalm tradition (81.8-11). The two northern guilds
expanded it formally during the Josianic reformation, to incorporate the
central ethical requirements of Yahwism. These we find already stated in
other ways in Hos. 4.2 or the Book of the Covenant: very likely there
were seven commandments, I, II, V, VI, VII, VIII, IX. This version
naturally contained Deuteronomic phrasing.

The present ten-word form did not take shape till the Exile. Then, in
Babylonia, the Merarites watched the beginnings of a crumbling into
assimilation, and inserted three further commandments. Jews were not
to let Yahweh's name go for nothing and bow the knee in the house of
Marduk; and they were to remember the sabbath day and keep it holy,
the sole practicable element of the traditional calendar, but the most frequent one, and the most effective defence of the national identity. In the
long run sabbath was Queen. The P-editors left their thumb-print by
phrasing the third and fourth commandments in the *third* person; it is no
longer Yahweh who is the speaker—'none other gods before *me*'—but
Moses about Yahweh—'*the LORD* will not hold him guiltless...*the LORD*
made heaven'. Also they have transferred much of the stress of the
Table on to the fourth commandment, which is now a quarter of the

length of the whole. Finally they added the more 'internal' command-ment, no. X, no coveting, which with its *son, daughter, manservant, maidservant...*, forms a kind of rhyme with no. IV. The later editors of Deuteronomy inserted the Table in ch. 5, with a few suitable amendments.

Commentators are agreed that much of the second commandment is directed against Israelite images of Yahweh, which must be pre-exilic; that some of the phrasing is Deuteronomistic; and that the creation story presupposed in the fourth commandment goes back to P's account in Genesis 1. Not much else is agreed: Noth (*Exodus*, pp. 160-68) attributes the Table generally to J, Van Seters to P; Noth is open to nameless antiquity, Van Seters argues for an exilic date. Mayes (*Deuteronomy*, pp. 160-72) in a thoughtful discussion, argues for a late date for the present Deuteronomy 5 form, with a series of Deuteronomistic redactions. Not only is the D-phrasing often striking, but he appeals to Gerstenberger's argument (*Wesen und Herkunft*, pp. 201-203) that tables of ten or twelve apodeictic laws are late developments. He approves E. Nielsen's dating of the original form to 622–560 (*Ten Commandments*, pp. 44-46). His conclusions are not far from those argued here.

The Covenant Law

The covenant of Israel with God is a theme of the Asaph psalter. In Ps. 50.6 his devoted ones have made a covenant with him with sacrifice; at 50.16 the wicked are reproached for taking his covenant in their mouth; at 74.20 he is prayed to have respect unto the covenant. The nation's forefathers kept not his covenant at 78.10, and were not faithful to it at 78.37. The formation of this covenant was set out, as we have just seen, in 81.8-11, including both Israel's duty to God, 'There shall no strange god be in thee', and his promise to them, 'Open thy mouth wide, and I will fill it.' The first commandment is given there, and there is reference to statute, ordinance and testimony (81.5-6), with reference to festal celebrations.

Of the various legal codes in the Pentateuch, two are generally taken to be pre-Deuteronomic: the so-called 'Book of the Covenant' in Exod. 20.22–23.33, and the short Table of so-counted ten commandments in Exod. 34.10-26. We have found some brief echoes of phrases in Exod. 23.1-8, on just judging, in Psalm 82 (pp. 163-64); but these should not be allowed to settle the argument in favour of Exodus 21–23 being of Asaphite origin in Bethel. If the Book of the Covenant was of Korahite origin in Dan, it would be familiar to Bethel priests, especially after 730. This indeed seems a more probable state of affairs: the Korahites have shown their ability to take over the Bethel traditions throughout Exodus, and just as they have ousted Aaron in favour of Moses, and Meribah in favour of Horeb, and pushed the Psalm 78 wilderness traditions on into Numbers, so we may expect that they will have given centre-place to their own legal traditions as the deliverance of Yahweh at the great theophany, and demoted the Asaphite code to a secondary position in Exodus 34.

This expectation is confirmed by a number of features in the Exodus 34 passage. First, the opening commandment is given only in a paren-thesis: 'Ye shall break down their altars, and dash in pieces their pillars, and ye shall cut down their Asherim; for thou shalt worship no other god...' (34.13-14): the D-exhortation is thus interrupted by an apology for the sole commandment of Ps. 81.10-11, which is also the first com-mandment of the Decalogue. Then the second commandment will be 'Thou shalt make thee no molten gods' (34.17): gods of מסכה, pouring (נסך), where the metal-worker coated the wooden image with molten gold or other metal from the crucible. The phrase is later displaced by the more usual פסל, an image (Exod. 20.4).

'A graven image and a molten image' (פסל ומסכה) is a hendiadys, and there is no distinction to be made in practice between the two (*ThWAT* 6.687-96). Molten images might on occasion be figurines cast in a mould, but Exodus 34 is concerned with larger idols made for public worship, like 'golden calves'.

The remainder of the Exodus 34 table is entirely calendrical, or expansions of the calendar. Commanded are: (3) the feast of Unleavened Bread; with appended laws (4) to sacrifice all first-born animals, and to redeem the human first-born (34.18-20); (5) sabbath every seventh day, with an interdict on work (34.21); (6) the feasts of Weeks and Ingather-ing—three festivals in all (34.22-24); (7) no leavened bread with the blood of the sacrifice (34.25a); (8) no Passover meat to remain till the morning (34.25b); (9) the first of the firstfruits to be sacrificed (34.26a); (10) no seething of a kid in its mother's milk (34.26b). With the initial two commandments this makes ten Words, which Moses is to write, and which comprise 'a covenant with thee and with Israel' (34.27-28).

The core of this code is laws (3) and (6), the three old Canaanite agri-cultural festivals, Unleavened Bread, Weeks and Ingathering, the barley, wheat and general harvest feasts. But between the first of these and the later two have been inserted a number of more Israelite matters. First, 'Seven days shalt thou eat unleavened bread, as I commanded thee, at

13. *The Mountain*   299

the time appointed in the month Abib: for in the month Abib thou
camest out of Egypt': the unleavened bread is associated with the
Exodus, with appeal to the tradition of Exod. 13.6-8. Second, 'All that
openeth the womb is mine', male ox and sheep; but asses may be
redeemed, and sons must be; as in Exod. 13.2, 11-16. The same associations are at work; just as the Korahite Deuteronomists introduced the
redemption of the first-born during the Passover story because that told
of the sparing of the Israelite first-born, so the same thought is operative
here—unleavened bread is an aspect of Passover. Third, 'Six days shalt
thou work', and then keep sabbath: the interval of seven weeks between
Passover and Weeks, שבעת, sevens, suggests the interposition of the
sabbath law here. Nearly half of the total code consists of these three
interruptions between the first annual festival and the later two.

After Ingathering follows a word of promise, 'For I will cast out
nations before thee...'; we are perhaps reminded of Ps. 81.11, 'Open
thy mouth wide and I will fill it.' Then there is a double command:
'Thou shalt not offer the blood of my sacrifice with leavened bread;
neither shall the sacrifice of the feast of the passover be left unto the
morning'. The second half of this is surprising: Passover was not mentioned among the three pilgrimage-festivals (חג), but it is clear that whoever wrote these words thought Passover and Unleavened Bread were
the same feast, as was understood by Matthew (Mt. 26.17-19). The first
half seems to be a rule for the observance of Passover also, since
unleavened bread is the special theme of the spring festival. The offering
of 'the first of the firstfruits of thy ground' (ראשית בכורי אדמתך) also
belongs at Paschal tide, on the third morning after Passover according to
Lev. 23.15; and the mysterious seething of the kid in its mother's milk
may refer to the Paschal kid also.

The present form of the code gives the strong impression that its
author is marrying his own Israelite festal tradition, which is centrally
about Passover, with the Canaanite agricultural calendar: and that
implies that he is an Asaphite, to whom the spring festival had been
Passover long before it had been Unleavened Bread. He places three
sizeable interruptions between Unleavened Bread and Weeks, two of
which carry Paschal overtones; and he appends to the whole four
subsidiary laws, one of which identifies Unleavened Bread with 'the
pilgrimage-feast of Passover', and at least two of the others are associated with the spring festival. The accent is overwhelmingly on Passover,

the feast which celebrates the central experience of the Joseph–Benjamin tribes, the Exodus.

Dan was the primary religious centre for (Northern) Israel rather than Bethel (Goulder, *Korah*, pp. 51-71), as long as it did not fall into enemy hands, being the more exposed. It might be expected therefore that the nation's code of common and criminal law would be kept in the national sanctuary at Dan; and thus that Exodus 21–23, which is substantially a manual for judges (מִשְׁפָּטִים, 21.1), should have been the Dan legal corpus. The Korahites have enrolled a bench of judges in Exodus 18 in preparation for their judges' handbook. This comprises two chapters of laws followed by an exhortation to just judging (23.1-9), and then two appendices. The first is a set of calendrical provisions, closely similar to those in Exodus 34 (23.10-19), and the second a D-type peroration (23.20-33).

The contorted Asaphite calendar has been taken over and simplified. The sabbath law comes first now, prefaced by a sabbath year law (23.10-12); but the editor has added in an echo of the old first Word— 'and make no mention of the name of other gods, neither let it be heard out of thy mouth'. Idolatry no longer seems much of a problem! There follow the three festivals, now without major interruption, though the Asaphite connection of Unleavened Bread with the Exodus is retained (23.15). Then come the four brief Words (7)-(10) as above; except that 'the meat of the feast of Passover' becomes 'the fat of my feast'. But this rule is more suited to Passover than other feasts because the Passover alone was eaten at night.

Noth (*Exodus*, pp. 189-92) takes Exodus 23 as the primary form of the calendar, and ascribes 'Passover' to a late gloss, and so forth. But the dependence is likely to be the other way. It is difficult to see why an Exodus 34 editor should take a logical order like 23.10-19 and muddle it; and 23.10-19 stands after the legal corpus has been completed and signed off, and is an addition.

Perlitt (*Bundestheologie*, pp. 203-32) supported by Nicholson (*People*, pp. 134-50) holds that Exodus 32–34 is a consistent unity, all stemming from the seventh century, probably from Josiah's time. For the narrative this seems convincing (see below). But the handling of the laws is less plausible. It was unwise of Noth to claim 34.10-28 as early and then to explain away most of these verses as Deuteronomistic expansions: his early code is really just (most of) 34.17-26. Perlitt and Nicholson cite Alt's view that this table is 'a later and heterogeneous compilation, containing priestly ordinances about cultic duties of lay-people' (p. 118 n. 95); but the stress on Passover, and the general disorder, are better explained as of early Bethel provenance. Psalm 81 provided not only the first commandment (81.11), but also 'testimonies' for worship (81.5).

More generally, Perlitt and Nicholson have canvassed a late date for the covenant idea, returning to Wellhausen's conclusion that it arose from the preaching of the great prophets. Perlitt sees it as a seventh-century phenomenon, Nicholson, who credits the texts in Hos. 6.7 and 8.1 (*People*, pp. 179-88), a century earlier. But the dating of the Asaph psalms to the 720s shows that the covenant was deeply rooted in Bethel by Hosea's time; and it also shows that ברית was a two-sided agreement, with promise as well as imposed duty. It is singular that neither Perlitt nor Nicholson takes these psalms into account.

It is the Asaphites who have had the guiding hand in ordering Deuteronomy. They have closed the opening paraenesis with a direction to Bethel, 'over against Gilgal' (Deut. 11.29-30; cf. pp. 47-49), and opened the closing chapters similarly with a liturgy in the same location (Deut. 27). But the Deuteronomic law corpus begins with the sanctuary law, as Exodus 21–23 is prefaced by the Korahite altar law of Exod. 20.24-26; and continues with expansions of the two northern codes in turn. Deuteronomy 12 tries to ensure the worship of Yahweh alone, with no other god, by centralizing the cult to Jerusalem. Deuteronomy 13 provides against anyone canvassing for the worship of other gods. Deuteronomy 14 lays down food- and tithing-laws to make a people holy to Yahweh. Thus far the first Asaphite commandments, the requirement of monolatry. Then in 15-16.17 comes the calendar, as in the Asaphite Exodus 34, but with some Korahite adjustments. First the sabbath year (15.1-11) as in Exod. 23.10-11; then the same as applied to Hebrew slaves (15.12-18), as in Exod. 21.1-11; then the sanctifying of firstling male animals (15.19), as in Exod. 34.19-20; then the festivals— Passover with Unleavened Bread (16.1-8), as in Exodus 34; Weeks and Tabernacles (16.9-17). Here the Asaph Table has had priority.

Blenkinsopp (*Pentateuch*, p. 211) suggests that Deuteronomy 14 may be 'one of several examples of late Priestly editing', modelled on Leviticus 11.

From Deut. 16.18 to ch. 26 the Korah code supplements. First, as in Exodus 18, comes the appointment of judges (16.18–17.13), with rulings for the supreme judge, the king (17.14-20), and priestly judges, Levites (18). What is to follow is a handbook for judges, secular and sacred. Then, with wandering steps, the Deuteronomists follow the path of their Korahite forebears, with suitable expansions. Here is not the place for a full account of the D-laws, but a table may suffice to show their general faithfulness:

Deuteronomy		Exodus	
19.1-13	Manslaughter and Murder Cities of Refuge	21.12-14	Manslaughter and Murder Cities of Refuge
19.21	Eye for eye, etc.	21.26-27	Eye for eye, etc.

[20–21.9 War, siege, unknown corpse, captive women]

21.18-21	Bad son stoned	21.15, 17	Bad son killed
22.13-30	Seduction, Adultery	22.16-17	Seduction
23.19-20	Loans without usury	22.26	Loans without usury
24.6	Millstone as pledge	22.27	Cloak as pledge

[23.19–24.22 Laws protecting the poor]

24.17	Perversion of justice	23.1-9	Perversion of justice
26	Firstfruits offered	23.19	Firstfruits offered

A frail attempt has been made in both codes to systematize sections on killing, women, property, the poor, and so forth; but this was not to be achieved before the days of the Mishnah. It is sufficient for our purposes that there is a visible, if intermittent, thread linking the second part of the D-corpus, Deuteronomy 19–26, with its Korahite forerunner, Exodus 21–23. The D-laws are an expanded combined version of the two old northern codes, first the Asaph, Bethel table from Exodus 34, and then the Korah, Dan code, the 'Book of the Covenant'.

The order of the D-laws ('apparently quite haphazard', Mayes, *Deuteronomy*, p. 49) has been discussed quite widely. C.M. Carmichael (*Laws of Deuteronomy*, 1974), establishes the link with Exodus 21–23, and argues persuasively for the widespread lack of system in ancient law codes. His attempts to account for the vagaries by partial appeal to historical associations have not, however, been so successful. J. L'Hour ('Législation'), stressed the recurrent formula, 'Thou shalt put away the evil from the midst of thee'; but this follows a variety of laws, and does not seem to account for the arrangement. R.P. Merendino (*Das deuteronomische Gesetz*, 1969), suggests that behind Deuteronomy 12–26 lie a number of earlier collections, some by subject (cultic, marriage, poverty laws), and some by formula ('abomination', purging, etc.); cf. also L'Hour, 'Les interdits' (1971). This is partly right, inasmuch as the cultic (12–14) and calendrical laws (15.1–16.17) are an expansion of the Exodus 34 table (with considerable paraenetic comment), while the laws on death, marriage, poverty, and so forth are an expansion of the Exodus 21–23 code. But the proposal of further collections based on form is speculative; see also Mayes's critique ·(*Deuteronomy*, pp. 49-55). G. Braulik ('Abfolge') proposes that Deuteronomy 12–25 is an exposition of the Decalogue in Deuteronomy 5: but this seems forced when the fifth commandment is 'expanded' to judges, kings and priests in 16.18–18.22.

After the Revelation

For the Asaph psalmists in the 720s the revelation at Meribah was what the burning bush at Horeb had been for the Korahites. Hitherto the unknown God had been their deliverer: now the unknown had revealed himself, 'I, Yahweh, am thy God (אנכי יהוה אלהיך) Which brought thee up out of the land of Egypt' (Ps. 81.11). No doubt in earlier times God had revealed himself as El: but by the eighth century Bethel was a solidly Yahwist shrine, and all that remained of El-worship was the use of the name for 'God', and its embedding in personal and tribal names (Israel, Bethel, Reuel, etc.).

The narrative version of the revelation, which has emerged from the above discussion, told of Yahweh's similar revelation of himself (Exod. 20.2), with a short table of ritual commandments centred on Passover (Exod. 34.17-26). This was revealed to Moses (earlier to Aaron) outside the camp at Meribah (the אלהים sections of Exod. 19–20). This disclosure of the divine identity then has a significant effect on the subsequent story, for God now no longer needs to be spoken of as אלהים, but may now be יהוה.

The Asaphite author continues his narrative then with this name in Exod. 24.3-8. Moses (earlier Aaron) came and told the people (no 'came down') all the words of Yahweh (i.e. Exod. 20.2; 34.17-26), and the people undertook to obey them. He 'wrote all the words of Yahweh'— perhaps they were inscribed on a scroll which had been held at Bethel. He built an altar and twelve pillars, and sent young men to sacrifice burnt-offerings and peace-offerings. It is noticeable that both at Deut. 27.2-7 and at Josh. 8.30-35, the two Shechem/Bethel ritual texts, the law is to be written down, with the setting up of (twelve?) great stones, the building of an altar, and the sacrifice of burnt-offerings and peace-offerings. As the Asaphite Moses was not a priest, and his father-in-law went away at Exod. 18.27, the sacrifices are performed by *young men*, who are almost certainly cultic assistants, servers (cf. New Testament νεανίσκοι). Then the covenant is ratified by a blood ritual reminiscent of the sanctification of priests in Leviticus. Half of the blood is dashed against the altar, as in Leviticus 9, and half is sprinkled on the people.

Noth (*Exodus*, p. 196) felt obliged to attribute 24.3-8 to J, despite its affiliations with the 'E'-passages in Exodus 19–20; the problem disappears if Exod. 34.17-26 is understood to be the Asaphites' ('E') revelation of Yahweh, as in Psalm 81. Perlitt

(*Bundestheologie*, pp. 190-203) followed by Van Seters (*Moses*, pp. 282-86) saw the covenant reading as no earlier than Josiah, again ignoring Psalm 81. Nicholson (*People*, pp. 164-78) sees an earlier tradition of a ritual like that consecrating priests. For the link with Deuteronomy 27 and Joshua 8, cf. Blenkinsopp, *Pentateuch*, p. 191. Perlitt drew attention to the links between 24.3-8, the closing of the revelation, and 19.3-8, its opening; but, as Nicholson notes, this does not imply the same authorship, and 19.3-8 should be seen as a Korahite anticipation of the older Asaphite closing ritual in 20.3-8.

The Korahites accepted this account, with minor glosses ('and all the ordinances', 'at the foot of the mountain'), but they encapsulated it in their own version. Moses is now ordered up the mountain a further time, and an additional layer of authority is set between God and the people: he is to be accompanied by Aaron, Nadab and Abihu and seventy elders, but the latter are to keep their distance from God while Moses alone draws near (24.1-2). The picture reflects seventh-century reality in Jerusalem: the king alone is at Yahweh's right hand, but there is a body of princes and priests who are men of influence in the time of Jeremiah. The whole party ascend the mountain, and they see God without harm, and eat and drink (24.9-11). Moses is then summoned to the peak, accompanied only by Joshua, while Aaron and the others are told to wait (24.12-14). The treacherous Korahites mean to betray their Asaphite allies; they have left Aaron behind to make him the scapegoat of the Golden Calf story to come. They have done with the old joint leadership by the hand of Moses-and-Aaron; they intend to have Moses and Moses alone for leader. The Stalinists followed their example with Trotsky in the 1930s.

The ascent is described in two phases. First the whole party go up, and receive the *visio Dei*; since this might imply peril of death, it is stressed that God did not lay his hand on the Israelite nobles (עֲצִילֵי בְנֵי יִשְׂרָאֵל). They saw the God of Israel without taking harm. However, they treated this enormous privilege with scant respect: 'they beheld God, and did eat and drink', as later they were to eat and drink and 'play' before the Golden Calf (24.9-11). However—or perhaps in view of this (וְ)—Moses and Joshua (hitherto unmentioned) are summoned to go up alone to receive the tablets, leaving Aaron and Hur to settle any problems (24.12-15a, 18b). It is likely that the narrative has been developed in two independent stages, which have been here combined; no doubt those who did so felt that Aaron's iniquity over the Golden Calf was the more heinous from his having just seen God.

Noth (*Exodus*, p. 194) took the eating and drinking to be the sealing of the covenant; but Perlitt (*Bundestheologie*, pp. 181-90) and Nicholson (*People*, pp. 121-33) note that this is not said, and that it could be merely a restatement of their not being in danger. However, the vision of God is a rare and marvellous privilege in Scripture; and we do not find Moses or Isaiah or Ezekiel or Enoch stuffing their faces in the middle of it.

The priestly author has transformed Moses' summons to the peak of (now) Sinai into a prolonged revelation of the blueprint for the tabernacle, and other matters (Exod. 25–31); opened by the glory of the LORD settling for a week on the mountain (24.15b-18a).

The Apostasy at Meribah/Horeb

Both Psalms 81 and 78 imply that the covenant was soon abandoned by the Joseph–Benjamin tribesmen. After his words of promise in 81.8-11 God continues, 'But my people hearkened not to my voice; And Israel would none of me' (81.12). When he had answered Israel in the secret place of thunder, God had been *proving* his people at the waters of Meribah (81.8), and we found the same idea in the Asaphite Exod. 20.20; nor did they pass the test. Ps. 78.34 speaks similarly of an earnest seeking for God, but it is soon said, 'But they flattered him with their mouth, And lied unto him with their tongue. For their heart was not stedfast with him, Neither were they faithful in his covenant' (78.36-37). The comment that the people 'provoked the Holy One (קדוֹשׁ) of Israel' (78.41) raises echoes of the Kadesh (קדשׁ)/Meribah story in Num. 20.1-13, where they did not trust him so as to sanctify him (להקדישׁני), and he showed his holiness (ויקדשׁ) there. I have outlined above (pp. 279-80) the process by which the Numbers 20 story, originally explaining Aaron's death as his punishment for the apostasy at Meribah, grew to its present form.

The Korahites had their own apostasy story, and it was important for them: it told how certain of the Levites had stood by Moses in his hour of crisis, and had been faithful to Yahweh, slaughtering their idolatrous relatives, and so winning a permanent priesthood, first at Dan (Judg. 17–18) and later throughout Israel (Deut. 18). The earliest account we have of their heroism is in Deut. 33.9: '[Levi] Who said of his father, and of his mother, I have not seen him; Neither did he acknowledge his brethren, Nor knew he his own children: For they have observed thy word, And keep thy covenant'. In recognition of such selflessness, Levi is to teach Jacob God's judgments, put incense before him, and holocausts on his altar.

The same incident is reflected in Exod. 32.26-29: 'Then Moses stood in the gate of the camp, and said, Whoso is on the LORD's side, *let him come* unto me. And all the sons of Levi gathered themselves together unto him. And he said unto them, Thus saith the LORD, the God of Israel, Put ye every man his sword upon his thigh, and go to and fro from gate to gate throughout the camp, and slay every man his brother, and every man his companion, and every man his neighbour. And the sons of Levi did according to the word of Moses: and there fell of the people that day about three thousand men. And Moses said, Fill your hand today to the LORD; for every man hath been against his son, and against his brother'. The Korahites have done their best to soften the savagery of the Deuteronomy 33 story: it was not *some* Levites who slaughtered other, apostasizing Levites—*all* the Levites were loyal Yahwists to a man. In the first telling they kill their brothers, companions and neighbours—that is brothers in the sense of fellow-Israelites: it is only in Moses' words at the end that they have killed their *sons* and brothers, now from their own families. As in Deuteronomy their reward is the priesthood.

The Korahites needed to expand their legitimating legend beyond this core, and the Josianic reformation gave them their inspiration. In 622 the centralizing policy which they had themselves urged in Deuteronomy 12 was adopted, and the principal of the surviving sanctuaries outside Jerusalem, at Bethel, was desecrated by being burned and crushed to dust (2 Kgs 23.15). The cultic focus at Bethel had been a pair of golden bulls, no doubt the base of the throne of God, since no such work is mentioned in 2 Kings 23; but Hosea makes it clear that these had been suspect a century before—'The inhabitants of Samaria shall be in terror for the calves of Beth-aven' (Hos. 10.5), 'the sacrificers of men kiss calves' (13.2). In 8.5-6, Hosea speaks of the calf in the singular—'He hath cast off thy calf, O Samaria...the calf of Samaria shall be broken'. This is a piece of unfair polemic, suggesting that the single calf was an idol.

Now that the Bethel cult was in disgrace, and the Bethel tradents, the Asaphites, presumably in retreat, their old northern friends were in a position to capitalize. Even in Asaphite tradition Aaron, their hero, had been compromised in an apostasy, and had died soon afterwards in consequence (Num. 20); he should be the leader of the idolatry in the

Korahite story too, and the idol should be a golden calf. There never was a golden bull at Dan: the cultic focus there was made of silver, and was an ephod with teraphim (Judg. 17.1-5).

The story now writes itself. Moses is comfortably away, up the mountain with God (24.18b), and Aaron, at the people's behest, organizes a collection of gold ornaments, and makes a molten calf. The old Asaphite revelation had been 'I, Yahweh, am thy God which brought thee up out of the land of Egypt' (Ps. 81.11): Aaron travesties this with his proclamation, 'These (אלה) be thy gods, O Israel, which brought thee up out of the land of Egypt' (Exod. 32.4). There is the same havering as in Hosea: the idol was both *a calf*, singular, as in Hos. 8.5-6, and *gods*, plural (like אלהים), as in Hos. 10.5 and 13.2. The autumn festival at Bethel had been in the eighth month, not the seventh month as at Jerusalem; so Aaron institutes a pilgrimage feast (חג) of his own, and builds an altar, and there follows an orgy of eating, drinking and sexual licence. Moses comes down the mountain to a scene of dancing and shouting: he burns the Golden Calf and grinds it to powder, as Josiah did the במה at Bethel (2 Kgs 23.15), strewing the dust on the water and making the people drink it for good measure. Then follows the massacre, in which Aaron is surprisingly spared, while the people are punished with a plague besides.

Although this was an act of treachery to their old northern colleagues, the Korahites were not without mercy. Their Aaron is a reluctant sinner. It is the people, not he, who initiate the horror; the festival that he proclaims is to Yahweh, not Baal as it might have been; from 32.7-20 his name is not mentioned, but all the blame is fixed on the people, who would have been destroyed in Yahweh's wrath, had Moses not interceded for them; the later Ephraimite hero, Joshua, is taken up the mountain with Moses, so the Asaphites retain some *amour propre*; in the interview between the two brothers (32.21-24), Aaron appears as a weak simpleton, not a villain. So even the hard-nosed Korahites, in their triumphant coup for the ascendancy, know how to temper the wind to the shorn lamb.

The passing of a century and a half, and the fall of Jerusalem, and the consequent exile, reconciled all parties in the Deuteronomistic orthodoxy: Israel's trials had been their own fault, a punishment from Yahweh for the cultic disorders of earlier times. All high places outside Jerusalem had been occasions of sin; and the worst such centres were those at the old northern national sanctuaries at Dan and Bethel. By 550 even the Korahites and Asaphites were loyal to Jerusalem: the dew of Hermon (and of 'Gerizim') had fallen on the hill of Zion. So the blame for the sin could be loaded paradoxically on Jeroboam the son of Nebat. The king who had made Dan the nation's religious capital, and Bethel its reserve, and had promoted the lines of Korah and of Asaph as priests, was excoriated by their descendants as the primal schismatic who enticed Israel to sin and disaster.

The tale in 1 Kgs 12.26-33 is a parody of Exodus 32, itself a parody of the historic features of Bethel worship mentioned above. Jeroboam makes two calves of gold, as there were at Bethel, and he says, 'Behold thy gods, O Israel, which brought thee up out of the land of Egypt', like Aaron before Sinai. He puts one calf in Dan and the other in Bethel, so they are molten idols, like Aaron's. Although he has set up the two images, only one is effective: 'for the people went *to worship* before the one, even unto Dan'. He ordains a pilgrimage-feast in the eighth month, as Aaron proclaimed a גח at Sinai. He institutes a non-Levitical priesthood, and sacrifices himself, so the cult is as illegitimate as one could imagine, like the dancing and licence which met the eyes of Moses and Joshua. The D-historians have already described the foundation of worship at Dan, with equal charity and truthfulness, in Judges 17–18: but its ephod was of silver and its priests were Levites, indeed of Mosaic ancestry. But all this is forgotten in the zeal of the moment: the silver ephod becomes a molten image of gold, and the Mosaic priesthood is replaced by priests from among all the people who were not of the sons of Levi.

This account is but a modification of the theory proposed by R.H. Kennett in 1905 ('Aaronite Priesthood'), and which has been widely followed: Exodus 32 is an attack on the Bethel bull-throne and its Aaronic priests. Kennett and many others have thought that Exodus 32 is a reflection of the incident in 1 Kings.12, and not vice versa. Van Seters (*Moses*, pp. 290-301) objects (i) that there is no evidence of an Aaronic priesthood at Bethel, nor that Aaron was regarded as a priest anywhere before P; and (ii) that the Jeroboam story is certainly not historical, but a fiction of the sixth century. Hence, he concludes, the Exodus 32 tale is dependent on DH, and 'J' must be exilic in date. It is not true that there is no evidence of a pre-exilic Aaronic priesthood. Ps. 99.6, 'Moses and Aaron among his priests' must be pre-exilic: Moses was honoured as a priest in Dan from the second millennium, but he is a priest no longer in the Pentateuch. But it was at Jerusalem, not at Bethel, that Aaron was regarded as the father of the true Israelite priesthood (cf. Goulder, *Korah*, pp. 65-71). It may be that the Exodus 32 story is partly motivated by the Korahites' resentment of false Zadokite claims to an Aaronic ancestry (as I there suggested), and their hope of supplanting them (Num. 16); but Aaron is dealt with kindly in Exodus 32, and he does not perform the sacrifices. So perhaps he is lampooned simply as being the old Asaphite hero, who was in trouble anyhow for disloyalty to the covenant (Num. 20); but it is likely that his folly is the more enjoyed for the discomfort it may cause the Zadokites.

Van Seters is correct in seeing the 1 Kings 12 story as the fabrication of DH, and that the treatment of the Golden Calf is related to the burning and grinding to powder of the Bethel high place in 2 Kings 23; but he ignores the antiquity of the massacre story, and does not recognize the primacy of Ps. 81.11 for 'I, Yahweh, am thy God...', and he trivializes the evidence from Hosea of a bull-throne in Bethel. The Golden Calf story belongs comfortably in the 620–600 period.

For the antiquity of the Levi blessing in Deuteronomy 33, cf. Mayes, *Deuteronomy*, pp. 402-404: Mayes takes 33.8-11 to be a compound of three traditions, not inserted in their present setting before 721, but vv. 8-9a 'may be considerably older'. Wolff (*Hosea*, pp. 171, 175) prefers LXX singular *calf* to MT plural *calves* at 10.5; but there would be an obvious motive for emending to the singular— how should the Beth-aven shrine have several calf-idols, and what about 8.5-6?

Leaving the Mountain

The sad tale of national disloyalty never stood alone: Israel could never have prospered without Yahweh's forgiveness. So Psalm 78 continues: '...Neither were they faithful in his covenant. But he, being full of compassion (רחום), forgave *their* iniquity, and destroyed *them* not: Yea, many a time turned he his anger away, And did not stir up all his wrath' (78.37-38). We can already discern the outline of the Exodus 33–34 narrative, with a hint of Yahweh's self-revelation at 34.6.

The old Korahite psalm tradition knew something similar at Dan; there also some reconciliation was narrated between Moses and God. Psalm 85, an early Korahite psalm (Goulder, *Korah*, pp. 102-20), seems to open with an appeal to God's forgiveness after such a fall. Ps. 85.3, 'Thou didst forgive the iniquity (נשאת עון) of thy people, Thou didst cover all their sin', recalls Exod. 32.32, 'Yet now, if thou wilt forgive their sin (תשא הסאתם)', and 34.7, where God is merciful, 'forgiving iniquity (נשא עון) and transgression and sin.' Ps. 85.4, 'Thou didst turn (thyself) from the fierceness of thine anger (השיבות מחרון אפך)', echoes Moses' prayer, 'Turn from the fierceness of thine anger (שוב מחרון אפך).' Ps. 85.14, 'Righteousness shall go before him (לפניו יהלך)' envisages one of four angelic (*quondam* divine) figures preceding Yahweh's ephod in procession. Similarly, Moses was promised in Exod. 32.34, 'behold, my angel shall go before thee', in his advance to the Promised Land. We

may note besides Yahweh's description of himself as an אל plenteous in
חסד ואמת (Exod. 34.6), and compare Ps. 85.8, 'I will hear what the God
Yahweh (האל יהוה) says', and 85.11, 'חסד ואמת shall go before him'.

The seventh-century Korahites thus had the outlines of a scene of reconciliation before their march to the Land. At first it is thought suitable
for Yahweh to have a dignified sulk (Exod. 33.1-7): the people is to go
forward, but he himself will not go with them, *only* his angel, following
Ps. 85.14. They mourn and strip off their ornaments to show earnest
repentance. The contrast of Yahweh's feelings towards the people and
towards Moses is then emphasized in 33.7-11: Moses would go to the
tent of meeting outside the camp, and there God would speak to him
face to face, with the pillar of cloud publicly advertising his presence, to
the awestruck amazement of all the people. The Asaphite leader Joshua
is included in these moments of revelation, as Moses' deacon (משרתו נער,
33.11).

This enables a more satisfactory arrangement to be negotiated. Moses
intercedes cleverly, and Yahweh agrees that his presence will go with the
people (33.12-16); that is good news indeed, for it assures their ultimate
triumph. But something further is required, for the Korahites have displaced the old Asaphite Decalogue (Exod. 34.17-26) in favour of their
own code and Decalogue (Exod. 20–23). Moses therefore asks God to
show him his ways (33.13), and God responds with a revelation of his
glory (33.17–34.16). Moses is protected from death by being hidden in a
cleft of the rock, and sees only the back of the divine glory (although he
has been used to speaking with God face to face). God declares his name
and nature (as in Pss. 85 and 78), and gives the assurance of his forgiveness (34.6-9), followed by the standard Deuteronomic commission to
drive out the Canaanites and destroy their shrines (34.10-16). Then can
be appended the remainder of the old Asaph cultic table (shorn of its
opening commandment, already given in Exod. 20.2-3/34.14). It can be
said that the first Decalogue had been inscribed by God on two tablets
which Moses had broken at the apostasy scene (32.15-19): but now he
will re-inscribe them on two further tablets (34.1). The unwary reader
does not notice that the second Decalogue is not the same as the first.

I have commented above on the claim of Perlitt and others that Exodus 32–34 is a
single, consistent, seventh-century story. Most of the narrative does indeed stem
from seventh-century Korahite hands—only the massacre story is earlier: but the
cultic law table is old Asaphite material. Blum (*Pentateuch*, pp. 45-60) argues the
unity of Exodus 19–20, 24, 32–34, but presses the evidence. All Israel is a kingdom

of priests in 19.6, and a particular, limited priesthood is ordained at 32.29 following the apostasy: but this is not at all linked to the apostasy. The people contribute their golden ornaments to making the image in 32.3, and these ornaments were the spoil of the Egyptians from Yahweh's great deliverance; but no irony is apparent.

At this point our evidence from the psalms ends: there is more to take us through the books of Joshua, Judges and Samuel, but for the Pentateuch that is all we have, and it will be suitable to draw the account to a close. The Asaph and the Korah psalm collections come from the eighth century, and are the earliest forms we have of the Exodus–Numbers tradition. It has been possible to trace the development of these two independent sources in seventh-century Jerusalem; and to see their further elaboration by Merarite (priestly, Jerusalem) tradents during the Exile. The seventh-century northerners were heirs to a proto-Deuteronomic style which we find in Psalm 78 and other Asaph psalms; hence the widespread occurrence of D-type phrasing in their story-telling. That is the whole history of the development of the Pentateuch, insofar as we are given a lead-in from the Psalter. But the later biblical books preserve some personal details of the Asaphites, which we should not neglect: it would be nice if we could identify the great faceless ciphers of the nineteenth century, J, E, D, Dtr and P, with a few actual human beings.

Chapter 14

The Sons of Asaph

The first part of this book has been a study of the Psalms of Asaph; but
I have postponed any examination of such evidence as we have of the
Asaphites from elsewhere in the Bible, and such an examination is
instructive. We have ten apparent fragments of the Asaph family line,
which I set out schematically here:

(1) 2 Kgs.18.18, 37 = Isa. 36.3, 22. During the Assyrian siege of
Jerusalem in 701, Hezekiah sent three plenipotentiaries to treat with the
Rabshakeh, one of whom was 'Joah the son of Asaph the chronicler'
(יוֹאָה בֶן־אָסָף הַמַּזְכִּיר). If *son* is intended literally, that gives: Asaph–Joah

(2) 1 Chron. 6.1-15 [16-30] gives a list of 'the sons of Levi', of which
the first mentioned family is that of Gershom/n; Asaph is not mentioned
here, but in (3) below his ancestry is traced back to Gershom. The line
runs: Gershom–Libni–Jahath–Zimmah–Joah–Iddo–Zerah–Jeatherai. In
6.2 [17] the sons of Gershom are Libni and Shimei.

(3) 1 Chron. 6.18-33 [33-48] gives a list of the families of the three
musical guilds set up by David. In vv. 24-28 [39-43], in second place,
come the forebears of Asaph: Gershom–Jahath–Shimei–Zimmah–Ethan–
Adaiah–Zerah–Ethni–Malchijah–Baaseiah–Michael–Shimea–Berechiah–
Asaph.

(4) 1 Chron. 9.14-17 gives a further list of Levites. The Asaph family
is mentioned second, and consists of: Asaph–Zichri–Mica–Mattaniah.
With Mattaniah are mentioned Bakbakkar, Heresh and Galal.

(5) 1 Chronicles 15 describes David's setting up of worship. In v. 17
Asaph is appointed, as it turns out in ch. 16, to be in sole charge of
the music. His father is given as Berechiah–Asaph. Berechiah (*bless/
Yahweh*) might be a rather suitable name for the father of one whose
calling was to do that.

(6) 1 Chronicles 25 gives a list of musicians who 'prophesy' by order
of the king. Verse 2 lists 'of the sons of Asaph' Zaccur, Joseph,

Nethaniah, Asharelah. These may be intended as Asaph's four sons either directly or indirectly.

(7) 2 Chronicles 20 describes a defensive campaign fought by King Jehoshaphat. The battle is turned by the prophecy of an Asaphite called Jahaziel, whose ancestry is given in v. 14: Mattaniah–Jeiel–Benaiah–Zechariah–Jahaziel

(8) 2 Chronicles 29 gives an account of Hezekiah's reformation. Among the Levites who arise to effect it are in v. 12 Gershonites, Joah and Eden. Their fathers are: Zimmah–Joah, and Joah–Eden. Of the sons of Asaph there are Zechariah and Mattaniah.

(9) Nehemiah 11 gives lists of those in Jerusalem at the time of the events described. (i) In v. 17 the chief of those to begin the thanksgiving in prayer is Mattaniah, whose forebears are: Asaph–Zabdi–Mica–Mattaniah. Also mentioned is Bakbukiah, 'second among his brethren'. (ii) In v. 22 the overseer of the Levites is Uzzi, with an ancestry: Mica–Mattaniah–Hashabiah–Bani–Uzzi.

(10) Neh. 12.27-43 gives an account of the celebration conducted by Nehemiah after the building of the wall in 445. The account is in the first person, and (i) in v. 35 includes Zechariah as 'a son of Asaph'. His forebears are given: Zaccur–Micaiah–Mattaniah–Shemaiah–Jonathan–Zechariah. In addition are named Zechariah's 'brethren', Shemaiah, Azarel, Milalai, Gilalai, Maai, Nethanel, Judah, Hanani, 'with the musical instruments of David, the man of God'. (ii) Nehemiah then appoints overseers of the treasury, two of whom are Levites, Pedaiah and Hanan (13.13). Hanan's forebears are: Mattaniah–Zaccur–Hanan.

For all their apparent dryness, these names contain some interesting information. (i) For historical reliability, we may begin with (10). Nehemiah is writing the account himself, and if the passage is part of the 'Nehemiah Memoir', he will have known Zechariah personally. Even if it is an insertion (as is often thought), there is still a high probability that Zechariah was present at the occasion, as the supposed glossator can hardly be writing long afterwards. While Zechariah's family memories may have been defective, the Asaphites were a significant and proud part of Israelite life, and the list is likely to be accurate for five generations. We may think of Zechariah as roughly thirty, and of each generation as roughly twenty-five years. If so, we may ascribe possible dates for the *floruit* of each character: Zaccur (575), Micaiah (550), Mattaniah (525), Shemaiah (500), Jonathan (475), Zechariah (450).

It is generally agreed that the text as it stands is not as Nehemiah wrote it: it has been edited at 12.32-36 (the names), and the description of the processions is in part incoherent. But Williamson (*Ezra, Nehemiah*, pp. 370-72) takes the names to be broadly reliable, and reconstructs the procession from them. The dignity given to the Asaphites, and the absence of the Korahites, are indications that, even if the names are an editorial gloss, they come from soon after the event.

There is some limited encouragement to give credence to this list. First in (10b) Hanan's grandfather is also called Mattaniah, and this could be the same as Zechariah's great-grandfather Mattaniah. But Mattaniah also recurs in the Chroniclers' Asaph genealogies, and in similar sequences. In (4) we have (Asaph)–Zichri–Mica–Mattaniah; in (9a) we have (Asaph)–Zabdi–Mica–Mattaniah; in (9b) Mica–Mattaniah. The Chroniclers will not have made the names up: they are familiar sequences which have been deployed from earlier times. It is also encouraging that Nehemiah's forms are not quite identical: Zaccur (זכור) for Zichri (זכרי)/Zabdi (זבדי), Micaiah for Mica. His friend Zechariah was not just copying the Chroniclers' tradition. There is another Zaccur in (6), and another in (10b). In (9b) Mica–Mattaniah are fifth and fourth names up from Uzzi, a supposed contemporary of Nehemiah, just as Zechariah is in (10).

Twenty-five years is a standard estimate for a generation. Of the kings of Judah there were 17 generations, father and son, from David to Josiah, covering just under four centuries (c. 1000–609), and averaging 23 years apiece; but perhaps kings tended to marry a little younger than commoners.

(ii) We may give historical credit to the suggestion that Joah in (1) was a son of our Asaph (whether as his father or the eponym of his clan), a real person who acted for Hezekiah. The analysis of the Asaph psalms yielded the conclusion that they were the composition of one man around 725, traditionally called Asaph. This Joah b. Asaph is active around 700, a generation later, so he lives at a suitable time to be the psalmist's son. He bears the name Joah, which is several times given in the Chroniclers' genealogies of the Gershom line [(2) and (8) twice], Asaph being of the line of Gershom: so it is less likely that the Joah b. Asaph in 2 Kings 18 is a coincidence. Furthermore he is called the מזכיר, rendered by RV mg as 'the chronicler'. In times before the nation's history was written down, there was need of an authorized repository for these vital traditions. Northern tradents had come south after 722, and the tradents of the Exodus stories were the family of

Asaph from Bethel: in the psalms the Selah passages were recited by one there referred to as the מנצח, the 'Choirmaster'; but he would be better described for public purposes as 'the remembrancer', מזכיר. David had a story to have publicly recited, and he had a מזכיר, Jehoshaphat son of Ahilud (2 Sam. 20.24) to recite it; his task להזכיר is noted in the heading of Psalms 70–71 (Goulder, *Prayers*, pp. 232-33).

We may therefore make a probable inference. Hezekiah welcomed the northern refugees, and was impressed by their traditions, their laws and their psalms. A man of the standing of Joah was treated in the same way that refugee Protestant theologians were treated in England in the reign of Edward VI. As Martin Bucer became professor at Cambridge, so did Joah become Hezekiah's official chronicler, the authority on past history and the man responsible for adding current events to it. As in David's time, this was one of the senior posts in the kingdom, and it was given to a Bethel refugee. With his family's wider experience of relations with the Assyrians, and very likely a knowledge of Aramaic, he would be a suitable delegate to treat with the Rabshakeh.

We may draw one further likely conclusion about Joah. In (2) there is a Joah b. Zimmah, and in (8) one of the leaders of Hezekiah's reformation is also Joah b. Zimmah. Furthermore (3) is clearly an expanded and 'improved' version of (2): the first parts of the two lines run:

(2) Gershom–Libni–Jahath–Zimmah–Joah–Iddo–Zerah
(3) Gershom–Jahath–Shimei–Zimmah–Ethan–Adaiah–Zerah.

Libni has been dropped, as carrying the (historical) association with the town of Libnah. Shimei was *brother* of Libni in 1 Chron. 6.2 [17], and there are Shimeites still in Zech. 12.13. Adaiah (עדיה) is a more Yahwistic form of Iddo (עדו). So it looks as if Ethan has been inserted in place of Joah by a promoter of Ethan the leading musician of the Merarites (see below); and if so, Joah was the son of Zimmah in the *Vorlage* here also. With so regular a paternity, it seems probable that Joah's historical father was in fact called Zimmah, and 'the son of Asaph' in 2 Kings 18 will be a reference to his ancestry. So this Zimmah is a man of some importance. If his son rose to such distinction, he is likely, with Eastern conservatism, to have been a senior Asaphite himself. He will have been one of the guardians of the E tradition.

Kurt Möhlenbrink ('Levitische Überlieferungen', p. 213) followed by Wilhelm Rudolph (*Chronikbücher*, p. 296) takes the names to refer merely to the time of the Chroniclers, and to have nothing to do with Hezekiah; but in view of the evidence cited above, this seems unduly sceptical.

(iii) If we accept these inferences as reasonable, there remain probably four missing generations, those of 675, 650, 625 and 600. The name Joah occurs three times in the Chroniclers' genealogies, two of them in Hezekiah's reign, (8), where there is an Eden (עדן) b. Joah and a Joah b. Zimmah. The other is in (2), where we have the line Zimmah–Joah–Iddo (עדו)–Zerah–Jeatherai. It might be then that the Chroniclers knew of Joah's activities in the time of Hezekiah, perhaps from 2 Kings 18, and of the line which we have in (2), to which it is partly similar; and that historically Joah's descendants ran Eden/Iddo–Zerah–Jeatherai. (The difference in spelling between Eden and Iddo is the tail of the ן.) If this were so, and it is a speculation, we could fill in three of the four blanks: Eden/Iddo (675), Zerah (650), Jeatherai (625).

There is a little support for this in 2 Chronicles 12 and 13. 2 Chron. 12.15 refers to the 'acts of Rehoboam,...written in the words of Shemaiah the prophet and of Iddo the seer, in reckoning the genealogies'; similarly in 13.22 the rest of the acts of Abijah are said to be written in the commentary (מדרש) of the prophet Iddo. It appears therefore that one of the men who had had responsibility for the national historical tradition was one Iddo, and that he had overworked the standard annals in a מדרש. If this Iddo were the son of Joah the מזכיר, he would have been well placed to do this work. Being familiar with the fuller northern historical tradition, he might take in hand to expand the Judahite annals on a similar basis, beginning with Rehoboam and Abijah, the first two kings of the divided Southern Kingdom.

(iv) Iddo is spoken of above as both prophet and seer (חזה). The Asaphites prophesy a number of times in Chronicles (1 Chron. 25.1), and most dramatically in 2 Chron. 20.14-17, when Jahaziel (root חזה *to see*) turns the battle as the Spirit of the Lord comes upon him. He begins, 'Hearken...thus saith the LORD'. It has sometimes been thought rather a comedown for the great prophetic tradition to be invested in a choirman; but it is not always noticed that the prophetic movement finds voice already in our Asaph psalms, several of which are designated by Gunkel as prophetic liturgies. In Psalms 50, 81 and 82 (and perhaps 75), the Asaph psalmist thinks fit to put considerable speeches into the mouth of God; and Pss. 50.7 and 81.9 both begin, 'Hearken, O my people'. The Asaphites knew that they were heirs to a prophetic ministry from Bethel days.

The same goes for other features of the sons of Asaph's ministry in Chronicles. It puzzles Nasuti (*Tradition History*, pp. 174, 182-86) that the sons of Asaph so often give praise and thanksgiving (תודה), whereas most of the Asaph psalms are national laments. But the Chroniclers had not read Gunkel, and the opening Asaph psalm bids, 'Offer unto God thanksgiving (תודה)... And call upon me in the day of trouble; I will deliver thee, and thou shalt glorify me... Whoso offereth the sacrifice of thanksgiving (תודה) glorifieth me' (50.14-15, 23). So it is not so surprising if, when Jahaziel has said his piece, the king has the people sing and praise the LORD, with the words, 'Give thanks (הודו) unto the LORD; for his mercy endureth for ever' (2 Chron. 20.21). These words, so often used by the sons of Asaph in Chronicles, are not in fact from the Asaph psalms, but (nearly) from Ps. 136.1; but they are a brief expression of the old Asaphite insistence on thanksgiving as the centre of worship and the key to national deliverance. It was besides the Asaph tradition which first used a psalm to expound Israel's history (Ps. 78), and the later historical psalms, 105, 106, 135, 136 are likely to be the compositions of their descendants: only the old Bethel psalms are labelled *Psalm of Asaph*, but Chronicles tells us that the later singers were mainly Asaphites and Korahites.

Nasuti has a useful chapter (*Tradition History*, pp. 161-91) on the late-biblical evidence for the sons of Asaph, drawing attention to the evidence for a historical figure Joah, among others; but his conclusions and mine have only a limited concurrence.

(v) This brings us to the central issue, which is much less speculative. It is a familiar feature of the Chroniclers' work that the centre of the stage is commonly occupied by the Levites. In the opening genealogies twenty verses are given to the priests (1 Chron. 6.1-15, 49-53) and thirty-three to the Levites (6.16-48). The consecration of the Temple site is greatly expanded with substantially two chapters on the Levites, especially the Asaphites and their singing (chs. 15–16). When David provides staff for the Temple, ch. 24 is given to the priests, and chs. 25–26 to the Levites, singers (25) and doorkeepers (26). In the great reforms of Hezekiah (2 Chron. 29) and Josiah (2 Chron. 30), it is the Levites who arise and take the work in hand. I have spoken of the Levitical lead in the battle in 2 Chronicles 20, and there are many smaller instances.

Why has there been this marked change in the position of the Levites over against Samuel–Kings? The answer has seemed obvious: the authors of Chronicles were Levites. But it is remotely unlikely that

Levites, who were second-class hierarchs, would have been able to force their way in to take over from priests the position of official tradents to the community. Numbers 16 implies indeed that the sons of Korah did at one point try to usurp the priestly prerogatives, and met with disaster (if not perhaps, historically, quite in the form described). No: the position of tradents had belonged to them from the beginning. The northern priests (as they had been), the guardians of the national history traditions at Dan and (especially) Bethel, had brought their treasures to Jerusalem in the 720s, and Joah of the sons of Asaph had been Hezekiah's מזכיר. The sons of Asaph and the sons of Korah had retained this guardianship over the centuries, and had thought of themselves for many years as 'the priests the Levites', the proper Levitical priesthood as against the non-Levitical Zadokites. They had pressed for parity in Deuteronomy 18, but without success. By the fourth century they accepted that they would never offer incense or sacrifice at the altar; but the sacrifice of thanksgiving was their prerogative, and the recitation in worship of the great *Heilsgeschichte*. So the Levites could hold their heads high. Let others cover their hands with blood; they had a spiritual ministry, and they had raised up a *monumentum aere perennius.* They had indeed.

(vi) So the 'Levites' had charge of the traditions from David to Ezra: and what about the traditions from Adam to Saul? The whole Exodus–Numbers story, and much more, had been the responsibility of the Asaphites from Bethel, and there had been Moses and Settlement traditions in the hands of the Korahites from Dan. Were they obliged to surrender these treasures into the hands of Jerusalem priests? We might think not: Joah was Hezekiah's chronicler, and Iddo his son wrote the expansions on Rehoboam and Abijah; and it is not perhaps likely that such persevering clans would have been forced to yield up the early period while retaining authority over the later. On the other hand, as we have seen, the old primary E tradition has experienced two massive expansions, each of an on-going kind. There has been the Korahite ('J') expansion, with a parallel statement in Deuteronomy; and an enormous re-working by P.

A preliminary answer may be offered to this dilemma. We may seek for *prima facie* evidence of authorship in such a work as the Pentateuch from two features: first, as in Chronicles, from the genealogies; and second from the laws providing for income. For no editor who gives the descendants of his heroes will be likely to omit the fact of his own relationship to them; and he will be a spiritual minister indeed who forgets to provide for his own family's living.

The line of the house of Levi is set out in Exod. 6.16-25, preceded by a verse each on the houses of Reuben and Simeon. The 'orthodox' family tree may be set out as described:

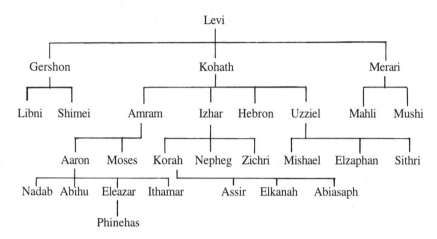

The picture is revealing. The family of central importance for the priesthood, and so for Israelite history with its later leadership by priests, is that of Aaron–Eleazar–Phinehas. But other famous families have been cut off: Moses' for example, or Ithamar's, which came to share the privileges of the line of Eleazar. There are, however, two families which achieve a surprising prominence. First, it turns out that the line of Aaron was not the senior Levitical line. That position was held by the descendants of Gershon, through Libni—or in other words, as we learn from 1 Chronicles 6, the Asaphites. They are not deprived of their position, as Nadab and Abihu are, for some sin: they just come from Levi's firstborn. But even more striking is the position of the Korahites. In the fifth generation only two families are set out, Aaron's sons and Korah's sons; Aaron is the eldest son of Amram, Kohath's first-born, and Korah is the eldest son of Izhar, Kohath's second-born. The Korahites arc in fact sometimes spoken of as alongside 'the Kohathites' (2 Chron. 20.19). We are left with the impression that in the eyes of the present writer the Korahites were pretty important people, nearly on a par with the high priests; and that in the eyes of an earlier writer the Asaphites were pretty important people, in some ways senior to the high priests. Either way, what we have is a couple of signatures on the corner of the canvas.

The same impression is given by the arrangements made in the

Pentateuch for paying the Temple staff. In Deut. 18.1-8 the priests are to have no portion nor inheritance, but are to live off the people's sacrifices; and these are to be shared 'if a Levite come from any of thy gates out of all Israel where he sojourneth' (v. 6). This was intended to enable the northern clergy, now without income, to be provided for; but in time it was understood to mean that priests and Levites share the offerings. What was more important in practice was the tithe, in effect a 10 per cent income tax on every Israelite, rich and poor. According to Lev. 27.32, 'the tenth shall be holy to the LORD': that is, it goes into the Temple treasury, but who gets it then? Num. 18.21 specifies, 'And unto the children of Levi behold I have given all the tithe in Israel for an inheritance, in return for their service which they serve'. So the Levites, 'the children of Levi', got it; and in New Testament times the Levites took the tithes, and gave a tithe of the tithe to the priests. So everyone was fairly treated, were they not?

For the practice of tithing in New Testament times, see E.P. Sanders, *Judaism*, pp. 146-69.

This happy division of the Gross National Product was already in force in the fifth century: Nehemiah's community vow included paying 'the tithes of our ground unto the Levites; for they, the Levites, take the tithes in all the cities of our tillage...and the Levites shall bring up the tithe of the tithes unto the house of our God, to the chambers, into the treasure house' (Neh. 10.37-38). Nehemiah had to enforce the rule, for he found Eliashib the priest embezzling the Levites' money (13.4-14). One does not need a PhD to divine who had a hand in laying down this division of the spoils. The historical and legal traditions were in the hands of Levites, and they legislated themselves a generous provision, 9 per cent of the national income.

A third possible criterion may be the relative numbers of the tribes given in Numbers 2 and 26; for, given that the figures are fictitious, it is likely that the tradent will have aggrandized his own tribe. Judah inevitably has the largest contingents, 74,600 leaving Egypt, 76,500 forty years later. The surprise is that the second largest tribe, in both chapters, is Dan, with 62,700 and 64,500. This calls for an explanation: perhaps the tradents were in part Korahite Levites, ultimately from Dan. I am grateful to Dr Errol Davies for drawing my attention to the figures.

(vii) And so to a final and decisive question: if the tradents were Levites, which Levites? As we have just seen, there were three clans of

Levites, claiming descent from Gershon, Kohath and Merari. We do not hear so much about Merari; but Chronicles (and Exod. 6) leave us with a puzzling impression over the other two lines, the sons of Asaph from Gershon(m) and of Korah from Kohath.

In many ways the Asaphites seem to be primary. They are the senior line: Gershon(m) was the eldest son of Levi. In 1 Chronicles 6 the Gershom line is set out first. In 1 Chronicles 9 there are no Korahites specifically mentioned: only the clans of Merari, Asaph, Jeduthun and Elkanah (who may be a Korahite). In 1 Chronicles 16 only the Asaphites are appointed to minister before the ark in Jerusalem; Heman and Ethan/Jeduthun, of the clans of Korah and Merari, are sent back to Gibeon (16.39-42), while the Asaphites sing a 28-verse psalmody. In 1 Chronicles 25 David appoints musicians, and the Asaphites are taken first (24.1-2). In 1 Chronicles 26 they miss out as doorkeepers in the Temple, but get first place in the important oversight of the Temple treasury (26.20-22). In 2 Chron. 5.12 they are first among the musicians at the dedication of Solomon's Temple. In 2 Chron. 20.14-17 it is Jahaziel the Asaphite whose prophecy wins the battle. The reader's first impression is that Asaph was the senior and most important Levite clan.

A closer attention to the minutiae shows, however, that this is not the end of the story. In 1 Chron. 6.1-15[16-30] the Korahites come second, but there are 20 of them to 15 Asaphites and eight Merarites. However, in a second account, 6.18-33[33-48] the Korahites come first, with 22 generations from Levi to Heman; while his brother Asaph stands on his right, with 15 generations to Levi, and their brethren the Merarites on his left, with 14 generations to Levi. Heman the Korahite comes first among the singers in 1 Chron. 15.19, even if he is left in Gibeon in ch. 16. Asaph may come first among the musicians in ch. 25, but only four of his sons play, and only six Merarites, against fourteen Korahites. In ch. 26 the Korahites lead the doorkeepers, and they keep the prestigious east gate, and the north gate, with ten staff in all out of eighteen. Even in 2 Chronicles 20, when the Asaphite Jahaziel has prophesied, it is the Kohathites and the Korahites who lead the response (20.19); and in 29.12 it is the Kohathites (= Korahites) who arise to put Hezekiah's reforms into action. For further detail of the in-fighting I refer the reader to my account in *The Psalms of the Sons of Korah*, pp. 77-84.

Although the Merarites come a poor third, they are not nowhere in the great game. They came first in the table in 1 Chron. 9.14; and they have managed to insinuate their champion Ethan into the place of Joah in the Asaphite genealogy in 1 Chron. 6.27[42]. So how are we to explain these somewhat erratic phenomena?

The normal explanation is in terms of redactions. Chronicles passed through a series of editions; and either one may say that 'the Chronicler' was an Asaphite whose work was later edited by a Korahite, or one may call 'him' a Korahite who has taken over Asaphite traditions. I have no quarrel with this general solution, but should only wish to clarify and expand it: for it surely does require an explanation of how one clan has managed to take over the traditions of another, and to insert a series of tendentious distortions in its own favour, even for those who think that the work was a scroll kept in a Temple safe and taken out for editing every twenty-five years.

Hartmut Gese's essay, 'Zur Geschichte der Kultsänger am zweiten Tempel' (1963), distinguishes three phases in the development of the Temple choir: (i) The Asaphites alone returned from the Exile before 515 (Ezra 2.41), and were the only singers, being neither Levites nor doorkeepers. They were descended from pre-exilic cultic prophets (cf. 1 Chron. 25.1-2; 2 Chron. 29.30). (ii) By 440 the singers *are* Levites (Neh. 11.15-18), who are distinguished from the priests and doorkeepers (11.3-19). A Jeduthun group has joined them, but the Asaphite Mattaniah is the leader. (iii) By the Chronicler's time (c. 330) there are three guilds, Asaph, Heman and Jeduthun, of which Heman becomes the most important in later redactions (1 Chron. 6, 25, etc.).

Gese accepts a little uncritically the late-biblical evidence: he is right in thinking that the Asaphites formed the fifth-century Temple choir, and that they had a position in the pre-exilic Temple; but this may be because there were Asaphites in the villages round Jerusalem (Neh. 12.28-29) who had never been away. An important part of the Korahite position was that the Asaphites were *merely* singers; hence their willingness to see Asaphites as David's sole choir in 1 Chron. 15–16. Gese gives no account of how the Heman (Korahite) and Jeduthun (Merarite) guilds came to infiltrate the long Asaphite monopoly; and he assumes that what was 'sung' was only psalms.

Our only reliable historical source for the period is the first-person section of the book of Nehemiah. In his description of the thanksgiving procession, Nehemiah gives the names of certain notables and priests, and of Zechariah the Asaphite (with his ancestry, given in (10) above), with six of 'his brethren' who are named (12.32-36); and there are further names of priests, and perhaps others, in the other half of the procession in 12.41-42. There is no reference to any Levite from the Korah or Merari clans. In 13.13 Nehemiah appoints two Levites to share in overseeing the Temple treasury; one of them is Hanan b. Zaccur b. Mattaniah; and we have seen that both Zaccur and Mattaniah are recurrent Asaphite names. Since Nehemiah goes to some trouble to specify his Levitical supporters, and gives ancestries for them alone, it is not an argument from silence to say that it is probable that in 445 the only Levites in Jerusalem were Asaphites. Nehemiah did not bring them with him: 'he sought them out of all their places, to bring them to Jerusalem to keep the dedication' (12.27). He carefully provides for them, and it is added 'For in the days of David *and Asaph* of old there was a chief of singers...' (12.46).

Nehemiah has cause to enforce certain biblical rulings—on usury and sabbath—which are common to our various traditions; but two laws are involved which are specific to Deuteronomy. One of these is the forbidding of intermarriage with Gentiles (Neh. 13.23-29): the interdict is in Deut. 7.3, and reference is made (Neh. 13.26) to Solomon's failure in this respect, described in Dtr 1 Kgs 11.1-3. The other law is cited: 'On that day they read in the book of Moses in the audience of the people; and therein was found written that an Ammonite and a Moabite should not enter into the assembly of God for ever...' (13.1-2). The text is at Deut. 23.3-5, almost verbatim; and furthermore the requirement to read the law 'in the audience of the people' at the autumn festival is also Deuteronomic, being specified for every seventh year in Deut. 31.10-12. So the tradition recited in Jerusalem in 445, and most probably cantillated by the Asaphites, included parts at least of the D-tradition.

Almost all critics attribute Neh. 13.1-3 to an editor: there is no 'I'; 'the people' take the required action; 'on that day' is suspiciously like the same phrase at 12.43, 44; Nehemiah's action against Tobiah is twelve years later according to 13.6. But Mowinckel (*Ezra–Nehemia*, II, pp. 35-37) followed by U. Kellermann (*Nehemia*, pp. 48-51) have suggested that 13.6 is a gloss, and that Nehemiah never had a second governorship. In any case, if 13.1-3 are a gloss, they are likely to be a nearly contemporary one (Williamson, *Ezra–Nehemiah*, pp. 380-81).

We find further extensive traces of Deuteronomy in Nehemiah's prayer in Neh. 1.5-11: 'I beseech thee, O *LORD, the great and terrible God* (Deut. 7.21), *that keeps covenant and mercy with them that love him and keep his commandments*... We *have dealt* very *corruptly* against thee (Deut. 4.25), and *have not kept the commandments nor the statutes nor the judgments which thou commandedst* thy servant Moses (Deut. 28.15). Remember the word that thou commandedst thy servant Moses saying, If ye trespass, *I will scatter you abroad among the peoples* (Deut. 4.27; 28.64); but *if ye return unto* me, *and keep my commandments and do them, though your* outcasts *were in the utter-most part of the* world, *yet will I gather them from thence and will bring them* (Deut. 4.29-31; 30.2-4) *unto the place that I have chosen to cause my name to dwell there* (Deut. 12.5). Now these are they servants and *thy people, whom thou hast redeemed by thy great power and by thy strong hand'* (Deut. 9.29). At 4.8[14] Nehemiah similarly addresses the nobles in D-phrasing: *'Be not ye afraid of them:* remember the Lord, *which is great and terrible'* (Deut. 7.21). Either Nehemiah himself was soaked in Deuteronomic language from his youth (which is quite likely), or the prayer was written for him by an Asaphic Levite who was.

For Ezra we are not so fortunate, but it is not so important. Hugh Williamson (*Ezra–Nehemiah*) thinks that there was a first-person Ezra memoir consisting of Ezra 7–8, Nehemiah 8, Ezra 9–10; and if so we have contemporary evidence from 397 or soon after, on the normal dating. Other commentators have been more sceptical; but even if they are right, we can still tell the interests and background of the author from the content. The affinities here are with the P-tradition.

The more sceptical view of Ezra taken by Rudolph seems to me more persuasive. Not only does the whole Ezra narrative sound artificial, with its fulsome decree from the king, huge weights of precious metal, grovelling confession, and so forth; but the story parallels the Nehemiah story, step by first-person step—Ezra's initiative, King Artaxerxes' support with royal bounty, the trouble-free journey, the successful mission (the establishment of the Torah by Ezra, of the wall by Nehemiah), the confession, the autumn festival, the mixed marriages. The date is part of the artificiality: 'the seventh year of Artaxerxes the king' was intended to push Ezra before Nehemiah 'in the twentieth year of Artaxerxes the king' (Neh. 2.1), and so give him priority. In fact we have no idea of Ezra's date, only that he is later than Nehemiah.

In Ezra 7.17 Ezra, descended from a long line of priests, orders the purchase of 'bullocks, rams, lambs with their meal offerings and drink offerings' for sacrifice in Jerusalem, a good way away, as is specified in Num. 15.4-13; and these animals are duly sacrificed in large numbers at 8.35. In 8.24-30 he separates twelve senior priests and weighs to them the gold and silver of the offering, with the gold and silver vessels; like the offering made by the people in Exodus 35, and the vessels of pure gold for the Temple specified in Exod. 25.23-40, and made by Bezalel in Exodus 37. Ezra says to the priests, 'Ye are holy unto the LORD, and the vessels are holy', as in Lev. 21.6, 22.2-3. In Nehemiah 8 he arrives in Jerusalem: the people gather as one man, and ask him 'to bring the book of the law of Moses, which the LORD had commanded to Israel' (8.1); Ezra has already been described twice as 'a scribe in the law of Moses/the God of heaven' (7.6, 21). This book clearly contains material new to the people, for they had not followed such specifications 'since the days of Jeshua the son of Nun' (8.17). The matters which are stressed as new are the observation of 1st Tishri as a feast (8.2-12); the cutting of olive, myrtle and palm branches for the celebration of Tabernacles 'as it is written' (8.15-16); and the observation of an extra, eighth day of the feast as עצרת, cessation day, 'according to the ordinance' (8.18). None of these prescriptions is given in Deuteronomy: they are 'written' in Lev. 23.24 and 23.39-42. Moreover the statement that the people had not dwelt in booths since the days of 'Jeshua' implies that they had so dwelt in the desert; in fact the Israelites had lived in *tents* in the desert, where there are not many trees, and the fiction of 'booths' made of branches in the desert is first found in Lev. 23.43.

All the points raised are in the priestly tradition of our Pentateuch, the last two in the so-called Holiness Code, and it is here that the centre of gravity lies. But Ezra 9–10 describes the notorious compulsory divorce policy arising from the princes' report that the people have not separated themselves, but act 'according to the abominations of the Canaanites, the Hittites, the Perizzites, the Jebusites, the Ammonites, the Moabites, the Egyptians, and the Amorites. For they have taken of their daughters for themselves and for their sons' (9.1-2). The ruling, and the list of Gentile peoples, are a powerful echo of Deut. 7.1-2, and it must be regarded as secure that the Ezra community's book of the law of Moses contained D- as well as P-material. The only, and significant, difference is that the interdict on intermarriage is clearly familiar but ignored, as against the calendrical laws in Nehemiah 8 which are unfamiliar and new.

Ezra, like Nehemiah, is much helped by Levites. Being at first accompanied by priests only, he sends by name for eleven Levites (Eliezer, Ariel, Shemaiah...) who in turn enlist a number of named Merarites (Sherebiah, Hashabiah, Jeshaiah), the first two of whom assist with the Temple vessels (Ezra 8.15-19, 24). In Neh. 8.4 he is supported by numerous named worthies (Mattithiah, Shema, Anaiah...), none of whom has the same name as those mentioned in Ezra 8; and a further group (Jeshua, Bani, Sherebiah...) 'and the Levites' expound the reading to the people (8.7-8). Sherebiah was the name of the Merarite (Mahlite) in Ezra 8.18, 24, and Jeshua could be the same as the Merarite Jeshaia, though 'and the Levites' might lead us to think that they were *not* Levites.

What is to be made of this apparent confusion? It seems best to think that the writer distinguishes 'the Levites' from 'the sons of Mahli the son of Levi' and 'the sons of Merari', who join 'the Levites' in Ezra 8.18-19; we then can make the same distinction at Neh. 8.7-8, taking Jeshua and Sherebiah to be the same as Jeshaiah and Sherebiah in Ezra 8.18-19, that is, Mahlites and Merarites being different from 'and the Levites' in the following phrase. Sherebiah is distinguished in Ezra 8.18 as 'a man of intelligence' (אִישׁ שֵׂכֶל), and in Neh. 8.8 he and the others cause the people to understand the law of God. In other words the Merarites are no longer 'proper' Levites, but just sons of Levi, in the same way that the northern priests began as 'the priests the Levites' and ended up as no longer proper priests, just Levites.

Furthermore, something similar seems to have happened over 'the singers'. In 1 Chronicles 16 the singing at the induction of the ark was done by the sons of Asaph alone; and at 2 Chron. 35.14-15 the Levites prepare the offerings, while 'the singers the sons of Asaph were in their place'. At 2 Chron. 29.12-13 the sons of Asaph are also distinguished from the sons of Gershon, their ancestors in 1 Chronicles 6 [(3) above]. Similarly, in Neh. 7.43-44 (= Ezra 2.40-41) the returning Israelites include 'The Levites: the children of Jeshua, of Kadmiel, of the children of Hodevah, 74. The singers: the children of Asaph, 148'. There are twice as many Asaphites as 'Levites', but the two classes are plainly distinct. (The writer here is, by common consent, different from the author of Ezra 7–10, and the Jeshua is not thought of as a Merarite). Among the errant marriers of foreign wives, again, there are six Levites, distinguished from Eliashib the singer (Ezra 10.23-24).

What is happening is an attempted takeover. In earlier times there had been three Levite clans, Asaph, Korah and Merari. The main body returning with Ezra were Korahites. They thought they were the only real Levites, and they describe themselves unashamedly as 'the Levites'. They had been supported by a small number of able 'sons of Mahli/Merari', from whom they distinguished themselves. The Asaphite Levites who had been so important to Nehemiah had lived in the villages round Jerusalem, and did not know the P-regulations; so they are demoted to being merely singers. It is not they who cluster round the podium expounding Ezra's reading of Leviticus 23; they had never heard of it, and are not numbered with the Merarites 'and the Levites'. They were just choirmen, very nice in their cassocks and surplices, singing their seventh-century anthems.

Now the reader will hardly have failed to notice an impressive three-way parallel. First, the earlier form of Chronicles gives pride of place to the sons of Asaph, but the redactions have been made in favour of the sons of Korah, with a corner for the sons of Merari. Secondly, the earlier 'return', that of Nehemiah in 445, was supported by Levites of the line of Asaph, and the Pentateuchal traditions of this community, both in the laws and in the devotional language, are exclusively Deuteronomic. The later return, that of Ezra commonly dated to 397, was supported by Levites of the clan of Korah, with help from Merarites; and their Pentateuchal traditions were not only Deuteronomic but markedly priestly. And thirdly, we found that the structure of the Pentateuchal narrative was basically that of E–D, edited in favour of Moses by 'J'; but finally much expanded and amended by P.

This suggests a central solution to the problem of the growth of the Pentateuch, which I will set out in a final chapter.

Chapter 15

CONCLUDING UNHISTORICAL POSTSCRIPT

In his admirably lucid outline, *The Pentateuch*, Joseph Blenkinsopp
counsels the wisdom of approaching his subject from the end, not the
beginning: J is lost in the mist, E is probably a fiction; what we have is
the clear final hand of P, and before it the massive work of D, which
seems even to have incorporated J. I have no doubt that the positive
statements about the last two schools are correct, but I intend nevertheless to ignore Blenkinsopp's advice. For, as I have argued in this book
and in *The Psalms of the Sons of Korah*, I think we have access to two
eighth-century northern sources, the Psalms of Korah and Asaph, and
with these it should be possible to present a better-grounded and more
satisfying account of the development of the Pentateuch. Furthermore,
the alignment of Asaph and Korah with D, and of Merari and Korah
with P, as was suggested in the last chapter, enables us to see the growth
of the tradition in much more realistic terms. We are in a position to
trace in outline the growth of the Pentateuch from eighth-century documents which we possess, and to watch the in-fighting between three
biblical clans whose affiliations we know.

History as we experience it is the product of the actions of defined
groups of people with named leaders and motives and intentions, with
threats and problems and interrelationships. We cannot hope to know
the Israelite communities of the pre-Christian centuries as we know the
movements of Victorian Britain: but even if many of the statements I
shall make are merely probable, and the account in places is more a
scenario than a sober history, we may hope to see events with a sharper
definition if they are described in terms of real people, rather than
the enormous standard ciphers looming out of the fog. Following
Kierkegaard, I have conceded that this chapter is unhistorical in that it
goes beyond what a professional historian would require in evidence.
But here, as often, I have taken Karl Popper as my guide. I cannot

guarantee the accuracy of the account I give; but I can offer a hypothesis that is clear, consistent and detailed, and this has the advantage of being more easily falsified, and so improved. There are not many accounts of the Pentateuch which propose the names of the authors of J, E, D and P.

The Asaphite Exodus–Kings

In the eighth century the principal religious centre of Israel was Dan. The people of God was spoken of there as Jacob, and the priesthood was descended from Jonathan b. Gershom b. Moses; the traditions which are clearly echoed in the Korah psalms from Dan are confined to parts of Joshua 24 (Ps. 44.2-9) and Exodus 32–33 (Ps. 85.2-9); and perhaps Genesis 28 (Ps. 46.11-12). The Danite priests gave not an inch to the Joseph tradents from central Palestine. They never call the people Israel, and they never refer to the Exodus. They had presided over the festival of a considerable empire for a quarter of a millennium, and they were not interested in parvenus.

Time puts down the mighty from their seat, and exalts briefly the slightly more humble. The Assyrian victory of 732 meant the cession of the city of God in the uttermost parts of the north, and the flight of its clergy to Bethel. For Bethel had been a holy place through the years for the central tribes; there God had been the shepherd of Israel leading Joseph like a flock; the temple there had been a royal house, and a kind of reserve national shrine when briefly Dan had been lost before. The coming of the Danite clergy as refugees meant the first impetus towards a national *Heilsgeschichte*, the fusion of two of the main tribal traditions.

There had been at Bethel, as there had not been at Dan, a continuous historical tradition, known to us through the Asaph psalms. It had started with the oppression in Egypt, and had run through, so far as our evidence goes, to the empire of Solomon; no doubt it continued thereafter in annals and legends. But what we also find in these psalms is a first attempt to meld the Bethel and Dan traditions together:

Thou hast... redeemed thy people,
the sons of Jacob and Joseph...
Thou leddest thy people like a flock
By the hand *of Moses and* Aaron (Ps. 77.16, 21).

The Asaphites are pleased to incorporate the traditions of the prestigious national priesthood into their own tribal saga, and the Korahites in their hour of need are driven to condescend. So the great concatenation begins: Jacob as well as Joseph was involved in the Exodus, and Moses, once a leader on the Midianite steppe, joins Aaron in the desert at Kadesh.

This first fusion of the Bethel–Dan traditions corresponds in part to the traditional E. It was put together at Bethel; it was the work of the 720s; it referred to God normally as אלהים, though also as יהוה, and also as אל, as had been done in both communities. It differed from the nineteenth-century E in having no Genesis: the story began in Egypt, from our Exodus 1. It was essentially the Bethel narrative, since it was formed at Bethel, and the Bethel story was much the richer. Its creators were the authors of the 'Psalms of Asaph'. Asaph was not the name of a man, but a fiction to make the psalms of Joseph more acceptable in Jerusalem. The name which the Chroniclers remembered as belonging to the time of King Hoshea was Zimmah (זמה, 2 Chron. 29.12); he is quite likely to have been the מנצח, the senior Asaphite who chanted the Selah passages in the psalms, and thus controlled any variations introduced into the tradition. The substance of the actual E is set out above in Chapter 8; but it differed from Wellhausen's E also in being not a written document, but a viscous tradition, varying a little in its recital at worship.

The Bethel priests did not have their way for long. Samaria fell in 722, and those in positions of authority who escaped deportation largely made their way to Jerusalem. Hezekiah welcomed the northerners, with their ancient priesthoods, their national prestige, their rich narrative and psalm traditions and sophisticated legal system. Joah the son of Zimmah he made his official chronicler (מזכיר, 2 Kgs 18.18, 37; 2 Chron. 29.12); and so the Exodus story began to belong to the southerners too. A national myth helped to reinforce the aspiration to a united nation, and Judah became a part of Israel. The Asaphite psalms were adapted for use in the new religious context. 'In Joseph is God known: His name is great in Israel' became 'In Judah...'; 'At Salem also is his covert: And his lair in Gerizim' became '...in Zion', Salem being assimilated with Jerusalem (Ps. 76.2-3).

Relations with the long-installed Jerusalem tradents need not have been difficult. They had the great saga of David to tell, and the annals of the southern kings; and there was no problem in incorporating these into the northern framework. This combination may be the work referred to by the Chroniclers as 'the words of Shemaiah the prophet and Iddo the seer in reckoning the genealogies' (להתיחש, 2 Chron. 12.15); and later as 'the commentary of the prophet Iddo' (מדרש, 13.22). Iddo was the son of Joah, and an Asaphite (2 Chron. 29.12). But the phrasing is sinister. A prophet, נביא, is a class higher than a seer, חזה; and Iddo rates as a prophet in 13.22. We must suspect the work of the ubiquitous Korahite final hand: the *midrash* had been the labour of a Korahite, Shemaiah, as well as the Asaphite Iddo (not necessarily in the same generation), and the former is being awarded pride of class as well as pride of place.

The Asaphite Genesis

The association of these men in producing our Samuel–Kings is not our present concern; but they and their colleagues, and those of the following generation, had two even more significant tasks, the prefacing to 'E' of the Jacob and other patriarchal narratives, and the adaptation of the old northern law codes. The first of these was achieved without much tension between the two guilds, but the second did arouse trouble, and ultimately the worsting of the sons of Asaph. The two projects went on side by side, and it will be convenient to take the composing of Genesis first.

There were loose traditions about Jacob going back before Hosea's time, but his relation to his family's settlement in Egypt had been left extremely vague. The Asaphites accordingly set about producing a coherent proem to their Exodus–wilderness–covenant corpus. If it has been right to trust the Asaph family's genealogy (1 Chron. 6.5-6 [20-21]), their representatives were Joah and Iddo, and since we have two clearly different hands at work, we may for simplicity attribute the Jacob and Abraham sagas in their original, Yahwist form to Joah, and the Joseph (Elohist) saga, with the Elohist expansions of Genesis 20–22, to Iddo. It might be that Iddo's son Zerah was the great Elohist rather than his father, but the work must have been done before the rise of Egyptian militancy at the end of the century.

Four traditions about Jacob went back to the previous century: (i) 'Jacob took his brother by the heel' (Hos. 12.3); (ii) 'Jacob fled into the field of Aram, and Israel served for a wife, and for a wife he kept [sheep]' (12.12); (iii) 'in his manhood he had strength with God; he had power over the angel and prevailed; he wept and made supplication unto him' (12.3-4); (iv) 'he found him at Bethel, and there he spake with us' (12.4). I have already suggested in Chapter 9 how the flesh was put on

these bones: there was no tension between the two communities—Jacob
was the eponym of the one, and Bethel and Shechem the sanctuaries of
the other, with the Transjordan centres of Mahanaim and Succoth.

With Joseph it was another matter. There was no tradition of how the
Joseph communities had come to be in Egypt, so Iddo and his colleagues had *carte blanche*. The tale which they have put together is a
possession for ever, combining so many of the most popular folklore
traits—the younger son survives his elders' plots, surmounts all
difficulties, rises from prison to premiership, and delivers his family.
Joseph has every virtue in his author's index: he is blessed by God with
prevenient grace, he is best-beloved of his father, he is candid, able, sex-
ually virtuous, courageous, the master of affairs, just, magnanimous and
warm-hearted. It did not worry Iddo that he was an intolerable prig. So
Joseph and Benjamin, the Asaphites' patriarchs, emerge as the heroes of
the story; and for his services Joseph is awarded an extra tribal place, as
his two sons, Ephraim and Manasseh, receive their grandfather's blessing. Throughout the story Egypt is treated with a respect remote from
the animosities of the Exodus narrative: it is complete well before
Pharaoh Neco.

It might seem that the Asaphite מזכיר would provoke jealousy from
his Korahite allies with so one-sided a tale. But then Jacob comes well
out of the story too. He is a soft-hearted old man who sees from the
start the transcendent virtues of his late-born son; he grieves his reported
death, lets his youngest, Benjamin, go to Egypt with the greatest reluctance; is much honoured by Joseph when the time comes, and is a figure
of dignity. The sons of Korah must have been well contented with the
tale. If the other sons do not cut much of a heroic figure, at least
Reuben, the eldest, intended well, and was foiled by a greater
providence.

Abraham was a third addition in a national history expanding backwards; but it is likely that one step followed closely upon another. The
character of the Yahwist Abraham closely mirrors that of Jacob, as do
many of his adventures—his visits to Shechem and Bethel, his deceitful-
ness, the barrenness of his (favoured) wife, the promises of progeny and
of the land—and we may think of Joah at work here also. At least it is
still an Asaphite telling the tale, as the stress on Shechem and Bethel
shows; for Abraham belonged in the Negev. Abraham's sojourn in
Egypt, with the famine, the plagues and the spoiling of Pharaoh, are
based on the Asaphite Exodus story; Hagarites and Ishmaelites were

among the enemies listed in the Asaphite Psalm 83; the themes of testing, and of trust in God, and of the power of prophetic intercession, are present in Isaiah and Jeremiah. We might then think that the great אלהים stories in Genesis 20–22 should be credited to his son Iddo, or whoever was the author of the Elohist Joseph saga: it is the same reflective mind which will not name God יהוה until his identity is revealed at Meribah, the same ability to draw a character of religious power and human magnanimity, the same narrative genius.

The Asaphite Deuteronomy

With the laws, there was more need for collaboration, for the Asaphites had only a calendrical table to contribute, and the elements of the nation's canon of law had been held at Dan. Nonetheless, here too the Asaphite מזכיר was in a position to pull rank. His first commandment (Ps. 81.11) was expounded in practical provisions in Deuteronomy 12–13; his calendar (Exod. 34.18-26), with proper stress on the Josephite Passover, in Deut. 15.1–16.17. Only then were the Korahites permitted to add, and extend, their old Exodus 21–23 laws (Deut. 19–26). Appeal is constantly made to the Josephite experience of the Egyptian oppression; and it may well be that the kindlier spirit of Deuteronomy 12–26 owes something to the fact that the legislators were refugees who had lost their homes, and were in consequence more sensitive to the pain of poverty. The Asaphites were also able to enclose their idealistic law system in an envelope of requirements that it should be promulgated at their old sanctuary between 'Mt Ebal' and 'Mt Gerizim' in the Arabah over against Gilgal—that is Bethel (Deut. 11.29-30; 27.1-26). They set the scene as Moses' deathbed testament, his final word from heaven, which cannot therefore be transcended.

If Mayes's analysis of Deuteronomy is accepted, the first edition consisted of the bulk of Deuteronomy 12–25, with a brief homiletic preface: this latter covered the behaviour appropriate on entering the Land, both in worshipping the redeemer from Egypt, and in extirpating, or at least not marrying into, the local peoples. There was stress on the rebellions in the desert, but no mention of Horeb, or of Moses, apart from the setting. Mayes's Deuteronomy-I therefore comfortably fits the Asaphic tradition, with its Yahweh-only theology (Ps. 81.11) and its catalogue of rebellions (Ps. 78) and its *Vergeltungsdogma*. There is no more of Moses than was already ceded in Ps. 77.21. The repeated 'Hear, O Israel...' (Deut. 6.4;

9.1) echoes Ps. 50.8, 81.9, 'Hear, O my people...' The requirement to instruct the children in the tradition (6.7, 20) is the burden of Ps. 78.1-8. So Deuteronomy-I was the creation of Zerah and Jeatherai, the last two Asaphite leaders of the first line, in the years running up to 622.

Mayes (*Deuteronomy*, p. 48) identifies 'the original book of Deuteronomy' as including the following: 4.45; 6.4-9, 20-24; 7.1-3, 6, 17-24; 8.7-11a, 12-14, 17-18a; 9.1-7a, 13-14, 26-29; 10.10-11; 12.13-15, 17-19, (20-28), 29-31; parts of 13.1-18; 14.2-3, 21; and nearly all of 14.22–25.16. I have added the Shechem/Bethel passages in chs. 11 and 27, which can only make sense with an Asaphite tradent in charge. Mayes's analysis owes something to the treaty theory of the form of Deuteronomy, and some curses at the end would be no harm.

The Korahite Revolution

But now the Korahites were gaining influence, and by an alliance with the Jerusalem priesthood, were beginning to outflank their northern colleagues. Three times in the year, in the old codes, all Israel was to see God's face (Exod. 23.17; 34.23); and to them that was understood to mean three national pilgrimages to Dan, where alone God resided in his sacred city. It had been difficult to control Baal worship in the multifarious shrines deplored by Hosea; nor could the Jerusalem priesthood prevent the worship of strange gods in the village high places around Judah. The Korahites proposed therefore that the first commandment be made enforceable by insisting on worship at the central sanctuary only; it may be that by amplifying Deuteronomy 12 they increased the stress on centralized worship (Deut. 12.1-7); and such a policy commended itself warmly to Shaphan the secretary and Hilkiah the high priest, officers under Josiah in the 620s.

So the Asaphite leaders concurred, little thinking that soon their own Bethel sanctuary would be recovered to Judah, and would fall under their ban. In the 620s the pressure of the Assyrian thumb was relaxed on Judah's windpipe, and Shaphan and Hilkiah determined upon a change of stance: independence in foreign policy, and the national religion, Yahwism, at home. So the northerners' book of the law was 'discovered' in the Temple, and the Deuteronomic revolution began. It was unfortunate for Jeatherai that the independent foreign policy had meant the recovery of Bethel, and he will have had the paradoxical satisfaction of having authorized the desecration and destruction of his family's sanctuary; for the crowning symbol of Josiah's new stance was the annihilation of Bethel. But an equally serious corollary was to follow, not mentioned in the book of Kings. We can tell that in the late seventh century the dominant voice among the tradents is no longer Asaphite but Korahite; and this can only mean that Josiah has appointed a Korahite מזכיר in the place of Jeatherai. It is now he who recites the national history at the Feast of Tabernacles each seventh year (Deut. 31.10-13); and he has not been slow to exploit his new position.

The detail of the Korahite developments I have expounded in Chapters 9–13 above. They did not much interfere with the Asaphite Genesis, though Judah becomes more of a figure in the Joseph saga. They prefixed a creation story (Adam and his family), and a flood story, both told in the light of closer relations with Mesopotamia in recent decades. They made Moses the sole hero of the Exodus, wilderness and covenant narratives. They introduced an element of bitter hatred of the Egyptians, probably in the years after Josiah's defeat at Megiddo. They demoted Aaron, first to be Moses' *fidus Achates*, then to be inaugurator of the Golden Calf, finally to be the scapegoat of Meribah. They transferred the great moment of national revelation from the oasis by Kadesh to Mt Horeb in Midian, their own place of origin. This involved a recasting of the wilderness narrative, and they reset the old Asaph rebellion stories to after the covenant. The basic story remains the old Asaph–Bethel–E story; but by superimposing their own Dan–Moses material, the Korahites have dramatically recast it, and the 'J' author, sought so diligently from Solomon's enlightened court to the Exile, is in fact a Korahite who flourished between 625 and 600.

The Bethel historical tradition ran from the Egyptian oppression to the Solomonic empire; it had no break that we can discern between Torah and Prophets—Psalm 78 runs the tale on without intermission. Nor did the labours of Joah and his descendants affect this. They prefixed Genesis and they inserted a fuller law-giving in Moses' mouth in Moab; but they knew no Tetrateuch, Pentateuch, or Deuteronomic history. The same is true of the Korahites. They have carried the tale back to creation, but it still goes on to current history. What is different, however, is the volume of material for the early period. By 600 the expanded narrative covers perhaps 75 per cent of our Genesis, 60 per cent of our Exodus, 10 per cent of our Numbers and half our Deuteronomy. So a Pentateuch is in process of formation: Deut. 31.11 requires the reading of 'this law' every seventh year at Tabernacles, and that is likely to be prefaced by the narratives of Egypt so often referred to in that law, but not perhaps succeeded by the matter following.

It is a mistake to think of either the E-version or the J-version as a document. They were the national history as told first by Asaphite, later by Korahite מזכירים at the autumn festival in seventh-century Jerusalem. No doubt they assumed a semi-fixed, viscous form with time; but the presumption that they were not committed to writing (apart from the Deuteronomic law book) offers an explanation for a double phenomenon. We have two histories of Israel from Saul to Jehoiachin. Once the Samuel–Kings history was in written form, it was difficult to amend; it was necessary to start again, and to compose a second history, Chronicles. Had the Korahite Pentateuch been written down and used at festivals for two centuries until the return of Ezra, it is difficult to imagine that its tradents would not have preserved it. The converse is in fact clearly evidenced. The Korahite text has been repeatedly expanded and amended, most obviously by the Merarites, but also by later generations of the sons of Korah. Attempts to distinguish the growth of oral traditions from written ones have not yielded any firm results. It is better to see the 'J' version as that which was formed at the end of the seventh century, and by constant recital at worship became familiar, and liable to only minor adjustment.

I have spoken of the 'J' and 'E' versions in deference to so long a scholarly habit. It should be stressed that these sigla do not imply the exclusive use of יהוה or אלהים by the two guilds. Both names for God were used in both the Asaph and the Korah psalms, אלהים being preferred in both in proportions of about 4:1. The Asaphites, in the Joseph narrative and in the later, more reflective chapters of the Abraham story, are more faithful to אלהים, which is retained intentionally in the Exodus story up till the revelation of Yahweh's name in Exodus 20. In general the change of name in the Korahite version is to be attributed to the Yahwist revolution, accepted from the prophets and enacted by Josiah. 'D' is similarly a muddling siglum. The Asaphites were already proto-Deuteronomists in their psalms; their language was Deuteronomic as they developed the narratives in the seventh century, and the covenant was the centre of their theology. The Korahites accepted all this: they are as Deuteronomic as their northern colleagues after a century of residence in Jerusalem, and the Deuteronomic laws are the laws of their two communities, restated in expanded Deuteronomic language. The 'Deuteronomists' are simply the Asaphites and Korahites of 650–600.

So the old E tradition was most likely recited by Zimmah at Bethel, and made the official *Heilsgeschichte* in Jerusalem with the appointment

of his son Joah as מזכיר by Hezekiah. It was elaborated with the addition
of a Genesis and a Deuteronomy by Joah's son and grandson, Iddo and
Zerah. Jeatherai was the last of the family to hold the office; we may
think that the line comes to an end with him for that reason. For names
of the J tradents we are not so well placed. We are looking for a leading
Korahite Levite from the time of Josiah. 2 Chron. 34.12 mentions
Zechariah and Meshullam, of the sons of the Kohathites (= Korahites),
as supervising the Temple repairs; in 35.9 the chiefs of the Levites (not
all Korahites) who give the Passover offerings are called Conaniah,
Shemaiah, Nethanel, Hashabiah and Jeiel. In 2 Chron. 12.15 the acts of
Rehoboam were written in the words of Shemaiah the prophet and Iddo
the seer: the fourth-century Korahites remembered one of their number
from monarchy times who had outclassed the Asaphite Iddo in composing the national annals. So perhaps J was called Shemaiah (שמעיה[ו]); if
so, few will grudge him his title 'the prophet'.

The Deuteronomistic History

Josiah and his reformation were as the grass which in the morning
groweth up, but in 587 were cut down and withered. The seventy leading citizens were killed, and most of the educated classes were taken into
exile, 4,600 in all according to Jer. 52.30. These will have included the
principal Levites, especially those of the dominant Korahite clan.

One of those who remained in the villages round the burned capital
had access to the old annals and prophetic legends, 'the *midrash* of the
prophet Iddo', as the Chroniclers spoke of it (2 Chron. 13.22). He wrote
the story up in the light of the Deuteronomic rebellion–punishment–
forgiveness theology which had been orthodoxy since Psalms 78 and 81.
The destruction of Jerusalem had been due to the false worship of earlier
times, serving strange gods on every high place, as Deuteronomy 12
forbade. Every king of Northern Israel had been implicated in this rebellion. The whole history has this message, implicit in its structure, and
expounded in many a comment and prophetic sermon. The author made
the point both transparent and authoritative by placing it first on the lips
of Moses. A historical recapitulation (Deut. 1–3) emphasized that rebellion over the spies ended in punishment, while obedience resulted in the
conquest of Transjordan; and a catalogue of blessings and curses (Deut.
28), of warning and promise (29–30) left the listener in no doubt of the
way in which he should walk.

The date of this history is not in much doubt. It ends on a note of pale hope, as King Jehoiachin, aged 55 and having suffered 37 years of imprisonment (597–560), is released to palace arrest in Babylon: the historian seems not to know of his death, or of the return under Cyrus, and should be writing in the 550s or 540s. Other details of the work's setting are less obvious. In view of the Levites' history as tradents of the Torah narrative, we should expect the D-historian to be a Levite. The stories that he tells in Joshua are of the capture of the territory of Benjamin; Joshua, the Ephraimite, is credited with the single-handed conquest of the land; in 8.30-35 he builds an altar at Bethel, between 'Mt Ebal' and 'Mt Gerizim', as was commanded in the Asaphite texts in Deuteronomy, 11.29-30 and ch. 27; in ch. 24 he binds the whole people in a covenant with Yahweh at Shechem. We should therefore tend to think of him as a surviving Asaphite.

Frank M. Cross (*Canaanite Myth*, pp. 274-89) argued rather persuasively that the main structure of the D-history should be credited to the reign of Manasseh: there is no peroration on the fall of Jerusalem; the stress is on the sin of Jeroboam, and on the election of David, and of Jerusalem. If so, then 'the midrash of the prophet Iddo' was Cross's first edition of the D-history.

The D-historian is preaching the *Vergeltungsdogma*, and he knows that worship outside Jerusalem was the trouble, supposed by some to include the worship of golden bull(s) at Bethel. So Bethel is included in Jeroboam's sad apostasies, and is duly destroyed by Josiah, with a prophecy of this destruction in 1 Kings 13. But it is striking that the book of Judges pulls to pieces the shrines at Dan, Gibeah and Shiloh, and delights to discredit Shechem, but has no ill tale to bear of the foundation of Bethel. Bethel was, in the Asaph–Korah tradition, an ancient and honoured sanctuary. Its altar was set up by Abraham (Gen. 12); it was the site of Jacob's dream, and was declared by God to be his house (Gen. 28); Moses had commanded worship to be offered there (Deut. 11, 27); Joshua had set up stones there, inscribed God's commandments and sacrificed (Josh. 8). Nothing was wrong with the place itself—only the false worship introduced by Jeroboam, and extinguished by Josiah.

So it is not surprising to learn that when Zechariah was prophesying in Jerusalem it was from Bethel that envoys came for consultation: for seventy years they had been mourning and fasting on the anniversaries of Jerusalem's fall in Ab and Tishri (Zech. 7.1-7). When the Temple was destroyed and the city burned, the Asaphites had gone back to their old

shrine at Bethel. They had loyally mourned Jerusalem's loss; and we
may think that they sustained the faith of the people of the land with
recitals of the old *Heilsgeschichte*, and readings from the more recent
Unheilsgeschichte. Deuteronomy and the D-history were never written
to be kept in files and chests. They are preachments, intended to be
proclaimed to a listening crowd renewing their covenant—elders,
officials, men, children, women and aliens (Deut. 29.10-15). The writing
of the D-history had two unintended effects on the development of the
Pentateuch. First, it was written down—if it had not been, then the
Chroniclers would have gently amended it, generation by generation, as
they did their own history of Israel. But in fact they had to make their
own new beginning; and that implies a fixed, written text of the Former
Prophets, and the promise, in time, of a fixed, written text for the Torah.
Secondly, although the D-historians have expanded Deuteronomy, their
systematic composition has begun with the book of Joshua; and in this
way they have unconsciously divided the old continuous Psalm 78 history into two phases, the Law and the Prophets. It was the genius of
Noth to see that the extensions to Deuteronomy made it the preamble to
the D-history, but he was mistaken in thinking that this was ever
thought of as an independent work. The D-historian could never have
ignored the long-established Genesis–Numbers traditions. His
amplifications in Deuteronomy 1–3, 28–30 are simply the easiest points
at which he can claim the authority of Moses for the teaching he is to
expound at leisure in Joshua–Kings.

So it seems likely that the D-historian was an Asaphite; and as I have
ventured possible names for E and D and J, it would be nice to see him
as a possible real human being also. When Nehemiah celebrated the
building of the wall of Jerusalem, Levites were an important part of his
procession; and all the Levites mentioned were of the sons of Asaph—
as, on the argument presented above, was to be expected. Their leader
was one Zechariah, b. Jonathan, b. Shemaiah, b. Mattaniah, b. Micaiah,
b. Zaccur (Neh. 12.35-36). A five-generation ancestry is impressive, and
we have seen that the names Mattaniah–Mica(iah)–Zichri/Zabdi have
recurred in other passages. It would seem that the line of
Zaccur/Zichri/Zabdi was the leading Asaphite family, going back to the
period around 575. Perhaps then it is they who have sustained the faith
of the people of the land after the catastrophes of the 580s, who have
gathered the faithful to worship at Bethel. If so, then the compiling of
the great D-history would be the work of Micaiah and his son Mattaniah

in 560–540. Since Mattaniah is the name most frequently remembered, we may credit him with the siglum Dtr.

The Priestly Expansion

The upper-class exiles of 597 and 587 will have included Korahites who knew the EDJ canon by heart, and perhaps some who had helped to compose it; but it also included priests like Ezekiel from the Jerusalem Temple, who might not appreciate the hitherto northern monopoly of recounting the national history. At all events an extensive rehandling of the tradition is in evidence in P, with a strong interest in the Tabernacle as a foreshadowing of the Jerusalem Temple, and an idealized legal system much concerned with the cult, and differing from the codes in Exodus 21–23, 34 and Deuteronomy 12–26. As the Chroniclers know three guilds of Levites, sons of Merari as well as of Asaph (Gershom) and Korah (1 Chron. 6.1-15[16-30], and *passim*), we may think that the Merarites are responsible for the P expansion. Its emphasis on sabbath (Gen. 1, the fourth commandment), and on Abraham's coming to the land from Ur of the Chaldees (Gen. 11), and on circumcision (Gen. 17), and on confession of sin with a view to return from exile (Lev. 26), all suggest a setting for P in the sixth century in Babylon.

P was never an independent document, as may be seen from its small compass in Genesis, and in Exodus 1–24. The Merarites simply retold the basic Genesis–Exodus story with minor expansions, and took over from Exodus 25, merely including three passages of the earlier tradition: the Golden Calf and its sequel (Exod. 32–34); the desert rebellions (Num. 10.29–14.45, with a few verses in Num. 20); and the Balaam–Sihon–Og traditions, of which we have no sign in the Asaph psalms. Their major work was done by Numbers 36, but they added a final chapter to Deuteronomy, and a considerable section to Joshua. I have argued above (pp. 245-52) that the Merarites were compelled to use sabbath worship as their opportunity to retell the sacred history, and that the Genesis story falls into twelve units suitable for recital on a series of sabbaths, as they are to this day. Unfortunately the Exodus–Deuteronomy readings are not, in the nature of the case, marked out with genealogies or short Merarite additions.

Heather McKay (*Sabbath and Synagogue*) has argued that sabbath worship cannot be firmly dated until well into the Christian era; but this conclusion is reached partly by making over-high demands on the evidence (sabbath study of the law is conceded), and partly by minimizing the evidence of Acts.

The Merarites' *Heilsgeschichte* was now twice the length of the EDJ version which they had brought with them; and it will have been in use not in a single centre like the Jerusalem Temple, but at a number of riverside- or house-meetings in different districts on the Chebar or the Euphrates. So it needed to be written down; and when Ezra returned to Jerusalem in the fourth century, he brought with him 'the book of the law of Moses' (Neh. 8.1-2). The book included specifications for worship on 1st Tishri, and at Tabernacles, which are found only in Leviticus 23; as well as a zeal against mixed marriages which comes from the older Deut. 7.3-4. So Ezra's book was not P, but EDJP, something rather close to our Hexateuch.

It may be that a careful study would reveal some likely names of sixth-century Merarites who would be candidates for the siglum P; but the work is large, and not unified—there is an independent H-code included, for example—and we may think that it grew gradually with the generations. We may be content to note that when Ezra gathered the returning exiles, he found no Levite among them (Ezra 8.15), so he sent to Iddo at the place called Casiphia; 'and according to the good hand of our God upon us they brought us a man of discretion, of the sons of Mahli, the son of Levi', namely Sherebiah. Iddo is an Asaphite name, so the guilds have been cooperating in their exile; and Sherebiah is of the sons of Mahli the son of Merari. Sherebiah will not be P, for there was no individual P, but a line of good men going back two centuries: but he is the man of discretion who brought the expanded P-version to Jerusalem, and we may be happy to know that the often austere and sometimes bleak P has a human face also.

Sherebiah's Pentateuch will not have been our Pentateuch exactly; indeed 'our Pentateuch' is not an exact term. Glosses and explanations and amendments were slipped in by copyists over the years, and it would be a bold hand to identify the Pentateuch of 300 BCE, say, with our Massoretic Text. The MT is but one form of a still viscous, now jelling, text-form, of which other, partly prior versions are preserved in the LXX and other translations. But here is a field into which even concluding unhistorical postscripts would be wise not to trespass.

For a recent critique of the *Hebraica veritas* theory, see Mogens Müller, *First Bible*.

BIBLIOGRAPHY

Ackroyd, P.R., 'Hosea and Jacob', *VT* 13 (1963), pp. 245-59.

Allen, L.C., *Psalms 101–150* (WBC, 21; Waco, TX: Word Books, 1983).

Alt, A., *Essays on Old Testament History and Religion* (The Biblical Seminar, 9: Sheffield: JSOT Press, 1989).

Anderson, A.A., *Psalms I–II* (NCB; London: Oliphants, 1972).

Avi-Yonah, M., and E. Stern (eds.), *Encyclopedia of Archaeological Excavations in the Holy Land, I–IV* (London: Oxford University Press, 1975–78).

Beyerlin, W., 'Schichten im 80. Psalm', in H. Balz and S. Schulz (eds.), *Das Wort und die Wörter* (Festschrift G. Friedrich; Stuttgart: Kohlhammer, 1973), pp. 9-24.

Birkeland, H., *Die Feinde des Individuums in der israelitischen Psalmenliteratur: Ein Beitrag zur Kenntnis der semitischen Literatur- und Religionsgeschichte* (Oslo: Grøndahl, 1933).

Blenkinsopp, J., *The Pentateuch: An Introduction to the First Five Books of the Bible* (ABRL; New York: Doubleday, 1992).

Blum, E., *Die Komposition der Vätergeschichte* (WMANT, 57; Neukirchen–Vluyn: Neukirchener Verlag, 1984).

—*Studien zur Komposition des Pentateuch* (BZAW, 189; Berlin: de Gruyter, 1990).

Boer, P.A.H. de, 'Psalm 81.6a: Observations on Translation and Meaning of One Hebrew Line', in W.B. Barrick and J.R. Spencer (eds.), *In the Shelter of Elyon* (Festschrift G.W. Ahlström; JSOTSup, 31; Sheffield: JSOT Press, 1984), pp. 67-80.

Booij, T., 'Mountain and Theophany in the Sinai Narrative', *Bib* 65 (1984), pp. 1-26.

—'The Background of the Oracle in Psalm 81', *Bib* 65 (1984), pp. 465-75.

Botterweck, G.J. *et al.* (eds.), *Theologisches Wörterbuch zum Alten Testament* (Stuttgart: Kohlhammer, 1987–).

Braulik, G., 'Die Abfolge der Gesetze in Deuteronomium 12–26 und der Dekalog', in N. Lohfink (ed.), *Das Deuteronomium. Entstehung, Gestalt und Botschaft* (BETL, 68: Leuven: Leuven University Press/Peeters, 1985), pp. 252-72.

Brenner, M., *The Song of the Sea: Exod. 15.1-21* (BZAW, 195; Berlin: de Gruyter, 1991).

Brown, J.P., 'The Mediterranean Vocabulary of the Vine', *VT* 19 (1969), pp. 146-70.

Brueggemann, W., 'Bounded by Obedience and Praise: The Psalms as Canon', *JSOT* 50 (1991), pp. 63-92.

—'Response to J.L. Mays, "The Question of Context"', in McCann (ed.), *Shape*, pp. 29-41.

Budd, P.J., *Numbers* (WBC, 5; Waco, TX: Word Books, 1984).

Budde, K., 'Ps. 82,6f', *JBL* 40 (1921), pp. 39-42.

Buss, M.J., 'The Psalms of Asaph and Korah', *JBL* 82 (1963), pp. 382-92.

Campbell, A.F., 'Psalm 78: A Contribution to the Theology of Tenth Century Israel', *CBQ* 41 (1979), pp. 51-79.

Caquot, A., M. Sznycer and A. Herdner, *Textes Ougaritiques*. I. *Mythes et Légendes* (Littératures anciennes du Proche-Orient; Paris: Cerf, 1974).

Carmichael, C.M., *The Laws of Deuteronomy* (Ithaca: Cornell University Press, 1974).

Carroll, R.P., 'Psalm LXXVIII: Vestiges of a Tribal Polemic', *VT* 21 (1971), pp. 133-50.

Childs, B.S., *Exodus: A Commentary* (OTL; London: SCM Press, 1974).

Clements, R.E., *Isaiah 1–39* (NCB; Grand Rapids/London: Eerdmans/Marshall Morgan & Scott, 1980).

Clines, D.J.A., *The Theme of the Pentateuch* (JSOTSup, 10; Sheffield: JSOT Press, 1978).

Coats, G.W., 'The Traditio-Historical Character of the Reed Sea Motif', *VT* 17 (1967), pp. 235-65

Cooke, G., 'The Sons of (the) God(s)', *ZAW* 76 (1974), pp. 22-47.

Crenshaw, J.L., 'Method in Determining Wisdom Influence upon "Historical" Literature', *JBL* 88 (1969), pp. 129-42.

Cross, F.M., *Canaanite Myth and Hebrew Epic: Essays in the History of the Religion of Israel* (Cambridge, MA: Harvard University Press, 1973).

Dahood, M., *Psalms I–III* (AB; New York: Doubleday, 1966–70).

—'The Four Cardinal Points in Psalm 75,7 and Joel 2,20', *Bib* 52 (1971), p. 397.

Davies, G.I., *The Way of the Wilderness: A Geographical Study of the Wilderness Itineraries in the Old Testament* (SOTSMS, 5; Cambridge: Cambridge University Press, 1979).

—*Hosea* (OTG; Sheffield: JSOT Press, 1993).

Day, J., *God's Conflict with the Dragon and the Sea* (University of Cambridge Oriental Publications, 35; Cambridge: Cambridge University Press, 1985).

Delitzsch, F., *Biblical Commentary on the Psalms I–III* (ET; London: Hodder & Stoughton, 1888) = (Leipzig: Dörffling & Franke, 2nd edn, 1867).

Dicou, B., *Edom, Israel's Brother and Antagonist: The Role of Edom in Biblical Prophecy and Story* (JSOTSup, 169; Sheffield: JSOT Press, 1994).

Dinsmoor, W.B., *The Architecture of Ancient Greece: An Account of its Historic Development* (London: Batsford, 3rd edn, 1950).

Duhm, B., *Die Psalmen* (HKAT, 14; Tübingen: Mohr [Paul Siebeck], 2nd edn, 1922).

Eaton, J.H., *Psalms* (Torch; London: SCM Press, 1967).

—'Notes on Questions of Philology and Exegesis in the Psalms', *JTS* 19 (1968), pp. 603-609.

—*Vision in Worship: The Relation of Prophecy and Liturgy in the Old Testament* (London: SPCK, 1981).

—*Kingship and the Psalms* (The Biblical Seminar, 31; Sheffield: JSOT Press, 2nd edn, 1986).

Eissfeldt, O., 'Das Lied Moses Deuteronomium 32:1-43 und das Lehrgedicht Asaphs Psalm 78 samt einer Analyse der Umgebung der Moses-Liedes', *Berichte über die Verhandlumgen der Sachsischen Akademie der Wissenschaften zu Leipzig* (Philologische/historische Klasse, 104.5; Berlin: Akademia, 1958).

—'Psalm 80', in R. Sellheim and F. Maass (eds.), *Kleine Schriften*, III (Tübingen: Mohr [Paul Siebeck], 1966), pp. 221-32.

Elbogen, I., *Der jüdische Gottesdienst in seiner geschichtlichen Entwicklung* (Hildesheim: Olms, 1967) = (Frankfurt, 3rd edn, 1931).

Emerton, J.A., 'Spring and Torrent in Psalm 74:15', in *idem* (ed.), *Volume du Congrès, Genève, 1965* (VTSup, 15; Leiden: Brill, 1966), pp. 122-33.

—'A Neglected Solution of a Problem in Psalm LXXVI 11', *VT* 24 (1974), pp. 136-46.

—'Judah and Tamar', *VT* 29 (1979), pp. 403-15.

—'Leviathan and *ltn*: The Vocalisation of the Ugaritic Word for the Dragon', *VT* 32 (1982), pp. 327-31.

—'The Origin of the Promises to the Patriarchs in the Older Sources of the Book of Genesis', *VT* 32 (1982), pp. 14-32.

—'The Priestly Writer in Genesis', *JTS* 39 (1988), pp. 381-400.

—'The Site of Salem, the City of Melchizedek (Genesis xiv 18)', in *idem* (ed.), *Studies in the Pentateuch* (VTSup, 41; Leiden: Brill, 1990), pp. 45-71.

—'The Text of Psalm lxxvii 11', *VT* 44 (1994), pp. 183-94.

Emmerson, G.I., *Hosea: An Israelite Prophet in Judean Perspective* (JSOTSup, 28; Sheffield: JSOT Press, 1984).

Farrer, A.M., *A Rebirth of Images* (London: Faber & Faber, 1949).

—*The Revelation of St John the Divine* (London: Dacre, 1964).

Finkelstein, I., *The Archaeology of the Israelite Settlement* (trans. D. Saltz; Jerusalem: Israel Exploration Society, 1988).

Fokkelman, J.P., 'Genesis', in R. Alter and F. Kermode (eds.), *The Literary Guide to the Bible* (Cambridge, MA: Harvard University Press, 1987), pp. 36-55.

Galling, K., *Die Erwählungstraditionen Israels* (BZAW, 48; Berlin: Töpelmann, 1928).

Gelston, A., 'A Note on Psalm 74:8', *VT* 34 (1984), pp. 82-87.

Gerstenberger, E., *Wesen und Herkunft des 'apodiktischen Rechts'* (WMANT, 20; Neukirchen–Vluyn: Neukirchener Verlag, 1965).

Gese, H., 'Der Dekalog als Ganzheit betrachtet', *ZTK* 64 (1967), pp. 121-38.

—'Zur Geschichte der Kultsänger am zweiten Tempel', in O. Betz *et al.* (eds.), *Abraham unser Vater* (Festschrift O. Michel; Leiden: Brill, 1963), pp. 222-34 = H. Gese, *Vom Sinai zum Zion* (BEvT, 64; Munich: Chr. Kaiser Verlag, 1974), pp. 180-201.

Gonzales, A., 'Le Psaume LXXXII', *VT* 13 (1983), pp. 293-309.

Goulder, M.D., 'The Fourth Book of the Psalter', *JTS* 26 (1975), pp. 269-89.

—'The Apocalypse as a Cycle of Prophecies', *NTS* 27 (1981), pp. 342-67.

—*The Psalms of the Sons of Korah* (JSOTSup, 20; Sheffield: JSOT Press, 1982).

—*The Song of Fourteen Songs* (JSOTSup, 36; Sheffield: JSOT Press, 1986).

—*The Prayers of David (Psalms 51–72)* (JSOTSup, 102; Sheffield: JSOT Press, 1990).

—'Asaph's *History of Israel* (Elohist Press, Bethel, 725 BCE)', *JSOT* 65 (1995), pp. 71-81.

Gray, J., *Joshua, Judges and Ruth* (NCB; London: Oliphants, 1967).

Gunkel, H., *Schöpfung und Chaos in Urzeit und Endzeit* (Göttingen: Vandenhoeck & Ruprecht, 1895).

—*Die Psalmen* (HKAT, II.2: Göttingen: Vandenhoeck & Ruprecht, 1929).

Gunkel, H., and J. Begrich, *Einleitung in die Psalmen* (Göttingen: Vandenhoeck & Ruprecht, 2nd edn, 1933).

Haglund, E., *Historical Motifs in the Psalms* (ConBOT, 23; Lund: Gleerup, 1984).

Hoftijzer, J., *Die Verheissungen an die drei Erzväter* (Leiden: Brill, 1956).

Houtman, C., *Exodus I* (Kampen: Kok Pharos, 1993).

—*Der Pentateuch. Die Geschichte seiner Erforschung neben einer Auswertung* (Kampen: Kok Pharos, 1994).

Jacquet, L., *Les Psaumes et le coeur de l'homme* (3 vols.; Namur: Duculot, 1977).

Jefferson, H., 'Psalm LXXVII', *VT* 13 (1963), pp. 87-91.

Johnson, A.R., *The Cultic Prophet and Israel's Psalmody* (Cardiff: University of Wales Press, 1979).

Junker, H., 'Die Entstehungszeit des Ps.78 und des Deuteronomiums', *Bib* 34 (1953), pp. 487-500.

Kellermann, U., *Nehemia. Quellen, Uberlieferung und Geschichte* (Berlin: Töpelmann, 1967).

Kelso, J.L., 'Bethel', in Avi-Yonah and Stern (eds.), *Encyclopedia*, pp. 190-93.

Kennett, R.H., 'The Origin of the Aaronite Priesthood', *JTS* 6 (1905), pp. 161-86.

Kirkpatrick, A.F., *The Book of Psalms I–III* (Cambridge Bible for Schools and Colleges; Cambridge: Cambridge University Press, 1891–1901).

Knierim, R., 'Exodus 18 und die Neuordnung der mosäischen Gerichtsbarkeit', *ZAW* 73 (1961), pp. 146-71.

Kraus, H.-J., *Worship in Israel* (ET; Oxford: Basil Blackwell, 1966) = *Gottesdienst in Israel* (Munich: Chr. Kaiser Verlag, 2nd edn, 1962).

—*Psalmen* (BKAT, 15; Neukirchen–Vluyn: Neukirchener Verlag, 5th edn, 1978).

Kselman, J.S., 'Psalm 77 and the Book of Exodus', *Journal of the Ancient Near Eastern Society of Columbia University* 15 (1983), pp. 51-58.

Lambert, W.G., and A.R. Millard, *Atra-Hasis: The Babylonian Story of the Flood* (Oxford: Clarendon Press, 1969).

Lewis, B., *The Sargon Legend: A Study of the Akkadian Text and the Tale of the Hero who was Exposed at Birth* (Cambridge, MA: American Schools of Oriental Research, 1980).

L'Hour, J., 'Une législation criminelle dans le Deutéronome', *Bib* 44 (1963), pp. 1-28.

—'Les interdits to'eba dans le Deutéronome', *RB* 71 (1964), pp. 481-503.

Lindars, B., *Judges 1–5: A New Translation and Commentary* (ed. A.D.H. Mayes; ICC; Edinburgh: T. & T. Clark, 1995).

Lohfink, N., 'Die Erzählung vom Sündenfall', in *idem, Das Siegeslied am Schilfmeer: christliche Auseinandersetzungen mit dem Alten Testament* (Frankfurt: Knecht, 1965), pp. 81-101.

Marcus, R., *Philo XI: Quaestiones in Genesim/Exodum* (LCL; Cambridge, MA: Harvard University Press, 1953).

Mathias, D., *Die Geschichtstheologie der Geschichtssummarien in den Psalmen* (Beiträge zur Erforschung des Alten Testaments, 35; Bern: Peter Lang, 1933).

Mayes, A.D.H., *Deuteronomy* (NCB; Grand Rapids/London: Eerdmans/Marshall Morgan & Scott, 1979).

Mays, J.L., 'The Place of the Torah-Psalms in the Psalter', *JBL* 106.1 (1987), pp. 3-12.

—'The Question of Context in Psalm Interpretation', in McCann (ed.), *Shape*, pp. 14-20.

McCann, J.C. (ed.), *The Shape and Shaping of the Psalter* (JSOTSup, 159; Sheffield: JSOT Press, 1993).

McKay, H., *Sabbath and Synagogue: The Question of Sabbath Worship in Ancient Judaism* (Religions in the Graeco-Roman World, 122; Leiden: Brill, 1994).

McKay, J.W., 'Exod.XXIII.1-3,6-8: A Decalogue for the Administration of Justice in the City Gate', *VT* 21 (1971), pp. 311-25.

MacLaurin, E.C.B., 'Joseph and Asaph', *VT* 25 (1975), pp. 27-45.

McNeile, A.H., *The Book of Exodus* (WestBC; London: Methuen, 3rd edn, 1931).

Merendino, R.P., *Das deuteronomische Gesetz: Ein literarkritische, gattungs- und überlieferungsgeschichtliche Untersuchung zu Dt. 12–26* (BBB, 31; Bonn: Haustein, 1969).

Mettinger, T.N.D., *The Dethronement of Sabaoth* (ET; ConBOT, 18; Lund: Gleerup, 1981).

—'YHWH Sabaoth—The Heavenly King on the Cherubim Throne', in T. Ishida (ed.), *Studies in the Period of David and Solomon and Other Essays* (Winona Lake, IN: Eisenbrauns, 1982), pp. 109-36.

—*In Search of God: The Meaning and Message of the Everlasting Names* (ET; Philadelphia: Fortress Press, 1988).

Millard, M., *Die Komposition des Psalters* (FAT, 9; Tübingen: Mohr, 1994).

Möhlenbrink, K., 'Die levitische Überlieferungen des Alten Testaments', *ZAW* 52 (1934), pp. 184-231.

Mowinckel, S., *Psalmenstudien I–VI* (repr.; Amsterdam: Schippers, 1966 [1921–24]).

—*Le Décalogue* (Paris: Alcan, 1927).

—*Studien zu dem Buche Ezra–Nehemia I–III* (Skrifter utgitt av Det Norske Videnskaps–Akademie; Oslo: Universitetsforlaget, 1964–65).

—*The Psalms in Israel's Worship I–II* (Oxford: Basil Blackwell, 1967).

Müller, M., *The First Bible of the Church: A Plea for the Septuagint* (JSOTSup, 206; Sheffield: Sheffield Academic Press, 1996).

Nasuti, H.P., *Tradition History and the Psalms of Asaph* (Ann Arbor: University of Michigan, 1985).

Nicholson, E.W., *God and his People: Covenant and Theology in the Old Testament* (Oxford: Oxford University Press, 1986).

Niehr, H., 'Götter oder Menschen—eine falsche Alternative, Bemerkungen zu Ps 82', *ZAW* 99 (1987), pp. 94-98.

Nielsen, E., *Shechem: A Traditio-Historical Investigation* (Copenhagen: Gad, 1955).

—*The Ten Commandments in New Perspective* (SBT, 2.7; London: SCM Press, 1968).

Noth, M., *Überlieferungsgeschichtliche Studien* (Tübingen: Max Niemeyer Verlag, 1943).

—*Überlieferungsgeschichte des Pentateuch* (Stuttgart: Kohlhammer, 1948).

—*Exodus* (OTL; London: SCM Press, 1962) = *Das zweite Buch Mose, Exodus* (ATD; Göttingen: Vandenhoeck & Ruprecht, 1959).

—*The History of Israel* (trans. P. Ackroyd; London: A. & C. Black, 2nd edn, 1960) = *Geschichte Israels* (Göttingen: Vandenhoeck & Ruprecht, 2nd edn, 1956).

—*Numbers* (OTL; London: SCM Press, 1968) = *Das vierte Buch Mose, Numeri* (ATD; Göttingen: Vandenhoeck & Ruprecht, 1966).

Olshausen, J., *Commentar zu den Psalmen* (Leipzig, 1853).

Ottosson, M., *Josuaboken* (Uppsala: Acta Universitatis Upsaliensis, 1991).

Pedersen, J., 'Passahfest und Passahlegende', *ZAW* 52 (1934), pp. 161-75.

Perlitt, L., *Bundestheologie im Alten Testament* (Neukirchen–Vluyn: Neukirchener Verlag, 1969).

Peters, J.P., *The Psalms as Liturgies* (New York: MacMillan, 1922).

Phillips, A., *Ancient Israel's Criminal Law* (Oxford: Oxford University Press, 1970).

Pritchard, J.B. (ed.), *Ancient Near Eastern Texts* (Princeton, NJ: Princeton University Press, 2nd edn, 1955).

Rad, G. von, *The Problem of the Hexateuch and Other Essays* (New York, 1966) = *Das formgeschichtliche Problem des Hexateuchs* (Stuttgart: Kohlkammer, 1938).

—*Genesis: A Commentary* (London: SCM Press, 1961 [1956]).

—*Old Testament Theology* (ET; 3 vols.; Edinburgh: Oliver and Boyd, 1962) = *Theologie des Alten Testaments* (Munich: Chr. Kaiser Verlag, 1957).

—*Wisdom in Israel* (London: SCM Press, 1972) = *Weisheit in Israel* (Neukirchen–Vluyn: Neukirchener Verlag, 1970).

Redford, D.B., *A Study of the Biblical Story of Joseph (Genesis 37–50)* (VTSup, 20; Leiden: Brill, 1970).

Rendsburg, G.A., *Linguistic Evidence for the Northern Origin of Selected Psalms* (SBLMS, 43; Atlanta, GA: Scholars Press, 1990).

Rendtorff, R., *The Problem of the Process of Transmission in the Pentateuch* (ET; JSOTSup, 89: Sheffield: JSOT Press 1990) = *Das überlieferungsgeschichtliche Problem des Pentateuch* (BZAW, 17; Berlin: de Gruyter, 1977).

Ringgren, H., 'Einige Bemerkungen zum 73. Psalm', *VT* 3 (1953), pp. 265-72.

Rudolph, W., *Esra und Nehemia: samt 3-Esra* (HAT, 1.20; Tübingen: Mohr, 1949).

—*Chronikbücher* (HAT, 1.21; Tübingen: Mohr, 1955).

Rudolph, W., and P. Volz, *Der Elohist als Erzähler: Ein Irrweg der Pentateuchkritik? An der Genesis erläutert* (Berlin: Töpelmann, 1933).

Salters, R.B., 'Ps. 82,1 and the Septuagint', *ZAW* 103 (1991), pp. 225-39.

Sanders, E.P., *Judaism: Practice and Belief 63 BCE–66 CE* (London/Philadelphia: SCM/Trinity University Press, 1992).

Schmid, H.H., *Der sogenannte Jahwist: Beobachtungen und Fragen zur Pentateuchforschung* (Zürich: Theologischer Verlag, 1976).

Schmidt, H., *Die Psalmen* (HAT: Tübingen: Mohr, 1934).

Schmitt, H.-C., *Die nichtpriesterliche Josephgeschichte: Ein Beitrag zur neuesten Pentateuchkritik* (BZAW, 154; Berlin: de Gruyter, 1980).

Shiloh, Y., *The Proto-Aeolic Capital and Israelite Ashlar Masonry* (Qedem, 11; Jerusalem, 1979).

Tate, M.E., *Psalms 51–100* (WBC, 20; Dallas, TX: Word Books, 1990).

Thompson, T.L., *The Origin Tradition of Ancient Israel*. I. *The Literary Formation of Genesis and Exodus 1–23* (JSOTSup, 55; Sheffield: JSOT Press, 1987).

Tournay, R., 'Notes sur les Psaumes', *RB* 79 (1972), pp. 43-50.

Van Seters, J., 'Confessional Reformulation in the Exilic Period', *VT* 22 (1972), pp. 448-59.

—*Abraham in History and Tradition* (New Haven, CT: Yale University Press, 1975).

—*Prologue to History: The Yahwist as Historian in Genesis* (Louisville, KY: Westminster/John Knox Press, 1992).

—*The Life of Moses* (Kampen: Kok Pharos, 1994).

Vervenne, M., 'The Question of "Deuteronomic" Elements in Genesis to Numbers', in F.G. Martinez *et al.* (eds.), *Studies in Deuteronomy* (VTSup, 53; Festschrift C.J. Labuschagne; Leiden: Brill, 1994).

Weiser, A., *The Psalms* (OTL; London: SCM Press, 1962) = (ATD, 14/15; Göttingen: Vandenhoeck & Ruprecht, 5th edn, 1959).

Wellhausen, J., *Prolegomena to the History of Israel* (Edinburgh: A. & C. Black, 1885) = *Prolegomena zur Geschichte Israels* (Berlin: Reimer, 1883).

—*Die Composition des Hexateuchs und der historischen Bücher des Alten Testaments* (Berlin: Reimer, 3rd edn, 1899).

Westermann, C., *Genesis: A Commentary* (ET; 3 vols.; Minneapolis: Augsburg, 1984–86) = (BKAT; Neukirchen: Neukirchener Verlag, 1974–82).

Whybray, R.N., *The Making of the Pentateuch* (JSOTSup, 53; Sheffield: JSOT Press, 1987).

Wildberger, H., *Jesaia Kapitel 13–27* (BKAT; Neukirchen: Neukirchener Verlag, 1978).

Willesen, F., 'The Cultic Situation of Psalm LXXIV', *VT* 2 (1952), pp. 289-306.

Williamson, H.G.M., *Ezra, Nehemiah* (WBC, 16; Waco, TX: Word Books, 1985).

Wilson, G.H., *The Editing of the Hebrew Psalter* (SBLDS, 76; Chico, CA: Scholars Press, 1985).

—'The Use of Royal Psalms at the "Seams" of the Hebrew Psalter', *JSOT* 35 (1986), pp. 85-94.

—'Understanding the Purposeful Arrangement of Psalms in the Psalter: Pitfalls and Promise', in McCann (ed.), *Shape*, pp. 42-51.

—'Shaping the Psalter: A Consideration of Editorial Linkage in the Book of Psalms', in McCann (ed.), *Shape*, pp. 72-82.

Winnett, F.V., 'Re-examining the Foundations', *JBL* 84 (1965), pp. 1-19.

Wolff, H.W., *Hosea* (Hermeneia; Philadelphia: Fortress Press, 1974) = (BKAT, 14.1; Neukirchen–Vluyn: Neukirchener Verlag, 2nd edn, 1965).

Wright, G.E., 'Shechem', in Avi-Yonah and Stern (eds.), *Encyclopedia*, pp. 1083-94.

Würthwein, E., 'Erwägungen zu Psalm 73', in *Festschrift, A. Bertholet zum 80. Geburtstag* (Tübingen: Mohr, 1950), pp. 532-49

Yadin, Y., 'Excavations at Hazor', *IEJ* 9 (1959), pp. 79-81.

Yaron, R., 'The Meaning of *ZANAH*', *VT* 13 (1963), pp. 232-37.

Young, W.A., *Psalm 74: A Methodological and Exegetical Study* (Ann Arbor: University of Michigan, 1979).

INDEXES

INDEX OF REFERENCES

OLD TESTAMENT

NEW TESTAMENT

OTHER ANCIENT SOURCES

INDEX OF SUBJECTS

INDEX OF AUTHORS

JOURNAL FOR THE STUDY OF THE OLD TESTAMENT
SUPPLEMENT SERIES